THE DEVELOPMENT OF POLITICAL THEORY

THE DEVELOPMENT OF
POLITICAL THEORY

---

by *Otto von Gierke*

TRANSLATED BY BERNARD FREYD, Ph.D.

HOWARD FERTIG

New York · 1966

HOWARD FERTIG, INC. EDITION 1966

Published by arrangement with W. W. Norton & Company, Inc.

Library of Congress Catalog Card number: 66-24346

PRINTED IN THE UNITED STATES OF AMERICA
BY NOBLE OFFSET PRINTERS

The first edition was published in the year 1880 as Number VII. of the "Untersuchungen zur Deutschen Staats- und Rechtsgeschichte," bearing the dedication: Herrn Geh. Rath, Prof. Dr. Johann Caspar Bluntschli.

CONTENTS

PREFACE TO THE FIRST EDITION

THE first part of this monograph was presented on the third of August, 1879, in honor of the eminent master in the sciences of politics and jurisprudence to whom this book is now dedicated by permission, at the celebration of the fiftieth anniversary jubilee of his Doctorate by the Faculty of Law of the University of Breslau. It deals with the life and doctrines of an almost forgotten German scholar whose political doctrine deserves in the writer's opinion a prominent place in the history of political science. Consideration is also given to the great importance of the juristic writings of this author for the history of legal systematism.

According to the plan announced at the close of that jubilee essay, there was to have been a second part devoted to the historical development of those ideas which are characteristic features in the politics of Johannes Althusius. By tracing backwards and forwards certain well-marked ideas on the State from this starting-point we should get a genetic account of those influential systems of thought which may be grouped under the phrase 'Nature-Right theories of the State.' Special attention was to be given to the hitherto neglected share of the Germans in this activity of more than five centuries.

This plan has now been carried out. As usually happens, while the original outline was kept within bounds, the second part has grown far beyond the estimated limits. Even so, this essay presents no more than a fragmentary section of the process of human thought.

This essay then does not go back beyond the political theories of the middle ages; it assumes a knowledge of the realms of ideas combined by these theories, of the ancient philosophy of

9

State and Law on the one hand and the Christian-Germanic mind on the other. It ends with the culmination of the influence of Natural Law (*Naturrecht*), marking the last decade of the eighteenth century as its boundary throughout. Within these bounds only certain essential ideas are traced in their successive phases and for this purpose are torn from the context of the various systems in which they appear; in order to show the external continuity in the development of ideas, the exposition of the internal unity in the systems of those who carry on this development has been wholly sacrificed. The history of the various ideas is moreover presented only in its theoretical aspect; the interaction, taking place always and everywhere, between the changes of theory and the movements of practical life is only glanced at. Lastly and above all, these political ideas are treated not in their full inwardness but chiefly in their juristic bearing. While there is otherwise no lack of excellent works dealing with the development of political ideas, it seems to the writer that there is a dearth of literature on the history of the legal formulation of ideas of the State. And yet the whole notion of Natural Law was essentially a juristic and even a quite one-sided juristic construction of Society and the State.

But even within these limits the writer has been able to carry out his plan only with some incompleteness, for which he must ask the reader's indulgence. The whole work has grown out of the researches of many years in the history of the theory of Corporations, and especially of the concept of the 'juristic person' which forms its keystone. The results of these extensive studies in the history of ideas will be duly published by the author in the continuation of his work, "Das deutsche Genossenschaftsrecht." The development, touched upon here, of theories as to the relation between subordinate groups and the sovereign Community will there be more fully set forth. There also the growth of the concept of 'ideal personality' will be studied on its native soil, will be traced in its various adumbrations, and will be appraised, with regard to public as well as private law, as an intellectual achievement shared in common by the history of political theories and the history of jurisprudence. There, lastly, the close and inseparable connection between the development of the Roman-Canonist theory of corporations and the growth of political theories will be shown in full detail. In particular, the original identity of the upgrowing modern doctrine of State and Society with the theory of corporations based on the texts of Roman and Canon law will be shown with reference to their medieval origin. A more complete picture will there be drawn from the political theories of the middle ages onward, while a few rough sketches are all that can be expected here.

Thus it remains in many respects a patchwork, a memorial essay of narrow appeal now published in an expanded form; yet the writer hopes that his labor has not been all in vain. While this attempt to write a history of ideas from a purely juristic standpoint covers only a small part of the elements of general public law, these contributions in this direction may claim at least the merit of a first beginning. In the light of the evidences here given, earlier views as to the origin of the deep-channeled streams of political thought must at any rate be taken under correction at various points. It will also be of general interest to find that for the most part they are much older than is commonly supposed. The German reader may observe with particular interest that his nation entered this field by no means, as is widely believed, in the role of mere stragglers. And among those whose achievements claim for the German mind an equal share in the development of the political ideas of modern Europe, it may be hoped that Johannes Althusius will not fall again into the undeserved oblivion in which he has been lost.

Lastly, it may be remarked that from this point of view the present essay is properly included in the series of "Untersuchungen zur deutschen Staats- und Rechtsgeschichte" edited by the writer.

PART ONE

LIFE AND DOCTRINES OF ALTHUSIUS

CHAPTER ONE

JOHANNES ALTHUSIUS

THE name of Johannes Althusius is at the present time well-nigh forgotten. This is the case, whether in spite of his being a German or perhaps just because of that fact.

In the history of political science little account is commonly taken of German literature of the times preceding the ever-memorable works of the genius of Samuel Pufendorf. It is rather supposed that before then, aside from the immense but indirect influence of the German Reformers upon politics, the Germans took a very small share in the clash of political ideas. The strictly pioneer works have doubtless been produced by other nations. But the German share was never slight in that process of European thought which, at once the effect and cause of political changes, gave rise to political theories. This holds true even for the middle ages, whose political theories, in a manner not yet fully appreciated, laid the groundwork of the modern idea of the State by fusing the reproduced ideas of antiquity with various elements taken from the medieval system of thought, whose organic unity was thereby dissolved. For while in pure jurisprudence, after the failure of the first attempts at a national science of law the medieval Germans were little more than receptive, even then they took their full share in the work of creating political theories.[1] Likewise in the sixteenth century and at the beginning of the seventeenth, the Germans stood nearly everywhere in the first rank in the various movements of political thought. To say nothing of the influence of religious ideas, an independent jurisprudence now flourished in Germany as in the neighboring countries, which slowly built up the structure of positive Public Law; here as elsewhere philological and historical study began to lead to the deepening of political thought; here as everywhere the antiquarian political essays of the humanists, the writing of practical handbooks on the art of government, and the discussion of the political questions of the day, were eagerly pursued; here flourished most of all the pure Law of Nature (*Naturrecht*) and along with it the abstract philosophic theory of the State.[2]

And at this time also as in the middle ages Germany took a most active part in the great conflicts of political opinion. In particular, the disputes as to the true 'subject' (or possessor) of sovereignty aroused in the second half of the sixteenth century found here a manifold echo. And while the prevailing movement toward absolutism had now no other champion worthy to set beside the Frenchman Bodin, the opposing principle of popular sovereignty was systematically worked out and most scientifically expounded by a German jurist. This German was Johannes Althusius.

In the year 1603 Althusius published at Herborn a systematic treatise on 'Politics,' including in this term general public law. In form this work is the earliest attempt at a strictly systematic and complete exposition of what is called Politics. More remarkable however is its content. The author adopts throughout the views of those publicists who had arisen chiefly during the recent civil wars in France, who had drawn from the principle of popular sovereignty the revolutionary consequence of a right of active resistance against rulers who violate their contract, and because of this had already received from their opponents the name of "Monarchomachi." [3] But what had previously been set forth in pamphlets and polemical works with a concrete aim, he clothed in the vesture of an abstract academic theory. He laid the groundwork of his theory in a broader and more rigorous fashion than anyone before him; he above all expounded the absolute inalienability of the sovereign rights of the people, as well as the nature of the underlying social contract, in terms which are reproduced with an often striking similarity in Jean Jacques Rousseau.

The Politics of Althusius naturally caused a great stir. In particular another German publicist, Henning Arnisaeus, opposed it with a lengthy argument to show that sovereignty is inviolable.[4] Without mentioning the name of this as of other opponents, Hugo Grotius sought to refute its basic principles at some length.[5] Many other publicists, earlier and later, attacked its fundamental ideas.[6] Nevertheless the book, as its eight editions indicate, gained a wide circulation and exercised a large influence. Several brief text-books of politics reproduced its teaching throughout.[7] In many political writings of a different school important passages are given in a more moderate form.[8] And as it was freely used and cited by writers on German public law in the treatment of political concepts, it gained a direct influence on the juristic construction of the Germanic Empire.[9] While in France and England many books which went no farther than this were burned by the hand of the hangman, it never incurred the displeasure of the public authorities. For the most part indeed this was owing to its purely theoretical form, but partly also to the freer spirit prevailing in Germany before the Thirty Years' War.

For the first time, about the middle of the seventeenth century Althusius was loudly assailed as the most pestilent of all the Monarchomachi and his Politics as a book worthy of the flames. Above all Hermann Conring in several of his political writings condemn the work in the sharpest terms.[10] In particular, in a dissertation defended by Naamann Bensen on the 'subject' of supreme power, he pointed to Althusius as the seditious architect of disorder,[11] and expressed his full agreement with a special rejoinder in which Bensen supported this thesis and especially the above accusation against a reply written by Johann Fichlau, a Prussian.[12] About the same time Peter Gartz, in his "Puritanischer Glaubens- und Regimentsspiegel" (Leipzig 1650), condemns the dogma of popular sovereignty as a product of Presbyterian error (p. 138 ff.), describing Junius Brutus and Althusius as the arch-heretics whose false doctrines had seduced himself in his youth (p. 197 ff.). Not less severely does Johann Heinrich Boecler condemn the work of Althusius as the most noxious fruit of Monarchomachism, which ought to be taken from the schools and given to the flames.[13] Ulrich Huber, in his moderately liberal work "De jure Civitatis," takes care to express his emphatic dissent from the leading ideas of Althusius, although (obviously in pious deference to a personal tie) he refrains from any harsh language.[14] Various German and French writers of the eighteenth century continued to cite and attack the outcast book as the leading system of Monarchomachism,[15] until after the middle of the century it was supplanted by the later English and French versions of the doctrine of popular sovereignty.

Since that time it has sunk into oblivion and has not been retrieved by the busy historical research of our century. In the histories of political ideas it is indeed touched upon with a few lines here and there.[16] But in the most extensive and important works devoted to this subject Althusius is treated with deep silence.[17] No one else at any rate seems to have considered a closer inspection of this dusty tome to be worth the trouble.[18]

And yet enough inducement for this could have been found in the direct connection which exists between the doctrine of the so-called Monarchomachi and the world-shaking theory of the Contrat Social. After all Rousseau found the ingredients already prepared from which he brewed his baneful potion; he merely performed the mixing and with the ferment of his fiery language increased its intoxicating power. Among the elements used by him a very large part was supplied by the older doctrine of popular sovereignty, while another part is taken from the doctrine of the Law of Nature already blended therewith by Sidney and Locke after the fashion of Grotius; the rest comes from the absolutist theory of Hobbes translated for the first time into the language of revolution by Rousseau.

But this is not all. In fact the Contrat Social shows a remarkable agreement with the Politics of Althusius in respect to several fundamental and salient ideas which do not occur at all in any of his predecessors, or at any rate in such precise terms. This argues a high degree of probability that Rousseau had read and made use of the book, well-known as it then was even in France. A strict proof can hardly be given, considering Rousseau's reluctance to quote and his talent for adapting borrowed ideas. Yet whoever makes a fair comparison of the two books will hardly fail to receive the impression that this is something more than a mere accident.[19]

Be that as it may, we hope these pages will show that the work of Althusius deserves attention for its own sake. It should be added that this gifted man can also claim a certain importance in the history of jurisprudence. And so may it be lawful to invoke his shade.

Of the events of his life only the outlines are known. It lies beyond the scope of this essay to attempt a fuller acquaintance. For our purpose it will suffice to summarize briefly the available facts.[20]

Johannes Althusius, whose name is later re-translated as Althus or Althusen but was really Althaus, was born in the year 1557 at Diedenshausen, a village in the countship of Witgenstein-Berleburg.[21] Of his parentage, his youth and the course of his studies nothing is known with certainty. He seems to have studied at the University of Basel and to have there taken the degree of a Licentiate and later of a Doctor of Laws.[22] There is reason to believe that he also went to Geneva to finish his legal education under Dionysius Godofredus, who was a Professor there after 1585.[23] In Geneva, especially at that time, he would doubtless have imbibed the stern Calvinistic spirit which appears in all his works.

In the year 1586 he accepted a call to the College of Nassau at Herborn, which had previously been devoted merely to the training of Calvinist theologians but was now enlarged by the establishment of a Faculty of Law. As the first teacher of Law at Herborn he inaugurated in the Christmas term his lectures on Institutes, later extending his teaching to the field of Philosophy. In November 1589 he became also a member of the Count's Chancery at Dillenburg (whereby his previous salary of 80 guilders was increased to 100). In 1594 he went as lecturer to the Academy at Steinfurt, but returned after a few months to the College at Herborn, only to be transferred to Siegen in the same year upon the removal of the College to that town. And when in 1599 the greater part of the College was removed back to Herborn, he stayed, together with two juristic colleagues (Ulner and Neurath), in the remaining part of the College at Siegen, where he had meanwhile been married. However, in spite of the remonstrances of his colleagues, supported by the town-council and the burghers, he soon complied with the wish of the Count and returned to Herborn, where his only other colleague in jurisprudence, Matthaeus, was incapable of performing his duties. Here in 1599 and again in 1602 he was Rector.

The year 1604 brought a complete change in his circumstances when he accepted the position of Syndic of the city of Emden.[24] He held this office until his death. He refused a call to the University of Leyden. He even declined, after long negotiation, a call to the University of Franeker, which in 1606 offered him its first Professorship of Law, with the then dazzling stipend of 1000 guilders.[25] In his office of Syndic he served with the utmost zeal and enthusiasm this flourishing port of East-Frisian commerce, and strove to put his theories into practice in the struggle for its freedom and autonomy. In the long struggle between the Counts of East Friesland and the Estates, during which the city of Emden in particular kept up a much closer connection with the Republic of the United Netherlands than with its own prince, and at times even acted as an independent republic under a Dutch protectorate, he could have no lack of opportunities for practical action in the spirit of his theory. During his whole tenure of office he seems to have been the very soul of municipal politics in the struggle for the Reformed (Calvinist) creed, the law of the land, and the rights of the burghers as against the prince and the nobility.[26] He enjoyed a high reputation in the city and undertook several diplomatic missions. He was well beloved by the Reformed clergy under the leadership of Menso Alting, and in 1627 he became an Elder in the Consistory. He died on the 12th of August 1638, at the age of 81, leaving a numerous family.[27]

Of the writings of Althusius the above-mentioned work on Politics, which is of chief interest to us, was published by Christophorus Corvinus at Herborn in 1603. Its title reads: "Johannis Althusii, U. J. D., Politica methodice digesta et exemplis sacris et profanis illustrata: cui in fine adjuncta est Oratio panegyrica de utilitate necessitate et antiquitate scholarum." [28] The author at that time still held his professorship, was not involved in any public affairs and had worked out his views by a purely theoretical method with no practical partisan aim. Yet it was probably the sentiments expressed in the Politics which procured for him the call to Emden, as his predecessor in the Syndicate, Dothias Wiarda, was removed from office just because he did not join the popular movement. In the following years Althusius largely rewrote and expanded his book, and here indeed the influence of his new practical occupation was felt. The much stronger second edition, published at Groningen in 1610, not only shows some differences of arrangement and a lengthy reply to recent attacks, but also contains many new sections and passages obviously occasioned by the affairs of East Friesland and the neighboring Netherlands, and partly evoked by the current disputes between Emden and the Counts of East Friesland. The historical and legal insertions are also much increased.[29] The third edition, which appeared at Herborn in 1614, enlarged only by supplements and citations from recent literature, agrees in substance with the second edition.[30] An edition printed at Arnheim in 1617 also styles itself the third edition, although it is a mere reprint of the Groningen edition of 1610. Under the title of a fourth edition the book was once more, during the author's lifetime, printed at Herborn in 1625 in the same form as in 1614.[31] After his death the book was again reprinted in 1643 at Leyden, in 1651 at Amsterdam and in 1654 at Herborn.

Besides the Politics Althusius wrote a series of juristic works, of which two undertook a systematic treatment of the body of civil law. The first of these appeared in 1586 at Basel under the title: "Jurisprudentiae Romanae libri duo ad leges methodi Rameae conformati et tabellis illustrati."[32] Being much used as a text-book, it went through a number of editions.[33] In a completely revised form it became the principal juristic work of Althusius (published at Herborn in 1617, and at Frankfort in 1618 and 1649): "Dicaeologicae libri tres, totum et universum jus, quo utimur, methodice complectentes, cum parallelis hujus et Judaici juris, tabulisque insertis atque Indice triplici; . . . Opus tam theoriae quam praxeos aliarumque Facultatum studiosis utilissimum."[34] His other juristic works deal only with special topics of law and need not concern us.[35]

Lastly, we have of Althusius a system of Practical Ethics,

which his cousin Philipp Althusius published under the title: "Joh. Althusii V. Cl. Civilis conversationis libri duo, methodice digesti et exemplis sacris et profanis passim illustrati" at Hanau in 1601 (2nd ed. 1611).[36]

In all these writings Althusius shows excellent learning in jurisprudence, theology, literature and philosophy. As a jurist he sums up the whole thought of his time, and is especially well acquainted with the works of the 'elegant' French school. In matters of theology, as a strict Calvinist he dwells with special preference on the Old Testament and brings the ancient Jewish institutions within the wide circle of his studies. His humanistic turn appears in a classical culture based more on Greek than on Roman literature, and thus he follows the taste of the time in a lavish use of Greek words and phrases. In philosophy he avows himself a follower of the Ramistic school, and applies himself chiefly to logic and ethics. His knowledge of history also has a wide range, though he doubtless stands in need of a properly historical criticism and a deeper historical insight.

The special power of his intellect lies in a peculiar gift for dialectics and systematism. He is readily satisfied with materials, however fragile, fashioned in the pattern of pure logic. He is the born radical doctrinaire. Like all men of this type he is more clear than deep, more acute than wise. His sentiments, bold as they often are, have a certain insipidity of tone; his extravagances are not the product of an overpowering fancy but of an intellect governed by one-sided logic. The bent of his mind, turned outward rather than inward, is averse from pure speculation. His whole attention is given to problems of educational method on the one hand and questions of public and private conduct on the other. His ideas show at all points the workings of a strenuous and ardent character. The extraordinary activity of his nature is shown in the restless zeal with which he labors to revise and improve his own writings, and in the force of his severe but often brilliant polemics; it reflects itself, so to speak, in the peculiar structure of his legal system, which starts with the concept of human activity and considers all legal institutions from the standpoint of the acts which create legal relations.[37] His style is lively and clear; it suffers from far-fetched conceits and the tedious accumulation of synonymous terms; when it rises by a sudden effort it develops a strong rhetorical effect.

NOTES

1. Thus—aside from the political elements in the Sachsenspiegel and other law-books, the partisan pamphlets written during the Investiture conflict and the Hohenstaufen wars, and the mere delivery of tradition (as in the work on the Roman Empire written about 1285 by Jordan of Osnabrück) —the two works of the Abbot of Admont, Engelbert of Volkersdorf, De regimine principum (between 1290 and 1327) and De ortu progressu et fine Romani Imperii liber (1307–1310) are excellent statements of the medieval-Aristotelian theory of the State. And among the adversaries of the Popes in the time of Lewis of Bavaria, the highly important foreigners William of Ockham and Marsilius of Padua are surpassed in statesmanlike and historical spirit by the German Lupold of Bebenburg, whose book De iure regni et imperii (1338–1340), full of original ideas with a future before them, should not be judged by the mistreatment of Riezler (Die literarischen Widersacher der Päpste zur Zeit Ludwigs des Baiers, Leipzig 1874). The well-known later work of Peter of Andlau, De imperio Romano-Germanico (1460), is indeed of slight importance. Among the Conciliarists Henry of Langenstein and Conrad of Gelnhausen take an important place in the history of political thought. Above all the grand effort of Nicolas of Cues, harmonizing two epochs in his Concordantia Catholica (1431–1433), to mold anew the medieval scheme of things, is a work of genius fit to rank with the Politics of Aquinas and the Monarchy of Dante. The writings of Gregory of Heimburg also should not be ignored in the history of political ideas.

2. We may here refer to the studies of Kaltenborn, Vorläufer des H. Grotius, Leipzig 1848, especially the sections on Oldendorp, Hemming, Winkler, and Meisner. Many of these political writings are also reviewed in Wilhelm Roscher, Geschichte der National-Oekonomik in Deutschland, Munich 1874, p. 32 ff. As to the value of the discussions, deductions and observations in public law, see H. Schulze, Einl. in das Deut. Staatsr., Leipzig 1867, p. 50 ff. There has yet been no thorough study of the influence of the German jurists of the sixteenth century on the development of the concepts of public law; among these Zasius, Fichard, Schürpff, Mynsinger and Gail should have special mention.

3. This name was given to them by Guilelmus Barclaius (William Barclay, a Gallicized Scot, 1546–1608) in his work De Regno et regali potestate adversus Buchananum, Brutum, Boucherium et reliquos Monarchomachos libri sex, Paris 1600 (I use the edition of Hanau 1612). Besides the three named, to each of whom he devotes two books, he includes Rossaeus (IV. c. 7), and even Luther (IV. c. 20). The works especially attacked are: (1) George Buchanan (1506–1582), De jure Regni apud Scotos dialogus, Edinburgh 1579 (2nd ed. 1580); (2) Hubert Languet (1518–1581), under the pseudonym of "Stephanus Junius Brutus," Vindiciae contra Tyrannos, Edinburgh 1579 (Paris 1631) [now usually ascribed to Philippe Du Plessis-Mornay (1549–1623)]; (3) Jean Boucher (d. about 1622?), De justa Henrici III abdicatione e Francorum Regno libri quatuor, Lyons 1591 (written in the struggle for the Ligue); (4) "Guilelmus Rossaeus" [not Rose, Bishop of Senlis, but William Rainolds (1544?–1594)], De justa Reipublicae Christianae in reges impios et haereticos authoritate, Paris 1590 (preface 1589; ed. Antwerp 1592; also for the Ligue).—The following are also usually classed among the Monarchomachi: (5) Franciscus Hotomannus (Hotman, 1524–1590), Francogallia, Geneva 1573 (Frankfort 1665); (6) the anonymous work published in French (Lyons 1576) and in Latin (Magdeburg 1578), De jure Magistratuum in subditos et officio subditorum erga Magistratus (I use the edition of Magdeburg 1604, compared with the copy printed at the end of the edition of the Vindiciae contra tyrannos, Hanau 1595, p. 203 ff.); (7) Marius Salamonius, Patritius Romanus, De principatu libri sex, Paris 1578; dedicated "ad Pomponium Beleurium, Regis in Sacro Consistorio Consiliariorum Praesidemque supremae Curiae Parisiensis"; a most remarkable dialogue between a jurist and a philosopher, with a historian and a theologian also taking part, on the maxim "princeps legibus solutus"; (8) Lambertus Danaeus (Daneau, a Calvinist divine, about 1530–1595), Politices Christianae libri septem, Paris 1596 (2nd ed. 1606); (9) Juan Mariana (1536–1624), De rege et regis institutione, Toledo 1599 (Frankfort 1611).—Next come (10) Althusius, (11) Hoenonius (see below, Note 7), and lastly (12) Milton.— The following are sometimes classed among the Monarchomachi: Calvin (1509–1564), John Knox (1505–1572), John Poynet (about 1516–1556) with his book "A short treatise of Politique Power and of the true Obedience which Subjectes owe to Kyngs and other civile Governours," and Thomas Cartwright (1535–1603); also David Pareus (Wängler, born 1548 at Frankenstein in Silesia, d. 1622) on account of his Commentary on the Epistle to the Romans, which was burned at Oxford in 1622. J. N. Hert 1651–1710), Comment. et Opusc., Frankfort 1737 (1st ed. 1700), I. 1 p. 307, makes the series begin with Marsilius of Padua.

4. H. Arnisaeus (of Halberstadt, d. 1636), De auctoritate principum in populum semper inviolabili (1611); see also his Doctrina politica (1606), c. 7 and 11, De jure majestatis libri tres (1610), I. c. 3 and 6, De republica (1615), II. c. 2 § 5. All these works, partly from new editions, are in his Opera omnia politica, Strasburg 1648.

5. Grotius (1583–1645), De Jure Belli ac Pacis, Paris 1625 (Amsterdam 1701), I. c. 3 § 8; see the Notes of Gronovius, the Commentary of C. Ziegler (Wittenberg 1666), and the Observations of Henniges (Sulzbach 1673), p. 164–220. Grotius sought in particular to show the possibility (denied by Althusius) of an alienation of sovereignty on the part of the people, by resort to the analogy of submission to slavery.

6. Such as Jacob Bornitius (Bornitz, of Torgau, afterwards living in Schweidnitz), De majestate politica, Leipzig 1610; also Partitionum politicarum libri quatuor, Hanau 1607, p. 40 ff. Georg Schoenborner (of Silesia, 1579–1637), Politicorum libri septem, Frankfort 1614 (4th ed. 1628). Alex. Irvinus (a Scotsman), De jure regni diascepsis, Leyden 1627. Theod. I. F. Graswinckel (1600–1666), De jure majestatis, The Hague 1642. Joh. Micraelius, Regia Politici scientia, Stettin 1654 (especially I. c. 10 and Qu. 1 ff., p. 108 ff.). Balth. Cellarius, Politica succincta, Jena 1658 (11th ed. 1711), c. 9. Johann Friedrich Horn (1620–1670), Politicorum pars architectonica de Civitate, Utrecht 1664. J. P. Felwinger, Diss. de majestate, in Dissertationes politicae, Altdorf 1666, p. 817 ff. S. Pufendorf (1632–1694), De jure Naturae et Gentium libri octo, 1672 (Frankfort and Leipzig 1744), VII. c. 2 § 14 and c. 6 § 4, De officio hominis et civis secundum legem naturalem libri duo, 1673 (Leyden 1769), II. c. 9. Joh. Christ. Becmann (1641–1711), Meditationes politicae, Frankfort-on-the-Oder 1672 (3rd ed. 1679), c. 12. Casp. Ziegler, De jure majestatis, Wittenberg 1681, I. c. 1 § 44 ff. Samuel Stryk (1640–1710), De absoluta principis potestate (Diss., Vol. XIV. nr. 7).

7. This is especially true of two other works published at Herborn soon after the Politics of Althusius: Phil. Henricus Hoenonius (De Hoen, jurist and statesman, 1576–1640), Disputationum politicarum liber unus, 1615 (this being already the 3rd edition); and Joh. Henr. Alstedius, De statu rerumpublicarum, 1612 (on Alsted, 1588–1638, theologian and philosopher in the College of Herborn, see C. D. Vogel, Archiv der Nassauischen Kirchen- und Gelehrtengeschichte, Vol. I., Hadamar and Coblenz 1814, p. 147–164).

8. Thus, in spite of various formal arguments against Althusius, in B. Keckermann (of Danzig, 1571–1609), Systema disciplinae politicae, Hanau 1607, I. c. 28 p. 425–435. Likewise Herm. Kirchner, Respublica, Marburg 1608, disp. II. § 1; and Z. Fridenreich (of Königsberg-in-der-

Neumark), Politicorum liber, Strasburg 1609, c. 10, 11, 26. Also M. Z. Boxhornius (d. 1653), Institutionum politicorum libri duo, Vol. II., Leipzig 1665, in his doctrine of sovereignty and tyranny takes the position of the Monarchomachi, although he was regarded, not without reason, as their opponent (I. c. 3 § 15 ff., c. 4 and 5, II. c. 4 § 45 ff.). In like manner Christoph Besold (1577–1638) in his Opus politicum; compare Diss. politico-juridica de majestate, Strasburg 1625, c. 1 ff., and Diss. de republica curanda, c. 7. Here also belong Diodor v. Tulden (about 1595–1645), De civili regimine, I. c. 11 ff. (Opera, Louvain 1702); Christ. Liebenthal (1586–1647), Collegium politicum, Marburg 1644, disp. VII.; Daniel Berckringer, Institutiones politicae s. de Republica, Utrecht 1662, I, c. 4.

9. Above all, the distinction of Majestas realis and personalis which was for a long time the prevailing theory (see below, Part II. Ch. III.), was taken directly from the doctrine of sovereignty held by Althusius and his school. This distinction appears fully developed for the first time in Dominicus Arumaeus (1579–1637) and runs through all the discourses produced by his own school in the Discursus academici de jure publico, Jena 1616–1623. Frequent reference is here made to the Politics of Althusius, as is easily explained by the fact that Arumaeus was a native of Friesland and began his studies at Franeker where the book was most admired (see below). Joh. Limnaeus (1592–1663), a pupil of Arumaeus, strongly advocated this theory and based the construction of the Empire upon it. Likewise Besold and many others.

10. Conring, Opera, Brunswick 1730, III. p. 17 (de autoribus politicis): "Habet hic quaedam haud contemnenda; . . . capitalem errorem habent hae politicae Althusii, quod nempe penes populum semper debeat esse summa reipublicae, quale quidem nec in toto orbe observatur." Ib. p. 43 (de civili philosophia, § 100): "Althusii et Hoenonii pernitiosa dogmata, seditiosae plebis tumultus alentia, a doctis viris jam dudum sunt profligata"; their teaching leads to the downfall of States. Ib. p. 421 (de civili prudentia, c. 14 § 104): "error pestilens et turbando orbi aptus." Ib. p. 881 (de regno, § 49). Compare p. 875 § 14, p. 1000 § 67 and p. 1070 § 16.

11. Dissertatio de subjecto summae potestatis, in Conring, Opera III. p. 909 ff. Compare p. 915 § 3: "Omnibus illis quantumvis multis palmam praeripit Johannes Althusius, reipublicae Emden quondam Syndicus, in sua (ut loquitur) Politica methodice digesta, . . . qui pestilenti velut sidere quodam afflatus eo impudentiae est progressus, ut ipsa illa seditiosorum hominum deliramenta in formam artis redigere sacraeque testimoniis scripturae incrustare atque sic pro veris et genuinis prudentiae civilis principiis venditare non erubuerit. Quod ipsum tam feliciter ipsi successit, ut asseclas haud paucos inveniret." Also p. 917 § 17, p. 925 § 51, p. 928 § 62.

12. The work of Fichlau, De imperio absolute et relate considerato ejusque jure, diss. de summae potestatis subjecto ab H. Conringio in lucem proditae opposita, 1650, is in Conring, Opera III. p. 955 ff.; it is there argued (p. 976–977) that Conring had grossly misrepresented the illustrious master Althusius, who ascribes the right of sovereignty to the "corpus universae consociationis" merely "ratione fundamenti" and "radicaliter," without denying its transference.—In his Vindiciae, ib. p. 929 ff., Bensen shows easily enough that Althusius expressly asserts the exclusive and inalienable sovereignty of the people (§ 21 p. 945–946).

13. J. H. Boecler (1611–1672), Institutiones politicae, Strasburg 1674, II. c. 1 p. 102 ff.; also Comment. ad Grotium, I. c. 3 § 8 ("orco damnandum" and poison for the young).

14. U. Huber (1636–1694), De jure civitatis, Leyden 1674 (4th ed. Franeker 1713), I. 2, c. 3 § 24 and c. 5–7, I. 3, c. 1 § 16 and 20.—Huber's wife was a granddaughter of Althusius (see below, Note 27).

15. See the long polemic of Brenneisen (1670–1734), Ostfriesische Historie und Landesverfassung, Aurich 1720, Preface § 17 and 19–20, also I. lib. VII. p. 436 ff.; for him Althusius is the leader of the anti-monarchists; an extract from his Politics is given as evidence. And then Heineccius, Praelectiones academicae in H. Grotii De jure belli ac pacis libros (1744, Opera VIII., 1) I. c. 3 § 8: he opposes the two extremes of Machiavellism and Monarchomachism, the latter of which was made into a system by Althusius, "vir doctus sed omni monarchae infensissimus." See Hert, loc. cit. p. 308; Justus Henning Boehmer (1674–1749), Introductio in jus publicum universale, Prague 1743 (1st ed. 1709), pars gen. c. 5.—That he was known in France is shown by the notices in Bayle, Dictionnaire historique et critique, Rotterdam 1702, I. p. 177; and Réal, Science du Gouvernement, Vol. VIII., Amsterdam 1764, p. 458–459: "un ouvrage qui méritoit le feu."

16. As in Schmitthenner, Zwölf Bücher vom Staat, Vol. I., Giessen 1839, p. 68, followed by F. Walter, Naturrecht und Politik, Bonn 1863, § 434. Also in Kaltenborn, p. 117.

17. As in F. von Raumer, Über die geschichtliche Entwicklung der Begriffe von Recht, Staat und Politik, 2nd ed. Leipzig 1832; J. Weitzel, Geschichte der Staatswissenschaften, Stuttgart and Tübingen 1832, whose silence reveals ignorance all the more as he is full of platitudinous verbiage on Buchanan (p. 140 ff.), Languet (p. 146 ff.) and Mariana (p. 153 ff.); L. A. Warnkönig, Rechtsphilosophie, Freiburg 1839, in the extensive historical sketches; Hinrichs, Geschichte der Rechts- und Staatsprincipien, 3 Vols., Leipzig 1848–1852; F. J. Stahl, Geschichte der Rechtsphilosophie, 3rd ed. Heidelberg 1856, though his remarks on the growth of the

doctrine of popular sovereignty (p. 289 ff.) are otherwise very good; Robert von Mohl, Die Geschichte und Litteratur der Staatswissenschaften, 3 Vols., Erlangen 1855–1858, where hardly any other important name is omitted; J. C. Bluntschli, Geschichte des allgemeinen Staatsrechts und der Politik, Munich 1864.—Even von Roscher, who reviews the political writers of Germany with prodigious learning (for this period see p. 144 ff.), omits Althusius.—Still less may we expect to find him mentioned by foreigners. The work of Baudrillart, Bodin et son temps, Paris 1853, makes no mention of him. Even the highly able work of Paul Janet, Histoire de la Science Politique dans ses rapports avec la morale, 2nd ed. Paris 1872, is in default.

18. Von Stintzing, in Allgemeine deutsche Biographie, Vol. I. (1875), p. 367, makes some correct remarks on the contents of the book. But when he says that Althusius was 'later wrongly regarded as a champion of popular sovereignty,' he can hardly have made a careful study of the inner structure of this system.

19. The leading passages of the Contrat Social (I use the 1st ed., Amsterdam 1762) which show a striking parallel to Althusius are in I. c. 4–6; II. c. 1–2, 4, 7; III. c. 1, 3, 10–11, 16. We shall refer to this again in Part II.

20. By far the most accurate and authentic information is in Vogel, op. cit., I. p. 165–173. Vogel's article on "Johannes Althus" is based partly on manuscript sources. He also makes use of the biographical sketch in Joh. Friedr. Jugler, Beiträge zur jurist. Biographie, Vol. II., Leipzig 1775, p. 270–276, as well as the material already used by Jugler in Emo Lucius Vriemoet, Athenarum Frisiacarum libri duo, Leeuwarden 1778, p. 134–135. He corrects the errors of Jugler. Unfortunately Stintzing, in writing the article on Althusius in the Allg. deutsche Biographie, was not acquainted with Vogel's article. In addition to Jugler, whose inaccuracy is rightly remarked, he makes use of the biography in (Emmo Joh. Heinr. Tiaden) Das gelehrte Ostfriesland, Vol. II., Aurich 1787, p. 278–293. Besides these works I make use of the information in Brenneisen.—Many errors occur in the article on "Althusen" in the Nouvelle Biographie Universelle (Paris 1855), II. p. 232–233; Althusius here becomes a "Jurisconsulte hollandais"; however, as to the contents of the Politics it is justly remarked that in part it expresses the principles which took effect almost two hundred years later in the French Revolution. Still more inaccurate is the article on Althusius in the New General Biographical Dictionary (London 1857), I. p. 366; but here also "the boldness of the democratical principles" is noticed.

21. Jugler, p. 270, makes the groundless assertion that Althusius was born, not in the district of Witgenstein (as is stated by Joh. Textor, Nas-

sauische Chronik, p. 11), but in Emden. Tiaden, p. 280, says that this is a 'well-founded' conjecture, supported by local tradition and also by the mention of East Friesland as 'the beloved Fatherland' in the preface to the "Ostfriesisches Recess- und Accordbuch" edited by Althusius. Stintzing, loc. cit., says doubtfully 'or in East Friesland,' while the Biographie Universelle decides for Emden. It is clear however that Jugler's conjecture is a mistaken inference from the position of Althusius as Syndic of Emden and his zeal in defending the freedom of that city. The words used by Althusius in the prefaces to the revised editions of the Politics and the Dicaeologica written in Emden, in speaking of his years of service rendered to the city, show clearly that he was not a native of that city nor of East Friesland; the impersonal tone of the preface to the collection of treaties anonymously edited by him argues nothing to the contrary. Moreover his whole family lived in the Reformed region east of the middle Rhine. His wife Margarethe (daughter of the financier Friedrich Neurath and Marie von Cronenburg, widow of Johannes Kesseler) was born at Siegen March 18, 1574 (died at Emden April 15, 1624); and when Althusius addresses the first edition of his Politics with a dedication to two of his relatives by marriage, Martin Neurath, U. J. D. Advocatus et causarum patronus Sigensis, and Jacob Tieffenbach, Advocatus Cambergensis, he sends his greetings not only to her kinsfolk but also to his own. His cousin Philipp Althusius, who published the "Civilis conversationis libri duo" at Hanau in 1601, lived at Corbach in Waldeck.

22. Vogel, p. 165. This accords with the fact that the first edition of his earliest book was published at Basel in 1586.

23. In the preface to the second edition of his Jurisprudentia Romana, Herborn 1588, he solicits the aid of the "virum bene de me meritum, Dionysium Gothofredum I. C. Genevensem excellentissimum" in the systematization of the civil law. In this connection he also mentions as specially qualified jurists Professor Hermann Vultejus of Marburg (1555–1634) and Professor Heinrich Bocer of Tübingen (1561–1630), but without suggesting any personal connection.

24. Tiaden p. 282, and Vogel p. 167. Stintzing is clearly mistaken in dating his inauguration as Syndic of Emden in the year 1601, as in 1602 Althusius was Rector at Herborn. The preface to the first edition of the Politics published at Herborn in 1603, while omitting to state where it was written, was clearly not written in Emden. His predecessor in the Syndicate, Doctor Dothias Wiarda, was indeed removed from office in 1601.—Réal makes him Syndic of Bremen; this error has been repeated, it occurs in the New General Biographical Dictionary, cited above.

25. In the dedication of the second edition of the Politics to the Estates

of West Friesland, dated February 21, 1610, Althusius mentions this honorific (honestis sane conditionibus) invitation as one of the reasons for the dedication. Perhaps the authorities of the university still hoped to obtain the services of this widely famous jurist. See Vriemoet, p. 134; Tiaden, p. 282; Vogel, p. 167.—The professorship was first offered to Dion. Godofredus.

26. See Brenneisen, op. cit., and the history of these years in Wiarda, Ostfries. Geschichte, Aurich 1791 ff., III. p. 469 ff. and IV. p. 1 ff.; also Tiaden, p. 292.—Brenneisen says that he, together with Ubbo Emmius (1547–1625), whose friend and counsellor he was, promoted the misconceptions and perversions of the constitution of East Friesland. As Syndic he had 'the direction of public affairs,' was often mentioned in the state-papers of Enno II and Ulrich II, and enjoyed 'great authority in his own city.' His doctrines may be recognized in all the contemporary documents of Emden and in the municipal transactions and proceedings of the Diet. See the extracts from documents given in Brenneisen, p. 458 ff.; among these the "Tractat," which was 'widely circulated throughout the country' under the title "Vindiciae juris populi contra usurpationem iniquam Comitis usque ad annum 1608, autore Ubbone Emmio," is said by him to have been written mainly by Althusius (a statement which is doubtless correct; this is shown especially by the arguments on the imprescriptibility of the people's rights, p. 450–451, and on the dissolution of the "vinculum" with the ruler resulting "eo ipso facto" from a breach of his contract, p. 452).—On the importance of the official position of Althusius and his personal influence see also Ubbo Emmius, De Frisia et Frisiorum Republica, Emden 1616 (Decas septima rerum Frisiacarum historiae), p. 384.

27. Details on his six children and their descendants in Vogel, p. 169–171. It is of some interest that a daughter of his son Hermann, named Agnes, married the eminent jurist Ulrich Huber at Franeker December 4, 1659 (see above, Note 14). A grandson of the same name as himself was Burgomaster of Emden in 1693.

28. This adjunct, which appears also in the later editions, has generally a separate pagination, and has no close connection with the subject-matter of the Politics itself.

29. The first edition contains 32 chapters in 469 pages octavo, the second edition 39 chapters in 715 pages quarto.

30. This edition contains 968 (including the Oratio, 1003) pages octavo. Here is found for the first time a division of the chapters into numbered paragraphs, which is repeated in the later editions (except that of Arnheim 1617). For this reason I use it as a basis for the present work, noting however all the variations of the earlier editions and comparing also the later editions published during the lifetime of Althusius.

31. Jugler, p. 273, remarks that here 'many violent expressions are omitted, which the author had inserted here and there in behalf of the city of Emden against its rulers.' This is quite incorrect. The edition of 1625 corresponds word for word with that of 1614, even in the page-numbering. —The edition of 1617 is omitted in Vogel, p. 172.

32. This book seems to have been the earliest separate publication of Althusius and was at any rate the direct cause of his call to Herborn.

33. For present purposes the second edition has been used as a basis; it was published at Herborn in 1588 by Corvinus (295 pages octavo besides the Tables). The second Basel edition of 1589 as well as the Herborn editions of 1592, 1599 and 1607 have also been used. According to Vogel later editions appeared at Herborn in 1623, 1640 and 1673.—To the Basel editions and the Herborn editions of 1592 and after, the Cynosura Juris of Johannes Reidamus is annexed. To the editions of 1592 and after, an "Epitome et brevis anacaephalaeosis dicaeologicae" is prefixed.

34. The book has 792 pages, large quarto. The Herborn edition has a shorter title; in the Frankfort edition of 1618 the same preface which in the Herborn edition bears the date, Emden March 1, 1617, is dated March 1, 1618. The two editions, both published by Corvinus, are otherwise in agreement.

35. They are enumerated in Jugler, op. cit.; Tiaden, p. 283 ff.; and Vogel, p. 171–173. I have not been able to obtain Gondelmann, Tract. de magis, veneficis et lamiis, Nuremberg 1616, which includes (p. 154–163) an Ad judicem admonitio by Althusius; according to Jugler it urges caution in prosecutions for witchcraft; that he should not be classed as an opponent of these prosecutions (as is done in the Biograph. Univ.) is shown in his Dicaeologica, I. c. 102–103. Mention should be made of the "Tractatus tres, quorum I de poenis II de rebus fungilibus III de jure retentionis," Cassel 1611 (quarto), published as transcribed lecture-notes by a pupil of Althusius, Christian Grau of Allendorf in Hesse. The book designated by Vogel as "Aphorismi de juris civilis studio, Aschaffenb. 1630 (12°)" bears instead the title: "Joh. Althusii aphorismi universi juris civilis vel repertorium . . . sub hac forma portabili editum studio Wolfgangi Sigismundi a Vorburg," and is nothing but a student's syllabus compiled from Althusius. —Althusius also edited an "Ostfriesisches Recess- und Accordbuch, d. i. Zusammenstellung aller Ordnungen, Decreten, Resolutionen u. s. w., zu verschiedenen Zeiten aufgericht und publicirt," Emden 1612, republished in 1620 and 1656; Brenneisen, pref. § 22, says that the editorial work is tainted with prejudice against the Count; Brenneisen's own book, however, is a mere polemic in behalf of the latter; I have only been able to obtain the 1656 edition.

36. This work (373 pages octavo) is as remarkable for the logical arrangement of its material as for its practical intelligence.

37. Jugler, p. 272, after praising the erudition of Althusius, deplores the faults of his 'moral character': 'A culpable impulse to discord and rebellion was too deeply rooted for him to fail to seize all occasions to give rein to his evil passions in the many quarrels of the city of Emden with its Counts and Princes at that time.' This is a mere figment whose source is too obvious for any value to be attached to it. Even Brenneisen, with all the warmth of his factual polemics, knows nothing of such motivations. On the other hand Ubbo Emmius, p. 244, writes concerning the Syndicate of Emden: "Hunc locum a multis annis tenet ac magna cum laude tuetur consultissimus et clarissimus vir, doctrina, virtute, fide singulari plane eximius et ingenii sui monumentis aeternum victuris illustris, Johannes Althusius, sincera ac peracta amicitia mecum conjunctus." In spite of this Vogel, p. 168, repeats Jugler's gossip without scruple, and adds as evidence: 'Even in Herborn outbreaks of this pestilent temper displayed themselves in him; he was at war with his colleague Matthäus, and only Count John the Elder could restore peace again.' We need not attempt to decide whether Althusius or 'Colleague Matthaeus' was in the wrong, and may content ourselves with the image of the personality which speaks in the writings themselves. But it is interesting to note how, in this as in so many other cases, virtuous indignation at a theory has led to aspersions on the character of its author. These notions reappear in Schmitthenner and Walter in the epithets 'violent' and 'quarrelsome.'

CHAPTER TWO

THE POLITICS OF ALTHUSIUS

WE shall now examine the content of the Politics of Althusius, which is primarily a methodical treatment of the idea of popular sovereignty as outlined by the author in the preface to the first edition.

In the dedication, addressed to two of his relatives who were practicing lawyers, he explains the plan and method of his work, discusses its difficulties and excuses its faults. His endeavor is to construct a complete and purified system of politics in strictly logical order. This requires on the one hand the dismissal of extraneous matters properly belonging to theology, ethics and law, and on the other hand the restitution to politics of topics which had been usurped by theology, philosophy and jurisprudence. In actual life and practice, of course, the various sciences are not to be separated and should even go hand in hand; but in matters of theory, without overlooking their inner connection, strict lines of demarcation should be drawn. Each science must solve its own problems by its own means; the solution of prior questions must be taken from other sciences. Thus philosophy and theology lay the groundwork of politics, as it is their province to establish the moral law of Nature and the revealed commands of God; but the application of the moral law, including the decalogue, to social life is a matter for politics. At the same time the latter has much to do with laying the groundwork of jurisprudence. The aim of jurisprudence is to deduce rights from facts, and to judge the acts of man by fixed rules ("de jure et merito facti in humana vita judicet"); the material facts of which it takes notice are not derived from itself but belong to other sciences. The aim of politics is to study the best means of instituting and conserving the life of human society ("ut consociatio, humanave societas et vita socialis bono nostro instituatur et conservetur mediis ad hoc ipsum aptis, utilibus et necessariis"); thus it deals with one of the essential factors in the genesis of law. Althusius on the one hand attacks Bodin and Gregorius for bringing purely legal questions into their political writings. On the other hand he accuses the jurists of trespass for invading the field of what we should now call General Public Law. He defines the region in question as the study of the origin, nature and elements of "majestas" or sovereignty. To jurisprudence he assigns only the derivation of particular legal relations from the rights of sovereignty and the contract made between people and ruler. For the rest, he takes the theory of the "jura et capita majestatis" as the proper theme and even the essential theme of politics, which stands or falls with it. To restore this to the domain of politics is his cherished purpose.

Here he differs altogether from the prevailing view as represented chiefly by Bodin. Expressing the ideas of a small minority he ascribes the rights of sovereignty not to the ruler but wholly and solely to the people. The rights of sovereignty belong necessarily and exclusively to the social body ("corpus symbioticum"); they are its spirit, its soul, the breath of its life; only when it possesses them does it live; when it loses them it perishes or at any rate forfeits the name of "Respublica." They are indeed administered by a chief magistrate, but the ownership and usufruct thereof belong inseparably to the people as a whole (populus universus, consociatio universalis, regnum ipsum). So much so indeed that even if the people itself wishes to renounce these rights and alienate them to another, it can never do this any more than a man can transfer his own life to another person.[1] As the people itself is the only possible source of sovereignty, it is the only possible permanent 'subject' (or bearer) thereof, and always maintains and preserves it and never dies. And whenever the agent ceases to exist or forfeits his right, the people resumes the exercise of these rights and delegates them anew. And as the very nature of these rights precludes any "commercium" or any individual ownership thereof, the ruler who usurps such an ownership ceases "eo ipso" to be a ruler and becomes simply a private man and a tyrant.

These arguments on popular sovereignty are repeated with slight alterations by Althusius in the preface to the second edition of his Politics (copied in the later editions). Not only do they appear more sharply defined in the otherwise abridged and revised version,[2] but they are also brought into close connection with the dedication of the revised work to the 'Honorable Estates of Friesland between Vlie-Strom and Lauwer-Zee.' In an eloquent apostrophe he declares that the liberty of Friesland and the other Netherlands rests secure on this basis, and that no nobler example could be found of a just, wise and valiant realization of his ideas than that which was displayed to all nations by the United Provinces in their glorious revolt against Spain.[3]

Althusius holds faithfully to this plan. The idea of popular sovereignty, whose consequences are worked out with iron rigor, forms the whole groundwork of the social structure which he now erects.

In the first chapter, after defining the subject-matter of politics as the organization of social life, he discusses the nature of "consociatio" in general. Here he sets forth the scheme which remained a pattern for later systems. Necessity leads to association; association itself is the product of a tacit or explicit contract. The parties to this contract become members of society ("symbiotici"), mutually bound in communion ("communicatio") in such things as are useful and necessary for social life. The association ($\chi o \iota \nu \omega \nu \iota a$) comprises interests, duties and rights. It is governed by two species of public laws ("leges consociationis"). Firstly, the fundamental social laws ("leges communicationis") define the terms and bounds of the association. Secondly, the administrative laws ("leges directionis et gubernationis") ordain the government of that sphere which has become social. Each society has its own "lex propria," but all societies have their "lex communis" defining rulers and subjects. Rulership is the service and care of the common welfare; obedience is the price paid for protection and defense. The efficient cause of all association and all government is the consent of the associates, and its final cause is the general welfare; at the same time its ultimate ground lies in the divine order of the world as manifested in nature.

In the subsequent chapters the author treats of the "species consociationis": family, corporation, commune, province and State. He always derives the larger and higher associations from the smaller and lower, and insists repeatedly that this is the only method which corresponds to their natural and historical relation. For it is by these steps that the development has taken place, each greater association resting upon lesser associations without which it could not exist, while they themselves can exist even without it (see for example c. 39 § 84). For each species of association he seeks then to determine the social sphere whose 'subject' is in every case the whole body of the associates, taking up next its government by representatives and executives. Every statement is followed by copious examples and illustrations taken from sacred and profane history.

The prime division of societies is the distinction between the "consociatio simplex et privata" which unites individual persons for a special common interest ("peculiare commune"), and the "consociatio mixta et publica" which unites the simple societies into an all-round political community ("politeuma").[4]

For the consociatio privata, Althusius first lays down a few general principles whereby it is treated throughout as a corporate body governed by a common will, with a unitary sphere of rights exercised under fixed rules, and having a unitary collective personality (c. 2 § 2–13). He classifies it further into the natural and necessary association of the family and the civil and spontaneous association of the corporation. Moral and economic duties are assigned to the family (thus he treats of domestic occupations, ib. § 14–36). He discourses at length on the marital community (§ 37–46) and the wider family-circle (c. 3, here also on nobility). The corporation ("consociatio collegarum") is defined as a unitary body, freely formed and freely dissolved, in which the collective body remains the bearer of the collective rights, but elects an executive to whom the management is entrusted and who thereby receives authority over the individual members (he is "major singulis, minor universis collegis"). The communion, looser or stricter according to the contract, comprises interests, services, laws and sentiment. The "communicatio rerum" deals with the corporate property, shares and beneficial interests of the members (c. 4 § 8–11); the "communicatio operarum" is expressed in the official functions of executives and syndics, the order of services, regulation of the vocations of the members, inspection and the like (§ 12–15); the "jus" of the association establishes corporative autonomy, jurisdiction, the power to punish and to make decisions (§ 16 22); lastly the "communicatio benevolentiae" completes the moral and social unity of the group (§ 23). After treating of the species of collegia, he gives a review of corporative organization among the Jews, Romans, Egyptians, Greeks, Gauls and Germans. In conclusion it is remarked that in contemporary States, for the most part, the several Estates are to be classed as "collegia generalia," and the ecclesiastical and secular courts, companies and gilds as "collegia specialia." [5]

Althusius holds that the "consociatio publica" or political community is a "universitas"; and following Losaeus he states some general rules applying to "universitates," particularly as to their formation according to the "jus gentium" and their self-identity amid changes of membership (c. 5 § 1–5). He divides these into the consociatio publica particularis and universalis.

Among the 'particular societies' he treats first of the local community (municipal corporation or commune). He begins by discussing the composition and organization of the commune; the definition, acquisition and grades of citizenship; the division of the citizens into rulers and ruled (§ 8–27). Here he says at the outset that every communal governing body, whether one man or many, must be regarded as a minister of the communal rights, chosen by election and removable at any time, with power over the individuals but not over the community itself ("jus in singulos non in universos cives"); and hence while the citizens swear allegiance it also takes the oath of fidelity to them. The same principle is applied to the various species of local communities.[6] Among these the three grades of rural communes, "vicus" (village), "pagus" (parish) and "oppidum" (borough) are first set forth (§ 28–39); then comes a lengthy description

of the constitutions of cities (§ 40–84), and of the special status
of particular kinds of cities, as imperial cities, provincial cities
and "civitates mixtae," metropolitan and colonial cities (c. 6 §
1–14).[7] Then returning to the consideration of communes in
general, he analyzes the nature of communal association ("communicatio civium"), in which he sees a "microcosmos" of the
structure of the State (§ 15–47). The social union again creates
a "communicatio rerum" in which the interests of the commune,
in accordance with the usual scheme, are divided into the spiritual
and the secular, and each of these into the "res universitatis in
specie" and the "patrimonium universitatis." Next comes the
"communicatio operarum," from which flow political and ecclesiastical offices, public works, guard-duty and military services,
industrial, commercial and agrarian vocations. And from the
"communicatio juris" the commune derives its capacity as an
autonomous communion of right and justice. And here also the
consummation is formed by the inner moral union of the members ("communicatio concordiae"). As soon as the community is
established it requires a government, which rests upon a delegation from the whole body, though in dependent communes this
does not take place without the co-operation of higher authorities
(§ 48–52).[8]

As the second species of "consociatio politica particularis"
Althusius treats of the "universitas provinciae," which he defines
as the incorporation of a larger but not independent territory
(c. 7 § 1–2). The provincial community is described as a compre-
hensive religious, political, economic and social unit (§ 3–64).[9]
But as to the administration of the "jus provinciale" he goes on
the principle that it is exercised jointly by the head and members
of the province, who together represent the province as a whole
(c. 8). The "membra provinciae" are the Estates of the territory,
these being divided into the "ordo ecclesiasticus" and the "ordo
saecularis." The ecclesiastical Estate is constituted according to
the Reformed model, in presbyteries, classical synods, and provincial synods (c. 8 § 6–39). The secular Estate is divided into
the nobility, burghers and commoners, each of these having its
own functions (§ 40–48). In many provinces indeed the Estate
of the commoners or peasantry is not admitted, but this is a

grievous wrong (§ 40). Each Estate organizes by delegation a representative college of deputies to take care of its own interests, and to assemble in conjunction with the other colleges in a general Diet to conduct the affairs of the whole province ("curam in negotiis vitae socialis provincialis," see § 49, and on the institution of Diets § 66–70). Over against the Estates there appears as head of the province the "Praeses Provinciae" or Count, who at the same time may rule over other provinces and may then be called Duke, Prince, Margrave or Landgrave. He is entrusted with this office by the "summus imperans" of the Empire; yet while remaining inferior he wields the powers of sovereignty independently, so that he "tantum potest in districtu quantum summus magistratus in regno" (§ 50–55). It is for him to act as chief executive of the province and to summon the Estates (§ 56–71); without their consent, however, he cannot lawfully undertake anything of importance (§ 50), and in case of dereliction of duty on his part the right of defection belongs to the whole community (§ 92). Althusius reviews the historical formation of provinces among the Jews, Romans, Gauls and Germans (§ 72–91). It is clear enough however that his 'province' is essentially a German territory, democratized as much as possible with special regard to East Friesland.[10]

He turns next to the State (politia, imperium, regnum, populus, respublica). He defines it as a "universalis publica consociatio, qua civitates et provinciae plures ad jus regni mutua communicatione rerum et operarum, mutuis viribus et sumptibus habendum, constituendum, exercendum et defendendum se obligant" (c. 9 § 1). Its constituent members are neither the individuals themselves nor the "collegia privata," but the cities and provinces which have agreed to unite and incorporate themselves into one body (§ 5). Their contract is the bond that holds the State together (§ 7). Such a completely federalized conception of the State does not of itself import the idea of a Federal State in the strict sense [*Bundesstaat*, as distinguished from *Staatenbund* or Confederation]; but the possibility of closer or looser Confederations of States and the organization of Federal Assemblies are fully treated later.[11]

The essential right of the State ("jus regni") which makes it

one body with one head is the "jus majestatis" (§ 19–27): "potestas praeeminens et summa universalis disponendi de iis, quae
universaliter ad salutem curamque animae et corporis membrorum Regni seu Reipublicae pertinent." The sovereign power of
the State, as Bodin rightly holds, is like the soul in the physical
body, strictly one and indivisible. Yet it is by no means the highest power, as Bodin infers, for it stands below the power of God.
Moreover it is not absolute but bound by legal limitations, even
though it may seem exempt from positive law so far as compulsion and punishment are concerned. But even this limited
sovereignty does not belong to any King or assembly of Optimates; it is produced and preserved by the people as a whole.
The individuals themselves are governed, but the whole body
governs ("non singulis, sed conjunctim universis membris et toto
corpori consociato regni competit"). So also it is said in the
Pandects: "quod universitati debetur, singulis non debetur."
Thus the physical body as a whole governs all its limbs. Hence
every disposition of sovereign power must be made by the "universa membra de communi consensu." Also, the people can
neither alienate nor dismember the rights of sovereignty. It can
delegate and distribute the exercise of these rights among various
'subjects,' as the division of administrative functions does not
touch the indivisible sovereignty which remains in the people
as the true 'superior.' [12]

This "jus regni" in the first place forms the content of the
"communio symbiotica universalis," and in the second place expresses itself in its "administratio."

Althusius first explains the content of the all-embracing community established in the State, while then he traces its expression in the several 'rights of superiority' belonging to the people.[13] The unity of the State expresses itself first of all in a
twofold manner, according as its end is the salvation of souls or
temporal welfare. In the first aspect it appears as an ecclesiastical
society devoted to religious faith, worship, morals and instruction (§ 31 ff.). As a secular society it sets up general rules by
virtue of the "jus majestatis saecularis generale" and enforces
them with rewards and punishments (c. 10), while by virtue
of the "jus majestatis saecularis speciale" it engages in practical

activity for the promotion of the general welfare (c. 11 § 1). This last function is again of two kinds. Firstly, it undertakes to provide the material means of social life, and thus in the common interest it concerns itself with trade and commerce, coinage, measures, weights, and language, and especially the imposition of ordinary and extraordinary taxes, burdens, services and official duties, as well as the grant of privileges (c. 11–15). Secondly, it undertakes to protect the social body and the "symbiosis universalis." Here the "communicatio auxilii" is of chief service, in giving charitable aid in perils of flood and fire and other cases of need, maintaining justice and police and military defense (c. 16), and also in the proper conservation and expenditure of the public treasure (c. 17 § 1 ff.). But this is also subserved by the "communicatio consilii" in general Diets of the Empire, in which the weightiest matters are decided by majority of votes (§ 55–61).[14]

In the eighteenth chapter Althusius discusses the exercise of these rights of sovereignty arising from the national community.[15] First he considers the State-authorities in general from the standpoint of the "administratores consociationis universalis"; then entering on an elaborate argument to prove his basic principle that in every form of constitution the holders of governing power, however great may be their authority over individuals, are subordinate to the sovereign community as a whole. He supplements this proof several times in later chapters, and resumes it once more in the penultimate chapter (c. 38) in discussing more fully the action to be taken against tyrants. His arguments, which are drawn from reason, holy scripture, positive law and history, are in large part identical with the arguments already developed in the middle ages and worked out by the earlier Monarchomachi. However there is no lack of new ideas. A wide field is covered by this vigorous but acute polemic, in which the principles of his opponents, particularly Bodin, Barclay and Arnisaeus, are confuted.[16]

According to Althusius the body of the people, just like any corporation in private law, has the power to appoint and authorize the ministers of its common rights, to fix terms and conditions and to prescribe oaths and obligations for them (c. 18 § 1–5).

Under the general principles of the law of corporations, such officers represent the people in so far as it cannot itself assemble and act in a body, and thus they have the powers and duties of guardians; but just because they are guardians they act only in behalf of the ward and appear as its "famuli et ministri," its mandataries and procurators whose authority is not their own but derivative. As the people is prior in time to its governors and is the source of their power, so it remains their superior and the bearer of a higher power ("potior et superior," § 6–14 and 92–106). But no relation other than such a mandate of the people is possible for a legitimate government. In the first place, as all men are by nature free and equal, no power can be derived from any other source than voluntary consent; hence, while the existence of government is required by right reason as well as by the Word of God, they also require that it be instituted by the common will (§ 16–24). In the second place, the community can never make an alienation of its sovereignty instead of the mandate; "jura majestatis, ut a corpore consociato inceperunt, sic individue et inseparabiliter illi adhaerent nec in alium transferri possunt" (ib. § 15, 84, 104, 123–124; c. 38 § 125–129). Althusius defends this basic principle very skilfully with the same weapons employed by the champions of absolutism who had also held that the right of sovereignty originally resided in the people and that it was a "jus individuum, incommunicabile, impraescriptibile." If this is true it must still remain in the people even though the people has made an agreement to alienate it. Hence it follows that all rulers, while they officially represent the whole people and bear its 'person,' have less power than the people (c. 18 § 26–27); that however free may be their governing power they nevertheless recognize the people as master ("populum seu regni corpus dominum agnoscere") and must serve the best interests of this master (ib. § 28–31; c. 19 § 2–3; c. 38 § 121–122 and 128); that they are bound by the laws of the realm and the limits of their mandate (c. 18 § 32–40 and 106); that when they exceed these limits they cease to be "ministri Dei et universalis consociationis" and become mere private persons, "quibus obedientia in illis, quibus suae potestatis limites excedunt, non debetur" (§ 41–46 and 105). This limitation is so inherent in the nature of government that even the formal grant of a "potestas absoluta" cannot change it; absolute power does not mean absolute despotism any more than liberty means license, but is simply a full power within the limits of the law; any mandate which goes beyond these limits would be null and void because "turpe, impossibile et contra jus naturale" (c. 38 § 128–130).

Althusius assumes throughout two grades of such officers, Ephors and the Chief Magistrate ("summus magistratus").

By the word "Ephors" (c. 18 § 48–122) he means all those magistrates, found everywhere under various titles, who by authority of the whole people have to exercise its rights as against the ruler.[17] They are the pillars of the State, who at once support the executive power and hold it within the limits of the law, and when it lapses by reason of vacancy or abuse they sustain the edifice themselves. The Ephors are originally chosen by popular election, but their office may become hereditary, and their appointment may even "ex populi concessione et beneficio" be left in the hands of the Prince or the Optimates. In any case they take the oath of office and are mere agents of the people. They form a college which acts by majority vote, and as such they exercise the "officium generale" of popular representation. In particular, by the mandate and in the name of the people they have power to elect the Chief Magistrate, to appoint a Regent in case of impediment and to govern the realm during an interregnum, and also to advise, admonish and correct the ruler. Moreover no important acts are valid without their consent, and in the weightiest matters the ruler must do what they decide; and above all they must protect the reserved rights of the people, resist every tyrannical encroachment, and in extreme cases depose the ruler; on the other hand they have to defend him against wrongful attacks. Besides this "officium generale" of the College as a whole, there is the "officium speciale" of the individual Ephors who exercise an "imperium limitatum" in their own provinces, under the supervision of the Chief Magistrate. This secures the benefits of a "mutua censura et observatio inter regem et ephoros." Lastly, after a brief survey of the various historic forms of the Ephorate,[18] he declares that this institution should be adopted universally. In default thereof all its functions must be performed by direct vote in the assembly of the whole people, regardless of any prescription of time or any usurpation (§ 123–124).

At the head of the State stands the Chief Magistrate, "qui secundum leges ad salutem et utilitatem universalis consociationis constitutus, jura illius administrat et executioni mandat" (c. 19 § 1). In relation to his inferiors he is regarded as chief, but he is still the mere "minister" of an "aliena potestas," as the "proprietas" of all the power which he exercises belongs to the "corpus universalis consociationis" (§ 2–5). His relation to the people is that of an obligatory contract mutually sworn to by a "consociatio mandans" and its "mandatarius" (§ 6–7). Whatever is not delegated to him is reserved to the people; it can and should bestow only a limited authority which may be revoked in case of abuse, so that it remains in all cases the imperishable "dominus" and in many things "major" (§ 7–23). The contract is composed of two parts. The first part is the "commissio regni," divided into the election and the solemn inauguration (§ 24–107). In the election by the Ephors, performed in the name of the people and under 'collegial' rules, the terms and conditions of rulership are settled as fundamental laws in the form of a "stipulatio." [19] The election may be entirely free, or it may be restricted by the constitution; thus it may be limited to a certain nationality or it may be determined by a law of succession instituted by the people. In any case the election is the constitutive act which creates the right of the ruler according to the Will of God and indeed as a right derived from God.[20] The second part of the contract with the ruler is formed by the taking of the oath of allegiance on the part of the subjects (c. 20). This completes the contract and makes it binding upon the ruler and the people until it is broken by one or the other. If it is broken by the people the ruler is absolved from his obligations. If the ruler breaks it the people, having bound itself only "sub conditione, si pie et juste imperaturus sit," is freed from all contractual obligations and may give itself a new ruler or a new form of government as it sees fit (§ 19–21).[21]

In the following chapters the author treats the administration of this system of government as the 'exercise of the sovereign rights of the people under the laws of the Empire.'

First he explains in seven chapters (c. 21–27, 1st ed. c. 16–22) the norms and guiding principles of government, whose observance he sums up as "prudentia politica." In connection with numerous examples of this he combines the standpoints of religion, ethics, law, and social politics.[22]

In ten chapters (c. 28–37, 1st ed. c. 23–31) he takes up the various branches of government.[23] This is primarily concerned with public affairs and the public property of the community. In connection with the previous classification of rights of sovereignty, he discusses the regulation of ecclesiastical affairs, including education, strictly in the spirit of a State-church (c. 28). Next comes the theory of the sanctions of law and their application in the administration of justice (c. 29). As "censura" a strict moral police-discipline is recommended (c. 30), and as "studium concordiae conservandae" an equally strict police-protection against disorder, with special reference to factions, assemblages and associations (c. 31). In the doctrine of the "procuratio mediorum ad vitae socialis commoditates necessariorum" he deals with matters of public economy and the apportionment of taxes, services and offices (c. 32). He discourses at full length on the convening at fixed periods of the "concilia universalia consociationis universalis," Reichstags or Imperial Diets,[24] and their formation under the positive public laws of the various nations of the world, especially of Germany (c. 33).[25] No less full is the treatment of the "cura et tractatio armorum" in peace (c. 34) and in war (c. 35–36), including many points of international law. After the administration of public affairs there comes the administration of public property, with a full exposition of its leading principle that all "res publicae et fiscales" are the property of the people and should be used only for the benefit of the people (c. 37 § 1–61),[26] as well the regulation and protection of the offices, Estates and corporations of the Empire (§ 62–78). The government, however, is concerned not only with the good of the whole but also with the good of the individuals, and while it wields the State's rights of superiority over persons and property, it must avoid any arbitrary encroachment on liberty or property.[27]

In the thirty-eighth chapter Althusius takes up the topic of abuse of power, with a very full discussion of tyranny and its remedies.[28] In this chapter, as has already been said, he seeks once more to establish the inalienable sovereignty of the people at all points and to fortify it against the latest attacks. According to him the Tyrant, in the strict sense of the term, is the legitimately instituted ruler who breaks the law or neglects his duty. The so-called "tyrannus absque titulo" with whom the tyrant is commonly identified (as distinguished from the "tyrannus quoad exercitium") is simply a public enemy whom any private person may seize and drive out (§ 27). He makes a special effort to fix upon the decisive marks which define the genuine tyrant.[29] Whenever these marks are present, the people should have the "jus resistentiae et exauctorationis" against a monarch as well as against the magistrate of a republic. This right is demonstrated by means of twelve arguments drawn from the nature of contract, of office and of mandate, the idea of popular sovereignty, the Law of Nature and the Word of God (§ 28–43); it is supported by precedents taken from sacred and profane history (§ 44–45), and defended against the attacks of Albericus Gentilis, Guilelmus Barclaius and Johannes Beccaria, as well as Bodin (§ 77–130). The exercise of this right, however, is granted only to the people collectively and to the Ephors acting in its name. Private individuals ("privati et subditi") have only the right of passive resistance and the natural right of self-defense in case of imminent peril (§ 65–68). But when the Ephors know that tyranny exists, when they have remonstrated in vain and have tried other peaceful means without success, they have collectively the right and the duty to throw off the tyrant and drive him out by force or to inflict the penalty of death (§ 53–64).[30] As individuals they have the right and the duty to protect their own provinces against tyranny, and if need be, to withdraw from the Empire, subject themselves to another ruler or declare their independence (§ 46–52). Indeed since the "regna universalis" is composed of families, corporations, parishes, boroughs, cities and provinces, when the contract of union is broken by its chief guarantor any of the component members of the State may secede and constitute itself an independent State (§ 76 and 110–114).

Yet according to Althusius this does not weaken but rather strengthens the power of the State by holding it within the limits of the law (§ 71–75).

The last chapter (c. 39, 1st ed. c. 32) treats of the distinction of various forms of the State, which are characteristically left to the last as mere "species summi magistratus." The chief magistracy is either "monarchicus" or "polyarchicus" (§ 1). Neither mixtures nor perversions give rise to new forms (§ 2). Bodin's distinction between forms of the State and forms of government is false; as sovereignty always belongs to the people, all distinctions of forms of the State are merely distinctions of administrative systems (§ 3). In a monarchy (§ 4–31) the ruler is a single physical person. The monarch, however, must necessarily possess a power limited by law and remains bound to the cooperation and control of popular organs. Thus no monarchy lacks aristocratic and democratic elements, while on the other hand all polyarchies show a monarchical element in some form of unitary apex. In this sense every healthy State-organism presents a mixture like the mixture of temperaments in man, so that an unmixed constitution is scarcely to be found in history or at any rate is not permanent. However, some one of the elements always predominates and gives its essential character to the constitution; hence properly speaking there can be no "forma mixta." Thus the Germanic Empire is a monarchy. The polyarchic magistracy (§ 32–44) consists of a number of persons taken together as a unit, which in order to govern must necessarily be formed into a College with fixed rules as to the presiding office, the conduct of business and the distribution of functions. In an aristocracy (§ 46–56) a small number of Optimates are "conjunctim et individue" entrusted with the exercise of sovereign powers. In a democracy (§ 57–82) the governing officers are elected and changed from time to time while the representatives of the provinces and communes, or of the corporations, curiae, centuriae, tribes or classes play the part of Ephors; the 'chief magistracy' here remains in the public assembly in which the people as a whole ("populus ipse instar unius") exercises the rights of sovereignty directly. Althusius traces the historical phases and variations of each of these forms of government. He also describes in the usual way their advantages and disadvantages, as well as the means of preserving them and the causes of their degeneration. As to the problem of the best form of government he offers no solution but merely reports the opinions of others.[31]

Such is the gist of this remarkable book. But before we proceed to judge its importance by a closer study of the history of the political ideas which it expresses, we may conclude our survey of the legal and political doctrines of Althusius with a glance at his juristic works.

NOTES

1. The passage is as follows: "proprietatem vero illorum et usumfructum adeo jure ad regnum seu populum pertinere contendo, ut hisce, etiamsi velit, se abdicare eosque in alium transferre et alienare nequaquam possit, non minus quam vitam quam quisque habet alii communicare potest." The preface to the later editions differs only in minor verbal points, yet here in the decisive passage referring to federal structure the "populus universus in corpus unum symbioticum ex pluribus minoribus consociationibus consociatus" is described as the 'subject' of sovereignty.

2. The train of ideas in the preface remains the same. He omits the reflections on the difficulty of formulating abstract principles and general rules amid the endless complexities of real life, which in the preface to the first edition precede the dedication to the friends who by their practical experience are best fitted to judge the book. There is added a fuller treatment of the political significance of the Decalogue.

3. In his contempt for Bodin he exclaims: "Neque enim, bello contra Hispaniae regem potentissimum suscepto, judicastis majestatis jura ita illi inseparabiliter cohaerere, ut extra illum non sint, sed potius eorum usum et exercitium iis abutenti adimendo, et quod vestrum erat repetendo, jura haec ad consociatam multitudinem et populum singularum provinciarum pertinere declarastis." He says that this is the chief reason for his dedication. It may be added that his examples are most largely taken from the constitution and history of the Netherlands. Lastly, he is moved by the good will shown by Friesland and its allies to the city which he serves, and to himself personally through the honor of the call to Franeker.

4. In the first edition the prime division appears in a different form as

the distinction of the consociatio particularis and universalis; the former being divided into the naturalis necessaria and civilis spontanea, and the latter into the privata in collegio and publica in universitate. It is highly significant that Althusius later gave up this antithesis between inferior societies and the State, and classified the latter as a sub-species of political communities.

5. The doctrine of collegia (c. 4) is gathered from the works of Bodin and Gregorius Tholosanus on the State, the monograph of Losaeus "De jure universitatum," and the juristic works of Bartolus, Paulus de Castro, Marcus, Gail, Mynsinger, Peregrinus, Menochius, Decianus and others.

6. Thus (§ 30–34) the affairs of the rural commune are managed by an "ex consensu vicinorum electus." In the city a "magistratus ab universitate constitutus" has the "imperium in singulos, non universos" (§ 49–52); a college of representatives has "non tantam potestatem, auctoritatem et jurisdictionem, quantam universitas" (§ 56); the weightiest matters, such as new taxes and changes of the constitution, require the consent of the general body of citizens (§ 61).

7. Besides the detailed account of the constitutions of cities and the internal organization of councils, he discusses in c. 5 § 70 ff. (following Botero and Hippolytus a Collibus) the causes of the growth of cities, and in c. 6 § 5 ff. the best plan for a capital city.

8. In the first edition the theory of communes is treated more briefly in a single chapter (c. 5).

9. These rubrics are the same as those given later under the heading of the State; but there the collective rights arising therefrom are "pleniora et majora."

10. The two extensive chapters on the "jus provinciale" are not given in the first edition, in which the province is merely mentioned in passing as one of the grades of association.

11. In c. 17 § 25–53 (1st ed. c. 7) there is a discussion of the "consociatio et confoederatio" of consociationes universales: when this is "plena" it forms "unum Reipublicae corpus;" when it is "minus plena," as in Switzerland, the Hanseatic League and the Netherlands, each member retains its sovereignty and under the terms of the contract is obligated only for defensio mutua, concordia (submission to the court of arbitration) and administratio communium jurium; herital fraternities and the relations of vassalage, guardianship and clientage are noticed as special kinds of "foedera."—A very full treatment of the "comitia sociorum confoederatorum" is given in c. 33 § 122–136 in the account of the federal constitution of the Netherlands (absent in the first edition).

12. These arguments, mingled with various attacks chiefly against Bodin,

and supported with a vast apparatus of learning, with texts of Scripture and rational demonstrations, appear in a quite similar form in the first edition, c. 7 § 12–27.

13. See c. 9–17. The classification of the jura majestatis given in c. 6–13 of the first edition differs materially. "Ecclesiastica" and "civilia" are distinguished here also, but the latter is subdivided into five branches providing for the maintenance of outward order (legislation, the power of reward and punishment, police protection, warfare, the power of alliance), and nine branches for the direct promotion of social life (jus commerciorum, usus monetae, idioma linguae, distributio munerum, dispensatio privilegiorum, defensio mutua, cura bonorum regni, usus comitiorum, constitutio ministrorum Reipublicae).

14. When in § 58 the right to be present and to vote is given to every membrum Reipublicae, it must be remembered that the 'members' are not the individuals themselves but the minor communities.

15. In the first edition the whole doctrine of the appointment, classification and functions of State-authorities is treated under the rubric of the "ultimum jus majestatis" of the whole community, which consists simply in the "constitutio administratorum" (c. 14–32).

16. The first edition naturally does not include the defense against the attacks evoked by the book itself. But in substance the arguments are already given here in the fourteenth chapter entitled "De Ephoris," at the close of which he also expounds the doctrine of the remedies for tyranny. All the basic ideas are stated here.

17. See the lengthy definition enumerating all their functions, in c. 18 § 48. The titles of office are stated in § 49: "patricii; seniores; status et regni primores; officiarii regni; pacti inter magistratum summum et populum initi vindices; custodes et defensores justitiae et juris, quibus magistratum summum subjiciunt et parere cogunt; censores summi magistratus; inspectores; consiliarii regni; censores honoris regii; fratres summi magistratus."

18. In § 110–122 there is a sketch of the constitutions of the national and provincial Estates of all the European countries, Germany receiving the fullest treatment. In the Empire the Electors as "ephori generales" are separated from the other imperial Estates or "ephori speciales."

19. The election of the Germanic Emperor is discussed at length, and the Electoral Capitulation is given in full, together with examples taken from other countries (§ 29–50). The assertion of Barclay that the monarch, being "legibus solutus," is not bound even by fundamental laws, is confuted (§ 51–69).

20. See c. 19 § 103–107, where he denies Barclay's proposition that

the "electio" is "populi" but the "constitutio" is "Dei," shows the identity of 'election' and 'institution' and asserts the principle that "electio populi est electio Dei."

21. Likewise in the first edition at the close of the fifteenth chapter, which corresponds to chapters 19–20 in the later editions.

22. According to the later editions the art of government requires both study and experience. This study comprises firstly, the divine, natural and positive laws which form the basis and the limits of governmental action (c. 21); herewith is a specially full discussion of the question, how far the law of the Old Testament is still binding at the present day and to what extent it is set aside as the "lex propria Judaeorum" (c. 22). Secondly, a knowledge of the nature and inclinations of peoples (c. 23) and their relation to government (c. 24–25) is necessary. Experience is based on one's own practice and the example of others (c. 26). Besides his own study and experience the ruler must take counsel with those who are wisest; thus in the usual manner there is a treatment of the "consiliarii magistratus" (c. 27).

23. The scheme of the first edition differs but little; it lacks the long chapter on the convocation of Imperial Diets, which is briefly touched upon at the close of c. 27.

24. The power to summon and preside, the publication and execution of the laws, belongs to the Chief Magistrate; all the Ephors are entitled to vote, or else all the membra regni; rules are fixed as to the place, time, division into "curiae," debate and voting, the subjection of absentees and of the minority, and other questions of parliamentary procedure; the idea of an assembly representing the sovereign people is strictly observed.—General Councils of the Church, which should be summoned by the Emperor, are included among "consilia extraordinaria" (§ 22–29).

25. Among the Jews (§ 31 ff.), Romans (§ 36 ff.), Greeks (§ 43 ff.), the ancient Leagues (§ 45), Germans (§ 46–110), French (§ 111), English (§ 112–117), Dutch (§ 118), Poles (§ 119), and other nations (§ 120); in Venice and other republics (§ 121); lastly federal assemblies in general and those of the Swiss and Dutch in particular (§ 122–136).

26. The Chief Magistrate is simply a responsible executive, bound by the law and having no power of alienation; at the same time he is entitled to receive from the public treasury a sustenance befitting his station. Whatever he acquires by war, alliance or marriage, he acquires not for himself but for the State (§ 117–118). As to the public wealth, its component parts and the ways of using it, see also c. 17 § 1–54.

27. See c. 37 § 79–116, with regard to the relief of the poor and the care of infants and the infirm; the inviolability of one's person, honor and

property, subject to the State's "jus compellendi et puniendi"; compulsory expropriation with compensation. The principle of liberty is formulated in § 80 and 82, that of the sacredness of property in § 111.

28. Corresponding to this is the much shorter concluding part of c. 14 in the first edition.

29. See § 1–26 and the arguments in § 131–134 against Arnisaeus, who had denied the very possibility of setting up decisive tests. The following examples are offered: alienation of domain; idolatry; the promotion of discord; subversion of the established institutions of Church and School; any direct damage to the whole State through abuse of power or neglect of duty; also many acts which do not ruin the State at once but are comparable to the scuttling of a ship or the casting away of a sail, mast or anchor.

30. The family of the tyrant should be spared as much as possible (§ 69).

31. At the close of the book, in the editions after the second (3rd ed. § 83–86), Althusius adds another brief vindication of his system. In particular he explains why he did not devote a special chapter to the theory of the decline and fall of States, and why he described the structure of subordinate communities first of all without at the same time applying to them the distinction of forms of government or working out a special "ars politica" for them.

THE JURISPRUDENCE OF ALTHUSIUS

AMONG the juristic writings of Althusius his systematic works deserve attention just because they are among the earliest attempts to set up a system of law wholly independent of the existing legal order.[1]

From the preface to the edition of the "Jurisprudentia Romana" published in 1588,[2] it seems that Althusius regards the systematizing of the subject-matter of law as a problem which had never yet been solved. For he suggests that he is the first to make the attempt, and solemnly invites the leading jurists of the time to take part in a work which is not to be completed by one man or even by one generation. While he occasionally cites the works of all the earlier 'methodists' (except Vigelius), it is evident that he does not regard these works as 'systematic' in his own sense of the term. In fact the systems of his predecessors differ from his own in that they adhere much more closely to the arrangement of the Civil Law. While the labors of Johann Apel were in general devoted to the dogmatic dialectical treatment of separate topics rather than to their systematic connection,[3] Conrad Lagus was the first to work out the idea of a systematic text-book, but in the main he followed the arrangement of the Institutes.[4] A like dependence on the system of the Institutes is shown in the unfinished Commentaries of Franciscus Connanus,[5] as well as the numerous 'methodical' writings of Professor Nicolaus Vigelius of Marburg,[6] and the Syntagma of Petrus Gregorius of Toulouse.[7] On the other hand, in the preface to the Jurisprudentia Romana, Althusius already gives a full and striking exposition of the faults of the system of Institutes, while in the body of the work he makes a wholly different arrange-

ment of the material.[8] His methodical principle is the purely
dialectical derivation of all classifications from the successive division of concepts. He states himself on the title-page that the
logical principles which guide him are the principles of Petrus
Ramus (1515–1572), who was at that time much admired as the
great champion of a 'natural' logic in opposition to Scholasticism.[9]
The so-called 'Ramistic method' had indeed been already applied by other jurists to particular topics; [10] but Althusius was
the first to employ it in the construction of a system.

The example of Althusius was followed by Professor Hermann Vultejus of Marburg,[11] whose work, published in 1590,
is systematized after a quite similar method but in a materially
different fashion; [12] while the famous Commentaries of Hugo
Donellus stand in closer relation to the system of Institutes,
which is indeed reduced to its essential principles and modified
in many points of detail.[13]

Althusius, however, devoted himself to the work of perfecting
his own system, being busied for many years in making it more
thorough and complete. Already in the year 1591 he gave to
Corvinus, his publisher in Herborn who desired a new edition,
a brief outline of his revised system which was prefixed to the
edition of 1592 and the later Herborn editions under the title of
"Epitome et brevis ἀναχεφαλαίωσις Dicaeologicae Romanae." The
project, then announced, of expanding this outline into a full account of the whole body of practicable law was not fulfilled until
the year 1617, when it was published at Herborn under the title
of "Dicaeologicae libri tres, totum et universum jus, quo utimur,
methodice complectentes" and in 1618 (adding to the title "cum
parallelis hujus et Judaici juris") at Frankfort.[14]

In the Dicaeologica the material is systematized to the last
degree. From the first principles down to the most minute details it is deduced with inexorable rigor, one might even say
fanaticism. At every point the successive division of concepts is
worked out by the force of dialectic. Often indeed the required
dichotomy can only be set up by recourse to somewhat arbitrary
antitheses, such as 'general' and 'special.' At almost every step
the antithesis between 'partition into members' and 'division into
species' is taken as the point of departure. Yet as a whole it is a

work of penetrating thought and shows an uncommon power of
intellect. And if on the whole this intricate and ingenious system
gained no lasting success, it served at least, as its author hoped,
to facilitate and clarify the study of law, and in fact several re-
arrangements first made by him became in course of time generally accepted.

This applies especially to the division (first occurring in the
Dicaeologica) of the science of law into a general and a special
part, which are distinguished in characteristic fashion as the doctrine of the "membra" and the "species" of jurisprudence.

As elements ("membra") of all legal relations a distinction
is drawn between the "negotium symbioticum" and the "jus."
Thus the general part (I. c. 1–34) is divided into two sections.

The first section deals with the "negotium symbioticum," that
is to say, the activity of human life as leading to the establishment of rights, the "factum civile" or the business of this world.
Its elements (membra) are Things and Persons, these being
here considered in so far as their qualities, conditions and striv-
ings involve legal differences, while the study of their physical,
political, ethical, theological, historical and logical nature belongs to other sciences (c. 1 nr. 9–10). Next comes the doctrine
of things, their partition into 'real' and 'ideal' parts and their
division into individual things and composite things, with further
subdivisions (c. 1 nr. 11–44).[15] Then comes a treatment of the
person as the "homo juris communionem habens." Having fixed
this definition he deals as usual with the two species, firstly individual persons and the influence of inherited and acquired status
(c. 5–6), and secondly natural and voluntary associations of persons (c. 7–8). Next comes the theory of the human act whereby
the person constitutes things as elements of social relations (c.
9–12). As requisites for the legally relevant act (distinct from
the "factum merum"), "voluntas" (along with dies, conditio
and modus, vis, metus and error, dolus and culpa and so on) and
"facultas" (potentia and auctoritas facientis) are recognized. Last
comes the consideration of the various species of "factum" (c.
12 nr. 12–17).[16]

The second section is devoted to "jus," which "ob factum
praecedens homini in re vel persona aliqua ad vitae hujus neces-

sitatem, usum et directionem constituitur." This is divided into
the theory of the "constitutio juris" or 'objective right,' and the
"species juris" or 'subjective right.'

The establishment of Right takes place by a rational deduction thereof from the essential nature of "negotium." Natural
Law is set up by the "recta ratio communis" according to the
general requirements of human society. Positive law is derived
from the "recta ratio specialis" according to the special requirements of a locally limited "vita socialis." The latter, in order
to be law at all, must keep in conformity to the first principles of
Natural Law, but at the same time in order to be positive law
it must differ therefrom in its adaptation to concrete relations.
Its species (written and unwritten law) are fully discussed. Then
comes a treatment of interpretatio naturalis and civilis (together
with Fiction).[17]

The "species juris" are "dominium" and "obligatio," which
are in general defined and distinguished as 'real right' and 'personal right.' Under "dominium" he treats of ownership, including so-called 'beneficial ownership' and "bonae fidei possessio"
(c. 18). To this is added the theory of possession as the "exercitium dominii" (c. 19) and the distinction of things by the
proprietary relations subsisting in them (c. 20–21). But on the
one hand, 'real rights' in the property of others ("servitutes," in
c. 22–24), and on the other hand "potestas" (c. 25–33), also
partake of the nature of ownership.[18] Under the rubric of "potestas" there is a treatment of liberty as "potestas sui ipsius" (c.
25) and the derivative rights of reputation, dignity, chastity and
bodily integrity (c. 26). Under "potestas aliena" comes a treatment of "potestas privata" (c. 27–31) and "potestas publica"
(c. 32–33) in symmetrical order.[19] Lastly, there is a general treatment of the second species of 'subjective right,' obligation (c. 34).

The special part is divided according to the "Species Dicaeologicae" into the "Dicaeodotica" and the "Dicaeocritica."

The "Dicaeodotica" is the theory of the distribution of rights
among men. It is divided into the Dicaeodotica acquirens and
amittens.

The theory of the acquisition of rights fills the rest of the first
book. After stating the general principles governing the acquisi-

tion of rights (c. 35) he proceeds to the acquisition of ownership (c. 36–63), including among the modes of derivative acquisition the general right of inheritance.[20] Then he speaks of the creation of relations of obligation. This takes place through contracts or through delicts. He gives a full treatment of the doctrine of the creation and operation of contracts and of the several species of contract (c. 64–97).[21] The conclusion of the first book comprises a treatment of delicts, expanded into a complete system of criminal law (c. 98–146).[22]

The theory of the loss of rights fills the second book of the complete work. It deals first with the extinction of rights in general (II. c. 1–11).[23] Then comes a discussion of the special modes of abrogation of ownership and possession (c. 12–13). Next come the singular modes of termination of obligations, such as their performance (c. 14–22). Lastly there is a treatment of discharge by "venia et gratia," limited to delictual obligations (c. 23).

The "Dicaeocritica" is the theory of rights in dispute and of their trial and adjudication. To this Althusius devotes the third book, in which he gives a systematic treatment of the whole law of Procedure, including the law of Actions.[24]

The work of Althusius, as has been shown in this review, is an encyclopedia not only of private law but of practicable law in general, and deserves attention in the history of the systematization of the law of Delict and Procedure. It is of special interest to note the way in which the author has worked Public Law into his system.

The reception of doctrines of public law in the system of civil law is not in itself peculiar to Althusius. As the whole exegetic literature since the Gloss upon the Corpus Iuris Civilis had brought the study of questions of public law within the sphere of the civil law, this arrangement was preserved by the 'methodists.' Of these but few attempted to sunder public law from private law as a separate domain;[25] on the contrary, this was regularly treated as coming within the bounds of private law and more especially the law of Persons.[26] But as these 'publicistic' admixtures had grown out of the external condition of the original texts, they remained all the more an incidental and occa-

sional adjunct. On the other hand, Althusius, who in the Jurisprudentia Romana had done much like his predecessors,[27] set to
work in full earnest in the Dicaeologica to incorporate the whole
body of public law into the Civilian system.[28] Here indeed, as he
asserted and maintained at all points the theories already developed in his Politics,[29] he had no difficulty in distributing the
relations of public law under the rubrics of private law. The result was a unified legal structure, erected wholly in the style of
private law and yet covering the groundwork of public law, the
like of which was hardly ever constructed before or since. And
yet at bottom this system but anticipates the last consequences of
that 'Nature-Right' doctrine of the social contract which was soon
to gain exclusive sway.

Althusius, in speaking of the 'subject' of rights with reference
to the classification of persons into "homines singulares" and
"homines conjuncti, consociati et cohaerentes," proceeds to explain the concept and nature of the collective person as a social
body.[30] As "species" of this, in agreement with the scheme of his
Politics, he treats first of the natural association of the family-
circle, narrower and wider (I. c. 7 nr. 10–40), and then the contractual association of the corporation, commune and State (c. 8).

In the theory of the "species juris," after having considered
Church-property and State-property with reference to public law
in discussing the distinction of things by their proprietary relations (c. 20–21), he gives a full account of 'public power' as the
second great species of "potestas aliena." [31] First he speaks of
"potestas publica universalis" or the sovereign power of the
State, whose origin, 'subject,' content and forms of exercise are
determined by him in full accord with his political system built
on popular sovereignty.[32] Then under "potestas publica limitata
(specialis, inferior)" he discusses (c. 33) "potestas provincialis"
combined with seigniory (under which rubric he treats the territorial princedom as a permanent and hereditary provincial
power), and also the "potestas officialis" conferred without territorial title.[33]

While so far he has held himself to the beaten track more or
less, he makes a bold departure when in his theory of contract
he introduces the 'publicistic' social contract among the species of

"societas." From the simple "societas bonorum" (c. 78) he distinguishes the "societas vitae," "qua συμβίωσις contrahitur et res, operae, ministeria atque bona ad συμβίωσιν illam conservandam conferuntur a sociis." Under the societas vitae privata or domestica he speaks of marriage (c. 79) and reception into the family-circle (adoption and unio prolium, c. 80). Under the societas vitae publica he treats at length of the consensual contract to which, in his theory, every social body and above all the State owes its existence (c. 81). In substantial accord with his Politics he explains the nature of the unity of the State,[34] and here also reaches the conclusion that the ownership of all sovereign rights, public property and institutions accruing from the contractual association belongs perpetually to the whole body of the associates (nr. 69). In like manner the delegation of executive or administrative power in public law is construed as a mandate (c. 83). In the theory of innominate contracts he constructs a "contractus socialis praestationis" related to the society, which again may be either private or public,[35] and regards treaties of alliance between independent communities on the one hand,[36] and agreements as to taxation among the members of a community on the other hand,[37] as contracts for social services under public law. Treaties of peace between communities are also included under innominate contracts (c. 87 nr. 44–46).

The effect is no less characteristic when in his theory of delicts Althusius speaks of tyranny as the extreme case of abuse of public power ("abusus potestatis publicae," c. 113), for which the penalty is deposition (nr. 3–20).[38]

Lastly, accusations of abuse of public power are also mentioned in the law of procedure under the head of Actions, as appertaining to the Ephors against the King or any other chief magistrate (III. c. 16 nr. 6).

For demonstrations and further discussions of all the propositions of public law received in the Dicaeologica, Althusius regularly refers to his text-book of Politics. It is all the more remarkable that, while the latter was afterward so often condemned as worthy of the flames, the Dicaeologica remained unchallenged and even in the eighteenth century could be unreservedly approved for the study of law.

NOTES

1. The systematic text-books of Althusius, often reprinted in the seventeenth century, were still highly esteemed and approved for use in the first half of the eighteenth century; see for example Georg Beyer, Notitia auctorum juridicorum, Spec. III. (Leipzig 1726), nr. 30 p. 103–106 (giving him preference over Connanus). Then they fell into neglect; yet Althusius was still known to historians of literature as one of the earliest 'methodists'; see for example Hommel, Litteratura juris, Leipzig 1761, § 69 p. 227 (where with all his contemporaries he is dismissed with contempt: "magna minatus extricavit nihil"); Jugler, op. cit.; Hugo, Lehrb. der civ. Litteraturgesch., Berlin 1812, § 213 (with many errors). Not until the nineteenth century was his name forgotten; thus he is ignored by Ratjen, Die Ordner des röm. Rechts, in Zeitschr. für Rechtsgesch., Vol. VIII. p. 277 ff.

2. Preface to the second edition, Herborn 1588. I have not been able to obtain the first edition of 1586.

3. J. Apel (1486–1536), Methodica dialectices ratio ad juris prudentiam accommodata, Nuremberg 1535. See Muther, Aus dem Universitäts-u. Gelehrtenleben, Erlangen 1866, p. 230–328.

4. C. Lagus (d. 1546), Juris utriusque traditio methodica, Frankfort-on-the-Main 1543 (I use also the editions of Lyons 1546, Basel 1553, Lyons 1562); the most distinctive idea is the division into a "pars prima philosophica" (theory of the sources of law in lib. I.) and a "pars secunda historica" (theory of the phases of law in lib. II.–VI.); but here follow persons, things, obligations, actions and procedure, and it is only in the last book that the "jus singulare" is separated. This last separation is absent in the otherwise similar "Compendium juris civilis et Saxonici," written by him in German about 1537 and edited in 1597 by Joachim Gregorii (I use the edition of Magdeburg 1602).—On Lagus see Muther, Zur Geschichte der Rechtswiss. und der Univ. in Deut., Jena 1876, p. 299–351.

5. F. Connanus (1508–1551), Commentarii juris civilis, Basel 1557 (1st ed. 1553). The only novelty is the separation of the law of marriage (lib. VIII.) and the law of inheritance (lib. IX.–X.). See also Ratjen, p. 282 ff.

6. N. Vigelius (1529–1600), Juris civilis universi absolutissima Methodus, Basel 1565 (last edition Frankfort 1628); Digestorum juris civilis libri 50 in 7 partes distincti, Basel 1568 ff. (filling up the framework of the Methodus with the content of the texts under specialized rubrics); Methodus juris controversi, ed. nova, Basel 1615; Partitiones juris (often ap-

pended). Under "Jus publicum" is set forth the doctrine of the sources of law, the courts, the administration of justice, the Church, the Fiscus, military affairs, cities, taxation and services (and again a detailed rubrication according to personae, res and actus). Then follows the "Jus privatum" in the trichotomy of persons (Dig. pars II.), things (ib. III.–IV.), and obligations and actions (ib. V.–VI.); the doctrine of the preservation, loss and recovery of rights being separated (ib. VII.). See Jugler, II. p. 79–97.

7. Petrus Gregorius Tholosanus (1540–1617), Syntagma juris universi, Lyons 1587 (1st ed. 1582). It is characteristic that he treats first (lib. 1–6) of things, and then (lib. 7–19) of persons (for in this order was the world created), and lastly (lib. 20–50) groups together under actions the modes of original acquisition (lib. 20), contracts (lib. 21 ff.), delicts (lib. 30 ff.), usucaption (lib. 40), inheritance (lib. 41 ff.), and procedure (lib. 47 ff.). See Jugler, IV. p. 67 ff.

8. After an introduction dealing with the nature and sources of law (lib. I. c. 1), he treats in the first book of "jus primum" or substantive law and in the second book of "jus ortum a primo" or actions and procedure. Under "jus primum" he separates acquisitio (c. 2–68) and amissio (c. 69–70). Under the acquisition of rights he treats first of its requisites, these being res (c. 2) and personae (c. 3), and under the latter voluntas and bona fides (c. 4); then come the "species." Here he divides all rights into "dominium" and "obligatio." Under dominium he considers ownership as annexed to possession (c. 5); as offshoots of this, the rights in the property of others (c. 6–7) and the "jus personae in personam et ejus bona per consequentiam" or potestas publica (c. 8–10) and privata (c. 11). And now he speaks of the division of things into res divini et humani, publici et privati juris, as following from the "ratione dominii et possessionis" (c. 12). Then he discusses the general requisites for the acquisition of ownership and lordship (c. 13), next the special modes of acquisition (c. 14–24), among these inheritance (and under this again the tutela testamentaria and legitima). He gives next a general treatment of obligatio (c. 25), proceeding to a separate treatment of contracts, including marriage, adoption and legitimation (c. 26–49), and delicts (c. 50–68). In the same independent manner he systematizes the doctrine of the loss of rights (c. 69–70) and of procedure (lib. II. c. 1–34).

9. Otherwise the Ramistic principles left the widest freedom to the individual as regards the mode of forming categories. The only common feature, strictly preserved by our author here as well as in the Politics, is the so-called "dichotomy," or the division of each concept into two specific concepts resulting from the affirmation and negation of a predicate. Although afterward the forcing of the various materials into the framework

of the Aristotelian four causes (efficient, material, formal, final) was taken as the criterion of the "Ramistic" school of jurisprudence (see Hommel, § 62), the earlier Ramists themselves, like their philosophical guides, broke away from the Aristotelian-scholastic dialectic of the four causes. And hence these play no part in Althusius himself. Contrariwise, the juristic application of the four causes was a very old thing (Stintzing, Krit. V. J. Schr., III. p. 625). Soon after indeed it was revived by the German jurists in a quite intolerable fashion and employed in the construction of what was in truth a purely scholastic method, and henceforth it was even combined with Ramistic principles.

10. Thus by Joh. Thom. Freigius (1543–1583); see Stintzing, loc. cit., p. 626. On the other hand Muther, loc. cit., p. 350, shows that his "Partitiones juris" (Basel 1571) is merely an extract from Lagus.

11. In the preface to the second edition of his Jurisprudentia (1588), Althusius says that his hope of attracting other scholars to this field has not deceived him: "Nactus enim sum σύνεργον insignem, praestantissimum virum Doctorem Hermannum Vultejum, in inclyta Academia Marpurgensi Professorem celeberrimum." As the system of Vultejus was first published in 1590, this may refer either to his lectures or to acquaintance with the plan of that work.

12. Vultejus (1555–1634), Jurisprudentiae Romanae a Justiniano compositae libri duo, Marburg 1590 (last ed. 1748). Here also the dichotomy is exhaustive. Right or Law (on its definition and sources I. c. 1–3) is divided into "jus absolutum" or substantive right (I. c. 4–78) and "jus relatum" or right in action (lib. II.). Jus absolutum is divided into "jus personarum" and "jus rerum." Jus personarum, having been treated as of the person in himself and in relation to other persons (I. c. 4–10), is divided into the pure right of person over person, or potestas publica (c. 11–15) and privata (c. 16–25), and the personal right conditioned by "res sive facta quasi medium," or obligation (c. 26–61). Jus rerum, after fixing the "rerum divisio," comprises the doctrine of real rights, of possession and ownership, as well as inheritance (c. 62–78).—See also Ratjen, p. 289 ff.

13. Donellus (1527–1591), Commentarii de jure civili (in the Opera, Florence 1840–1847, Vol. I.–VI.); Donellus himself published only the first eleven books in 1588 and 1590, the complete work appearing in 1596. The dichotomy may also be recognized here. After the introduction dealing with law in general (lib. I.–II. c. 8) there follows in the first part (lib. I.–XVI.) the "cognitio juris," in the second part the "ratio juris obtinendi" or procedure (lib. XVII.–XXII.). Substantive private law (including the "jus agendi") is divided into the "proprie nostrum," which again is located either in the person (doctrine of status and guardianship in lib. II. c. 9–18

and lib. III.) or in external things (ownership including inheritance in lib. IV.–IX. c. 9, rights in the property of others in lib. IX. c. 10–XI.), and the "jus quod nobis debetur" (law of obligations including marriage in lib. XII.–XVI.).—See also Ratjen, p. 283–289.

14. In the dedication to the Burgomaster and Council of the city of Emden, dated March 1, 1617, the author says that this work grew out of the long-desired expansion of his often reprinted Jurisprudentia Romana but had become in fact an "opus paene novum et a priore in multis diversum." In the year 1601 Philipp Althusius, in the preface to the "Civilis conversationis," says that his cousin employs all his spare time in working on the Dicaeologica.

15. Individual things are classified into corporeal (immovables and movables, principal things and appurtenances, fruits and expenditures, in c. 1–2) and incorporeal (c. 3); incorporeals by nature are acts, by statute are all fungible things, for in these value appears as substance (here come the species of value, the measures of value, and money). Composite things are bodies συνημμένα or διεστωτα, the latter being aggregates of corporeal things alone or also of incorporeal things, and these again being the hereditaments of living persons or of decedents (c. 4).

16. This relegation of the general theory of things, persons and acts to a Preliminary Part, whose germ is visible already in the Jurisprudentia Romana (see above, Note 8), while familiar to us at the present day, was first made by Althusius. It occurs again to some extent in Jean Domat, Les Loix Civiles dans leur ordre naturel, Paris 1735 (first published 1689–1697), Traité des loix and Livre préliminaire; but only after the end of the eighteenth century did it gradually come to prevail, through the medium of the systems of Natural Law. The same is true of the division of persons into individual persons and collective persons, which so far as I can see does not occur anywhere in the theory of the 'subject of rights' before Althusius.

17. The "Index capitum" at this point concludes the "pars prima," to which it gives the heading "de generalibus." The "pars altera," in which he places the doctrine of the "species juris," forms thus the transition to the special part.

18. The transition is very artificial; the division into res divini and humani juris, and of the latter into communes and propriae and further into publicae and privatae, comprises a "distributio generalis" of things; their "distributio specialis" leads to usus rei alienae and to potestas.—The making absolute of the quality common to rights in things and rights in the person of oneself and others is not, to say the least, clearly brought as the reason for taking them together.

19. Potestas privata is twofold, according as it confers a "jus in personam

et rem" or merely a "jus in personam"; the former again is domestica (plena over slaves, minus plena over freedmen and serfs in later law, as well as in marital and paternal power), or administratoria (tutela and cura); the latter is correctoria et moderatoria (toward younger kinsfolk and pupils) or clientelaris. Potestas publica is universalis (sovereign power) or particularis (official power). See below, Notes 31–33.

20. Chapters 35–63 form the "pars tertia"; this includes occupatio (c. 36), traditio (c. 37), fructuum perceptio (c. 38), conjunctio rerum (c. 39), utilization (c. 40), usucapio (c. 41–42), successio (c. 43–63); under successio to potestas there comes the acquisition of the powers of guardian and curator by the various modes of "delatio," in c. 54 and 60–62.

21. Denoted in the Index as the "pars quarta." Beginning with contracts in general (c. 64–67); then contracts under the Roman scheme (c. 68–89), in which marriage (c. 75), adoption (c. 80) and "societas publica" (c. 81) are included, and under innominate contracts (c. 87–89) various contracts occurring in modern law find a place; then pacts (c. 90); lastly quasi-contracts (c. 91–95) and "contractus mediati" (liability on contracts of persons under power and agents, c. 96–97).

22. Denoted in the Index as the "pars quinta"; beginning in c. 98–100 with the general theory of delicts and punishments, and treating in c. 101–146 the "species delictorum" in strictly systematic order.

23. The modes of extinction, universal or at least common to several classes of rights, are here given as actus contrarii (II. c. 2), release and renunciation (c. 3), compromise (c. 4), the tendering of a decisory oath (c. 5), lapse of time (c. 6), natural (c. 7) or civil (c. 8–9) extinction of the thing or person, restitutio in integrum and res judicata (c. 10), and also the modes of termination of hypothec and guardianship (c. 11).

24. Lib. III. c. 1–5 discuss (after defining the general notions) the administration of justice; c. 6 treats of the parties; c. 7–20 of actions (including accusations); c. 21–24 of the exceptions; c. 25–26 of the defendant's answer and the litiscontestation; c. 27–45 of the proof; c. 46 of the final process; c. 47 of the judgment; c. 48 of the execution; c. 49 of the citation; c. 50 of contumacy; c. 51 of power of attorney; c. 52 of cautions and oaths of surety; c. 53 of the interlocutio judicis; c. 54 of the modes of summary process; c. 55–57 of legal remedies.

25. Such a separation is made for the first time in the system of Vigelius (above, Note 6). Likewise Donellus places the "jus divinum" in lib. II. c. 4 and the "jus publicum" in c. 5–6 with a brief sketch of their content, before the "jus privatum."

26. Thus Lagus, in the "jus personarum" in lib. II. c. 21–23, treats of "potestas et dignitas publica," the forms of State, the vicissitudes of the

Roman Empire. Gregorius, in the law of persons in lib. 15–19, speaks at length of the ecclesiastical and secular Estates. Vultejus, in the theory of status in c. 6, mentions the "cives cum imperio," and under rights in personam, before potestas privata, discusses potestas publica ecclesiastica (c. 11) and politica (c. 12–15), including the theory of the forms of State, offices and services.

27. In lib. I. c. 3 he defines the State under the rubric of "homines conjunctim considerati," together with the family, corporation and commune; in c. 8–10 he treats more fully of potestas publica, the rights of sovereignty, the forms of State, offices and services.

28. The following passage from the preface refers most clearly to the insertion of matters of public law: "Quaedam etiam materiae hucusque ex agro juridico exterminatae exulabant, quasi ἀπόλιδες, jure civitatis juridicae indignae; his possessionem suam, quae injuria illis erat adempta, tribui easque ad proprios lares reduxi soloque suo natali restitui."

29. These do not appear anywhere in the Jurisprudentia Romana; indeed the remarks on sovereign power (I. c. 8) agree with Bodin almost word for word. But even in the preface to the Dicaeologica a republican spirit breathes in the dedication to the Burgomaster and Council, who had navigated Emden's ship of state safely through the storms of recent years and had won for this city the freedom almost of an imperial city.

30. With citations from Holy Scripture he emphasizes more strongly than in the Politics the organic nature of human societies; the "conjunctio hominum" produces "unum corpus," in which a harmonious organization (συμμετρία) assigns to each member its functions, the complete union of wills produces a soul and a heart, in word and deed a "syncretismus" of the individuals takes place and advantages and disadvantages are shared in common; by reason of this unity the individuals are no longer regarded "per se et in se," but the body resulting from their conjunction is regarded as one person.

31. In the definition of "potestas publica," c. 32 nr. 1, he uses these words: "quae data est alicui a corpore consociationis . . . ad negotia, res et personas corporis consociati curandum et administrandum." In c. 25 nr. 3 he has already repeated with regard to all potestas the proposition of the Politics: "imperare nihil aliud est quam inservire aliorum utilitatibus."

32. The power of the State is delegated "a consociatione universali"; it is bound by the "leges Decalogi et regni"; it consists in the administratio or exercitium of the "jura et negotia consociati corporis," whose "proprietas" remains in the consociatio universalis (c. 32 nr. 3–5). Hence the division into administratio ecclesiastica and civilis, and of the latter into the care for "conservanda disciplina interna" and for "commoditas vitae so-

cialis" and so on (nr. 6–19). Lastly the forms of government (nr. 20–22).

33. Here he explains the territorial princedom as an administrative office derived from the Imperial power, bound by its ordinances and held to accountability. Furthermore there is not only an immediate but also a mediate "potestas provincialis" (nr. 4).—Official power (nr. 10–42) is "publica vera" (imperium and jurisdictio) or "publica modo quodam" (vicaria and compromissaria).

34. Here he divides the "jus symbioticum" into the εὐνομία καὶ εὐταξία or the obligation of submission to the public leges and poenae, and the βιάρκεια καὶ βοήτεια or the communicatio of res, labores, consilia and auxilia. In expounding the idea of "symbiotici" he treats at length of the acquisition of citizenship and its grades, and in discussing "communicatio" he treats of munera personalia, realia and mixta.

35. See I. c. 87 nr. 22 ff.; from a "contractus socialis praestationis privatus" he derives the obligations of service between parents and children, kinsfolk, patron and freedmen.

36. See I. c. 87 nr. 33–36 and the reference in c. 81 nr. 71.

37. See I. c. 87 nr. 37–43. No taxation can be lawful unless "omnium membrorum Reipublicae consensu et communi decreto, in conventu publico solemniter celebrato atque indicto." Even unanimity is requisite. The assessment of property must be at a uniform rate.

38. This crime is committed when "magistratus summus vincula consociationis solvit et fundamenta ejus evertit." Tyranny is "generalis" (such as usurpation of absolute power, total incapacity, wickedness and the like), or "specialis" (as in ecclesiastical affairs, suppression of the Estates, imposition of unjust burdens, squandering of the public treasure, oppression of individuals). The punishment is "privatio potestatis publicae;" the tyrant is regarded as "privatus" and there is against him a "jus resistendi." Akin to tyranny is indolence and neglect of duty, whose punishment is extraordinary but may likewise be deposition.—As a matter of course, criminal law deals also with the "delictum universitatis" according to the theory of that time (c. 100 nr. 19–31), as well as the "laesio publicae potestatis" (c. 131–133, including "collegia illicita," c. 133 nr. 26–29).

PART TWO

HISTORICAL DEVELOPMENT OF THE POLITICAL
IDEAS EXPRESSED IN THE POLITICS OF
ALTHUSIUS

CHAPTER ONE

RELIGIOUS ELEMENTS IN
THE THEORY OF THE STATE

AS religious ideas have at all times played a leading part in determining the course of political theories, so the Politics of Althusius grew in the soil of a definite religious view of the world. It bears the stamp of the Calvinistic spirit throughout. As such it forms a link in the chain of those monarchomachist writings (see Part I., Ch. I. Note 3) which were produced by the Huguenots, Puritans and German Reformers. It patently agrees with them in a number of points wherein the Catholic group of Monarchomachi differs altogether.

In the first place it is a common trait of all the political writers of the Calvinist school that they seek and find in Holy Scripture not only the religious and moral truths regulating social life but also models for the governance of Church and State. Thus it is that their arguments are mostly framed in the fashion of the Old Testament. In Althusius this goes so far that he heaps up everywhere texts and historical examples taken from the Bible, emphasizes even in the preface the political application of the Decalogue, proposes to himself as a life-work the introduction of the Jewish law into all the branches of jurisprudence, and even declares that the ancient Jewish State was the best approximation to his ideal State that ever existed.[1] At the same time this leads to the complete rejection of the Canon law, wherein again Althusius goes so far that neither in his political nor in his juristic works does he quote any text of the Corpus Iuris Canonici or mention a single Canonist among the many authors cited.

Another common trait of these writers is the institution of a presbyterial and synodal form of church government, such as is fully described by Althusius with its claim to universal adoption. Thus they conceive Church and State as normally one and the same, it being the duty of the State to maintain the pure and true religion.[2] The idea of religious liberty is as completely foreign to them as to almost all men of their time.[3]

And lastly, in the construction of civil government there are certain positive traits common to these writers which go back to the teachings of Calvin and come out particularly in the doctrine of Ephors and their rights and duties as against unrighteous rulers.[4]

Thus they are sundered by sharp lines of division from the contemporary Catholic (and especially the Jesuit) Monarchomachi, who insist upon the Canon law, the superior origin of the Church and its independence of the State. But after the German Reformation took a decisive turn toward princely absolutism [*Obrigkeit*], the soil of the Lutheran creed produced no political system in which the rights of the people were put in the foreground.

While the common religious basis shows itself unmistakably in the Calvinist writers as a group, there are at the same time wide differences among them as to the application of theological standpoints to political doctrine. In this respect there is a sharp contrast between the Politics of Althusius and the work which otherwise is most nearly akin to it, the Vindiciae Contra Tyrannos. "Junius Brutus" sets his whole doctrine on a purely theological basis, proceeding from this in his own way to a covenant with God which bears the stamp of the verbal contract of Roman law.[5] Althusius on the other hand deduces his system in a rational way from a purely secular conception of society; for him biblical texts are merely examples, and the events of sacred as well as profane history serve as illustrations of the results which have first been reached by rational inference. Among the other Calvinist Monarchomachi theological, juristic and historical arguments are found in combination; sometimes, as in the book De Jure Magistratuum, these elements may be evenly mixed; or the historical mode of argument may predominate, as in Hotman and Buchanan; [6] or, as of course in the theologians, the theological viewpoint may remain in the foreground.[7] But none of them makes even the remotest anticipation of the later apriorist and rationalist theory of the State, in the same way that Althusius does with his dialectical deduction of the whole system of politics from a few axioms which are held to be self-evident.[8] And besides, the earlier writings take a more or less confessional color from their concrete aim of defense against religious oppression, while the Politics of Althusius, with its systematic ordering of the whole life of the State, is a purely secular book in content and purpose.

And thus it may be said that in spite of its stern Calvinistic spirit the Politics of Althusius shakes off the whole theocratic conception of the State. In order to measure its position from this aspect we must review the history of the theocratic idea.

The genuinely medieval system of thought was in its heights and depths imbued with the theocratic idea. Its view of the world starts with the idea that the universe is one Organism (macrocosmus) animated by one Spirit and molded by one Law in which, by virtue of the all-pervading divinely ordained harmony, every partial unity (microcosmus) presents an image of the universal whole. Thus the theory of human society must take the divinely created organization of the universe as the prototype of the first principles which govern the construction of human communities.[9] Whence it follows that the starting-point of all social construction is the principle of unity ("principium unitatis"), from which every plurality takes its origin, in which it finds its norm, and to which it returns.[10] Hence the totality of Mankind, being conceived as a partial unity with a final cause of its own within the universal whole,[11] appeared as a single State founded and monarchically governed by God Himself,[12] which must express itself equally in the two correlative Orders of the Universal Church and the Universal Empire; [13] and every partial unity, ecclesiastical or secular, derived its own essential oneness from this primal Unity.[14] Hence also the representation of each social aggregate by a single monarchical head corresponded to the divinely willed order of the universe.[15] Hence lastly the office of the ruler or magistrate, of every rank, was regarded as a mandate emanating directly or indirectly from God, and as a proximate or remote image of the divine Government of the World.[16]

This view of the world was shaken for the first time by the clerical party itself, after Gregory VII declared that the State was a work of Sin and the Devil. The effect of this was simply to emphasize the idea that the State needs to be consecrated by the divinely founded Church, from which the sinfully begotten State must first receive its right to exist and its 'true' being.[17] And all the more strongly did the supporters of the State uphold the immediately divine origin of civil government as their leading principle, while on the other hand even the most militant champions of the Hierarchy tended more and more to admit the divine (at least the mediately divine) origin of the State and of Lordship.[18]

Yet already in the middle ages the theocratic idea suffered a continuous process of decline and dissolution. It was the philosophical theory of the State, influenced by antiquity, which gradually cut the ground from under its feet. As the origin of the State is traced back to a natural impulse or to acts of human will, the idea of a divine foundation fades away; the divine Will indeed remains as the efficient cause but recedes into the position of a "causa remota." [19] And as the authority of all rulers is derived from the will of the general body of the ruled, the idea of the immediately divine appointment and mandate of the person of the ruler disappears; the maxim that 'all power is of God' remains valid, but is reduced to the doctrine that the people receives directly from God the power and capacity to create a government which by these things alone, partakes of the divine sanction.[20] And furthermore as the free choice of the form of government to be established is left to the people, the divine right of monarchy is extinguished; the colorless principle is evolved that according to times and circumstances one or another form of government may conform to the divine plan of the world.[21] Lastly, in this domain there enters into the heritage of scholastic philosophy the Humanist movement, whose political ideas, with a more or less antique-heathen coloring, abandon even in form the whole theocratic basis.[22]

It was the Reformation itself which gave new life to the theocratic idea. With all their differences of viewpoint Luther, Melanchthon, Zwingli and Calvin agree in emphasizing the Christian Vocation and hence the divine right of princely power. On the one hand they place the spiritual domain in more or less decided subjection to the State, and on the other hand they measure the rightfulness of the State by the performance of its religious duty, thereby adding a new interpretation to the teaching of Paul [Rom. xiii. 1] that all power is of God.[23]

Thus it was the most ardent opponents of the Reformation, especially the Dominicans and Jesuits, who now strove with all the weapons of the spirit in behalf of a purely secular construction of the State and Rulership. They did this not only to set the State in sharper contrast to the Church (in which at the same time they raised the theocratic idea to the highest pitch), but also to deduce from this contrast between the products of man and of God the necessity of a subordination of the secular power to the spiritual power.[24] But so far as its relations to the Church were not involved, they worked out a theory of the State which was free from all dogmatic assumptions, was purely philosophical in its basis and secular through and through. This applies not only to the genuine Monarchomachi of this group.[25] The great theorists of this school also agree that political society is rooted in the Law of Nature; that by the Law of Nature the united community is vested with sovereignty over its members; that all rights of rulership are derived from the will of the community, which is by the Law of Nature empowered and bound to transfer its own power.[26] Of course they do not give up the principle that the State is grounded in the Will of God and that all power is of God; but more and more they develop for this principle an interpretation which does not conflict at any point with the construction of the State by the pure law of reason, and which holds simply that in the last resort nature and natural reason, together with the relations, rights and duties based upon them, are emanations from the Divine Being.[27] This doctrine appears in its full maturity in the ingenious and profound Suarez. According to Suarez, sovereign power arises immediately and necessarily with the 'politic and mystical Body' itself, which the individual men

bring forth by an act of union conforming indeed to natural reason and thus to the Will of God, but at the same time purely
voluntary.[28] Yet it is not the individuals themselves whose will
produces the sovereignty of the whole body over its members;
for they do not previously possess the powers which belong to
the whole body (such as the power of life and death and of binding the conscience) nor can they, when deciding to form a community, prevent it from being sovereign. And perhaps even God
—although as "primus auctor" He remains the source of all
power—does not Himself give this power to the united People
by a special act (as to the Pope). On the contrary, for the people
sovereign power arises "ex vi rationis naturalis"; God gives it
as "proprietas consequens naturam," "medio dictamine rationis
naturalis ostendentis, Deum sufficienter providisse humano gen-
eri et consequenter illi dedisse potestatem ad suam conserva-
tionem et convenientem gubernationem necessariam." Just as the
individual man, by the mere fact of his existence, is free and has
power over himself and his limbs, so the body politic, by the
mere fact of its existence, has power and dominion over itself and
therefore over its own members. Just as the parent of a child
gives him only existence, and God through this medium gives
him freedom under the laws of reason, so is the sovereignty of
the community derived from the Author of Nature through the
medium of a free act of human will. And just as the father may
or may not procreate the son, but if he does he can only procreate
him as a free human being; so in this case, it is only for the creation of the community that human will is necessary: "ut autem
illa communitas habeat potestatem praedictam, non est necessaria
specialis voluntas hominum, sed ex natura rei consequitur et ex
providentia auctoris naturae, et in hoc sensu recte dicitur ab ipso
immediate collecta." [29] It is directly from this that Suarez, in
arguing (as Grotius did later) from the analogy of a renunciation of liberty, deduces the mutability and transferability of the
people's sovereignty. Yet it is left to the free discretion of the
people whether it shall itself retain the supreme power in whole
or in part, and whether and on what conditions it shall transfer
this to one person or to several; hence whoever has a legitimate

rulership holds it directly from the people and only indirectly from God.[30]

Over against such theories, not only the Protestant publicists [31] but also the Catholic anti-Jesuits [32] maintained the tenets of the divine origin of the State and the divine mandate of the civil power. The Calvinist Monarchomachi also entered the lists on this side.[33]

But just so far as the doctrines of contract and popular sovereignty are taken in earnest, these tenets must necessarily lose their importance for the construction of the State itself. Of course they remain of the greatest importance for defining the relation of the State to the Church and religion; they form the basis for contesting the claims of the Hierarchy, for the treatment of the Church as a State-institution, and for the religious mission of the State, culminating in the denial of liberty of conscience.[34] But otherwise they are again reduced, as under similar presuppositions in the middle ages, to the colorless expression of the general religious view that the State is an integral part of the natural and moral order of the world derived from God. Hence they may also be combined, easily enough, with a derivation of the State from the pure Law of Nature, which approaches closely to the Jesuit theory of the State and goes far beyond this only in bringing the Church itself into the system of Natural Law. And here the Politics of Althusius presents itself as the logical outcome of this development. For all references to the divine causation may be eliminated from this work without making the slightest difference in the basis of the State. It is indeed significant that the reference to God is nowhere, even formally, the starting-point of the argument, but appears for the first time in the conclusion, and there chiefly as a defense against attacks based on the divine right of princely power. The State is the product of a free contract and the form of the State is determined by a free choice; but the impulse to associate and to institute rulers comes from Nature and Nature's God.[35] The people elects and gives power to the ruler, but at the same time God through the medium of the people gives him his right and mandate.[36] And whenever the ruling power commits a breach of the contract made with the people, it loses all divine authorization, while the people, in performing the act of deposition, at the same time executes the Divine Will.[37]

It was the struggle against the doctrine of popular sovereignty which in the seventeenth century, as so often since then, inspired various efforts to restore a strictly theocratic conception of the State. The immediately divine origin and godlike nature of personal majesty were again asserted, and hence the absolute sacredness and inviolability of sovereignty.[38] The most scientific as well as the most thorough-going attempt at such a restoration was made by a German. This was Johann Friedrich Horn, of Brieg in Silesia, with his "Politicorum pars architectonica de Civitate." Horn exposed with extraordinary acumen the defects of the prevailing theory of contract and argued that the power of the State could not possibly be derived from the individual. On the other hand he drew the last consequences of individualism, while he rejected as absurd every conception of society as an organic whole and even the concept of 'juristic person' itself. From such premises he logically inferred that "majestas" cannot be explained otherwise than as a transcendental dispensation, that it is a faithful image of the Divine Majesty, and that its bearer as "Pro-Deus" is responsible only to God Himself. With the same rigor he argued that the 'subject' of majesty can only be a single human individual and hence that monarchy alone is the original and normal form of the State. All restrictions on the sovereignty of the monarch were swept away as conflicting with the unity, inalienability and ubiquity of majesty, which is destroyed by the slightest diminution and can no more be imparted to another person than the will or intellect of man can be imparted to a dog. He explained the republic as an artificial semblance of monarchy, in which it is impossible to find any 'subject' of majesty or any real State-power at all. What is here produced is the mere appearance of such a power with a series of more or less similar operations through a network of the legal relations of individuals ("mutuae obligationes singulorum"), while that which is the "opus Dei omnipotentis" can never originate in this way.[39]

Such attempts at restoration, however, could not avert the inevitable downfall of the theocratic idea in the political thought of the seventeenth century. The spirit of Natural Law was too strong for this. Its fate was sealed when the champions of the Ruler's Sovereignty, independent of Church and People alike, not only took over but carried to the highest pitch the pure 'Nature-Right' construction of the Jesuits and Monarchomachi. The vast authority gained by the system of Hugo Grotius stifled all opposition. And why should even the most extreme absolutists need to trace the State and its power to a supernatural source, after Hobbes had erected his all-devouring despotism by pure reason on the basis of contract and had exalted his commonwealth, though verily earth-born, to a "Mortall God"? [40] In Germany however, after the pure 'Nature-Right' basis of the State had long been accepted as an axiom,[41] Pufendorf dealt the decisive stroke. When he placed his system of philosophical politics, fashioned in the moderate and enlightened spirit of the new absolutism, wholly on the ground of the Law of Nature, and expressly rejected the theocratic idea,[42] he opened the dogmatic era of the law of reason with its countless 'natural systems of general Public Law,' which amid all their differences of viewpoint agreed in rejecting all transcendental notions of the State and Sovereignty.[43]

This is not the place to pursue this development further or to deal with the revival of the theocratic idea in the eighteenth and nineteenth centuries. Nor is it needful for us to study the strenuous debates carried on since the middle ages over the true nature of Natural Law, although the conception of the relation of Natural Law to God was important in fixing the position of the religious element in the theory of the 'Nature-Right' State.[44] As to this it need only be said here that as Natural Law extended its dominion it was at the same time emancipated from religious ideas and became rationalized. Already medieval schoolmen had hazarded the saying, usually referred to Grotius, that there would be a Law of Nature, discoverable by human reason and absolutely binding, even if there were no God, or the Deity were irrational or unjust.[45]

NOTES

1. A similar statement occurs in the book De jure Magistratuum, q. 6 p. 64. "Junius Brutus," Vindiciae contra tyrannos, and Danaeus, Polit. Christ., also start from this position.

2. Thus also Hotman, Francogallia, c. 21; De jure Mag., q. 10 p. 109 ff.; Junius Brutus, q. I., II. and IV.; Hoenonius, Disput. polit., disp. V. Among the Protestant advocates of popular sovereignty John Milton (Areopagitica, 1644, in Prose Works, London 1848, II. p. 49 ff.) was the first to suggest the separation of Church and State, while John Locke (Letters on Toleration, 1689, in Works, London 1801, Vol. VI.) gave it his strong support. On the other hand Rousseau with his "religion civile" (Contrat Social, IV. c. 8, and Lettres écrites de la Montagne, I. c. 1) holds to the original Calvinistic views.

3. As the principle of tolerance was but seldom suggested in the middle ages, particularly by Marsilius, Def. pac., II. c. 9–10, so after the Reformation its advocates, such as "Martinus Bellius" (Castalion), De haereticis, an sint persequendi, Magdeburg 1554 (see Janet, II. p. 139–149), remained isolated. The idea of religious liberty was first asserted by Milton, op. cit., and more decidedly by Locke, op. cit.; but at the same time it was taken up and carried to victory by the more or less absolutistic champions of religious Territorialism ["cujus regio ejus religio"], such as Benedict de Spinoza (Tractatus theologico-politicus, 1670, c. 14–15 and 20; Tractatus politicus, 1677, c. 3 § 10 and c. 6 § 40); Pufendorf (De habitu religionis christianae ad vitam civilem, 1687, § 30 ff.); and above all Christian Thomasius (Institutiones jurisprudentiae divinae, Frankfort and Leipzig 1709, written in 1687, III. c. 6 § 144–163; Dissert. of 1695, 1697 and 1699, in Dissertationes, Halle 1723, nr. 27, I. p. 975 ff., nr. 37, II. p. 154 ff., and nr. 44, ib. p. 318 ff.; Fundamenta juris naturae et gentium ex sensu communi deducta, Halle and Leipzig 1705, III. c. 6 § 12).

4. See Joh. Calvin, Institution Chrestienne (1st ed. 1541), in the Corpus Reformatorum, Vol. XXXII., book IV. c. 20 "du gouvernement civil"; here indeed civil government is described as a divine ordinance and hence in § 24 ff. resistance even to tyrants is repudiated; but according to § 31 this applies only to "personnes privées"; when there are "Magistrats constituez pour la defense du peuple, pour refrener la trop grande cupidité et licence des Rois," as the Ephors in Sparta, the Tribunes in Rome, the Demarchs in Athens, and today perhaps in every kingdom the three assembled Estates, they have not only the right but the duty "de s'opposer et resister à l'intem-

perance ou cruauté des Rois, selon le devoir de leur office"; indeed they may be accused of perjury on account of any "dissimulation, par laquelle malicieusement ils trahiroyent la liberté du peuple, de laquelle ils se devroyent cognoistre estre ordonnez tuteurs par le vouloir de Dieu." Here we have clearly the germ of the Ephor theory of Althusius, which is already found full-grown and even with the same generalized use of the word "Ephori" in Junius Brutus (p. 89 ff., 148 ff., 300 ff.), and also later in Hoenonius (II. § 46 ff. and IX. § 44 ff.); it is also taught in much the same form by Hotman, c. 19; De jure Mag., q. 6 p. 22 ff.; Danaeus, III. c. 6 p. 221; Alsted, p. 56 ff.

5. In q. I. the idea of contract comes from God. In q. II. God is the stipulator, while the people as universitas (following l. 22 Digest, de fidej.) and the king are joint promissors and thereby become "correi debendi," each being bound "in solidum," "ne quid detrimenti Ecclesia capiat." God demands from each the "rem integram" and punishes each for the other's default. But this presupposes that the people and the king have toward each other the right and duty of resistance and correction; in particular the people will not be decimated by God but justly punished for suffering godless rulers (p. 84 ff.). Likewise the several provinces and cities with their rulers are promissors to God, and have in like manner the right and duty of active resistance in case of damage to the Church (p. 99 ff.). But private men have only the duty of passive resistance, not armed "defensio ecclesiae," as "quod universitas debet, singuli non debent" (p. 115). In q. III., besides the right of resistance to religious tyranny, there is indeed the right of resistance to a ruler who damages the temporal State, which is deduced from a second contract made between the people and the king; but the twofold pact between God and king and people on the one hand and between king and people on the other hand belongs to the self-same act of the "constitutio Regis" (p. 248 ff.). Likewise in q. IV. the duty of neighboring princes to intervene in case of religious oppression is deduced from the "ecclesia unica" (p. 329 ff.), and in other cases of manifest tyranny, from the nature of humana societas" (p. 348 ff.). One need but compare this mode of argument with the Politics of Althusius in order to notice the diametrical opposition.

6. Yet Leopold von Ranke (Abhandl. u. Versuche, erste Sammlung, Leipzig 1872, p. 226) goes decidedly too far when he says that Buchanan did not intend to develop a universally valid theory at all, but only the positive public law of Scotland; it is true that Buchanan refers to the differences of constitutions, but the sovereignty of the people, the subjection of the ruler to the law, and the right of resistance are supported by rational arguments holding good for every rightfully instituted State.

7. Thus in Calvin, Knox, Poynet, Cartwright, Wängler and Alsted; but in Danaeus, despite his theological style, an Aristotelian rationalism prevails (I. c. 3, 4, 6; II. c. 4; III. c. 6).

8. In this respect Hoenonius falls short of his model, and clings to the "duplex pactum" of Junius Brutus (II. § 1–5).

9. This idea is most clearly developed in Dante (1265–1321), De Monarchia libri tres (ed. by Carol. Witte, Vienna 1874), especially I. c. 7. It is again developed in full splendor by Nicolaus Cusanus (Nicolas of Cues, 1401–1464), De concordantia catholica (in Schard, De jurisd. imp., p. 478 ff.), especially I. c. 1–4. But see already Johannes Saresberiensis (John of Salisbury, 1120–1180), Policraticus (1159), ed. Leyden 1639, IV. c. 1–4, V. c. 2–6, VI. c. 21; Hugo Floriacensis (Hugh of Fleury), Tractatus de regia et sacerdotali dignitate (1100–1106), ed. in Steph. Baluzii Miscellaneorum liber quartus, Paris 1683, p. 9 ff., I. c. 1; S. Thomas Aquinas (d. 1274), De regimine principum (Opera, Antwerp 1612, Vol. XVI.), I. c. 12; Alvarus Pelagius, De planctu ecclesiae (ed. Lyons 1617), I. a. 37 R; Somnium Viridarii (1376 or 1377), ed. in Goldast, Monarchia, I. p. 58 ff., I. c. 37–48.

10. The application to the Order of Human Society of propositions taken from Augustine and teaching the principle of 'unity before plurality' is made by Aquinas in particular, loc. cit., I. c. 2, 3, 12. But see already Hugo Floriac., I. c. 1. Then above all Aegidius Colonna Romanus, De regimine principum (1280–1316), ed. Venice 1498, III. 2 c. 3. With the greatest genius Dante, I. c. 5–16; and Nic. Cus., loc. cit. See Alv. Pel., I. a. 40; Johannes Parisiensis, Tract. de potestate regia et papali (about 1303; in Schard p. 142, and Goldast II. p. 108), c. 1; Antonius Rosellus (d. 1466), Monarchia (in Goldast, I. p. 252 ff.), II. c. 5–7; Laelius, in Goldast II. p. 1595 ff.; Petrus de Andlo, De imperio Romano-Germanico (ed. Nuremberg 1657), I. c. 8.

11. See Dante, I. c. 3–4 and III. c. 16.

12. One corpus mysticum, one universitas, one respublica, communitas, politia, populus unus, regnum unum, the ecclesia in the widest sense; see S. Bernard, Epistola ad Conr. Reg., in Goldast II. p. 67–68; Hugo Floriac., I. c. 1, II. p. 46 and 50; Thom. Aquin., Opera IV. p. 48, q. 8 a. 1 and 2; Engelbert of Volkersdorf, De ortu, progressu et fine Rom. Imp. (ed. Basel 1553), c. 15, 17 and 18; Dante, I. c. 3, 5–9; Lupold of Bebenburg, De iure regni et imperii, c. 15; Petrarca, Epistolae (1350–1370), in Goldast II. p. 1345, nr. 7 and 8; Alv. Pel., I. a. 13 F, a. 37 Q and R, a. 40 and 45; Augustinus Triumphus, Summa de potestate ecclesiastica (1324–1328), ed. Rome 1583, I. q. 1 a. 6; William of Ockham, Octo quaestiones (1339–1342), III. q. 1 and 9, and Dialogus (1342 or 1343), III. tr. 2, lib. 1, c. 1,

and lib. 3, c. 17 and 22 (in Goldast, II. p. 314 ff.); Somn. Virid., II. c. 305–312; Nic. Cus., III. c. 1 and 41.

13. In the great controversy between the papalist and imperialist theories the medieval mind remained at one with itself in so far as the dualism of the two Orders and Swords must find its solution in a higher unity ("ad unum reduci"). The papalist view perceives in the "argumentum unitatis" the middle term and conclusion of all arguments for the supremacy of the Church (see especially Boniface VIII [in the bull Unam Sanctam of 1302], c. 1 Extrav. comm., 1, 8; Joh. Saresb., loc. cit.; Thom. Aquin., De reg. pr., I. c. 14–15, and Opera lll. p. 227, q. 60 a. 6 ad 3; Alv. Pel., I. a. 40 and 54; Aug. Triumph., I. q. 1 a. 6, and q. 22 a. 3). The secularist view is but seldom carried to the opposite extreme (Marsilius Patavinus, Defensor pacis, 1324–1326, ed. s. l. 1622; in hypothetical form, Ockham, Octo qu., III. c. 3 and 8, Dial. III. tr. 2, l. 1, c. 1, and l. 3, c. 17 and 22). It finds this unity presented above all in the supermundane Head of the Body of Mankind (Hugo Floriac., I. c. 2, and II. p. 46 and 65; Dante, III. c. 12; Joh. Paris., c. 18–19; Quaestio in utramque partem (in Goldast, II. p. 95 ff.), p. 103 ad 4–5; Ockham, Octo qu., I. c. 1 and 18, Dial. III. tr. 1, l. 2, c. 1 and 30; Somn. Virid., I. c. 38, 46, 48, 102, and II. c. 102, 305–312; Ant. Ros., I. c. 42). And furthermore it points to the inner unity in the mutual support and supplementation, the mutual dependence, the 'harmonious concord' of sacerdotium and imperium (Hugo Floriac., prol., I. c. 3, 12, and II. p. 50; S. Bernard, loc. cit.; Sachsenspiegel, I. a. 1, and Gloss ad h. 1. and ad III. a. 57; Eng. Volk., op. cit., c. 22; Joh. Paris., c. 14; Quaestio, p. 105 ad 11; Ockham, Octo qu., I. c. 3 and 14; Somn. Virid., I. c. 49 55; Ant. Ros., III. c. 15–18; Nic. Cus., III. c. 1, 12 and 14; other citations in Höfler, Kaiserthum und Papstthum, Prague 1862, p. 121 ff.). See also Friedberg, Die mittelalterlichen Lehren über das Verhältniss von Kirche und Staat, Zeitschr. f. Kirchenrecht, VIII. p. 69 ff.—Then when each of these two Orders is taken by itself the divinely instituted, outward and visible unity of the Spiritual Realm was but very rarely questioned in the middle ages (as by Ockham, Octo qu., I. c. 1 and 30, and III. c. 2 and 8, Dial. III. tr. 2, l. 1, c. 3 and 8, l. 3, c. 17; and in substance by Mars. Pat., loc. cit.; for the first time in decisive fashion when John Wyclif and John Hus demanded a more inward, less external, conception of the Church; compare for similar views Joh. Gerson, Opera, II. p. 88). On the other hand indeed the necessity of a single Universal State was in principle already disputed in France (Joh. Paris., c. 3, 16, 22; Disputatio inter militem et clericum about 1303, in Schard, p. 686–687; Somn. Virid., I. c. 36, 73, 80, 96; Gerson, De pot. eccl., c. 9, II. p. 328; see also Mars. Pat., I. c. 17; Ockham, Dial. III. tr. 2, l. 1, c. 1–10 and l. 2, c. 6–9).

14. See for example Aegid. Col., II. 1 c. 2; Eng. Volk., c. 15, 17, 18; Dante, I. c. 3 and 5; Aug. Triumph., I. q. 1 a. 6; Ant. Ros., I. c. 6; Nic. Cus., II. c. 27–28.

15. The arguments for preferring the monarchical form of government in Church and State culminate always in the "exemplum totius universi gubernationis, quae fit per unum Deum supremum," in the fittest representation of the unity by the "per se unum," and in the prototype of Universal Nature. See especially Thom. Aquin., De reg. pr., I. c. 2 and 5, Op. XXI. p. 487 and 507; Aegid. Col., III. 2 c. 3; Dante, I. c. 5–14 and especially c. 15; Joh. Paris., c. 1; Alv. Pel., I. c. 40 D and 62 C; Gerson, IV. p. 585; Somn. Virid., I. c. 187; Nic. Cus., III. praef.; Laelius, loc. cit. p. 1595 ff.; Ant. Ros., II. c. 5–7; Petr. Andl., I. c. 3 and 8;—independently and with some divergence, Eng. Volk., De regimine principum, ed. Huffnagl, Ratisbon s. a., I. c. 11–12.

16. For Papacy and Empire no proof is needed; the generalization is clearly expressed in Dante, loc. cit.; Petr. Andl., I. c. 2 ("subalterna quadam emanatione"), and II. c. 9; Tengler, Laienspiegel (1509), p. 14, 17, 56.

17. See the doctrine (taken partly from S. Augustine, De civitate Dei, l. 15 c. 1, and l. 19 c. 15) of Gregory VII in his Epist. lib. VIII., nr. 21, in Jaffé, Monum. Gregor., p. 456. Also Alv. Pel., I. a. 36, 37, 56 B, 59 F–G, 64 D–E; Aug. Triumph., I. q. 1 a. 1 and 3, q. 2 a. 7, II. q. 33 a. 1; Ptolemaeus Lucensis, in the continuation of the work of Thom. Aquin., De reg. princ., III. c. 10.

18. Hugo Floriac., prol., I. c. 1, 4, 12, II. p. 66–68, indeed describes the doctrine of the human, and therefore sinful, origin of kingly power as a wide-spread heresy, which conflicts with the text "non est potestas nisi a Deo." But see Joh. Saresb., IV. c. 1, p. 208–209, and VI. c. 22, p. 391–395; Ptol. Luc., III. c. 1–8; Alv. Pel., I. a. 8 and 41 C–K, with the distinction in I. a. 56 B.—On both sides the dispute, as regards both Emperor and King, turns in general on the question whether their power was "immediate a Deo" or "mediante Ecclesia."

19. See Thom. Aquin., I. c. 1 and 13; Ptol. Luc., III. c. 9 and IV. c. 2–3; Aegid. Col., III. 2 c. 32, also III. 1 c. 1 and 3–6; Eng. Volk., De ortu, c. 1; Joh. Paris., c. 1; Gerson, IV. p. 648; Nic. Cus., III. praef.; also Ockham, Dial. III. tr. 2, l. 1, c. 27; Mars. Pat., I. c. 15.

20. Joh. Paris., c. 11 and 16: populo faciente et Deo inspirante. Mars. Pat., I. c. 9: God is "causa remota." Ockham, Dial. III. tr. 2, l. 1, c. 27: imperium a Deo et tamen per homines. Ant. Ros., I. c. 56. Nic. Cus., II. c. 19, III. praef. and c. 4: in Church and State the voluntary submission of men establishes the material force, and God lends the spiritual power; it is surely divine, and not merely human, when an assembled multitude decides as if

it were one heart and one soul (II. c. 5 and 15). Jacobus Almainus (d. 1515), De auctor. eccl., c. 1 (in Gerson, Opera, II. p. 978 and 1014): God gives the power to the communitas so that this power may be lent to the ruler.

21. Already the borrowing of the Aristotelian doctrine of the forms of government, their conditions and advantages, threatened the divine right of monarchy. But now it is expressly said that no form of government is more divine than another, and that it all depends on the "dispositio gentis"; thus Ptol. Luc., II. c. 9 and IV. c. 8 (in the "status integer" of human nature the "regimen politicum" would indeed be preferable); Eng. Volk., De reg. pr., I. c. 16; Ockham, Octo qu., III. c. 3 and 7, Dial. III. tr. 2, l. 1, c. 5. It is likewise asserted that the "unitas principatus" is also possible and necessary in a republic; Mars. Pat., I. c. 17 and III. concl. 11; Ockham, Dial. III. tr. 2, l. 3, c. 17 and 22. Ockham says indeed that the State which comprises all mankind may rightly be in the form of a Republic instead of under an Emperor; Dial. III. tr. 1, l. 2, c. 2, 12–14, 16–17, 25, 30.— Even with regard to the Church the divine ordinance of monarchical government was called in question by Ockham (Octo qu., III. c. 3, 6, 8; Dial. III. tr. 2, l. 1, c. 1, 4, 9, 13), and denied by Mars. Pat. (II. c. 15–22, III. concl. 32 and 41). Among the Conciliar pamphleteers Randuf, De modo uniendi ecclesiam (about 1410, in Von der Hardt, Mag. Concil. Const., I. p. 68 ff., and Gerson, Op. II. p. 161 ff.), c. 5, maintains (following the hypothetical method of Ockham, Dial. III. tr. 1, l. 2, c. 20–27) that the Council has the right to alter or abolish the monarchical government of the Church; for views which are similar, though attacked by him, see Petrus de Alliaco (d'Ailly), in Gerson, Op. I. p. 662 ff.; Gerson, ib. II. p. 88; Joh. Breviscoxa, ib. I. p. 872 ff.

22. Aeneas Sylvius (Pius II), De ortu et auctoritate Imperii Romani, 1446, in Schard p. 314 ff., sometimes repeats the traditional phrases, but they have become empty words. Franciscus Patricius Senensis (d. 1494 as Bishop of Gaeta) in his "De institutione reipublicae libri IX" (Strasburg 1595) eulogizes the republic, and in his later work "De regno et regis institutione libri IX" (ib.) prefers monarchy, all in the manner of antiquity. A complete and deliberate break with the theocratic idea was made in a realistic spirit by Niccolò Machiavelli (Il Principe, Venice 1515), and in an idealistic spirit by Sir Thomas More (De optimo reipublicae statu deque nova insula Utopia, Louvain 1516).

23. On Luther and Zwingli see Bluntschli, p. 46 ff.; on Melanchthon see Hinrichs, I. p. 11 ff., and Kaltenborn, p. 11 ff.; on Calvin see Baudrillart, p. 33 ff.—It need hardly be added that the dogmas of the fanatical dissenting sects were also of a theocratic color.

24. See Dominicus Soto (a Dominican, 1494–1560), De justitia et jure libri decem, Venice 1602 (1st ed. 1556), I. q. 1 a. 3, IV. q. 4 a. 1–2, X. q. 3 a. 1; Franciscus Victoria (Dominican, d. 1546), Relectiones tredecim, Ingolstadt 1580, Rel. I. q. 5 nr. 8, and Rel. III.; Ferdinand Vasquez (1509–1566), Controversiarum illustrium aliarumque usu frequentium libri tres, Frankfort 1572, c. 8, 20, 21, 27; Didacus Covarruvias y Leyva (1512–1577), Quaest. practic. (Opera, Vol. III.), I. c. 1; the argument of the Jesuit Lainez, 1562 [at the Council of Trent], in Ranke, p. 227; Leonhardus Lessius (Jesuit, 1554–1623), De justitia et jure libri quatuor, Antwerp 1612 (1st ed. 1606), II. c. 5, and III.–IV.; Ludovicus Molina (Jesuit, 1535–1600), De justitia et jure, Mainz 1659, II. disp. 21 and 29; Robert Bellarmine (1542–1621), De membris ecclesiae militantis, III. 6, De Summo Pontifice lib. V., and De potestate Summi Pontificis in rebus temporalibus adversus Barclaium (Rome 1610); Franciscus Suarez (Jesuit, 1548–1617), Tractatus de legibus ac Deo legislatore, Antwerp 1613, III. c. 3, c. 6–8, c. 10 nr. 2–6, IV. c. 3 and 19, V. c. 14 nr. 3.—Also Boucher, I. c. 5–8 and 18, II. throughout; Rossaeus, c. 3–11; Mariana, I. c. 10.

25. In Salamonius neither God nor the Church is mentioned at all; in Mariana only occasionally; the arguments of Boucher and Rossaeus, so far as the independence of the Church is not in question, are almost identical with those of the Huguenots, especially Languet.

26. Thus Victoria, Rel. III.; Covarruvias, loc. cit., nr. 2 ("lege naturali"); Soto, I. q. 1 a. 3, and IV. q. 4 a. 1–2; Lainez, loc. cit.; Vasquez, c. 42–43 and 47; Molina, II. d. 21–31; Suarez, III. c. 1–4; Bellarmine, loc. cit.

27. See Victoria, III. nr. 4, 6–8: God, on account of human need, implanted the natural instinct of association, and hence the State is "a jure naturali, ergo a Deo"; yet from the same source comes the power of the "ipsa Respublica" over its members, together with the right and duty of transferring this power to Kings and Princes; hence the power of the latter is also "a Deo et jure naturali."—Soto, I. q. 1 a. 3: the spiritual power is derived from God, the civil power from the people; the text 'by me kings reign' [Prov. viii. 15] means only that "a Deo tanquam naturalis juris auctore donatum mortalibus est, ut unaquaeque Respublica seipsam regendi habeat arbitrum, ac subinde, ubi ratio, quae spiramen est divini numinis, postulaverit, in alium suam transmittat potestatem, cujus legibus providentius gubernetur"; also at more length, IV. q. 4 a. 1–2: the spiritual power is derived immediately from God, "neque facta est a republica neque per rempublicam derivata"; "potestatem civilem . . . Deus per legem naturalem, quae suae sempiternae participatio est, ordinavit"; for God gave to every man by nature the right of self-preservation, to make this practicable

added the instinct of association, and gave to the "congregata Respublica" the understanding that it must institute some form of government and give it magisterial power; thus the "ordinatio civilis potestatis" is from God, "non quod Respublica non creaverit principes, sed quod id fecit divinitus erudita"; this is the reason why there may indeed be one spiritual, but not one secular supreme head of all Mankind (which indeed has never assembled together).—Molina, II. d. 22 § 8–9: natural reason, given by God, leads to association in the "corpus Reipublicae"; this has "jure naturali, ergo a Deo immediate" power over its members; d. 23: as all cannot exercise this power, "lumen naturae docet, in Reipublicae arbitrio esse positum, committere alicui vel aliquibus regimen et potestatem supra seipsam, prout voluerit expedireque judicaverit"; thus arise the forms of the State; d. 26: the "potestas Regia" is thus derived from the "jus positivum," but indirectly from the "jus naturale"; d. 27: thus from God.—Still more colorless is the derivation of secular power from God in Bellarmine (compare Ranke, p. 228).

28. Suarez, III. c. 1 (origin of the State), and c. 2 (proof that "ex natura rei" no one man, but the community itself, is sovereign).

29. III. c. 3 nr. 1–6. The relation of this quite excellent reasoning to the doctrine of the State-contract will be resumed in Ch. II.

30. III. c. 3 nr. 7; c. 4 throughout (Saul and David were exceptions).— Everywhere Suarez works out the contrast to the Church: the ecclesiastical power comes directly from God, the secular power through the Law of Nature; God has instituted monarchy in the Church and popular sovereignty in the State; the Church is supernatural, the State is natural; the Church is necessarily universal, the State is necessarily particular; see I. c. 7 nr. 5, c. 8 nr. 9, III. c. 3 nr. 8, c. 6, IV. c. 1 ff.

31. Such as Joh. Ferrarius (councillor to the Prince of Hesse and professor at Marburg), De Republica bene instituenda, Basel 1556, German version by Abraham Saur, Frankfort 1601, c. 1 (God is the original cause of society, it does not spring from 'natural curiosity'), and c. 3 (civil power is from God and is 'God's handmaid') ; G. Lauterbeck, Regentenbuch, 1559, II. c. 1 and 20; Jac. Omphalus (of Andernach), De civili politia libri tres, Cologne 1565, I. c. 3 and II. c. 1; Theod. Reinking, Biblische Polizei, in drey Stände, alsz Geist-, Welt- und Häuslichen abgetheilt, II. ax. 1 ff., and Tractatus de regimine (1616), 3rd ed. Marburg 1641, I. cl. 1 c. 1 ff.; Arnisaeus, De jure maj., I. c. 3 § 1–3, II. c. 6, and De subjectione et exemtione clericorum (against Bellarmine; with a wholly medieval aspect of the duo fora immediate dependentia a Deo).

32. Such as Petrus Gregorius Tholosanus, De Republica (1586), Frankfort 1609, VI. c. 1–3, VIII. c. 1, XXIV. c. 7, XXVI. c. 5 and 7;

Barclay, op. cit., I. and II., III. c. 2, 4–16, V. c. 7–8, and De potestate Papae, Hanau 1612 (against Bellarmine). See also the other polemics against Bellarmine in Goldast, III. p. 565–1134.—On the other hand Bodin nowhere goes into these questions.

33. In this respect they openly follow the teaching of Calvin, loc. cit., § 2–4, 8 and 31.

34. Thus also in Althusius, Politica, c. 9 § 28 ff., and c. 38.

35. See especially c. 1 nr. 12 and 32 ff.—How different in the Vindiciae!

36. See especially c. 19 nr. 51 ff.; nr. 67 ff. ("Rex et ephori a Deo constituuntur et a populo, a Deo mediate et a populo immediate; uterque a Deo et populo sua potestate et officio privatur, a Deo quidem mediate, a populo immediate"); nr. 103 ff. The argument against Barclay's distinction "electio Dei, constitutio populi" applies equally, as Althusius omits to mention, against Junius Brutus, who also says "populus reges constituit, Deus eligit." Althusius on the other hand is never tired of repeating that the people alone is the creator of all government, God acting only in and through the people.

37. See the passages cited in Note 36, also c. 28. With some similarity De jure Mag., p. 14 ff.—Still farther goes Milton, Defensio pro populo Anglicano, London 1651, c. 2 p. 15: while God is the mediate source of kingly power, the right of the people is also from God, and when the people makes itself free this is also God's Will; likewise c. 4 ("unctus Dei" is the populus), and c. 5.—Algernon Sidney (1622–1683), Discourses concerning Government (1680–1683), Edinburgh 1750, c. I. § 6 and 17, says no more than that God has given to men freedom and the freest choice of social institutions and forms of government.

38. To this effect Barclay and Arnisaeus, though not in so many words. Much more decidedly Graswinckel, De jure maj., c. 1–3 (majestas immediate a Deo, non a populo; its genesis can be explained only by divine grace); c. 7 and 11. Likewise Claudius Salmasius (1588–1653), Defensio regia pro Carolo I Rege Angliae, Paris 1651, c. 2. See also King James I, Works, London 1616. Sir Robert Filmer, Patriarcha, 1680 (with the well-known derivation of all kingly power from Adam, which Suarez, III. c. 2 nr. 3, had confuted beforehand, and hence with lively polemics against Suarez and Bellarmine). Felwinger, loc. cit., p. 817 ff. Wandalinus, Juris regii ἀνυπευθύνου et absolutissimi . . . libri sex, Copenhagen 1663–1667. Valentin Alberti, Compendium juris naturae orthodoxae theologiae conformatum, Leipzig 1678, c. 14 § 3–4 (Majestas a Deo semper confertur immediate Magistratui, concurrente tamen civitate seu populo quoad designationem personae sive personarum; thus is the "potestas Dei vicaria et

summa"). Joh. Jac. Mullerus, Institutiones politicae, Jena 1692, I. c. 7 § 62–65. Pelzhoeffer de Schoenau, Arcanorum Status libri decem, Frankfort 1710, II. c. 3.—Then Fénelon (1651–1715), Essai sur le gouvernement civil, 3rd ed. London 1723, chap. VI. and concl. p. 181–183. Bossuet (1627–1704), Politique tirée des propres paroles de l'Écriture Sainte, Brussels 1710 (1st ed. 1709), I. a. 1, II. a. 1–2, V. a. 1.

39. See especially I. c. 4 § 3–6, II. c. 1 § 2–21, c. 9 § 1, c. 10 § 11–15, c. 11 § 1–5, III. c. un.—Horn's absolutism vies with that of Hobbes, even though it is moderated somewhat by the religious idea; see II. c. 2–6 (absolute power over persons; dominium eminens as true ownership; derivation of all private ownership from the State's grant); c. 10 § 4–15 (no legal limitations; the advocates of "majestas realis" should be put to death, and plebeian neighbor-states ought to inflict this punishment on them by international law); c. 12 § 2–13 (passive obedience); c. 3 § 7 and c. 5 § 3 ownership of church-property by the State, and absolute "jus sacrorum").—There can be no better proof of Horn's keen insight than the way in which he not only exposes the inner contradiction in Barclay, Salmasius and Grotius, between the idea of contract and the absolutist consequences (II. c. 1 § 17), but above all argues that the political theory of Hobbes is just as revolutionary, and in its last consequences just as favorable to popular sovereignty, as the doctrine of the Monarchomachi themselves.—I have nowhere found any appreciation of Horn, though Pufendorf attacks him in a most elaborate and vigorous fashion (De officio, III. c. 6 § 20, c. 8 § 4; De jure Nat. et Gent., VII. c. 3 and c. 5 § 5); just another illustration of what was said at the beginning of this monograph.

40. The warning of Horn (see preceding Note), which reads almost like a prophecy of the new turn given by Rousseau to the ideas of Hobbes, went unheeded.—Spinoza's theory of the State, with all its philosophical profundity and its reservation of spiritual freedom, remains closely akin to the politics of Hobbes.

41. The formulas most commonly used were that the State and its power are "a Deo et natura" and that rulership is derived "mediante humana institutione" from God. Thus Keckermann, op. cit., p. 9 ff.; Otto Casmannus (d. 1607), Doctrinae et vitae politicae methodicum et breve systema, Frankfort 1603, c. 3–4; Matthias Bortius, in Arumaeus, I. nr. 30, c. 5 § 1–2 and c. 6 § 1–2; Hilliger, ib. II. nr. 13 c. 3; Gryphiander (d. 1652), ib. V. nr. 6, § 15 ff. and 21 ff.; Schoenborner, I. c. 4; Werdenhagen, Univ. introd. in omnes respublicas, Amsterdam 1632, II. c. 2; Adam Contzen (1575–1635), Politicorum libri decem, Mainz 1620, I. c. 3 § 3 and c. 5 ff., V. c. 20; Aaron Alex. Olizarovius, De politica hominum societate libri tres,

Danzig 1651, III. c. 2; Bornitius, Partit., p. 32 ff.; Knichen, Opus politicum, Frankfort 1682, I. c. 1 th. 2, and c. 8 th. 2; Boecler, Inst. pol., I. c. 1 and II. c. 1.

42. Pufendorf, De jure Nat. et Gent., VII. c. 3, De off., II. c. 6 § 14 (God has only given to the people the power by which it produces sovereignty).

43. Pufendorf was followed in essentials by Thomasius; see Inst. jur. div., III. c. 6 § 67–114: the two extreme views, that sovereignty comes from the people alone (although with divine sanction) and that it comes directly from God, are both wrong; God is the creator, but He produces it through the "consensus populi"; Fund. jur. nat., III. c. 6 § 9–10; see his controversy with Masius on this question, in Hinrichs, III. p. 184 ff. Similarly Hert, Diss. de modis constituendi civitates (Comment. et Opusc., I. 1 p. 286 ff.). G. G. Titius (1661–1714), Specimen juris publici Romano-Germanici, Leipzig 1705 (1st ed. 1698), VII. c. 7. Nic. Hier. Gundling (1671–1729), Jus naturae et gentium, Halle 1728 (1st ed. 1714), c. 35 § 18–36, Ausführlicher Discours über das Natur- und Völkerrecht, Frankfort and Leipzig 1734, c. 34. J. H. Boehmer, Introd. in jus publ. univ., pars spec. I. c. 2 § 24–29 (not immediate a Deo, but ordinatio divina approbans).—But now even the opposing advocates of the godlike nature of Majesty mostly introduce the mediation of the people; thus Henr. de Cocceji (1644–1719), Prodromus justitiae gentium, Frankfort-on-the-Oder 1719, and Samuel de Cocceji (1679–1755), Novum systema justitiae naturalis, 1740, III. § 612 ff. See also Henr. Ernestus Kestner (1671–1723), Jus naturae et gentium, Rinteln 1705, c. 7.—The Catholic systems in part follow Suarez closely; thus Franz Schmier, Jurisprudentia publica universalis, Salzburg 1732, I. c. 2 s. 4 § 2–3, II. c. 1 s. 3 § 1–3.—Christian Wolff and his school have no further need for any serious attack on the transcendental origin of government.

44. For the period from the Reformation to Grotius reference may be made to Kaltenborn; for the later period and especially for the controversies aroused in Germany by Pufendorf and Thomasius, see Hinrichs. But the historical development of the idea of Natural Law in the middle ages remains obscure in many respects. Hitherto, attention has been chiefly given to the controversies between the principles of faith and reason and as to the respective spheres of divine and human action. Almost forgotten, however, is the great debate running through all scholastic thought, which touches the deepest questions of legal philosophy and lives today in other forms, as to whether and how far will (voluntas) or rational insight (intellectus) is the essence of Natural Law and hence ultimately of all law. The older

view, which is more especially that of the Realists, explained the "lex naturalis" as an "actus intellectus" independent of the will—as a mere "lex indicativa," in which God is not a lawgiver but a teacher working through the reason—in short, as the dictate of reason as to what is right and just, grounded in the Being of God but unalterable even by Him. (Thus already Hugo de S. Victore Saxo, in the days of Calixtus II and Henry V, Opera omnia, Mainz 1617, III. p. 385, de sacramentis I. p. 6, c. 6–7; later Gabriel Biel, d. 1495, Almainus and others.) The opposite view, starting from pure Nominalism, saw in Natural Law a mere divine precept ("lex praeceptiva"), which is right and binding merely because God as the lawgiver wills it so (thus Ockham, Gerson, d'Ailly). The prevalent opinion was of a mediating sort, though it stood nearer to the Realist principle. It regarded the substance of Natural Law as a judgment touching what is right, a judgment necessarily flowing from the Divine Being and immutably determined by the "natura rerum" which is comprised in God; yet the binding force of this Law, but only its binding force, was traced to the Divine Will (thus Aquinas, Cajetanus, Soto, Suarez II. c. 6 § 5–14). In similar ways was decided the question, what is the constitutive element of Law (or Right) in general? Most of the Scholastics therefore taught that what makes law to be law is only the "iudicium rationis, quod sit aliquid iustum." Thus with even greater sharpness Soto, op. cit., I. q. 1 a. 1, and Molina, Tract. V. d. 46 § 10–12; see also Bolognetus (1534–1585), De lege, jure et aequitate (in Tractatus universi juris, I. p. 289 ff.), c. 3; Gregorius de Valentia, Commentarii theologici, Ingolstadt 1592, II. disp. 1, q. 1 punct. 2. The opposite school taught that law becomes law merely through the will that this or that shall pass for law and be binding; or they laid all the stress on a command (imperium) given to those subject to the law. Others again held that "intellectus" and "voluntas" are equally essential. But Suarez (who reviews at length all the older opinions) distinguishes at this point between Positive Law and Natural Law, and in the case of the former sees the legislator's will (but not the legislative command) as the constitutive, while reason is only a normative, element (I. c. 4–5 and III. c. 20). In the later philosophy of law the derivation of all law from will and the conception of both Natural and Positive Law as mere command was well-nigh universal. But Leibniz (1646–1716), who in so many ways went deeper than his contemporaries, and who perhaps for this reason so often turned his eyes backwards toward medieval modes of thought, attacked this 'will-theory' with forceful words aimed against Pufendorf and Cocceji. He denied that the element of compulsion is essential to the concept of law, and argued that "Recht" is prior to "Gesetz" ('law is law not because God has willed it, but because God is just'); see Opera, ed. Dutens, Geneva 1768, IV. 3, p. 275–283, also p. 270 ff., § 7 ff. and § 13.

45. It is the German Gabriel Biel who in his Collectorium sententiarum, Tübingen 1501, lib. II. dist. 35, q. un. art. 1, after explaining that Natural Law is merely "indicans," not "praecipiens," and that God is not its legislator by the power of Will but is the Author of Reason and therefore its ultimate source, proceeds as follows: "Nam si per impossibile Deus non esset, qui est ratio divina, aut ratio illa divina esset errans: adhuc si quis ageret contra rectam rationem angelicam vel humanam ut aliam aliquam si qua esset: peccaret. Et si nulla penitus esset recta ratio, adhuc si quis ageret contra id quod agendum dictaret ratio recta si aliqua esset: peccaret." Similar utterances of Gregorius, Almainus and Anton. Cordubensis are cited and opposed by Suarez, II. c. 6 § 3 ("licet Deus non esset vel non uteretur ratione vel non recte de rebus judicaret, si in homine esset idem rectae rationis dictantis dictamen, . . . illud habiturum eandem rationem legis, quam nunc habet"). Compare the well-known passages in Grotius, op. cit., proleg. nr. 11, and I. c. 1 § 10.

THE DOCTRINE OF THE
STATE-CONTRACT

INTO the heritage of the theocratic idea there entered every-where the doctrine of the State-Contract, which was destined to tyrannize over the minds of men for centuries. In the historical development of this doctrine the Politics of Althusius is of epoch-making importance. It may be said that Althusius raised the idea of contract to the level of a theory, in so far as he was the first to construct in a logical way a scientific system of general politics on the assumption of definite original contracts. Thereby he produced a work of genius which may none the less be called original even though, as in all such cases, the materials were gathered and partly put into shape before his time.

Althusius takes as the basis of his theory the division of the processes of will assumed to institute the State into two parts, the Social Contract and the Contract of Rulership. This division was commonly accepted until the end of the eighteenth century and was first attacked by Hobbes. The distinction of these two contracts was stated much earlier, but never with such juristic sharpness.[1] In any case each of these may be separately studied in its genesis and history. That which is logically posterior is taken first, simply because it is historically anterior.

I. The Contract of Rulership

The assumption of a Contract of Rulership as the legal basis of civil power became accepted in the middle ages as almost beyond dispute.

Its earliest traces may be followed up to the time of the Investiture conflict.[2] It was favored by religious ideas of an original state of Nature wherein there was neither ownership nor rulership. Many remembrances of events in the history of Germanic law came to the aid of this theory, as also the contractual form which agreements between Princes and Estates had given to many of the rights and duties coming within the sphere of public law. But its victory was decided chiefly by the conception being formed as to the origin of the highest of earthly powers, which was taken as the model of all rulership.

Jurisprudence, on the basis of its ancient texts, had always accepted the doctrine that the Imperial power, as successor to the Imperium of the Roman Caesars, was founded originally on an act of transference performed by the people in the Lex Regia.[3] It was the champions of the secular power who broadened this foundation when, in opposing the papal claims, they removed the constitutive power from the Pope's co-operation to the will of the people, even in the later changes of the Empire as recorded in the tales of medieval historians.[4] They argued that as the Empire proceeded from the people, so at every vacancy of the throne it escheats or reverts to the people.[5] Hence in an extreme case the people may transfer the Empire from one nation to another; and thus in the 'translation' of the Empire from Greeks to Germans the true authority lay in the "consensus populi" mentioned at the coronation of Charles the Great, while the Pope merely declared and executed the people's will.[6] Thus at every vacancy the election of the new Emperor belongs to the people, and the choice by the College of Electors takes place purely in the name of the people by virtue of an authorization given by it once for all.[7]

But that which was true of the greatest society on earth must be the effluence of a principle grounded in Divine and Natural Law. Since the end of the thirteenth century indeed it was held as an axiom of political philosophy that the legal basis of all government lies in the voluntary or contractual subjection or submission of the governed.[8] In accordance with this it was said to be a principle of Natural Law that the institution of the ruler belongs exclusively to the people.[9] From this it was inferred that pure elective monarchy is in better accord with Divine and Natural Law than hereditary monarchy, and just for this reason it prevails in the Empire as in the Church.[10]

For a long time the clerical party maintained that the State was the product of violent conquest or successful usurpation. But on the other hand, while admitting that such was its origin in concrete cases, it was said that a retroactive legitimation by the express or tacit consent of the people was indispensable if the ruler was to have a good title to rulership.[11] And when others held that an organic development of the State from the Family was possible, and derived hereditary monarchy from the succession to paternal power,[12] the prevailing doctrine traced all regal succession back to an initial grant of the people's power to a whole dynasty as such.[13]

This theory, framed in the middle ages, not only remained unshaken in the later centuries but became more and more an essential element of the whole 'Nature-Right' theory of the State. In the sixteenth century and at the beginning of the seventeenth it was not only taken by the Monarchomachi as the basis of their whole system,[14] and fully maintained by the clerical writers;[15] it was also adopted by publicists and jurists of widely different schools,[16] was held by Bodin as a self-evident postulate,[17] was accepted by the earliest teachers of positive German public law,[18] and was left untouched by most of the champions of unlimited monarchy themselves.[19] Then when Grotius, Hobbes, Pufendorf and Thomasius had based all sovereign power on the Contract of Submission,[20] the contractual basis of government became an established dogma.[21] Its few opponents could gain no success, as they had nothing to put in its place but the restoration of the theocratic idea.[22]

The real dispute turned more and more on the meaning and terms of the Contract of Rulership.

This dispute also reaches far back into the middle ages. It first took a strictly juristic form in the dispute of the Glossators [in the twelfth century] as to the legal nature of the ancient "translatio imperii" from the Roman people to the Princeps.[23] One school explained this as a definitive and irrevocable alienation of power,[24] the other as a mere concession of its use and exercise.[25]

The dispute was generalized and led to the most widely different theories of the relation between ruler and people. On the one hand from the people's abdication the most absolute sovereignty of the prince might be deduced, and in this sense even the Hohenstaufen could admit the foundation of rulership in the will of the people.[26] On the other hand the assumption of a mere "concessio imperii" led to the doctrine of popular sovereignty. Between these there was room for various interpretations of the contract in the sense of a sovereignty which was either divided or bound by limitations and conditions.

In the later centuries this dispute continued. There were efforts to make the juristic nature of the contract of rulership more definite; on the one hand the assumed alienation was more sharply analyzed, on the other hand the idea of a delegation or mandate was developed and was at last put by Althusius in the form of a purely functional contract. But now above all the hitherto accepted mode of argument, starting from the contractual volition and thus being essentially an ascertainment of the presumed intention of the contracting parties, was opposed with ever sharper accentuation and ever greater success by the logical deduction of those terms of the contract which are alone possible in the nature of things. In this respect a new epoch is marked by Bodin and Althusius, the former as deducing from the nature of government itself the necessarily full and unconditional transfer of sovereignty to the ruler, and the latter the impossibility of diminishing the people's sovereignty by any contract of rulership.

While in these same disputes is rooted the whole controversy as to the 'subject' of sovereignty, this topic will be left to the next Chapter. Yet we must here remark that in working out the idea of the contract of rulership, all adherents of the contract theory drew certain common consequences in favor of the people as well as the ruler, with which, maintaining the strictly contractual standpoint, the radicalism of Hobbes on the one hand and of Rousseau on the other made a breach.

With regard to the people's rights, even the staunchest believers in the contractual alienation of sovereignty could not deny the original sovereignty of the people, since the people must itself possess these rights before it can alienate them.[27] They could not do otherwise than concede to the people a perfectly free choice of the form of government to be erected.[28] Lastly, they could not deny the consequence that the people's original sovereignty and original right of election must come into full force anew when the contract is terminated by the extinction of the instituted ruler (such as the reigning dynasty in an hereditary monarchy).[29]

Yet the people, in order to possess and transfer sovereignty, must be a 'subject' of legal rights and capacities. The contract theory agreed from the very beginning that the people, even before the appointment of a ruler, existed as a constituted "universitas," and that in framing the contract of rulership it acts as a single body endowed with juristic personality under the rules of corporation law.[30] But if the people and ruler are the original contracting parties, and if the contract theory is strictly followed out, they must always be regarded, even in the perfected State, as two distinct 'subjects' of rights bound in mutual obligations. From this it was inferred that the people continues to exist as a corporation, immortal and self-identical amid changes of its members, and the obligation of the original contract continues for later generations; the people of today is indeed the same people that originally entered into legal obligations.[31] Likewise it was universally held from the beginning that the people in its totality is somehow the 'subject' of a legal right to demand the fulfillment of the ruler's duties and the due observance of the limitations of his power.[32] Thus the doctrine of the contract of submission, even when least favorable to the rights of the people, led always to the recognition of mutuality in the relation of ruler and people; but it purchased this result at the cost of a dualistic disruption of the State's Personality.

In this dualism Hobbes detected with the eye of genius the weak point of the accepted doctrine, and here he inserted the lever of his iron logic in order to eliminate not only the dualism of the State's personality but also every right of the people. When he included the contract of submission in the original contract of union made by the individuals getting themselves out from the "war of every man against every man," he replaced the contract between people and ruler by a "covenant of every man with every man." [33] For only a moment does the multitude by this union of wills become itself a person, expiring as such in the self-same act by the necessary giving up of all will and all personality to the ruler.[34] When the State is instituted the whole personality of the people is merged in the person of the sovereign ruler, be it the natural person of one man or the artificial person of an assembly. Only in and through the ruler is the people a person, without him it is a mere multitude, and hence it cannot be regarded as the 'subject' of any right against the ruler.[35] Thus also the individuals have no rights whatever as against the sovereign power, which is absolute by its very nature; nor can they derive any rights from the original covenant, as they did not contract with the ruler, but simply with all other individuals to renounce, jointly and simultaneously, all rights and all liberties in favor of this third person.[36]

In the contract theory of Spinoza we may here pass over the derivation of the concept of right from the concept of power, the formation of civil society through the motive power of reason, the limitation of the State's authority by the limits of its power and the considerations of its own reason, and the consequent reservation of the spiritual freedom of the individual. Otherwise it differs in essentials from the theory of Hobbes only in that it conceives the abdication of all natural rights by all the individuals as a subjection to the community which is thereby united in one body, and thus regards the other forms of the State as mere modifications of democracy, which is set up as the normal form.[37]

It may be added that the Hobbesian concentration of the basis of the State in a contract of submission, made directly by the individuals, gained other adherents, but all of them deduced from this contract a legal right (at least an imperfect legal right) of the individuals as against the ruler.[38]

In general, however, the doctrine maintained the separation of the contract of union and the contract of submission, and thus held that the latter was always made between the people already constituted as a person and the future ruler.[39] In particular Pufendorf strengthened this construction by inserting between these two contracts another fundamental decree in which the united community behaved already as a juristic person.[40] At the same time the idea grew more and more prevalent that the personality of the perfected State is fully and completely merged in the personality of the ruler. Yet while Pufendorf and a few followers deduced with Hobbes the extinction of the people's personality, and recognized only the individuals as bearers of established contractual rights against the ruler,[41] the majority followed Huber in reserving to the people a continuous personality separate from the State's personality represented by the ruler, and hence upheld the assumption of a relation of obligation between the bearer of the State-power and the subject community as such.[42]

Thus indeed all the absolutist explanations of the contract of submission showed themselves unable to eradicate from the contract theory what Horn had perceived to be its immanent revolutionary germ, which was destined to unfold itself when the day came that the people, having learned of its original sovereignty, began to lament its loss!

On the other hand, so long as the idea of a contract of rulership distinct from the contract of union stood erect, it always set, at least in theory, certain insuperable bounds to the popular caprice even in the systems teaching popular sovereignty. For it stipulated the recognition of a right of the ruler somehow independent of the rights of the people. It was agreed that the contractual appointment of a ruler is absolutely necessary and inheres in the nature of the State as a society of governors and governed.[43] But in whatever way this act might be performed, so long as it is a contract it must provide a contractual right for the ruler himself. And thus even the Monarchomachi granted a permanent right of rulership to the instituted ruler and his family under the settlement, a right which could indeed be forfeited by breach of contract but until then must be respected by the people. The above exposition has shown how Althusius himself worked out the whole system of contract, in favor of the ruler as well as against him, in the form of a Legal and Constitutional State based on mutuality.[44]

Thus it was in truth a revolutionary act when Rousseau struck out the contract of rulership from the contractual theory. It was not wholly without preparation that this stroke fell.[45] But Rousseau first asserted distinctly and argued with inexorable logic from his radical premises, that there neither is nor can be a contract of rulership; that the "institution du gouvernement" is not a contract but a simple "commission"; that it is not at all a bilateral act but is composed of a legislative and an executive act of the sovereign Community.[46] Just here, however, lay the really new fundamental idea of his theory, from which there followed all the propositions first announced by him and unheard before. For the destruction of the contract of rulership cleared the way for the destruction of every right of the ruler; and from the permanent and absolute omnipotence of the assemblage of the people, suspending the executive power and the whole jurisdiction of government as soon as it is assembled, he developed his program of permanent revolution.[47]

The contract of rulership survived this attack, but its living power was broken. In Germany especially, the philosophical construction of the contract theory by Fichte and Kant was too much influenced by Rousseau to permit of the resumption of the older dualistic construction. The only question was how much or how little of the substance of the obsolete contract of submission should be carried over into the social contract.

II. The Social Contract

The doctrine of the Social Contract was but imperfectly worked out before Althusius, yet its groundwork had already been laid.

On the basis of the patristic fusion of biblical and antique ideas the medieval doctrine commonly supposed an original state of Nature without any "States," in which the pure Law of Nature prevailed with liberty and equality of all persons and community of all goods. It was agreed that the politic or civil State was the product of changes made at a later time. By way of investigating the nature of these changes, men at first satisfied themselves with general discussions of the way in which "dominium" had made its appearance in the world and the legitimacy of its origin; and in their concept of "dominium," Lordship and Ownership were blended. Yet the question of the origin of government was more and more separated from the question of the origin of private property. And when the first of these questions was answered by the postulate of a contract of submission as above described, we may see coming to the front the prior question: how did it happen that this community itself, whose will, expressed in an act of transfer, was the origin of the State, came to be a single body competent to perform legal acts and possessing a transferable power over its members?

The answer to this question however was uncertain and vacillating during the middle ages and for a long time after. It was influenced by the long-standing dispute as to whether civil society was a mere consequence of the Fall of Man, or whether it would also have come into being, though in a freer and purer form, if mankind had increased in numbers while yet in a state of innocence.[48] More weighty was the collateral question as to whether the legal basis of the State is to be sought in mere positive law, or in the "ius naturale" or else in the "ius gentium" derived therefrom.[49] The statements in classical literature on the origin of civil society were largely inconsistent and could be interpreted in various ways. From this was evolved a mass of ideas which were divergent and often uncritically combined.

The idea that civil society was originally created by a direct Act of God did not vanish all at once; the special unity of a single Nation or State was often explained simply as an emanation and a vestige of the unity of the human species as originally created.[50] Yet in the middle ages the prevailing view was that God was only indirectly the creator of political society, as He had implanted in man the 'political' nature discovered by Aristotle. Hence Nature was introduced as a more proximate cause of the State. There were always advocates of the view that the nature of man had directly and necessarily produced political society; the more closely men followed Aristotle, the more decidedly were they led to a theory of organic development which taught that the State had grown by a natural process through the gradual enlargement and consummation of that aboriginal community, the Family.[51] But already in the middle ages a different view steadily gained ground, that Nature (like God) acted only as "causa remota" or "causa impulsiva": that is, as the source of a human need for and an impulse toward the social life, or in short as a more or less compelling motive for the foundation of the State; while the union of men in a political bond was itself regarded as a free and rational act of human will.[52] Sometimes there appears the notion that the State is an Institution which was founded, as other human institutions were founded, by certain definite founders, whether peacefully or by force.[53] But there prevailed more and more the hypothesis of an original creative act of will of the whole uniting community.[54] This collective act, if there had been a technical legal concept for it, would have had to be characterized as the "self-constitution of a corporation." We find indeed the germs of such a concept.[55] They remained inchoate, however, as even the juristic theory had no such developed concept to offer, for in spite of the distinction between "universitas" and "societas" the single act whereby a community unifies itself was confused with an obligatory contract made by a number of individuals. In like manner the doctrine of the publicists brought the supposed act of political union under the category of a contract of partnership or 'social' contract.[56]

Thus the idea that the basis of political society is a social contract was already expressed in the middle ages. Yet on the whole it remained without further development. It was but seldom that its individualist consequences were brought out, by making the isolated individual historically prior to society,[57] and logically deriving all societies from the individual.[58]

Even in the sixteenth century the theory of the Social Contract was but partially matured.

The dominant school of publicists, under the influence of Aristotle, maintained a hostile or indifferent attitude toward the new idea.[59]

On the other hand, it was favorably received by the school of Natural Law which was now growing up independently. As the threefold classification of law into jus naturale, gentium and civile was supposed to reflect a threefold structure of society, it was supposed that the "societates domesticae" (which were known even in the state of nature) were a purely natural growth, the "societas humana" underlying the "jus gentium" was explained as a vestige of the original unity of mankind, and the "societas civilis" with its resultant "jus civile" was traced back to an act of union which was only indirectly caused by nature through man's social instinct. For the most part men were satisfied with the statement of such general positions.[60] Only the Catholic school of Natural Law went more closely into the nature of the contract of political union. Yet it sought to lead the development of this idea along wholly new lines. It emphasized in various ways that the body politic was created not only by the free and deliberate assemblage of its members, but by virtue of the natural instinct of union implanted in man by God or according to the dictates of natural reason, and hence according to the law of nature.[61] It also engaged in the notable attempt (already mentioned in another connection) to divest the social contract theory of its original individualist character, by arguing that while the body thus produced owes its existence to the alienation of the wills of individuals, it derives sovereign power over its members not from the individuals but directly from the law of nature by virtue of the rational nature of things, and thus from God.[62] Thereby, however, this theory was reduced to a mere moment of transition in the historical development of the social contract. For when it once made the individual the creator of the State it could not permanently reject the derivation of the State's power from the rights of the individual.

The Monarchomachi had no reason to demur at this conclusion. Yet they themselves but incidentally took up the idea of the social contract,[63] and did little or nothing to develop it. This may be explained by their practical aim, which was satisfied with establishing the contractual relation between people and ruler, while the study of the construction of society itself seemed to be only of theoretical interest. Thus Hotman and the author of the book "De Jure Magistratuum" have nothing to say on the origin and nature of political society; and the same is true of Junius Brutus, even though he holds a prominent place in the history of the contract of rulership.[64] Other writers of this group, such as Buchanan and Mariana, expressly state that the community which contracts with the ruler is the product of an act of union of men originally living separately, but fail to discuss the nature of this act.[65] Salamonius alone works out somewhat more closely the idea of the contract which establishes the "societas civilis"; but even he makes use of this only in discussing the legal status of the ruler.[66]

Such was the position of the Social Contract idea when Althusius made his contribution. A glance at the preceding account of this (p. 35 ff. and 58) justifies the statement that Althusius must be regarded as the creator of a genuine theory of the Social Contract. He sets up at once, as the constructive principle of his political and social system, the idea that all human association rests on a contract of the associates. At the very beginning of his Politics he bases the generic idea of "consociatio" on the tacit or express consent of the associates. Even for the family-relations, while recognizing them as natural and necessary, he maintains the fiction of a contractual basis. But for its full development he applies the idea of contract to corporations, communes and the State, which he regards throughout as relations which are freely entered into even though conditioned by the social nature of man. Here he assumes throughout an underlying formal "contractus societatis," which he places without hesitation under the rules of the civil law. Then when he analyzes in detail the terms of the contractual association existing in every species of community, he is enabled to make the attempt, never before undertaken in this way, to draw a sharp line between the spheres of rights of the individual and the community, as well as of narrower and wider societies. From the pure concept of the social contract he builds the structure of a community vested with all the political rights of superiority over its members, turning next to the contractual relation between it and its officers. Thus also he applies the category of "societas" to the perfected State, and resolves its whole content into a sum of legal relations of obligation. In accordance with this he requires for the extension of the political community beyond its previous domain a new contract and therefore unanimous agreement of the members. And thus he brings out into the sharpest relief the last philosophical consequence of the idea of contract and derives all the rights of the community from the inborn rights of the human individual. Even the State's rights of superiority are in the last analysis simply the product of individual rights which are voluntarily given up and communalized. He moderates this individualist principle only by the theory that the State does not derive its powers directly from the individual, but through a series of indispensable mediating links.

With the erection of such a theory of the social contract Althusius was in advance of his time. Yet in the main, the ideas developed by him were destined in the course of the seventeenth century to win an almost complete victory. The idea of the social contract was indeed opposed not only by the adherents of the theocratic idea, who equally opposed that of the contract of rulership,[67] but also, as before, it was more or less expressly rejected, or at most admitted as a minor element, by the publicists who followed Aristotle while yet for the most part accepting the contract of rulership.[68] But the school of Natural Law, growing more and more dominant since Grotius, received it whole into its own theory of the State. Yet Grotius himself, while stating his definition of the State and a series of leading deductions in phrases often reminiscent of Althusius,[69] altogether failed to attempt any strictly rational proof of the axiom which seemed to him self-evident.[70] And after the second half of the century all 'Nature-Right' theories of the State, however influential, simply stated and developed in various ways the social basis which was always taken for granted.

To be sure, that keen thinker who was the first after Althusius to analyze fully the supposed contractual basis of civil society challenged the idea of a "social contract" in the strict sense and all the consequences drawn from it. For Hobbes, as is said above, construed the very first act of union of the isolated individuals as a universal contract of submission to a ruler who is vested at once with exclusive power. Nevertheless the single original contract substituted by him, which bound the contracting parties to abdicate at once their inborn natural rights in favor of a third person, remained a "covenant of every man with every man" for the establishment of a relation common to all. Thus he was really not very far from the concept of the "contrat social." In fact the closely related contractual theory of Spinoza made a direct transition to this concept. And the same is more or less true of all the various turns which the Hobbesian idea of the single and direct contract of submission of individuals took among its adherents.[71]

Also the dominant theory, developed in Germany by Pufendorf and his followers, holding that prior to the act of submission there was an act of union of individuals which created rights independently, all the more decidedly subsumed the latter under the category and the rules of the social contract.[72] It defined and treated the State as a "societas," which as the most perfect, most composite and most permanent society, takes the highest place in the scale of societies but never transcends the concept of a society.[73] Thus, after the manner of Althusius, it worked out an ever wider and more independent General Part of the 'Nature-Right' theory of Society. In this, with a fuller identification of "societas" and "universitas" [construing both alike as mere sums of individuals], it set up and unfolded a unitary concept of society based on contract, purely 'individualistic' and thus preserving the idea of a "societas." Then it treated general public law as a mere sub-section of the Special Part of the Law of Societies, in which this theory was applied to the several species of societies.[74] But to be consistent with its assumption that the foundation of the State requires not only the social contract but also the contract of submission, it drew the distinction, growing ever more essential, between the ordinary "societas aequalis" and the "societas inaequalis" characterized by the separation of "imperans" (ruler) and "parentes" (subjects), and treated the development into the latter form as the essential mark of the State.[75] Thus it could now assert the principle that while the contract of union produces of itself an 'equal' society, yet this is only the substrate of a State, and that it is only by the contract of submission that the change into an 'unequal' society is produced and the State is brought forth.[76] But with this distinction it gained a handle whereby the Law of Societies, in its application to the State, could be freely modified with reference to the special characteristics of the "societas inaequalis," and could be adapted to the requirements of the absolutist system which bore more or less the impress of it.[77]

But meanwhile the doctrine of the social contract was developed in England, especially by Sidney and Locke, in the sense of popular sovereignty.[78] The English theory gave the contract of rulership only secondary importance if it did not drop it alto-

gether; it regarded the State as essentially completed with the
social union of the individuals. Thus the idea of the social contract not only occupied the center of the political system (as in
Althusius), but prepared itself for that exclusive dominion which
Rousseau claimed for it.

Before taking up Rousseau's relation to his forerunners we
must glance again at the results of the tangled and ramifying
development of the social contract for the conception of the relation between the individual and society. For this was the point
in which the world-historical importance of the whole doctrine
lay.

Of course even in this point there were sharp disputes among
the adherents of a doctrine which was so variously construed and
made to serve such different political tendencies. Yet there was
a certain agreement in questions of principle as a necessary logical
consequence of the common premise. And if there was some
divergence here and there on one or another side, yet on the
whole the current of thought swept onward in one and the same
direction.

Ever more distinctly did the theoretical derivation of society
from the individual present itself as an essential feature of the
doctrine of the social contract. One must always, if one is to be
consistent, come to the conclusions that the individual is prior
to society, that every society is the product of a sum of individual
acts, and that all social right and even the power of the State is
an aggregate of individual rights which have been separated out
and put together.[79] It was a hopeless task when various teachers
of Natural Law again and again opposed this theoretical individualism, and sought once more to start from the idea of the
whole, or else to derive the State's rights of superiority from a
source independent of the individual without breaking with the
idea of the origin of the State in an act of union of 'stateless'
men.[80]

But the doctrine of the social contract must necessarily give a
further explication of this individualist basis of the State, to the
effect that the legal basis of all civil subjection is placed in the
free will of the individual. For it started with the assumption of
a pre-political state of Nature (while losing itself in countless

disputes in picturing this state), but was always agreed as to the original liberty and equality of men and consequently the original sovereignty of the individual. Of course even for the state of Nature it provided some legal restraint of the individuals, as this was produced by the pure Law of Nature itself; but the sovereignty of the individual seemed to be no more abolished by this than the sovereignty of the several nations was by international law (which indeed was ever more generally defined and construed as a pure law of nature applying to nations living as "personae morales liberae" in the "status naturalis").[81] And if for the state of nature itself a natural society of men was often assumed instead of hostile or indifferent isolation, yet the adherents of the social contract expressly referred all their thoughts back to a formally organized "societas" vested with some power over its members.[82] Obviously the leap from the state of nature to the "status civilis" or "socialis" could not rightfully be done in any other way than by the sovereign individual voluntarily giving up his own sovereignty. And strictly speaking the doctrine of the social contract is verbally equivalent to the fiction of such acts, if indeed words are to correspond to ideas. Of course the adherents of this doctrine assumed in general a more or less compelling "causa impulsiva," which determined the wills of men to exchange the state of nature for the social state. But while they were engaged in many controversies, according as they regarded an innate social instinct or some external stimulus as the deciding factor,[83] and at the same time assigned a greater or lesser share to conscious reflective reason,[84] they were here discussing only the remoter causes of the State, the hidden springs and prime movers of the directly creative contract.[85] Hence they agreed in placing the legal basis of the State wholly and solely in the "consensus" which forms the substance of this contract, which they conceived as a declaration of will which, despite any prior internal or external necessity, was legally free and therefore binding.[86] Hence without more ado they reckoned the State (as we have seen done by Althusius) among the "societates voluntariae." They admitted that as an empirical fact a society might possibly be founded and held together by external force alone, but they let it gain its lawful existence only from the express or implied consent of its members.[87] Ever more clearly they worked out their distinctive principles, that the original contract of union requires that the participants be unanimous;[88] that each individual has an inherent right to hold aloof and to remain in the state of nature;[89] that the validity of the principle of majority rule in constituted societies is to be grounded simply in the unanimous agreement, whether express or presumptive, originally made to this effect.[90] And lastly they could not avoid the consequence that for every later member of the community, whether native-born or immigrant, the individualist contractual basis of subjection is restored by the assumption of a "pactum tacitum." [91]

The social contract theory left the greatest room for differences of opinion in the consequences which were drawn from it as to the legal relation between the individual and the constituted community (as represented by the ruler). For in this matter everything depended on what content was attributed to the consent of the parties, whether this was necessary in the nature of things or presumptively willed. Here was free scope for subjective opinion and practical tendency to assert themselves. Yet in general the logical development of the concept of 'society' brought forward the idea which chiefly distinguishes modern from ancient political thought, which is reflected in all the medieval systems, is fully displayed in the Politics of Althusius and is continued by Grotius and his school: the idea of certain inalienable rights of the individual which even the State must not infringe. Even under the ordinary rules for the interpretation of contracts, it must be presumed that in forming the social contract the individual has given up his natural sovereignty only so far as is indispensably required for attaining the purpose of society. But while ever since the middle ages men were agreed that the function of the State is limited, they differed in defining the sphere of powers assigned to the State, according as they held to the older theory of well-being in one or another of its nuances or already approximated the theory that the purpose of the State is merely legal. Nevertheless there arose the doctrine that the anterior Law of Nature is modified but not abolished by the State, that the original natural rights of liberty and equality must

continue so far as compatible with the civil state, and lastly, that
this gives to the individual true legal rights against the State,
though these may be imperfectly protected. Thus it was that
when Hobbes with radical boldness championed the opposite side
in all these points, he proposed his own formula for the original
contract, stifling the social contract in its birth, and argued the
possibility of the downfall of all natural rights in the State, the
necessary abdication of all natural liberty by the individual, and
the absolute 'rightlessness' of the subjects as against the ruler.[92]
Yet even Hobbes was constrained to make certain reservations
for the individual,[93] and Spinoza rose on a like basis to the postulate of a political order which recognized the spiritual and moral
freedom of the individual as its purpose and its limitation.[94] The
dominant schools of Natural Law, however, in direct opposition
to Hobbes, maintained the old view of the social contract together with the old theorems as to the continuance of the original
natural rights of the individual. And now for the first time there
grew up the system of the inborn and inalienable rights of man,
which finally became the very essence of the whole doctrine of
Natural Law. The idea of the 'Legal State' (*Rechtsstaat*) as
constructed by Huber and others was a movement in this direction; [95] it was accepted in principle despite all absolutist leanings
by Pufendorf,[96] Thomasius,[97] Boehmer [98] and other such writers; [99] in England it took its classical shape from Locke; [100] in
Germany Wolff and his followers dressed it out in elaborate
scholastic detail.[101] At this point the theory that the State exists
only for the guaranty of security and legal protection, which had
been made popular by Pufendorf, Locke and Boehmer, offered
a fitting handle whereby the scope of the rights untouched by
the State-contract could be gradually widened. At the same time
the struggle for liberty of conscience which Thomasius, Locke
and Boehmer fought out on the basis of this theory gave it the
consecration of an ideal aim. When Locke made personal liberty
and property prior to all social organization, and treated these
as the two inviolable rights which are entrusted by the individual
to the State simply for protection, the groundwork was laid for
a future theory of purely individualistic economics. And when
Wolff in his great system of Natural Law, which was dominant

for a long time, brought out the distinction between those in-born rights which survive in civil society from the liberty and equality of the state of nature and which the individual cannot lose either by his own surrender or by the force of law, and those rights which are acquired in civil society, the way was open for the historical process which closed in the official 'Declaration of the Rights of Man.'

Thus the theory of the social contract had already been worked out in a rich variety of forms when Rousseau wrote his fiery book. Rousseau, as already said, made a truly revolutionary departure when, striking out the contract of rulership, he declared that the social contract is the one and only legal basis of the State and that it is quite incompatible with any other basis of the relations of public law. Yet in order to give this omnipotent and exclusive contract of union the form of a revolutionary program he needed but to combine the elements which were ready to hand. Thus in essentials he completed the picture of the social contract by bor-rowing from his democratic forerunners the purely social frame-work adapted to the liberty and equality of all members, and filling this up with the absolutist content of the Hobbesian con-tract. He says that voluntary agreement is the only possible rightful source of the social bond which limits natural rights (and even of the family-tie among adults), and hence is the act by which alone the people becomes a people (I. c. 1–5). He con-strues the State's rights of superiority simply as the product of an absorption by the community of the innate rights of the origi-nally sovereign individuals,[102] bases all political subjection on the free consent of the individuals,[103] and treats the constituted State throughout as a society identical with the sum of the associ-ated individuals.[104] Lastly, he assigns to the State a purely in-dividualist end, which is nothing else than the substitution of a social equivalent for the liberty and equality of the state of nature which the world, sadly enough, had lost.[105] But the only rational and rightful way to attain this end is by providing in the con-tract of union for 'the total alienation of each associate with all his rights to the whole community.'[106] Thus despite all individu-alist beginnings and endings, there is the absolute despotism of the Sovereign displayed in every majority vote, from which

Rousseau reclaims the idea of man's indefeasible natural rights only by a series of inconsequences and sophisms.[107]

At this point we may refrain from pursuing the further evolution of the social contract theory in detail. It was ever more widely diffused,[108] its structure became ever more mechanical, rationalist and individualist. In this respect Rousseau's formulation exercised a growing influence. This is manifest even in such writers as Scheidemantel and Schlözer, who held fast to the old assumption of a constitutive contract of rulership separate and distinct from the social contract,[109] and is otherwise marked by the disappearance of this assumption. The dominant school of Natural Law agreed only in opposing Rousseau's notion of the complete absorption of the individual by society, and sought already to gain an unshakable basis for the inalienable rights of man, which it pushed more and more decidedly into the foreground, by restricting the social act of union to a limited part of the individual's personality.[110] In this way Beccaria, by presuming that the portion of liberty sacrificed by the individual is the least possible, deduced from the social contract the wrongfulness of capital punishment.[111] And Humboldt, by carrying out to its last consequences the idea that the State is merely a means for serving the ends of the individual, argued for the utmost possible restriction of the 'limits of the activity of the State.' [112] And while the French Revolution in its course was more and more driven to realize the despotic ideas of Rousseau, yet in this point Sieyès himself, who otherwise even outbids the radical-mechanical construction of his master, raises a plea in behalf of the individual.[113]

The culmination of the idea of the social contract together with its inherent abstract individualism was reached by Fichte in his earlier philosophy of Law and the State, in which he based the whole legal and political order upon the freest consent of the sovereign individual, a consent which is renewed at every moment.[114] He did not shrink from the consequence that each individual has the right to withdraw from the State at any time, and any group of persons has the right to form a 'State within the State,' as it is the 'inalienable right of man' to 'cancel his contracts unilaterally whenever he wishes'! [115] And in equating the sovereign general will with the sum of the sovereign individual wills, he even went so far as to deny in all seriousness the legal validity of the acts of majorities; sometimes he strongly insisted on absolute unanimity and sometimes he conceded, as the only resource, the treatment of dissentients as non-members! [116] And yet, abstract individualism always comes so near to radical State-absolutism that in spite of everything Fichte showed even in his earlier writings a strong practical tendency toward the latter.[117] And so clastic was the theory of the State-contract that Fichte, when later developing what he himself called the 'higher' view of the State, and reducing the individual to a mere 'instrument' of the State which lives on for the whole human race,[118] could preserve the essential features of his earlier 'Nature-Right' theory of contract with a few modifications.[119]

The idea of the social contract gained its one last triumph when Kant took it as the basis of his abstract 'State of Right and Reason' (*Rechts- und Vernunftstaat*).[120] Even Kant could not avoid the atomistic and mechanical view of the State, as this was the logical consequence of the idea of contract.[121] Yet he himself introduced into the theory a number of elements which marked the beginning of its downfall. When he divested the State-contract of all historical reality as a 'fact,' and claimed for it only the practical reality of an 'idea of reason' by which alone the State can be construed *a priori* and 'the rightfulness of it can alone be conceived,' [122] he separated the question of the legal basis of the State from the question of its origin, and as regards the latter at least he opened the way for a deeper historical view. And further, when he declared that entrance into political society is a binding precept of reason, the observance of which is an enforceable legal duty of individuals living in the state of nature,[123] he prepared for the philosophical transition to a theory which placed the legal basis of the State in its rational necessity alone. When lastly (like his predecessors) he treated the sovereign general will as merely the aggregation of the individual wills, and yet through his distinction of "homo phaenomenon" and "homo noumenon" replaced the summation of empirical wills by the summation of rational wills,[124] he broke off what was in practice the most dangerous point of the conception of the State as an individualistic society, and ended with the postulate of a regulation of the empirically given State by the abstract principles of the sovereign Law of Reason.[125]

The philosophical revision made by Kant secured a new lease of life for the 'Nature-Right' doctrine of the State-contract.[126] But already it met with invincible opponents in the historical school of law and in a legal philosophy which with all its divergent tendencies started once more from the idea of the whole and the community. To these combined attacks it finally succumbed.[127] It succumbed, and yet we of this day enjoy the fruits which, amid the unspeakable errors and dangers for which it is blamed, it won in the struggle for the ideas of Freedom and Right.

NOTES

1. In the middle ages this distinction is suggested in Joh. Paris., c. 1, and Dante, I. c. 6; it is distinctly formulated in Aen. Sylv., c. 1 ("societas civilis") and c. 2 (institution of "regia potestas"). In the sixteenth century it is most clearly expressed by Covarruvias, I. c. 1; Victoria, Rel. III.; Molina, II. d. 22–23; its elaboration in Suarez is later than the Politics of Althusius.

2. See Manegold of Lautenbach (in Sitzungsber. der Bair. Akad., 1868, II. p. 325 N. 63): "Nonne clarum est, merito illum a concessa dignitate cadere, populum ab eius dominio et subiectione liberum existere, cum pactum, pro quo constitutus est, constet illum prius irrupisse?"—The antipapal party also traced monarchy back to the people's will, but held that when once expressed this became a "necessitas" and is irrevocable; see the declaration of the anti-Gregorian cardinals [1408] in Sudendorf, Registrum, II. p. 41.

3. [The Lex Regia (l. 1 Dig. 1, 4, and Inst. 1, 2, 6) says: "Quod principi placuit legis habet vigorem; utpote cum lege regia, quae de imperio eius lata est, populus ei et in eum omne suum imperium et potestatem conferat."] See Glossa Ordinaria on l. 9 Dig. 1, 3, l. 1 Dig. 1, 4, l. un. Dig. 1, 11, l. 2 Cod. 8, 53, l. 11 Cod. 1, 17 v. "solus imperator"; and on I. Feud. 26; also Jacobus de Arena, Inst. de act., nr. 5 p. 277; Cinus on l. 4 Cod. 2, 54; Innocent IV on c. 1 x. 1, 7 nr. 1–2 [papa habet imperium a Deo, imperator a populo]; Baldus on l. 1 Cod. 1, 1 nr. 1–12.—Also Dante,

III. c. 13–14; Lup. Beb., c. 5 p. 355 [olim tenuit monarchiam imperii populus urbis Romanae; postea transtulit in ipsum imperatorem]; Ockham, Octo qu., II. c. 4–5, Dial. III. tr. 2, l. 1, c. 27–28; Aen. Sylv., c. 8; Ant. Ros., I. c. 32 and 36.

4. The clerical party, which agreed as regards the foundation of the Empire, avoided the consequences by the assumption that since the advent of Christ the rights of the people had passed to Him and from Him to Peter and his successors.

5. See for example Lup. Beb., c. 5; Ockham, Octo qu., II. c. 14, Dial. III. tr. 2, l. 1, c. 22; Ant. Ros., I. c. 64.—In this matter the earlier jurists were indeed so bound by the spell of the ancient texts that in their eyes the "populus Romanus," to which the Empire must revert, was the populace of the City of Rome as it existed in their own day. And about the middle of the twelfth century the followers of Arnold of Brescia made a serious attempt to derive practical results from this; see the letter of the Senatus Populusque Romanus to King Conrad, in Jaffé, Monum. Corbeiens., p. 332 ff., and the letter of Wezel (1152), ib. p. 542; also Otto of Freising, Gesta Frid., I. c. 28 and II. c. 21. Lupold of Bebenburg, c. 12 and 17, was the first to assert distinctly that the Imperial People consists of the "totus populus imperio Romano subiectus;" compare Ockham, Dial. III. tr. 2, l. 1, c. 30.

6. Joh. Paris., c. 16; Mars. Pat., II. c. 30; Ockham, Octo qu., II. c. 9, IV. c. 5 and 8, Dial. III. tr. 2, l. 1, c. 20; Theodoricus de Niem, in Schard, p. 788–792; Aen. Sylv., c. 9.—Compare Lup. Beb., c. 12, as to the people of the City of Rome acting alone.

7. Mars. Pat., II. c. 26 ("concessio populi"), and III. concl. 9 and 10; Lup. Beb., c. 5 and 12 (Otto III de consensu principum et populi); Ockham, Octo qu., VIII. c. 3; Nic. Cus., III. c. 4 ("populus Romanus habet potestatem eligendi imperatorem per ipsum ius divinum et naturale; . . . unde electores, qui commune consensu omnium Alemannorum et aliorum qui imperatori subiecti erant, tempore Henrici II constituti sunt, radicalem vim habent ab ipso omnium consensu, qui sibi naturali iure imperatorem constituere poterant"); Ant. Ros., I. c. 48 ("collegium universale fidelium"). —The Pope's share in the institution of the Electoral Princes is traced back to a mandate of the people (Ockham, Dial. III. tr. 2, l. 1, c. 30), or explained by the co-subjection of the church in secular matters (Nic. Cus., III. c. 4). At the same time it is argued that as the whole people of the Empire is represented by the Electors, their act of election has all the effect of an election made directly by the people, and hence confers the full rights of an Emperor independently of the Pope; Mars. Pat., II. c. 26; Ockham, Octo qu., VIII. c. 1–8 and IV. c. 8–9, Dial. III. tr. 2, l. 2, c. 29; Nic. Cus.,

III. c. 4.—Lup. Beb., c. 5–6 and 12, draws his well-known distinction here.

8. Eng. Volk., De ortu, c. 2, is the first to say that all regna et principatus originated in a "pactum subiectionis" which satisfied a natural instinct and want. Compare Mars. Pat., I. c. 8, 12, 15. Ockham, Dial. III. tr. 2, l. 2, c. 24 and 26. Aen. Sylv., c. 2. But especially Nic. Cus., II. c. 12: the binding force of all laws rests on the "concordantia subiectionalis eorum qui ligantur"; II. c. 13: all power flows from the free "subiectio inferiorum"; III. c. 4: it arises "per viam voluntariae subiectionis et consensus"; II. c. 8 and 10.

9. Eng. Volk., op. cit., c. 10; Mars. Pat., I. c. 9 and 15; Lup. Beb., c. 5 and 15; Ockham, Octo qu., II. c. 4–5, V. c. 6, VIII. c. 3, Dial. III. tr. 2, l. 3, c. 5–6 (if once there has been a departure from the "omnia communia" of the pure law of nature, we have as a principle of the modified law of nature "quod omnes, quibus est praeficiendus aliquis, habeant ius eligendi praeficiendum, nisi cedant iuri suo vel superior eis ordinet contrarium"); Nic. Cus., III. c. 4 ("ius ·divinum et naturale"); Ant. Ros., I. c. 69.— For this an appeal was also made to the doctrine laid down by the jurists, that according to the ius gentium every free people may set a Superior over itself; thus Baldus on l. 5 Dig. 1, 1 nr. 5 and 8; Paulus Castrensis on l. 5 Dig. 1, 1, lect. 1 nr. 5 and lect. 2 nr. 17–18.

10. Otto of Freising, II. c. 1; Thom. Aquin., XXI. p. 495 and 501; Aegid. Col., III. 2 c. 5; Mars. Pat., I. c. 16; Lup. Beb., c. 5; Ockham, Octo qu., IV. c. 5 and 9, VIII. c. 3; Bartolus, De regimine civitatis, nr. 23; Baldus on l. 5 Dig. 1, 1 nr. 11–15; Nic. Cus., III. praef. and c. 4.— Compare the Miles in Somn. Virid., I. c. 187.

11. Special pains were taken to prove (following Augustine, De civ. Dei, V. c. 15) that the world-dominion of the Romans, though gained by force of arms, was nevertheless "de iure" (see especially Dante, II. c. 1–11; Petrarca, Ep. VII. p. 1355 ff.; Baldus on l. 1 Cod. 1, 1; Aen. Sylv., c. 3–5; Petr. Andl., I. c. 4–10; and even Ptol. Luc., III. c. 4–6; Alv. Pel., I. a. 42). But here men had recourse more and more to a retroactive "subiectio voluntaria" of the subjected peoples or to a "consensus maioris partis mundi"; see Eng. Volk., c. 11; Ockham, Dial. III. tr. 2, l. 1, c. 27; Ant. Ros., V. c. 1–30.

12. Aegid. Col., III. 1 c. 6, supposes three possible origins of a State: the purely natural way of an outgrowth from the family, the partly natural way of "concordia constituentium civitatem vel regnum," and lastly mere force and conquest.

13. Eng. Volk., c. 10; Mars. Pat., I. c. 9; Lup. Beb., c. 15 p. 398; Ockham, Octo qu., V. c. 6.

14. Before Althusius it was most fully developed by Junius Brutus,

q. III. p. 248 ff. See further Buchanan, p. 16 ff. and 78; De jure Mag., q. 5; Danaeus, I. c. 4 p. 41 ff.; Hoenonius, II. § 1–5, IX. § 5. Also Sala-monius, I. p. 16–30; Boucher, I. c. 10–17; Rossaeus, c. 1 § 2–3, c. 2 § 3–6; Mariana, I. c. 8.

15. Covarruvias, I. c. 1 nr. 2–4; Victoria, III. nr. 7–8; Soto, I. q. 1 a. 3, IV. q. 4 a. 1; Vasquez, c. 47; Lainez, loc. cit.; Bellarmine, loc. cit.; Molina, II. d. 23; Suarez, III. c. 4 (no power is justly possessed unless it "legitimo et ordinario jure a populo et communitate manasse constat": through a "translatio" by the "consensus communitatis," which is "debitus" after a just war and may be "tacitus" after an unjust war, while "successio" is never the root but only the outgrowth of the power given "immediate a populo"). See above, Ch. I. Notes 26, 27, 30.

16. Such as Melanchthon in the year 1523; Richard Hooker (d. 1600; see Ranke, Zur Geschichte der Doktrin von den drei Staatsgewalten, loc. cit., p. 240 ff.); Botero, Della ragione di stati, Venice 1559, I. c. 2; Boxhorn, I. c. 3 § 15 ff. (rulership, while contrary to Nature, rests on a continuing agreement between imperans and subditi); Casmannus, c. 3–4 and 10; Bornitius, Partit., p. 47 ff., and De maj., c. 3 (consensus populi spontaneus aut coactus, expressus vel tacitus, verus vel quasi); Fridenreich, c. 10–12 ("consensus universorum"); Micraelius, I. c. 10 § 9–11.—Among the jurists may be cited Alciatus on l. 15 Dig. de V. S. (Opera, II. p. 1047), and Cujacius, Opera (Venice 1758), IX. p. 677 and 846.

17. Jean Bodin, De Republica libri sex, Lyons 1586 (1st ed. in French, Paris 1576; I use 2nd Latin ed. Frankfort-on-the-Main 1591), c. 8.

18. Such as Vultejus, op. cit., I. c. 11; Fridericus Pruckmann (of Frankfort-on-the-Oder), Paragraphi "soluta potestas" tractatus, 1591 (in Opuscula politico-juridica, Frankfort-on-the-Main 1672); Tobias Paur-meister a Kochstedt (1553–1608), De jurisdictione imperii Romani libri duo, Hanau 1608, I. c. 17 nr. 5 ff. (imperium . . . ab ipso populo socie-tatem imperii contrahente in magistratus primarios . . . transfertur); Bor-tius, in Arumaeus, I. nr. 30, c. 2 § 3–15, c. 5 § 3–5, c. 6 § 2; Hilliger, ib., II. nr. 13 c. 3; Frantzken, ib., IV. nr. 41 § 39 ff. (populi consensus expressus vel tacitus); Besold, Diss. I. praecogn. philos., and Diss. de majestate, s. 1 c. 2 § 5.

19. See Barclay, III. c. 2 and IV. c. 10; "Waremund de Erenbergk" (Eberhard v. Weyhe, 1553–1633), Verisimilia . . . de regni subsidiis ac oneribus subditorum, Frankfort 1624 (1st ed. 1606), c. 3 p. 43 ff.; and even Claudius de Carnin, Malleus tripartitus, Douai 1624, I. c. 9–10.— Also Arnisaeus, De rep., II. c. 2 § 5, and De jure maj., I. c. 3 and 6, who yet, besides the "libera populi voluntas et electio," also regards succession to the original paternal power, the foundation of the State, and just war

as in themselves sufficient titles to power, and only in case of unjust acquisition requires a tacit consent; hence it is not rightly that "soli populo attribuitur ex jure naturae potestas imperii constituendi."

20. Grotius, I. c. 3 § 8, 13 and 17, and c. 4 § 15 (but indeed only normally; "bellum justum" and colonization of one's own land are also modes of acquiring dominion); Thomas Hobbes, De cive [1642], c. 5, Leviathan [1651, Latin version 1668], c. 17; Pufendorf, De jure N. et G., VIII. c. 1 ff., De off., II. c. 5 ff.; Thomasius, Inst. jur. div., III. c. 6 (voluntary or involuntary, express or tacit).—See also Spinoza, Tract. pol., c. 5 § 6 and c. 7 § 26.

21. See Huber, op. cit., I, 2 c. 1; Berckringer, I. c. 4; Becmann, c. 12 § 4–6; Hert, Elem. prud. civ., I. s. 3, and especially Diss. de mod. const. civ., s. 1 § 3 ff. ("pactum de imperio" is necessary even in case of conquest), and s. 2 (argument against those who weaken the contractual basis of imperium); Titius, Note on Pufend. De off. (1703), II. c. 6 § 8, and Specim. jur. publ., VII. c. 7 § 17 ff. (pactum reciprocum inter imperantem et futuros subditos); Gundling, Jus nat., c 35, Disc., c. 34; Kestner, c. 7 § 3; Christian Wolff (1679–1754), Jus naturae methodo scientifica pertractatum, Frankfort and Leipzig 1740–1750, VIII. § 36 ff., Institutiones juris naturae et gentium, Halle 1754, § 833 ff. and § 972 ff.; Joh. Gottl. Heineccius (1681–1741), Elementa juris naturae et gentium, c. 6 § 112–113 and § 139; Daniel Nettelbladt (1719–1791), Systema elementare universae jurisprudentiae naturalis, Halle 1785 (1st ed. 1748), § 1132 ff.; Gottfried Achenwall (1719–1772), Jus naturae, 1781 (1st ed. 1750), II. § 96–98; Joach. Georg Daries (1714–1791), Institutiones jurisprudentiae universalis, Jena 1776 (1st ed. 1746), Praecog. § 24, and Jus nat. § 659; Joh. Adam v. Ickstatt (1702–1776), Opuscula Vol. II., Munich and Ingolstadt 1759, Op. 1, c. 1 § 7–11; W. X. A. v. Kreittmayr (1705–1790), Grundriss des allgemeinen und deutschen Staatsrechts, Munich 1770, I. § 3, Anmerkungen über den Codicem Maximilianeum Bavaricum Civilem, I. c. 2 § 6 nr. 1; Heinr. Gottfr. Scheidemantel (1739–1788), Das Staatsrecht nach der Vernunft und den Sitten der vornehmsten Völker betrachtet, Jena 1770–1773, I. p. 56 ff. (but also possibly by war without any contract of union or of submission); August Ludwig v. Schlözer (1735–1809), Allgemeines Statsrecht und Statsverfassungslere, Göttingen 1793, p. 73 ff., and others.—Likewise the Catholic systems, such as Schmier, loc. cit., II. c. 1 s. 3 § 3; Franc. Jos. Heincke, Systema juris publici universalis, 1765, I. c. 2.—Boehmer, op. cit., P. spec. I. c. 1 § 14–26, while regarding violence and love of power as the motives for the foundation of States, yet holds fast to the contractual "submissio voluntatum" as the legal basis of rulership (ib. III. c. 2). On the other hand David Hume (1711–1776), Political

Discourses, 1752 ("Of the Original Contract"), while admitting an original contract as the historical beginning of government, denies the contractual ground of the obligation of obedience at the present day.—That Frederick the Great shared the belief in this dogma is shown in the Considérations of 1728, Oeuvres, VIII. p. 25, Antimachiavel of 1739, ib. p. 59 ff. c. 1 (ed. of 1834, p. 10), Essai sur les formes de gouvernement of 1777, ib. IX. p. 196 ff.

22. Of the writers mentioned in Ch. I. Notes 38 and 39, Graswinckel, Horn, Alberti, Filmer, Mullerus, Pelzhoeffer and Fénelon expressly reject the contract of submission, while Salmasius, c. 6–7, and the two Cocceji (ib. Note 43) accept it; Bossuet, I. a. 3 prop. 1–6, makes government originate from a universal renunciation of liberty, so that the "multitude en se soumettant" produces the sovereign; yet this is not a contract, as nature impels to a full and irrevocable submission; sovereignty is neither at first nor later in the multitude, therefore it comes from God; see also Cinq avertissements aux Protestants, XLIX., L., LII., LVI.

23. But see already the opposing utterances in the Investiture conflict, above (Note 2).

24. Accursius, in Gloss. Ord. on l. 9 Dig. 1, 3 v. "non ambigitur," decides in favor of this view, while the Gloss on l. 11 Cod. 1, 14 v. "solus imperator," mentions it but does not decide. So also Gl. on I. Feud. 26 v. "an imperatorem." Hostiensis, Summa de constitutionibus. Bartolus on l. 11 Cod. 1, 14 nr. 3–4 ("omnis potestas est abdicata ab eis"). Baldus on l. 8 Dig. 1, 3 nr. 5–11, l. 8 Dig. 1, 14 nr. 1–3, and l. 11 eod. nr. 6, I. Feud. 26 nr. 15, and II. Feud. 53 (the translatio was an "alienatio pleno iure"; otherwise the Emperor would not be "dominus" but "commissarius populi"). Angelus Aretinus on § 6 Inst. 1, 2 nr. 5–6. Joh. de Platea on Inst. 1, 2 nr. 51. Marcus, Decisiones, I. q. 187.

25. See this opinion in Gloss on l. 9 Dig. 1, 3, and l. 11 Cod. 1, 14, loc. cit., where the "concessio" is assumed by analogy with "iurisdictio delegata" in l. 1, i. f., Dig. 1, 21, and on I. Feud. 26, loc. cit. Also Cinus on l. 12 Cod. 1, 14. Christoforus Parcus on § 6 Inst. 1, 2 nr. 4. Zabarella on c. 34 § verum X. 1, 6 nr. 8 Paul. Castr. on l. 8 Dig. 1, 3 nr. 4–6, and l. 1 Dig. 1, 4 nr. 4 (concessio of usus, but no translatio of substantia). Ockham, Octo qu., IV. c. 8.

26. See for example the address of the Archbishop of Milan to Frederick I in Otto Fris., IV. c. 4, and the letter of Frederick II in Petrus de Vineis, Epistolae, Basel 1566, V. c. 135.

27. The original sovereignty of the people was most fully supported by the Jesuits in assailing the transcendental origin of the State. See especially Molina, II. d. 22; Suarez, III. c. 2–3; Schmier, II. c. 1 s. 3 § 2; Victoria,

III. nr. 7; Vasquez, c. 47; and the citations from Martinus Navarrus and Martinus Ledesmius in Suarez, c. 2 nr. 3. At the same time it was also posited by Bodin, I. c. 8; Barclay, III. c. 2 and IV. c. 10; Grotius, loc. cit.; Fridenreich, c. 10–11; Huber, I. 2 c. 1, and Opera minora, I. nr. 2, and others. Among later writers see especially Kestner, c. 7 § 3; Wolff, Jus nat., VIII. § 29–34, and Inst., § 979 (imperium civile originally as proprietas and res incorporalis in the people); Achenwall, II. § 98 (likewise), and § 99–100; Nettelbladt, § 1132 ("originaliter penes omnes cives simul sumptos"); Ickstatt, loc. cit. § 7; Hume, loc. cit.

28. For the middle ages see Ch. I. Note 21; then Victoria, III. nr. 15; Soto, IV. q. 4 a. 1; Bellarmine, III. 6; Molina, II. d. 23 § 1–14; Suarez, III. c. 3 nr. 8, and c. 4; Schmier, loc. cit. § 3; and even Bodin, I. c. 8, II. c. 1 ff.; Bortius, loc. cit., c. 2 § 14; later, with special significance, Wolff, Jus nat., loc. cit. § 36 ff., Inst., § 982 ff.; Nettelbladt, § 1132; Achenwall, II. § 93 and 96.

29. See for example Bortius, loc. cit. § 3–15; Micraelius, loc. cit.; then Hert, De mod. const. civ., I. § 11–12 (in case of a mere "dissolutio secundi pacti" the "populus conjunctus pacto primo" remains and has now to erect a new "pactum secundum"); Boehmer, P. spec. III. c. 4 (specially full account of how the people's rights, being in abeyance "stante imperio," display themselves all the more fully "vacante imperio"); Daries, loc. cit., Jus nat. § 775.

30. In the middle ages Ockham (Dial. III. tr. 2, l. 1, c. 27, vouching Gloss on c. 6 x. 1, 2) seeks to prove the legal validity of an establishment of the world-monarchy by vote of a majority of the nations, on the ground that as mankind acted in this case as a "universitas," the necessary or useful acts of the majority are binding; in like manner Anton. Rosellus, V. c. 2, vouching Dig. 3, 4, Innocent IV and Bartolus. Marsilius, I. c. 15, says in general that the "anima universitatis" is the "principium factivum" of the State. Then Junius Brutus especially works out the thought that the people makes the contract as a "universitas" ("conjunctim non divisim"), as in this case according to l. 22 Dig. de fideiuss., "unius personae vicem sustinet," q. II. p. 75 and 84 ff., III. p. 248 ff.; likewise the other Monarchomachi, of whom even Althusius refers throughout to the rules of Roman law on corporations. The Dominicans and Jesuits stand wholly on the same ground; see for example Victoria, III. nr. 14 (major pars); Soto, IV. q. 4 a. 2 ("publicus conventus" is requisite); Molina, II. d. 22 § 8–9, and 23. Even Bodin, I. c. 8 nr. 82 ff., and Grotius, I. c. 3 § 8, start openly from acts of submission of the people constituted as a juristic person, and in general there was no doubt uttered in this matter before Hobbes. See also Pruckmann, p. 90 ff. (contract "cum universitate vel communitate"), and p. 111 nr. 25 ff.—It is

on this that the advocates of popular sovereignty base the proposition "populus tempore prior" which they use as an argument, while their opponents do not deny this proposition but only its argumentative force.

31. Thus especially Junius Brutus, q. III. p. 171 ff.; compare Althusius, Polit., c. 19 § 74 ff., c. 9 § 16, c. 38 § 65 ff.

32. The advocates of popular sovereignty take this for granted. But even its opponents, until the time of Hobbes, agreed in recognizing some rights of the people against the ruler (even though in the opinion of many these rights were not enforceable), and also agreed in ascribing these to the whole body of the people conceived as a collective person. Likewise throughout the middle ages (see below, Ch. III.). Also Vasquez, c. 47; Soto, I. q. 1 a. 3, q. 7 a. 2, IV. q. 4 a. 1–2; Molina, II. d. 23 § 6–10; Suarez, III. c. 4, V. c. 17. And even Bodin, I. c. 8, and more decidedly Grotius, I. c. 3 § 13 ff., and c. 14. See Pruckmann, p. 90 ff.; Fridenreich, c. 18.—Even Arnisaeus, De jure maj., I. c. 6, concedes at least an "obligatio inaequalis."

33. Hobbes, De cive, c. 5, Lev., c. 14 and 17 (formula: "as if every man should say to every man, I authorise and give up my right of governing myself, to this man, or to this assembly of men, on this condition, that thou give up thy right to him, and authorise all his actions in like manner").

34. De cive, c. 7 and 12, Lev., c. 18; for Democracy see especially De cive, c. 7 § 7, for Aristocracy ib. § 8 ("patet populum ut personam unam, summo imperio ad hos [optimates] translato, non amplius existere"), for Monarchy ib. § 11 ff.

35. De cive, c. 5–7 and 12, Lev., introd. and c. 17–18; hence the saying "Rex singulis major, universis minor" is absurd, for "universi" means either the collective body as one person ("civitatis personam," which is the same as the sovereign), or else simply the "multitudinem solutam" which is the same as "singulos" or "every one" individually.—The reasonings on the difference between "people" and "multitude" are specially admired by his followers.

36. De cive, c. 6–7, Lev., c. 18–19; see also the formula of the covenant (above, Note 33) and the characterization of this pact as "a real unity of them all, in one and the same person" (Lev., c. 17).

37. Spinoza, Tract. theol.-pol., c. 16, Tract. pol., c. 5 § 6, c. 6, c. 7 § 26, c. 11 § 1–4. That is to say: "unusquisque omnem, quam habet, potentiam in societatem transfert; quae adeo summum naturae jus in omnia, hoc est summum imperium, sola retinebit, cui unusquisque, vel ex libero animo vel ex metu summi supplicii, parere tenebitur"; thus arises Democracy, the "coetus universus hominum, qui collegialiter summum jus ad omnia, quae potest, habet"; it is the most natural and most perfect form. Yet it is added that the foundations and rights of sovereignty are just the same if it is pos-

sessed by King or Nobles. Even here a normal and rational rulership arises only from the pact which "libera multitudo instituit," not by war. But nothing is said as to whether there is here a second pact or whether the first pact may be monarchical or aristocratic.—That even Spinoza identifies the State's personality with the Ruler's personality is shown in the reasonings in Tract. theol.-pol., c. 16, Tract. pol., c. 2 § 15, c. 3 § 1–2 and 5, c. 4 § 1–2, as well as Ethica, IV. prop. 18 schol., where the unity of the social body rests on the principle that the will of the State is taken as the will of all.—Just as decidedly does he deprive the individual of every actual right against the State; Tract. theol.-pol., c. 16–17, Tract. pol., c. 2 § 15, c. 3 § 2–5, c. 4 § 1–6.

38. Nearest to Hobbes stands Adrian Houtuynus, Politica contracta generalis (The Hague 1681, see § 99 nr. 14: "corporis et personae jus omne abierit in summum Imperantem"). Compare Titius, Specim. jur. publ., VII. c. 7 § 17 ff., and IV. c. 10 § 2 ff., Note on Pufend. De off., II. c. 6 § 8 (absolvitur omnis civitatum structura unico pacto, quod inter imperantem et futuros subditos initur; this pact is reciprocal, and is successively renewed or else perpetually continued with the accession of new "paciscentes"). Gundling, Jus nat., c. 35, and c. 3 § 52, Disc., c. 34 (following Hobbes almost entirely). Also Hume, loc. cit., who, however, argues from the individualistic structure of the original contract that it does not bind future generations, and hence that it cannot be the legal ground of the obligation of obedience at the present day.

39. Huber, De jure civ., I. 2, c. 1 and 3. Becmann, c. 12 § 4. Wolff, Jus. nat., loc. cit. § 4 ff., Inst., § 979 ff. Nettelbladt, loc. cit. Schlözer, loc. cit., p. 63 ff. (pactum unionis) and p. 73 ff. (pactum subjectionis).

40. Pufendorf, De jure N. et G., VII. c. 2, De off., II. c. 6 (in the decretum the majority rules; those who are born later are bound by it without more; foreigners accede to it by a pactum tacitum on entering the country). Pufendorf's two pacts and one decretum found great favor in Germany. They were accepted by Thomasius, Inst. jur. div., III. c. 6 § 26–31; yet in his Fund. jur. nat., III. c. 6 § 2–6, he says that it is still doubtful "an constitutio ita subito et uno quasi continuo actu facta fuerit." Also Kestner, c. 7 § 3 (the pactum unionis has already the effect "ut paciscentes una quasi persona fiant"); Hert, De mod. const., s. 1 § 2–8; Schmier, I. c. 2 s. 4 § 3; Heineccius, loc. cit. § 109–113; Ickstatt, loc. cit. § 7–11.—Also Achenwall, II. § 91–93, who however changes the decree into a "pactum ordinationis."

41. According to Pufendorf the "persona moralis composita" arises in the State, as elsewhere, only from the "moralis translatio voluntatum et virium," by which the will and act of the ruler are taken as the will and

act of all; hence the "voluntas imperantis" is identical with the "voluntas civitatis," while on the other hand that which is willed and done by "omnes excluso Rege" is a "voluntas et actio privata, non civitatis," and is not an act at all but a multitude of acts; without the ruler the people is not a person but a mere multitude, since by its subjection "populus ut persona moralis expiravit." And indeed, since the people becomes a person only as the State and the State is identical with the ruler, one may say without paradox that "Rex est populus"; De jure N. et G., VII. c. 2 § 5–6, 13–14, De off., II. c. 6 § 5–6, 10–11; compare De jure N. et G., VII. c. 4 § 2, c. 5 § 5, VIII. c. 10 § 8, De off., II. c. 7. If in the limited monarchy the ruler is bound by the concurrence of other organs, this makes no difference, for even here "omnia quae vult civitas, vult per voluntatem regis, etsi limitatione tali fit, ut non existente certa conditione Rex quaedam non possit velle aut frustra velit"; it is merely a "conditio sine qua non" of his act; even a lex commissoria is compatible with this; De jure N. et G., VII. c. 6 § 9–13, De off., II. c. 9; (in the same words Kestner, c. 7 § 14). Yet since the people has expired only as a "persona moralis" and not as a sum of "personae physicae," the ruler under the contract of submission is always bound by the Law of Nature, and under special stipulation also by the constitutional rights of the citizens, and the teaching of Hobbes that he can do them no injury or injustice is false; De jure N. et G., VII. c. 5 § 8, c. 6 § 9 ff., c. 8, De off., II. c. 9, and already Elem. jurispr. univ., I. def. 12 § 6.—In this matter Thomasius follows Pufendorf throughout; on the State's personality see Inst. jur. div., III. c. 6 § 26–28, 31, 62–64, 115, 157, Fund. jur. nat., III. c. 6 § 7, and on obligation Inst. jur. div., I. c. 1 § 103–113. Similarly Boehmer, P. spec. I. c. 3 § 1 note 0, § 15 ff. (on the State's personality), and ib. c. 5 and III. c. 1–2 (on the bilateral obligation, which is "imperfecta" only for the ruler and "perfecta" for the subjects). Ickstatt, c. I § 14–15 and 66. Darics, Jus nat., § 661. Kreittmayr, Grundriss, I. § 2–3 and 5.

42. Thus on the one hand Huber argues that by virtue of the transference the voluntas imperantis is the voluntas civitatis, that the "civitates per eos qui habent summam potestatem personae fiunt," and even that "summa potestas est ipsa civitas"; see op. cit., I. 3 c. 1 § 32, c. 2 § 14, c. 6 § 26, I. 9 c. 5 § 51, 65–72. But on the other hand he seeks to prove, as against Hobbes and Spinoza, that in the translatio imperii the populus is "unum quid," that it retains the "jus personae" and remains a "universitas," "quamvis nec congregatus sit neque sciat tempus futuri conventus," and hence that it may have rights against the ruler, and that in particular it may reserve such rights in the original contract or gain them by later contractual agreements; ib. I. 3 c. 4 § 8–83, c. 5 § 58–59; also I. 2 c. 3 § 17 ff., c. 4 § 1 ff., c. 5 and 8, I. 9 c. 5. Compare Berckringer, c. 4 § 7 ("persona

potentia, imo actu, sed possibili"). Hert, loc. cit., s. 1 § 3 p. 288, and § 5 p. 291 (the State is a person only through the summa potestas as its animating soul, nevertheless "personam populo et corpus posse tribui, quatenus primo pacto continetur"), and s. 2 p. 298–306 (polemic against weakening the contractual nature of the "pactum secundum"); also the objection of Hert, Treuer and Titius (obs. 557) in the commentary on Pufend. De off., II. c. 6 § 10. Compare Schmier, I. c. 3 nr. 3, 28–34 and 62–72, with II. c. 2 s. 1 § 2–3, s. 2 § 3, c. 4 s. 1 § 1–2; Wolff, Inst., § 975 ff.; Heineccius, § 115, 129–134, 139, 149; Achenwall, II. § 101 ff., 109–110, 152 ff., 174, 187, 203 ff.; Nettelbladt, § 1122, 1163, 1200–1201 (as against the princeps the populus is a "persona moralis," which may be completely "subdita" and yet have its own power), 1210–1212, 1217, 1220, 1267–1270; Scheidemantel, III. p. 364–375, also p. 341 ff.—Of these later writers it is often difficult to tell whether they assign constitutional rights to the individuals or to the community, as in general the phrase 'moral person' comes more and more to mean only the sum of individuals taken together in any legal relation. Characteristic of this are the discussions in Schlözer, p. 43, 73 ff., 93 ff., 113.

43. Democracy alone made difficulties here. When with reference to this form of State many said that the people may in its discretion retain or transfer the rulership, they still assumed that besides the contract of union a special agreement was required for the erection of democracy; see Suarez, III. c. 4 nr. 1, 5–6, 11; Schmier, II. c. 1 s. 3 § 3, and especially II. c. 4 s. 2 § 3 (by the reversion of sovereignty the people does not at once become a "perfecta Democratia," but merely gains the opportunity to ordain this or another form of the State); Wolff, Jus nat., § 37 ff., Inst., § 982; Nettelbladt, § 1132; Achenwall, § 96–98. Others construed even here a formal "translatio imperii" to the majority or to the popular assemblage perpetuated as a single 'subject'; see Molina, II. d. 23 § 12; Soto, IV. q. 4 a. 1; Victoria, III. nr. 1, 6–8; Fridenreich, c. 18; Micraelius, c. 10 § 9 ff.; Huber, I. 2 c. 3 § 25 ff.; Pufendorf, De jure N. et G., VII. c. 2 § 8, c. 5 § 6, De off., II. c. 6 § 9 (the decretum is followed here also by a formal "pactum subjectionis," in which the "singuli" appear as "paciscentes" with the "populus" and transfer the rulership "in concilium ex universis constans in perpetuum"); Becmann, c. 12 § 4 ff.; Hert, p. 286 ff. and 317 ff.; Kestner, c. 7 § 3; Heineccius, § 129 ff.; Daries, Praecog. § 24, and Jus nat. § 658–660; Ickstatt, § 8 ff.—On the other hand the Monarchomachi, with their tendency to wipe out the distinction between monarchs and the magistrates of a republic, were inclined to place the act of installing republican governing bodies on a level with the contract of rulership; thus especially Althusius, c. 39; see also Rossaeus, c. 1 § 2; Milton, Defensio (1651),

c. 6; Sidney, c. I. s. 10, c. II. s. 4 and 20; Locke, Two Treatises of Government (1690), II. c. 10 § 132.

44. In this Althusius agrees with the following: Junius Brutus, q. III. p. 260–264 (contractus mutuus obligatorius; breach of contract makes the populum seditiosum, regem tyrannum); De jure Mag., p. 29 ff. (mutua obligatio), and p. 74 ff.; Salamonius, I. p. 11; Danaeus, I. c. 4 p. 41, III. c. 6 p. 214 ff. (contractus populi cum Principe et ejus familia ab initio quidem fuit voluntatis, postea autem factus est necessitatis); Rossaeus, I. c. 1 § 4, c. 2 § 6 (obligatio reciproca) and § 11; Boucher, I. c. 18 ff.; Mariana, I. c. 6; Hoenonius, II. § 1–5, § 39 ff.; also Hotman, Francog., c. 13 and 25, and Quaestionum illustrium liber, q. 1; less definitely Buchanan, p. 16 ff. and 78, whom Rossaeus, I. c. 1 § 4, reproves for having overstepped these bounds.—Even Sidney, c. II. s. 32, upholds the rights of the ruler, which ill accords with the proposition advanced by him in c. III. s. 36, "the general revolt of a Nation cannot be called a Rebellion."

45. A weakening of the contract of rulership followed on the one hand from the logical development of the concept of mandate, as the mandator may indeed revoke the mandate, and on the other hand from the necessary appeal, in case of breach of the contract, to the sovereign people as judge in its own cause. From the first point of view Milton declared that the people may depose the king even without any other cause than its desire for a change of government (The Tenure of Kings and Magistrates, 1649, in Prose Works, II. p. 14). From the second point of view Locke arrived at a right of revolution which is decisive in the last resort; op. cit., II. c. 19, especially § 240–242; also c. 11 § 141, c. 13 § 149–150.—See also preceding Note as to Buchanan and Sidney.

46. Rousseau, III. c. 1 (not a contract but only a "commission"); c. 16 ("il n'y a qu'un contrat dans l'État, c'est celui d'association: celui-là seul en exclut tout autre; on ne saurait imaginer aucum contrat public qui ne fût une violation du premier"); c. 17 (instead there is first the law, "qu'il y aura un corps de Gouvernement établi sous telle ou telle forme," secondly "l'exécution de la loi," for which the Sovereignty is suddenly converted into a Democracy); also c. 3–6 on the establishment of the various forms of government.

47. III. c. 1 (the Government is in fact a second "personne morale" within the "personne morale" of the State, and within this whole it possesses as an intermediate body a certain unity and power of its own, but as against the Sovereign it has no will of its own and only a derivative and subordinate existence; its commission is always revocable); c. 10; c. 14 (suspension of all authority by "le peuple légitimement assemblé en Corps souverain"); c. 18 (every regular assemblage of the people is to be opened

with these two questions: "s'il plaît au souverain de conserver la présente forme de Gouvernement," and "s'il plaît au peuple d'en laisser l'administration à ceux qui en sont actuellement chargés").

48. The first view is held in the middle ages by the high clericalist school, following Gregory VII (see above, Ch. I. Note 17), and also by Frederick II in Petrus de Vin., Ep. V. c. 1; Gerson, IV. p. 647 ff., and others; later for example Molina, II. d. 21; and then again Thomasius, Inst. jur. div., III. c. 1 § 4–10, c. 6 § 2–25; Boehmer, P. spec. I. c. 1; Heineccius, c. 6 § 100–105. The second view is held under the influence of Aristotle by Thom. Aquin., Summa theologica, I. p. 383; Ptol. Luc., III. c. 9 and IV. c. 2–3; and later Suarez, III. c. 1 nr. 12; Danaeus, I. c. 4; Arnisaeus, Polit., c. 2, De rep., I. c. 1 p. 1–4; Keckermann, p. 12; Hoenonius, I. § 4; Knichen, I. c. 1 th. 2, I. c. 8 th. 2; Conring, Exerc. de urb. Germ., c. 9–15; Alberti, c. 14 § 1.—In his own way Gryphiander, loc. cit., § 21 ff. and 66 ff.

49. For the origin in mere positive law, the high clericalist school of the middle ages; later for example Boxhorn, I. c. 2 § 3–8, c. 3 § 15 ff. For the foundation in Natural Law, see Joh. Paris., c. 1 ("ius naturale et gentium"); and later most of the clerical writers, as Victoria, III. nr. 7; Soto, IV. q. 3 a. 1; Covarruvias, I. c. 1 nr. 3; Suarez, III. c. 1; likewise Bolognetus, c. 18; Greg. Thol., I. c. 2 § 6, XIX. c. un.; Buchanan, p. 11 ff.; Danaeus, I. c. 3; Althusius, c. 1 § 22 ff., and all the writers cited in Ch. I. Notes 41–43. For the derivation of the State from the jus gentium see Molina, II. d. 18 § 17 and d. 20; Lessius, II. c. 5 dub. 1–3.

50. For the medieval view see above, p. 71–72; later for example Greg. Thol., I. c. 3; Gryphiander, § 12–15 and § 163; Bossuet, I. a. 1 prop. 1–5, and a. 2 prop. 1–3; Kestner, c. 7 § 2–3.

51. The process of purely natural growth is treated, as for example in the middle ages by Aegid. Col., III. 1 c. 6, as the most normal mode of origin of the State; and Mars. Pat., I. c. 3, combines such a view with the idea of creative human activity. Later Greg. Thol., I. c. 2 § 1–6 and XIX. c. un., not only pours out his scorn on the 'ridiculous' notion that men at first led a solitary life like wild beasts in the jungles and mountains, but also gives a full positive statement of the theory of development: by nature there has always been "aliqua societas vel communitas vitae" among men, and in a natural way the society, as it "natura coaluit," also completes itself by the several stages of the familia, vicus, pagus, regnum and imperium. In like manner Besold, Diss., I. c. 3, describes the "origo civilis societatis": it is "in utero naturae concepta, in ejus gremio enutrita," it is erected by the jus naturale and is only preserved and improved by the "cura et industria hominum"; it is only violence and unreason that have here and

there led to an isolated life contrary to nature. Thus in essentials Arnisaeus, Polit., c. 2–6, De rep., I. c. 1–5; Bolognetus, c. 13; also Keckermann, p. 12 ff.; Fridenreich, c. 2 (as a tree with many branches grows out of its roots, so has the State grown out of "consociationes domesticae"); Schoenborner, I. c. 4 ff.; Conring, loc. cit., and many other Aristotelians.

52. Already Thom. Aquin., however great may be the stress that he lays on the nature of man as "animal politicum et sociale in multitudine vivens" (thus Op. I. p. 383, V. p. 264, De reg. pr., I. c. 1), makes mention of the "ratio constituens civitatem" (XXI. p. 366); compare Ptol. Luc., III. c. 9 and IV. c. 2–3. Aegid. Col., III. 2 c. 32, says expressly: "sciendum est quod civitas sit aliquo modo quid naturale, eo quod naturalem habemus impetum ad civitatem constituendam; non tamen efficitur nec perficitur civitas nisi ex opera et industria hominum"; compare III. 1 c. 1 ("opus humanum") with c. 3–5. Eng. Volk., De ortu, c. 1: ratio imitata naturam. Joh. Paris, c. 1. Gerson, IV. p. 648. Nic. Cus., III. praef. Aen. Sylv., c. 1, 2 and 4: human reason, "sive docente natura sive Deo volente totius naturae magistro," invented and erected the State, Rulership, Empire. Patric. Sen., De inst. reip., I. 3, goes so far as to speak of all social life as a series of 'inventions' which mankind made "duce natura" as a result of giving thought to common utility ("de communi utilitate cogitare"); compare III. 5.

53. Violent compulsion is treated as the constitutive principle of the State by the clericalist writers cited above, Ch. I. Note 17; see also Ptol. Luc., IV. c. 3. On the other hand Thom. Aquin., I. c. 13, assigns to the kingly office the creation of the State after the model of the divine Creation of the World.

54. Aegid. Col. (see above, Note 12) regards the foundation of the State by force as also possible, but less normal.

55. In particular Mars. Pat., I. c. 15, takes as the "principium factivum" of the State the "anima universitatis vel eius valentioris partis" and gives a lengthy account of how the reason dwelling within the whole body brings forth the social organism, consciously imitating herein the life-giving process of Nature.

56. It was of special importance that, following Cicero, De republica, I. 25, 39 ["populus autem non omnis hominum coetus quoquo modo congregatus, sed coetus multitudinis iuris consensu et utilitatis communione sociatus"], the State was defined as a "societas," as "humanae multitudinis coetus iure, consensu et concordi communione sociatus" and the like; see for example Dominicus de S. Geminiano on c. 17 in Sexto, 1, 6 nr. 7; Randuf, c. 7 p. 171; Theod. de Niem, Nemus unionis, ed. Basel 1566, tr. V. p. 261. Compare the suggestion of the social contract in Joh. Paris., c. 1, and its elaboration in Aen. Sylv., c. I; and Patric. Sen., loc. cit., I. 3.—

Any influence of the contractual theory of the Epicureans (see R. Hildenbrand, Geschichte u. System der Rechts- u. Staatsphilosophie, Vol. I., Leipzig 1860, p. 515 ff.) is out of the question.

57. Thus according to Aen. Sylv., loc. cit., "societas civilis" was founded by men who had previously been roaming about in the wilderness; likewise according to Patric. Sen., loc. cit., men originally living in isolation first decided to live together as a result of rational thought.

58. Thus Mars. Pat., I. c. 12, Ockham, Dial. III. tr. 2, l. 2, c. 26–28, and Nic. Cus., II. c. 8, 10, 12–13 and III. c. 4, derive all political subjection from the voluntary self-binding of the individual.

59. Thus the writers mentioned above, Note 51; see especially the polemics of Gregorius and Besold. Even Bodin knows nothing of the social contract; his definition of the State (I. c. 1 nr. 1), his discussions on the family as the basis of the State (I. c. 2–5), and his description of the formation of the State by a gradual outgrowth from the family or by colonization (IV. c. 1) indicate rather an opposite view.

60. See for example Joh. Oldendorp (1480–1561), Juris naturalis gentium et civilis isagoge, Cologne 1539, tit. 2; Connanus, Commentarii, I. c. 4 nr. 4 ff., c. 5 nr. 1 and 4, c. 6 nr. 2–3, c. 7 nr. 1–2; Bened. Winkler (1579–1648), Principiorum juris libri quinque, Leipzig 1615, I. c. 10, II. c. 9–10, V. c. 3–4 ("multitudo . . . sese consociat," introduces order and government and thus produces "societas civilis et civilia jura"). See also Claudius Cantiuncula, in Institutiones Paraphrasis, Lyons 1550 (1st ed. 1530), p. 101.

61. See Note 27 of preceding chapter and Note 49 of this chapter. Thus Victoria, III. nr. 4, argues vigorously against the idea that the civitas is an "inventum" or "artificium"; it is "a natura profecta" and may well be likened to the corpus humanum.

62. See the perfected doctrine in Suarez (above, p. 73 ff.); its groundwork already in Victoria and Soto (above, Ch. I, Note 27), as well as in Covarruvias, I. c. 1 nr. 2–3; but especially in Molina, II. d. 22, according to whom the "homines convenientes" as parts of the "corpus totius Reipublicae" are indeed the "conditio sine qua non" but not the creators of the executive, legislative and judicial powers of this Body, but rather "longe diversa fit potestas, quae ex natura rei consurgit in Republica, a collectione particularium potestatum singulorum" and "eam non habet Respublica autoritate singulorum, sed immediate a Deo."

63. Among them Danaeus must be reckoned an opponent of the contract theory, as in I. c. 3 he expounds the formation of society according to the Aristotelian scheme and herewith says that the State has a "causa remotior Deus, proxima ipse affectus naturalis."

64. For just this reason the broad statement of Janet, II. p. 158, that

the Vindiciae is the earliest exposition of the contract theory, is untenable.

65. According to Buchanan, p. 11 ff., civil society arose from primitive "vita solitaria" not simply for the sake of utility but by the force of "vis naturae" and the "lex divina ab initio rerum nobis insita conveniendi in unum coetum causa." According to Mariana, I. c. 1, men who were originally isolated were impelled by "imbecillitas et indigentia" to establish civil society. Rossaeus, c. 1 § 1, holds that men were induced to associate by natural reason. See also Boucher, c. 10 ff., on the original liberty and equality of men. Also Hoenonius, I. § 4 ff., according to whom the impulse to associate came primarily from God and Nature, and from necessity as the "causa minus principalis."

66. Salamonius, after having (I. p. 35 ff.) construed all law as an express or tacit contract ("consensus in idem, pactum et stipulatio"), explains (p. 38–42) that the civitas as a civil society necessarily presupposes the existence of "pactiones" and "leges," as every society requires a previous agreement in order to fix the conditions and declare the will whereby it is bound; that in the State as in any other society these fundamental contracts create an obligation not of the society toward itself but of all the "socii" toward one another; lastly that the ruler of the society, and in the State itself the Prince who is appointed as "praepositus vel institor societatis," shares in this obligation.

67. See above, p. 76 and Note 22 of present chapter; especially the works of Filmer, Horn and Bossuet, as well as Alberti, c. 2 § 9 and c. 10 § 1; Fénelon, Ch. VII.

68. As is remarked above (Note 51), Besold, Arnisaeus, Keckermann, Fridenreich, Schoenborner and Conring set up a formal theory of organic development. More or less the same position is taken by many other publicists of this school, who content themselves with expounding the gradual development of the Family, Commune and State after the usual scheme; thus Joh. Crüger, Collegium politicum, Giessen 1609, disp. I.; W. Heider (1558–1626), Systema philosophiae politicae, Jena 1628 (written 1610), p. 25 ff.; Christ. Gueinzius, Exercitationes politicae, Wittenberg 1617–1618, exerc. II.–X.; Koenig, Acies disputationum politicorum, Jena 1619, disp. I.; Werdenhagen, II. c. 13 ff.; Tulden, De civ. reg., I. c. 5; Micraelius, I. c. 8 ff.; Olizarovius, III. c. 2 ff.; Knichen, I. c. 1 th. 2, c. 8 th. 2.— The opposition to the contract theory is often expressed by rubricating the State as a "societas naturalis perfecta"; thus Joh. a Felde, Elementa juris universi, Frankfort and Leipzig 1664, p. 4; Sam. Rachelius, Inst. (1681), IV. tit. 31; Mullerus, I. c. 1 ff.—At the same time there were also publicists who described the State as a "societas civilis et voluntaria" in contrast to "societates naturales," thereby showing themselves adherents of the idea of

contract; thus Henr. Velstenius, Centuria questionum politicarum, Wittenberg 1610, dec. II.–V.; Christ. Matthias, Collegium politicum, Giessen 1611, disp. 4–5, and Systema politicum, Giessen 1618, p. 20 ff.—Paurmeister, I. c. 17 nr. 3 ff., expressly says that in the natural equality of men the State could only arise from "mutua conventio": "ut enim omnium aliarum rerum societas contrahitur, sic quoque imperii sive ἀρχῆς πολιτικῆς"; every πολιτεία however is just a "κοινωνία sive societas"; compare ib. c. 3 nr. 10: "primum istud ex societate et libera conventione populi contractum imperium"; c. 30 nr. 1–3: the respublica terminates like other societies by "contraria voluntas."

69. See Proleg. nr. 15–16; the definition of the State, I. c. 1 § 14; the derivation of the principle of majority rule from the presumed intention of those "in societatem coëuntium," II. c. 5 § 17; the general theory of "consociatio" as the creator of privatum et publicum jus in personam, ib. § 17 ff.; the treatment of the "consociatio qua multi patres familiarum in unum populum ac civitatem coëunt" as the perfectissima societas, which "maximum dat jus corpori in partes" and relates to all external human acts in themselves or may relate to them according to circumstances, ib. § 23; the designation as the perfectissima societas, ib. § 23; the analogy with the privata societas as regards the right of citizens to withdraw from the State, ib. § 24; the discussions on the State's right to alienate parts of its domain, wherein the State is characterized as a corpus voluntate contractum; the decision is drawn from the presumable intention in entering this societas, and the part is treated as prior to the whole, II. c. 6 § 4 ff.; also the derivation of the power of punishment, which was "initio penes singulos," ib. c. 20; the denial of the State's right to the lives of individuals, as they had in themselves no such right and hence could not transfer it, III. c. 2 § 6; lastly ib. c. 20 § 8.

70. In any case Schulze, Einl., § 45 N. 1, is wrong in calling him the 'creator of the contract theory.'

71. See above, Notes 33–38.

72. See above, Notes 39–40. The peculiar analysis of the constitutive contract in Huber, I. 2 c. 1 § 1 ff. (in the establishment of the state of peace by the "conjunctio multorum cum foedere se non laedendi," of the civil State by the fusion of all wills in one, and of the form of government by a constitutional contract) gained no wider acceptance. Pufendorf characterizes the act of union as a "pactum singulorum cum singulis, quod in unum et perpetuum coetum coire velint, suaeque salutis ac securitatis rationes communi consilio ductuque administrare"; see Elem., I. def. 12 § 17 and 26, De jure N. et G., VII. c. 2 § 7, De off., II. c. 6 § 7. In like manner all the adherents of Pufendorf's trichotomy; see Thomasius, Inst. jur. div., III.

c. 6 § 29; Kestner, c. 7 § 3; Hert, De mod. const., s. 1 § 2 (singuli cum singulis paciscuntur de cohabitatione et mutua conjunctione quum voluntatum tum virium), and Elem. prud. civ., I. s. 3; Schmier, I. c. 2 s. 4 § 3; Heineccius, II. § 110; Ickstatt, c. 1 § 7 ("pactum de conferendis viribus"); Achenwall, II. § 91. In like manner the idea of the social contract is expressed in Boehmer, P. spec., I. c. 2 § 3–12, and c. 3 § 1; Becmann, c. 4–5 (translatio juris mutua); J. G. Wachter, Origines juris naturalis, Berlin 1704, p. 34; Wolff, Inst., § 972, Jus nat., VIII. § 4 ff.; Daries, Praecog. § 24, and Jus nat. § 651, 655 and 659; Nettelbladt, § 1124 and 1180 ff.; Kreittmayr, loc. cit. § 3.

73. Thus Pufendorf, De jure N. et G., VI.–VII., De off., II. c. 2–5, and Elem., I. def. 12 § 17; Thomasius, Inst. jur. div., I. c. 1 § 97 ff., c. 6 § 6, III. c. 1 ff.; Hert, De mod. const., s. 1 § 1 ff. ("princeps societatum"), Elem. prud. civ., I. s. 1 § 6 ff.; Becmann, c. 11; Schmier, I. c. 2 s. 1–4 (societas composita, perfecta, inaequalis); Boehmer, P. spec., I. c. 3 § 1 note 0; Heineccius, II. c. 1 § 11 ff., and c. 2–6; Wachter, p. 34; Wolff, Jus nat., § 14 ff., Inst., § 975 ff.; Achenwall, proleg. § 97 and II. § 85 ff.; Daries, Jus nat., § 660 ("omnis civitas est societas"); Nettelbladt, Syst. nat., § 1114 ff. ("societas cujus finis est salus publica"), and Syst. pos., § 848; Kreittmayr, § 2, and Anm., loc. cit. nr. 2.

74. See the general theory of "personae morales compositae" as identified with "societates," and its application to the State in Pufendorf, De jure N. et G., I. c. 1 § 13 ff., and VII. c. 2 § 6 ff.; also Elem., I. def. 4 § 3 ff., and II. def. 12 § 26. Similarly Becmann, c. 4; Thomasius, op. cit., I. c. 1 § 91 ff.; Hert, Disc. de plur. hom. pers. un. sustin. (Op. II. 3 p. 55), s. 2 § 9–11; Boehmer, P. spec. I. c. 2 § 1 ff. (general theory of "societas," which is conceived as "persona moralis"); Heineccius, II. § 13–25 (likewise). But it was Wolff above all who worked out the general 'Nature-Right' theory of societies in the sense of the "societas" resting on contract and at the same time construed as a "persona moralis" (Jus nat., VII., and Inst., § 836–853), applying this to every species of society and lastly to the State. In this he is followed by Achenwall, proleg. § 82 ff., I. § 43 ff., and II. § 2–40 ("societas in genere") and § 85 ff. (jus publicum universale as the application of the natural law of societies to the greatest societas); Daries, Praecog. § 17 ff., and Jus nat. § 517–561, compared with § 654 ff.; Nettelbladt, Syst. nat., § 326–414 ("Jurisprudentia naturalis generalis socialis"), and § 1114 ff. ("jus publicum universale" as its application to the State), together with the corresponding sections on the special law of societies as applied to families, corporations, communes and churches, also Syst. pos., § 846 ff. (here even the "universitas" is defined as a "societas plurium quam duorum").

75. The distinction occurs first in Grotius, I. c. 1 § 3; and under other names in Hobbes, Lev., c. 22; further in Pufendorf, De jure N. et G., VII. c. 5 § 20; Thomasius, I. c. 1 § 93 ff., and c. 2 § 27 ff. (yet, as the only true societas inaequalis according to him is the covenant with God, he describes the State, which he otherwise defines as a "societas naturalis summum imperium continens," as a mere "societas mixta") ; Hert, loc. cit. (societas aequatoria and rectoria), Elem., I. s. 1 § 6 ff., and De mod. const., s. 1 § 1 ff.; Schmier, I. c. 2 s. 4; Wolff, Inst., § 839; Heineccius, II. § 19. But it was especially Boehmer, loc. cit., who worked this out scientifically and deduced from it all the special attributes of the State as contrasted with other societies and particularly the Church; see also his Jus eccl. Protest., I. c. 31 § 42 ff. This distinction plays an equally fundamental role in Daries, § 550 ff. and 651 ff.; Achenwall, II. § 22–40; Nettelbladt, Syst. nat., § 354 ff., and others.

76. According to Pufendorf (De jure N. et G., VII. c. 5 §′6) and his followers, even after the fundamental decree following the contract of union there are only the "rudimenta civitatis," which become a State by the contract of submission. Daries, § 651 ff., gives the technical name of "anarchia" to the original societas aequalis, which becomes a "societas civilis" only when imperium is established. This does not exclude the supposition that within the political societas inaequalis there is a continuance of the societas aequalis among the subjects; thus for example Boehmer, P. spec. III. c. 3.

77. Above all, in this way the independent rights of the lesser societies, while theoretically deduced from the structure of society, were in practice diminished at pleasure. In particular the so-called 'collegial' system was evolved for the Church and at the same time, being recognized merely as a "societas aequalis," it could be turned into the paths of Territorialism so far as the State's rights of supremacy over it were concerned. This position was held particularly by Boehmer, whose teachings prevailed for a long time.

78. See Milton, loc. cit., II. p. 8 ("all men naturally were born free"; in consequence of disorder "they agreed by common league to bind each other from mutual injury"; "hence came cities, towns, and commonwealths"). Sidney, c. I. s. 10, c. II. s. 4–5 and 20. Locke, II. c. 7 ff. (common consent). Locke indeed calls the State "one body politic," but with him the idea of the body politic and society coincides with, and exhausts itself in, a contractual relation of the associated individuals (see especially c. 8 § 95–99).

79. In this Hobbes and Spinoza (see above, p. 103), as well as Grotius

(above, Note 69), most of the German teachers of Natural Law (above, p. 104), and even Paurmeister (above, Note 68), agree with the Monarcho-machi. But the latter gave these propositions the earliest and afterward the most precise formulation; see above, Notes 57–58 and 65, and especially the remarks on the Politics of Althusius; also the statements on the source of civil authority in Milton, loc. cit., II. p. 9 ("this authority and power of self-defense and preservation being originally and naturally in every one of them and unitedly in them all"); Sidney, c. I. s. 2, 9 and 10, c. II. s. 1–2, 4–5 and 20 (the originally sovereign, free and equal individuals "recede from their own right" and thereby form society and government); Locke, II. c. 7–9, especially § 88–89.

80. Here belongs the Catholic theory already noticed, which derives only the State's existence and not its rights from the social contract; see above, Note 62; likewise Schmier, II. c. 1 s. 3, and Heincke, I. c. 2 § 9 ff.— Then Kestner, c. 7 § 3, for whom the imperium of all particular societies flows from the original right of the society of the totum genus humanum. Also Praschius, Designatio juris naturalis ex disciplina Christianorum, Ratisbon 1688, who bases the Law of Nature on the principles of love and self-sacrifice, hence makes the part subordinate to the whole and the special purpose of the part subordinate to the general purpose of the whole, and says such things as the following: "natura non intendit ultimo in singulos homines, sed societatem"; God willed "non singulos homines, sed societatem"; "societas, quae ex pluribus unitis constat, magnificentiae divinae est convenientior et naturae Dei, qui est unus ac trinus, proprior." Similarly Placcius, Accessiones juris naturalis privati et publici, Hamburg 1695. Dav. Mevius, Prodromus (1671).—But the foremost exponent of this duality is Leibniz, who starts from the organic whole of the spiritual universe culminating in the World-Empire of God and derives law from the community (Bruchstück vom Naturrecht, in Guhrauer, I. p. 414 ff., Einl. zum Cod. jur. gent., in Dutens, IV. 3 p. 287 ff.), but at the same time defines the State as a contractual society (Caesarinus-Fürstenerius, c. 10), bases its power of punishment on a promise of every individual to obey the laws and judgments (Nova methodus, II. § 19), and finds the basis of all civil law in the "conventio populi" (ib. § 71).—Also the two Cocceji (H. de Cocceji, Prodromus, and S. de Cocceji, Novum systema § 612 ff.) assume a direct derivation from God of the sovereignty belonging to the social body as against its members, but make it arise historically from the contract of union of the housefathers who under jus naturale were vested by God with imperium over the members of their families.—Just as little does Montesquieu abolish individualism; see for example Esprit des Lois (1748), XI.

c. 6: the legislative power is inherently in the people as a body, "comme dans un État libre tout homme qui est censé avoir une âme libre doit être gouverné par lui-même."

81. It is obvious that the Hobbesian "law of nature" ("lex naturalis"), which simply comprised the theorems deduced by reason from the instinct of self-preservation and led to the "right of every man to everything" ("jus omnium ad omnia") by virtue of the sovereign right of each man to judge of the fittest means to his own self-preservation, was in truth no legal limitation at all; De cive, c. 1 ff., Lev., c. 13–14. Just as little was Spinoza's 'natural right' as identified with power; Tract. theol.-pol., c. 16, Tract. pol., c. 1–2. And the individual remained naturally sovereign when with Thomasius, Fund. jur. nat., I. c. 5–7 (departing from the earlier Inst. jur. div., I. c. 1–2), the Law of Nature was construed as a "norma," but no more than a "norma consilii" with "obligatio interna." But even though the majority still held that the lex naturalis must be regarded as a true "lex" deduced by reason and therefore with external binding force,—whether for the rest the ground of its obligation were found in the Will of God or the Being of God or the nature of things or the nature of man,—yet they recognized as the legal consequence of its violation (apart from any divine or natural punishment) only the right of every other individual to self-defense or at most to vengeance, and in any case assigned to the community no resulting power of punishment. See Oldendorp, tit. 2; Winkler, II. c. 10; Balth. Meisner, De legibus, Wittenberg 1616, lib. III.; Grotius, I. c. 1 § 10; Huber, I. 1 c. 2 ff.; Richard Cumberland, De legibus naturae (London 1672), especially c. 5; Pufendorf, De jure N. et G., II. c. 3, De off., I. c. 3; Placcius, lib. I.; Mevius, III. § 13; Kestner, c. 1; Heineccius, I. c. 1 ff. and II. c. 1; H. de Cocceji, op. cit.; S. de Cocceji, op cit., I. § 56 ff. Further Locke, II. c. 2 ff. (violation of the law of nature places the executive power in the hands of every individual), and c. 12 § 145–146 (the Law of Nations subsists between bodies which are in the state of Nature); then especially Boehmer, P. gen. c. 1, c. 2 § 3 ff., P. spec. I. c. 3 § 22; Gundling, Jus nat., c. 1 and 3; Wolff, Jus nat., I. and IX., Inst., § 39 ff. and 1088 ff.; Achenwall, proleg. § 7–60 and II. § 210 ff.; Daries, Praecog., § 11 ff., 29 ff. and 790 ff.; and Nettelbladt, § 111 ff., 208 ff. and 1403 ff., all of whom follow out in detail the analogy, mentioned in the text, of the unsocial "jus mere naturale" and the Law of Nations; and lastly Montesquieu, I. c. 2 ("lois de la nature," derived "uniquement de la constitution de notre être," are valid for "un homme avant l'établissement des sociétés").

82. While Hobbes and Spinoza, loc. cit., depicted the state of nature as a "bellum omnium contra omnes," the prevailing opinion held to the traditional idea of a primeval communion of peace and right among men;

thus see Boehmer, P. gen. c. 1; Schmier, I. c. 1; Montesquieu, I. c. 2; also Pufendorf, De jure N. et G., II. c. 1–2, De off., II. c. 1 (but this peace is insecure); and Thomasius, Inst. jur. div., I. c. 2 § 51 ff., c. 4 § 54–72 (while later, in Fund. jur. nat., I. c. 3 § 55, he opines that it was "nec status belli, nec status pacis, sed confusum chaos"). After Grotius men also assumed an original relation of "socialitas," and disputed as to whether this was the effect or cause of the law of nature; compare Hert, De socialitate primo naturalis juris principio, Comm. et Opusc., I. 1 p. 61 ff., and ib., II. 3 p. 21 ff.; Mevius, III. § 13 and IV. § 35. But some understood this as the mere "naturale desiderium societatis" (thus Huber, I. 1 c. 2 ff., and Montesquieu, loc. cit.), others as a natural and unregulated sociality, and expressly warned against the confusion of "socialitas" with "societas" (thus Thomasius, loc. cit.). In any case the society of the state of nature was explained as nothing else than a natural social tie connecting the peoples in a wider aspect despite their own sovereign liberty. Locke himself (II. c. 2) means nothing more than this by his "state of Nature," though indeed the phrase "naturalis societas gentium" is more often used in this sense (compare above, Note 60, and Thomasius, Inst. jur. div., III. c. 1 § 38 ff., Fund. jur. nat., III. c. 6 § 5; differently indeed and contradicting his own premises, Wolff, Inst. § 1090 ff., with his "civitas maxima"). And on the other hand, wherever we find the assumption of an original "societas" in the sense of a formal association, we may be sure that we have to do with an opponent of the doctrine of the social contract; thus Gryphiander, loc. cit. § 12 ff.; Horn, I. c. 4 § 3–6; Alberti, c. 2 § 9 and c. 10 § 1; Bossuet, Pol., I. a. 1 prop. 1–5. It should also be noted that the idea of a primeval community of goods, which according to the older theory must clearly be taken as a legal bond already connecting the individuals, lost this meaning when nothing more was admitted than the so-called "communio primaeva negativa," that is, the simple negation of private ownership; see for example Pufendorf, De jure N. et G., IV. c. 4–5, De off., I. c. 12; Thomasius, Inst. jur. div., II. c. 9 § 58 ff.; Boehmer, P. spec. II. c. 10; Wolff, Inst., § 183 ff.; Achenwall, I. § 106 ff. But the most logical step toward individualism was taken by Locke when, while denying all dominion over persons in the state of nature except paternal power, he made private property arise by the law of nature from the individual's own labor (including occupancy), II. c. 5. From other points of view Alberti also held that private property existed from the very beginning (c. 7 § 19).

83. The originally dominant and never wholly discarded theory held with Aristotle that man is an "animal natura sociale," and hence regarded his natural instinct as the force impelling him to associate; at most it admitted "indigentia" and "metus" as playing a secondary role; see above, Notes 52,

60 (especially Winkler), 61, and 65 (Buchanan and Hoenonius) ; likewise Althusius, c. 1 § 31 ff.; Schmier, I. c. 2 s. 4 § 2 ("appetitus societatis naturalis") ; Heincke, I. c. 1 § 1 ff. ("ipsa lex naturalis" as the "causa impulsiva"). As an extension of this theory there is the doctrine of sociality in Grotius and his followers; see Boecler, Inst., I. c. 1; Hert, loc. cit.; also Huber, I. 2 c. 1 § 1 ff. (the idea of justice and the "naturale desiderium societatis"). But besides this there was always another view, which held that man is by nature an antisocial being and that the idea of association first awoke in him through need or through fear or else through both together; see above, Notes 52 and 65 (Mariana). This view was worked out in the harshest form by Hobbes; according to him man is by nature not sociable but self-seeking and ambitious, but amid the intolerable results of this natural instinct the fear of one another induces the persuasion that the natural state must be abandoned; De cive, c. 1 ff., Lev., c. 13–14. In essentials the same view is expressed by Gundling, Jus nat., c. 3 § 11 ff. and c. 35 § 1 ff. (with greater stress on the idea that the social state is unnatural and artificial) ; Kestner, c. 7 § 3; Daries, § 657; and even Thomasius, Inst. jur. div., III. c. 6 § 2–25 and c. 1 § 4–10 (it is no "impulsus internus" which produces the State, as nature impels rather to liberty and equality, but the "impulsus externus" of fear and need). By way of mediation Pufendorf, De jure N. et G., II. c. 1–2, VIII. c. 1, De off., II. c. 1 and 5 ("socialitas" as the first cause, "metus" as the second; Grotius in stressing the former and Hobbes the latter are both right but one-sided). A quite new variation of the materialistic view was developed by Boehmer, P. spec. I. c. 1: the cause of the formation of States is man's innate propensity to violence, as this led to the gathering of bands of robbers and these were confronted by societies for mutual protection. He is followed by Heineccius, II. c. 6 § 100–104, and Kreittmayr, § 3.

84. At first there sometimes prevailed the idea of an impulse instinctively determining the will. But already in the middle ages human reason is generally regarded as a factor, and indeed the State is sometimes described as a deliberate invention; see above, Note 52. The later teachers of Natural Law often say outright that natural reason impels men to associate. Likewise Althusius assumes throughout a conscious act of the will. Hobbes and his followers naturally cannot dispense with the mediating link of a rational insight into the precariousness of the state of nature; see also Becmann and Gundling, loc. cit. This element comes into the foreground in Spinoza, Tract. theol.-pol., c. 16, Tract. pol., c. 3–4. In Sidney, c. II. s. 4, and Locke, II. c. 7 and 9, there is no question of any motive for the formation of the social contract other than rational deliberation, which leads to the conviction that this act is expedient. In Germany the same standpoint is

taken by Wolff, Jus nat., VIII. § 1 ff., Inst., § 972; also Achenwall, II. § 93.

85. Thus the believers in the social instinct say that Nature is only the "causa remota" of the State; or they say that the State arises "ex natura" but "mediate per pacta" (thus S. de Cocceji, III. c. 5 § 200); or else they argue that despite the natural instinct the "pactum" remains the necessary "modus constituendi" (thus Schmier, I. c. 2 s. 4 § 3; Heincke, I. c. 2 § 1). In like manner the advocates of another "causa impulsiva" themselves treat "consensus" as the indispensable, and juristically the only relevant, middle term in the formation of society; see for example Gundling, loc. cit., c. 35 § 1 ff. —On the other hand it is said by the opponents of the social contract theory that God or Nature are immediate causes of the State; see above, Notes 51, 63 and 68; also Obrecht, Disputationes, d. 1, and Gueinzius, Exerc., X. q. 1; Arnisaeus, Polit., c. 2, De rep., I. c. 1 nr. 1 ff., and Werdenhagen, op. cit. II. c. 2, add fear and need as the "causa secundaria"; Conring, De urb. Germ., c. 8 ff., De cive, c. 44 ff., expressly combats the view that "sponte convenerunt homines" or "quasi metu coacti," and makes them coalesce "naturae innato instinctu" exclusively.

86. With full precision Althusius, c. 1 § 28–29, sets forth as the "causa efficiens" of "consociatio politica" the "consensus et pactum civium communicantium," but as its "forma" the "consociationem per collationem et communicationem ultro citroque factam." On the other hand Hobbes, loc. cit., also takes pains to prove that the covenant which is dictated by fear is yet a juristically free and binding act of will. In like manner Boehmer, loc. cit., denies the idea of an "absoluta necessitas" in the formation of States. Sidney, loc. cit., takes his stand simply on free will: "Freemen join together and frame greater or lesser societies and give such forms to them as best please themselves"; there is no other ground of political subjection than consent. Not less absolute is Locke, II. c. 8 § 95: "Men being . . . by nature all free, equal and independent, no one can be put out of this estate and subjected to the political power of another without his own consent"; compare § 99: political society requires "nothing but the consent of any number of freemen capable of a majority, to unite and incorporate into such a society; and this is that and that only, which did or could give beginning to any lawful government in the world." In Germany then above all Wolff, loc. cit., and Achenwall, loc. cit., emphasize the "liberum arbitrium" of individuals uniting themselves into a State.

87. Until then according to Sidney, c. III. s. 31, a society exists only "de facto" (compare c. I. s. 8, 10, 11, 16, 20, c. II. s. 1, 5, 7, 31, c. III. s. 18, 25); according to Locke, II. c. 8 and 17, there is only the form of a society; see also Huber, I. 2 c. 1 § 14–26; Hert, De mod. const., s. 1 § 4.—More

profoundly says Suarez, III. c. 1 nr. 11, that force as an empirical fact may found a State, "sed hoc non pertinet ad intrinsecam rationem seu naturam talis principatus, sed ad hominum abusum."

88. See especially Pufendorf, De jure N. et G., VII. c. 2 § 7 and c. 5 § 6 (against Hobbes, De cive, c. 7 § 5), De off., II. c. 6 § 7; Locke, loc. cit.

89. See Pufendorf, loc. cit. (any one may remain "in libertate naturali," but then he stands outside of civil society). Locke, II. c. 8 § 95 and 96. Schmier, I. c. 2 s. 4 § 2: with all the natural necessity for the State, it is yet for the individual a matter of free choice whether he "inter socios se jungere et imperium alienum agnoscere velit."

90. Thus first Grotius, II. c. 5 § 17 (above, Note 69); Pufendorf, Elem., I. def. 12 § 17, De jure N. et G., VII. c. 2 § 15 ff., c. 5 § 6, De off., II. c. 6 § 12; Thomasius, Inst. jur. div., III. c. 6 § 64; Locke, II. c. 8 § 97 ff.; Ickstatt, II. 1 c. 1 § 66 ff.

91. As for immigrants, first Pufendorf, De jure N. et G., VII. c. 2 § 20, De off., II. c. 6 § 13 (above, Note 40); as to native-born citizens (for whom men otherwise acquiesced in the binding of the sons by the fathers), first Locke, II. c. 8 § 113–122 (voluntary contract of union as each man comes of age, but thenceforth binding for life).—Just here comes the polemic of Hume, loc. cit., against basing political subjection at the present day upon consent.

92. Hobbes, De cive, c. 5–7 and 14, Lev., c. 17–19, 21, 24 and 26.

93. Certain acts cannot by their very nature be forbidden; Lev., c. 21.

94. For him also the abdication of the individual in favor of the community is absolute ("omne suum jus in eam transtulerunt"), and any right of the former against the latter is impossible; yet natural right still exists in so far as the limits of power remain the limits of right; spiritual and moral freedom however remains beyond the effective reach of power; hence it is not and cannot be transferred; when it is alienated, man is no longer man and the State, whose purpose is the development of man's true nature, becomes irrational; see Tract. theol.-pol., c. 16, 17, 20, Tract. pol., c. 3 § 6 ff., c. 4 § 4, c. 5 § 1–7, Epist. 24.

95. See Huber, I. 2 c. 3 § 27 ff., and I. 2 c. 4 § 1–25, as to the legal restraints on the majority in a democracy, which arise from contractual reservations, partly tacit (self-understood) and partly express, in favor of the individual; and in like manner for the other forms of government, ib. c. 5 and 8; also I. 3 c. 4, the analysis of the tacit and the express limitations of State-power; I. 9 c. 5, as to the continuance and validity of Natural Law in the State.—See also Besold, Diss. de majestate, s. 1 c. 1 § 5, and Tulden, c. 11, on the restriction of the majority in a democracy by the fundamental contract (below, Ch. III. Note 131).

96. See Pufendorf, Elem., I. def. 12 § 6, De jure N. et G., VII. c. 1, 8–9, De off., II. c. 5, c. 9 § 4, c. 11 (continuance of the Law of Nature, and the resulting "obligatio imperfecta" of the ruler to treat the individual as "homo" and "civis").

97. See Thomasius, Inst. jur. div., I. c. 1 § 103 ff., and especially the passages cited above, Ch. I. Note 3.

98. See Boehmer, P. gen. c. 2 § 8 ff., P. spec. I. c. 1, c. 2 § 20 ff., c. 5, III. c. 2 § 1 ff. (despite the necessary abdication of "libertas et aequalitas" the jus naturale, being inalienable, remains otherwise intact; religious liberty above all is tacitly reserved).—Similarly Heineccius, II. § 132 ff. and § 184.

99. See Schmier, III. c. 3, on the limitations of the State's power as to personae, bona and jura, wherein the principle is worked out that in the State the Law of Nature is not abolished but unfolded, and that "libertas naturalis" continues in all matters which are not comprised in the State-contract; also I. c. 4 and V. c. 2. Further Gundling, c. 1 § 51 ff. (distinction between inborn and acquired rights and duties), and c. 3. And Hert, De mod. const., s. 1 § 6: the society of cives inter se as well as quoad imperantem extends only "quatenus ad finem societatis obtinendum expedit."—See Gerh. Noodt, Diss. de religione ab imperio jure gentium libera (1706), Opera, I. p. 634 ff.— Joh. Strauch, De juris naturalis et civilis convenientia (Opuscula, Halle 1729), nr. 16 p. 535 ff.

100. According to Locke the State is simply an outgrowth of the state of Nature and an institution for the protection of natural rights; the individuals have not transferred to it all rights but only the power of punishment and the administration of justice, to be exercised in accordance with the natural rights of the individuals; the fundamental rights of the individual cannot be alienated or transferred; it is absurd to suppose that any "rational creature" has given up more of the "equality, liberty and executive power" of the state of Nature than is required for the purpose of the State, "the better to preserve himself, his liberty and property"; "the power of the society" never extends farther than "the common good"; see II. c. 7, c. 9 § 131, c. 11 § 134 ff., c. 12.—Sidney also holds that only a part of natural liberty and equality is given up; c. I. s. 10, c. II. s. 4 and 20.

101. Wolff's whole system rests on the distinction between the pure law of nature as existing in the state of nature and the law of nature as modified by the State-contract; in the latter the original liberty and equality are abrogated so far as this is required for the erection of the State, but otherwise remain unimpaired; since the State's power extends 'no farther than those acts which are proper for the promotion of the general welfare,' there is even in the State a large sphere in which the 'Nature-Right' sovereignty of the individual

still continues; hence the rights and duties of man in the State are classified as inborn and acquired; a part of these inborn rights is 'so closely bound up with man that it cannot be taken from him;' see Politik, § 215 and 433, Jus nat., I. § 26 ff., VIII. § 35, 47, 1041 ff., Inst., § 68 ff., 980, 1075 ff.— Quite similar ideas are worked out by Achenwall; see I. § 63 ff. (continuance of the "jura connata" of the "status originarius" in the "status adventitius," so far as they are compatible with the imperium), II. § 98 ff. (limits of the State's power), § 107 ff. (continuance of libertas naturalis with regard to "actiones civiliter indifferentes"). Likewise Nettelbladt, § 111 ff., 193 ff., 208 ff., 1104 ff.; Kreittmayr, § 32 and 36; and many others.

102. Rousseau, I. c. 6; also I. c. 7, on the "tacitement" transferred power of coercion of any future individual will which refuses to obey the general will; II. c. 5, on the derivation of the State's power of life and death from the contract of the individuals.

103. See IV. c. 2; the propositions here set forth,—as to the requisite unanimity of civil association, which is described as "l'acte du monde le plus volontaire," the right of recusants to hold aloof, thereby becoming "étrangers parmi les citoyens," the effect of residence in the territory as implying consent, the contractual basis of the principle of majority rule,—are all found in his predecessors. See also III. c. 10: when the government breaks the social pact by usurping the sovereignty, "tous les simples citoyens, rentrés de droit dans leur liberté naturelle, sont forcés, mais non obligés d'obéir."

104. This conception lies at the root of the whole book, despite all the arguments as to the nature of the community as a unitary body endowed with personality (I. c. 5–7, II. c. 2 and 4, III. c. 1) and on the distinction (II. c. 3) between the 'general will' ("volonté générale") and the 'will of all' ("volonté de tous"); compare the habitual treatment of 'all' and 'every' as equivalent (as in II. c. 4), the numerical calculation in III. c. 1, the discussions in III. c. 11, 12, 15 and 18.

105. See I. c. 6; also c. 8–9 as to the replacement of "liberté naturelle" by "liberté civile," of the right to everything by the protection of lawful ownership, and of natural equality by legal equality. See also the earlier Discours sur l'origine et les fondements de l'inégalité parmi les hommes (1753).

106. See I. c. 6; these clauses are so completely determined by the nature of the act that the smallest modification would make them null and void; since all are equal no man can reclaim anything; each man is free, seeing that he acquires the same power over every other man as that other does over him, thus receiving an equivalent for what he has lost; hence the formula: "Chacun de nous met en commun sa personne et toute sa puissance sous la suprême direction de la volonté générale; et nous recevons en corps chaque membre

comme partie indivisible du tout." Compare I. c. 9, on the giving up and receiving back of real property.

107. The Sovereign itself is not legally bound by the fundamental contract (I. c. 7), and may even dissolve it (III. c. 18); its power is absolute (II. c. 4); guaranties for the individual are impossible (I. c. 7). Nevertheless there are "bornes du pouvoir souverain" in the personality of the members and the "droit naturel dont ils doivent jouir en qualité d'hommes"; for each man alienates only "tout cela dont l'usage importe à la communauté"; and while the Sovereign "seul est juge de cette importance," yet it follows from the nature of the general will ('all' being at the same time 'every'), and chiefly from the nature of the social contract, whose basis is destroyed by any violation of equality, that the Sovereign neither wills nor can will any transgression of these limits (II. c. 4, also I. c. 7 and II. c. 6).

108. Even Frederick the Great accepted the "pacte social"; Essai sur les formes de gouvernement, Oeuvres IX. p. 195 ff.; compare ib. p. 215. Cajetan Filangieri (1752–1788), La Scienza della Legislazione, Naples 1780, I. c. 1 ff., follows Rousseau entirely.—It is most significant that Justus Möser (1720–1794), with all his opposition to the theories of the state of nature and the rights of man, was unable to give up the idea of the social contract; see Patriotische Phantasien, Berlin 1778–1786, II. nr. 62 p. 298–316 (the well-known comparison with the Aktiengesellschaft or joint-stock company), also I. nr. 32, 56, II. nr. 1, III. nr. 60–61, IV. nr. 51 and 61, Vermischte Schriften, Berlin 1797, I. p. 306 ff., 313 ff., 335 ff.—Likewise Herder, Ideen zur Geschichte der Menschheit (1784–1785), IX. c. 4, although he describes the state of nature as social.

109. Scheidemantel, I. p. 44 ff., 56 ff., 68 ff. (the State is not necessitated by the nature of man, and the Law of Nature imposes no inevitable obligation to give up liberty). Schlözer, p. 3 ff., 63 ff., 73 ff., 93 ff. (the State as a free invention and a machine; the social contract as a "unio virium" shows itself in the course of centuries to be insufficient; experience and philosophy lead to a "unio voluntatum" in the "pactum subjectionis" and thus to the State).

110. See for example Scheidemantel, III. p. 172–343; Schlözer, p. 31 ff. and 93 (the State is invented merely to 'insure' the rights of man); the ideas of the latter are made still more individualistic by Christian v. Schlözer, Kleine Schriften, Göttingen 1807, p. 11 ff., especially § 9–14.

111. Cesare Bonesana Beccaria (1738–1794), Dei Delitti e delle Pene, Monaco 1764, § 2.

112. Wilhelm v. Humboldt, Ideen zu einem Versuche die Grenzen der Wirksamkeit des Staats zu bestimmen (1792), Breslau 1851. Nothing is more indicative of the spirit of this essay than the proposal of a law expressly

declaring 'that every moral person or society is to be regarded as nothing more than the sum of its existing members' (p. 130).

113. Emmanuel Sieyès, Politische Schriften, vollständig gesammelt von dem deutschen Uebersetzer, 1796. See for the contract theory in general, I. p. 129 ff. and 432 ff.; comparison of the State to a joint-stock company, I. p. 283 ff. and 445 ff.; full identification of political society with 'the united members themselves taken together,' and of the general will with the 'general sum of the wills of all the individuals,' I. p. 144 ff. and 205 ff.; declaration that 'the happiness of the individual is the sole purpose of the social state,' II. p. 32; argument for the rights of man as the inalienable original rights of the individual, which are not given up in the social state and must not be infringed by the State, I. p. 413 ff., 427 ff., II. p. 3 ff.; inclusion of private property in this category, I. p. 459 ff., 485 ff., II. p. 35; protest against magnifying the idea of sovereignty, as it only comprises what is needed, II. p. 374 ff.

114. Johann Gottlieb Fichte (1762–1814), Sämmtliche Werke, Berlin 1845–1846, VI. p. 80 ff. (Beiträge of 1793), p. 12 ff. (Zurückforderung of 1793), III. p. 191 ff. (Naturrecht of 1796–1797).—The individual will is the only lawgiver (VI. p. 80 ff.); the freedom of the individual and the realization of his natural rights is the sole purpose of the State (VI. p. 101 ff., III. p. 111 ff. and 148 ff.); though the existence of the State is required by nature and reason, entrance into it is a matter for the free will of the individual (III. p. 201 and 369); the individual is but partly merged in society —not wholly, as Rousseau thinks (III. p. 204 ff.); the rights of man cannot be alienated or renounced (VI. p. 159 ff.).—Compare the hypothesis of a preparation for the contract of union (*Vereinigungsvertrag*) by the contract of property (*Eigenthumsvertrag*) and the contract of protection (*Schutzvertrag*), and their consummation in the contract of citizenship (*Staatsbürgervertrag*) to be made by each individual with the whole community (III. p. 191 ff.).

115. Werke VI. p. 105 ff., 148 ff., 159.

116. Werke III. p. 16, 164, 178 ff., 184 ff.—And otherwise the State's will appears throughout as a sum of wills and the State itself as a sum of individuals; compare ib. p. 105 ff., 150 ff., 183 (absolute right of revolution); VI. p. 39 and 103 ff.—To be sure Fichte seeks to prove the idea of a 'real whole,' which arises from the contracts, appears as an 'organic' being and takes a place independent of the individuals; but this 'whole' is nothing more than the 'totality of the members' and differs from a 'real' multitude only in that its components are indeterminate; after all this is a purely mechanical, not an organic, concept; hence even the State cannot be a real "person"; see

Werke, III. p. 202 ff. and 250; likewise Rechtslehre (1812), Nachgelassene Werke, Berlin 1834, II. p. 507 ff. and 638, but especially p. 632.

117. Above all by his socialistic ideas, whose germ appears already in Naturrecht (Werke III. p. 210 ff.) in the derivation of property from contract, and is developed in Der geschlossene Handelsstaat (1800), ib. p. 387 ff., and Rechtslehre, Nachg. Werke II. p. 528 ff.

118. See Grundzüge (1804–1805), Werke VII. p. 1 ff., 147 ff., 157 ff., 210; Rechtslehre, Nachg. Werke II. p. 537 ff.; Staatslehre (1813), Werke IV. p. 402 ff.—Along with this the steady enlargement of the State's functions (civilization of the race, education, morality, culture); see Werke IV. p. 367, VII. p. 144 ff., 428 ff., Nachg. Werke II. p. 539 ff.

119. See Rechtslehre, Nachg. Werke II. p. 493–652.

120. Immanuel Kant (1724–1804); the works here considered are cited from Sämmtliche Werke, in chronologischer Reihenfolge herausgegeben von G. Hartenstein; here are given the essay "Ueber den Gemeinspruch: das mag in der Theorie richtig sein, taugt aber nicht für die Praxis" (1793), VI. p. 303–346; the essay "Zum ewigen Frieden" (1795), VI. 405–454; the "Metaphysik der Sitten" (1797–1798), VII. p. 1–303 (Rechtslehre, p. 41–173).

121. He also starts from the autonomy of the rational individual, whose will is its own lawgiver (VII. p. 20 and 133). Hence a lawful bond among men can only be based upon contract (VI. p. 329, 409, VII. p. 133 § 47). The 'pact of civil union' whereby the people constitutes itself a State has for its terms the total surrender of inborn external freedom with its immediate and undiminished resumption as a legally conditioned freedom (VII. p. 133 § 47). The purpose of this civil union is solely the establishment of an assured Reign of Law (VI. p. 322, 330 ff., VII. p. 130 § 44, 136 § 49), that is, the conditions for the union of the external freedom of one with the external freedom of others (VI. p. 322, VII. p. 26 ff.). Right (including the right of property) is prior to the State and is only made peremptory by it (VII. p. 130 § 44; compare p. 53 ff. § 8–9, p. 63 ff. § 15–16). Even in the State the objective 'Law of Reason' ("Vernunftrecht"), given *a priori*, governs (VI. p. 338, 413, VII. p. 34, 131), and accordingly the subjective rights ('belonging to every man by virtue of his manhood') of liberty, equality and autonomy remain inalienable, and anything contrary to them (such as hereditary nobility) is contrary to law (VI. p. 322 ff., 416 ff., VII. p. 34 ff., 147ff.). The State itself is defined as the 'union of a multitude of men under just laws,' hence as the sum of the united individuals (VII. p. 131 § 45), and is conceived as a 'mechanism' (ib. p. 157 and 158). The sovereign is the general will, which is alone empowered to legislate, is conceived throughout as

the sum of the individual wills (as the 'concurrent and united will of all'), and derives its rightful power just from this, that the autonomous will of each person decides for itself (VII. p. 131 § 46, also p. 54 § 8, 62 § 14–17, 106 § 41; VI. p. 327 ff. and 416–420). That the votes of the majority and of representatives suffice, is 'assumed as by general consent, hence by a contract' (VI. p. 329).

122. VI. p. 329, 334, 416 ff., VII. p. 133 § 47; also the arguments for the aprioristic existence of the idea of the civil state in the state of nature, VII. p. 62 ff. § 14–17.—Suggestions of the merely ideal existence of the contract occur already in Thomasius, Fund. jur. nat., III. c. 6 § 2–6; Becmann, Consp. doctr. pol., p. 16; Kreittmayr, § 3, and Anm., loc. cit. nr. 2.

123. VI. p. 320 and 415, VII. p. 54 § 8, 130 § 44, 107 § 41; also his deeply cherished plan to make this principle of the duty of associating apply to States which among themselves still live in the state of nature, VI. p. 415 ff., VII. p. 162 § 54, 168 § 61.

124. VII. p. 36, 153, 158–159; also above, end of Note 121.

125. VI. p. 329–339 and 416 ff., VII. p. 136 ff., 158 ff., 173.

126. Kant is followed by Rotteck (Vernunftr., I. § 61, II. § 19 ff.), and Welcker (in connection with the idea of organic development, Letzte Gründe, p. 80 ff., Encykl., p. 119 ff.); while Wilh. Jos. Behr stands wholly upon the older theory (Angew. Staatsl., § 18 ff.). The transition to the theory of the pure Law of Reason is made by K. S. Zachariae (Vierzig Bücher vom Staate, 1st ed. p. 61 and 116 ff., 2nd ed. I. p. 49 ff.).

127. Even in its flowering-time the contract theory did not lack important opponents (such as J. H. G. v. Justi, Die Natur und das Wesen der Staaten, Berlin, Stettin and Leipzig 1760, p. 40 ff.; Adam Ferguson, Essay on the History of Civil Society, 1767, I. c. 1 ff.; F. K. v. Moser, Neues patriot. Archiv., I., 1792). But its final downfall was determined—apart from the historical, theocratic and naturalistic theories of the Restoration (Edmund Burke and Friedrich v. Gentz, Adam Müller, A. v. Haller)—by the victory of the historical school of law over natural law, and by the philosophical attacks of Fries, Schelling, Hegel and Schleiermacher.

THE DOCTRINE OF POPULAR SOVEREIGNTY

I. In the Middle Ages

WE have seen that the evolution of the doctrine of the State-contract led at an early time to the general idea of the People as the original 'subject' of public power. At the same time it has been seen that the more precise expression of the idea of the contract of rulership led to a theory in which even in the constituted State the ruler and the people remain two distinct correlative 'subjects' of rights. And we have already shown that as to the relation between ruler and people in public law, opposite theories issued out of the old controversy on the nature of the grant of rulership as a "translatio" or a "concessio."

The theory of a mere 'concession' gave birth in the middle ages to the doctrine of Popular Sovereignty.[1]

To be sure, throughout the middle ages even the 'transference' theory allowed to the people as a whole an active political right of its own, by which the ruler's authority was strictly limited.[2] Political institutions being what they everywhere were, such an admission was almost unavoidable. From several viewpoints indeed this was held to be compatible with the right of the people to depose the ruler in case of necessity.[3] But in any case the adherents of this theory declared that the ruler is "maior populo" and the true "superior," claimed for him the sole and exclusive right to the "imperium," and with special emphasis denied that the legislative power continues in the people.[4]

On the other hand the concession theory also recognized an independent right of the ruler, of which he could not be deprived so long as he was faithful to his contract. But it left to the people the substance of the power whose exercise was transferred, and hence it set up the universal principle "populus maior principe." [5] From this especially it inferred that the community still retains a legislative power over and above the Prince and a continuing control over the exercise of the ruler's office.[6] And with the greatest emphasis it asserted the further consequence, that if the ruler neglects his duties the people may sit in judgment upon him and depose him by right and doom.[7]

With these principles, first developed with reference to the Empire and then generalized, the people was declared to be the true sovereign, whatever might be the form of the State. Yet for the most part men held fast to the medieval principle that Monarchy is the normal and the best form of government. In truth, however, the monarch was placed on a level, in principle, with the magistrate of a Republic. This appears equally in all the political systems erected on this basis, though otherwise they were imbued with an extremely different spirit.

With all the consistency of democratic radicalism Marsilius of Padua erected an abstract scheme, identical for all governments, of a division of powers between the "universitas civium" and the "pars principans." For him the sovereign is always and exclusively the legislator, but the legislative power is and necessarily remains in the people, and is exercised in the assembly of the citizens entitled to vote or their elected representatives. By means of legislation the popular will produces the State with its whole organization, constitution and distribution of offices; in particular it erects the office of the Principate for the conduct of purely executive business, of which the "universa communitas" cannnot itself take care. But the ruler remains subordinate to the legislator; "per auctoritatem a legislatore sibi concessam" he is the State's "secundaria quasi instrumentalis seu executiva pars." Hence he is appointed, corrected, and if need be supplanted by the legislator. And lastly, since the "universitas ipsa" is to act by his agency, his whole administration should be conducted in the fullest possible accord with the popular will ("iuxta subditorum suorum voluntatem et consensum").[8]

And even Lupold of Bebenburg, monarchical and moderate

as his tendency is, teaches expressly that the People of the Empire is "maior ipso principe"; that it can make laws (especially if the throne be vacant or the Emperor negligent), depose the Emperor and for sufficient cause transfer the Empire to another nation; also that every particular nation has just the same rights against its own King.[9]

With equal decisiveness Nicolas of Cues, who undertakes to give a modern content to the medieval idea of the world-society of Mankind, worked out in all its gradations the principle of popular sovereignty. In his theory no earthly power has any legitimate or divinely willed origin other than the voluntary agreement of the governed. In narrower and wider societies alike the constituted ruler is but the minister of the collective rights and the bearer of the collective will ("quasi in se omnium voluntatem gestans"). Only by recognizing himself to be the creature of this collective body does he become the father of the individuals ("dum se quasi omnium collective subiectorum sibi creaturam cognoscit, singulorum pater existat"). Just as before, he remains subject to the law-making power; this necessarily belongs to the collective body by the very nature of law, whose binding force is derived from the consent of those who are bound. And as he is elected by the community, he only receives "administratio" and "iurisdictio" within the scope of his mandate. Even in this he is under continuous control, and in case he exceeds his official power he may be judged and deposed by the people. And these principles are imprescriptible divine and natural law, so that no mere positive law can derogate from them.[10]

In like manner during the fifteenth century, in all the theoretical arguments whereby men seek to defend the rights of the Estates against the growing power of Monarchy, recourse is had to popular sovereignty as a first principle.[10a]

This theory gained a still higher and wider significance by being transferred to the Church in the great struggle between Pope and Council. When the doctrine of papal absolutism, even at its zenith, could not quite eliminate the idea of a right of the ecclesiastical Community (as represented by the Council) which at certain points broke through the monarchical principle,[11] the growth of this germ on a purely Canonical soil produced a theory in which, without prejudice to the normal superiority of the Pope, a superiority of the Community in exceptional cases might be made good.[12] And from the beginning of the fourteenth century the anti-papal doctrine advanced toward a much bolder version, in which the arguments of positive law were combined with the application to the Church of those theoretical constructions of the State and Society which were believed to be based on Natural Law. In this way John of Paris already placed the Pope on a level with the head of an ordinary corporation.[13] But above all Marsilius of Padua and William of Ockham transferred the political doctrine of popular sovereignty to the Church, in which they not only ascribed all the powers of a true sovereign to the Community represented by the Council,[14] but—here they differ from all the later Conciliar theorists—they even called upon the laity to take an active part in forming the sovereign collective will.[15]

This full-grown theory of the indestructible 'Nature-Right' sovereignty of the ecclesiastical community was erected into a system by the writers of the great Conciliar Age, who again restricted active membership to the clergy, and was made an official program at the Councils of Pisa, Constance and Basel.

For d'Ailly, Gerson, Zabarella, Andreas de Randuf, Theodoricus de Niem and many of their contemporaries, the whole constitution of the Church is based on the idea that the plenitude of ecclesiastical power is in substance indivisible and inalienable, and is vested in the "ecclesia universalis" represented by the Council, while the exercise of this power belongs to the Pope and the Council in common.[16] When these writers attempt to define more precisely the relation of Pope to Council there are many differences among them; but on the whole they agree in ascribing to the Pope the ordinary exercise of a supreme and monarchical power of government, and to the Council a more original and a fuller power which is to be employed in regulating, correcting and if need be supplanting the papal power.[17] Thus in the more important acts of government the co-operation of the Council is requisite; it should take action against abuse of the papal power, and may have to judge the Pope, depose him and even inflict physical punishment on him.[18] For this purpose it may assemble and constitute itself by its own authority, without the Pope and even against him, though normally it should be summoned by him.[19] During a vacancy of the See, its "potestas suppletiva" puts it in the place of the absent monarch, and then "per se ipsum vel per organum aliquod vice omnium" it can exercise his powers of government.[20] And in principle the election of the new Pope belongs to the Council, and when the Cardinals, as is the regular practice, perform this function, they act only as representatives of the Council.[21] Yet it is believed that these propositions do not infringe the monarchical constitution of the church,[22] but simply that the introduction of aristocratic and democratic elements produces a 'mixture,' which was commended in ancient times as the 'best polity.'[23] But this only shows how completely the idea of monarchy has been dissolved by the idea of a sovereignty of the people standing above all forms of government. For the other ecclesiastical organs are regarded as mere delegates of the General Council: an assembly which binds them unconditionally by its acts, which in case of collision is the sole representative of the church, and indeed stands above the Pope.[24]

It is, however, Nicolas of Cues who in the most universal fashion works out the principle of popular sovereignty in the church. For him this principle is an imprescriptible rule of "ius divinum et naturale" and he sets up a complete parallelism between the structure of the Church and the structure of the State.[25]

Yet similar ideas are not only laid down by the later ecclesiastical publicists of the Conciliar school,[26] but come to prevail more and more even in the expositions of Canon law based on positive law.[27]

This powerful movement within the constitutional doctrine of the church, as it has just the church's constitution in view, is naturally sustained and determined largely by ideas relating specifically to the church. To this extent it lies beyond the scope of our monograph, and thus it could only be touched upon here without attempting to bring out its full inwardness. Yet at the same time—and for this reason it could not be wholly omitted—it forms an important chapter in the historical development of

'Nature-Right' theories of the State. For one of its great features is just this, that in course of time the Church is ever more sharply and distinctly conceived and construed as a 'Polity,' which must be governed by the constitutional model which had already been framed for the State by combining antique ideas with the basis of Natural Law. In the end indeed the Church is said to be charged with the mission of realizing the ideal of a perfect political constitution.[28] Here indeed, while it utilized, established and developed the idea of an inalienable and imprescriptible sovereignty of the whole Community, based on Divine and Natural Law, it contributed immensely to the success of the political doctrine of popular sovereignty. For this reason the earliest scientific reaction in favor of the Papacy, the reaction led by Turrecremata, began quite fitly with the denial of the principle of popular sovereignty, which it denounced as radically false and impossible.[29]

But before we pursue the further development of this doctrine we must make a twofold analysis of that idea drawn from medieval theory which we have denoted by the highly ambiguous phrase 'Popular Sovereignty.' We must first ask what the medieval theory understood by the 'People' taken as the 'subject' of supreme power. And secondly we must examine how far the concept of 'Sovereignty' was developed with reference to the rights in dispute between people and ruler.

1. When 'People' is taken in the sense of the organic body which becomes a 'person' in the State, the concept of the People's sovereignty goes over into the concept of the State's sovereignty. It would seem that the medieval theory must have been put through such a transition.

For if an organic conception of human societies was to some extent directly implied in the original thought of the middle ages, which everywhere started from the idea of the whole, so also the later philosophic theory of the State, under the influence of biblical allegories and antique models, carried out universally the comparison of mankind at large and every smaller society to an animate body.[30] The old idea that mankind united in Church and Empire is a single organism, a "corpus mysticum cuius caput est Christus," [31] was still held by all parties as something sacred, while they made use of it in widely different juristic arguments.[32] And even Nicolas of Cues, whom we must name among the leading champions of popular sovereignty, fashioned once more in new and splendid forms the ideal vision of this great Organism spanning Heaven and Earth, to connect therewith his whole system of Church and State. Thus every separate spiritual or secular society, and above all the State, was described as a "corpus mysticum," which indeed as a "corpus morale et politicum" differs in many respects from a "corpus naturale et organicum" yet corresponds to it in the essential features.[33] Some there were who soon strayed into a superficial anthropomorphism and earnestly sought to ascertain which organ of the physical body corresponds to each organ of the State.[34] But with or without such crude conceits, the spirit of the organic conception was at the same time unfolded in a variety of forms and was worked up into the principle that the essence of the State consists in the unity of a common life which, as in the case of natural organisms, results from the harmonious coherence of the parts, which are properly differentiated, disposed and vested with special functions.[35] And from this principle there was already developed with more or less sharpness the conception of individuals as members of the living collective body; [36] of distinctions of rank and estate as the organic differentiation and grouping of elements; [37] of societies mediating between the individual and the universal Community as necessary articulations; [38] of the constitution as the organization which unites the many into a one; [39] of constitutional powers as organic functions; [40] of the branches vested with these functions as organs; [41] of the ruler as that highest governing organ which every organism requires.[42]

But despite all such elaborations the medieval organic theory of the State halted without reaching its final goal, which alone would have enabled it to govern the purely juristic construction of the State. Thus it was that this theory might here and there conceal but could not hinder the steady progress of an atomistic and mechanical construction of the State.

For in the question as to the 'subject' of the State's power, which determines all juristic constructions of the State, the organic idea gains its usefulness and relevance only in so far as it issues in the legal concept of the personality of the unitary whole.

But no such result was attained in the middle ages. It is true that the professional lawyers of the middle ages were already operating—and sometimes in a very precise fashion—with the concept of the ideal 'right-subjectivity' of the State.[43] But the concept that they were using was merely the 'juristic person' of the Civilian-Canonist theory of corporations, an instrument produced in the workshop of private law, which was ever more commonly regarded as a creature of pure thought ("persona repraesentata"), a fiction ("persona ficta") set up by an "artificium iuris," and, with whatever differences of interpretation, was connected in a purely external and mechanical fashion with the aggregate of real persons.[44] On the other hand the publicists, properly so called, of the middle ages hardly ever—and this is quite remarkable—make any direct application of the concept of personality to the Church or the State. When they make an indirect use of it by accepting its consequences they depend altogether on the Civilian-Canonist theory of corporations. There is not the slightest trace of the thought which would seem to lie so near at hand: that of deepening the concept of the juristic person by combining with it the concept of the social organism, of treating the substantial living unity ascribed to the latter as at the same time a 'subject' of rights, and thus replacing the phantom of the "persona ficta" by the concept of a real Group-Personality.

Thus indeed it was impossible for the medieval theory to rise to the thought of the State's sovereignty. On the contrary, in the inquiries as to the 'subject' of the State's power the unitary personality of the State well-nigh wholly disappeared behind the visible bearers of official power. And as between the two 'subjects' of rights, embodied or supposed to be embodied in the ruler and the popular assembly, the only dispute was as to which had the higher and fuller right.

In so far as the ruler was made the 'subject' of the State's power, the Civilian-Canonist idea of the 'fictitious person,' of the type which had long been realized in the Church, enabled men to distinguish the rights which belonged to the ruler in his official capacity from those which belonged to him in his private capacity.[45] But for this purpose they employed, not the concept of the personified State, but rather the concept of the personified

Office or "dignitas" [such as the English 'Crown'], since the ruler's office, outlasting its temporary holders, was constituted the permanent bearer of a distinct sphere of rights and duties.[46] But in any case, in the discussions on the 'subject' of the State's power within the sphere of competence expressed by this "dignitas," the State's personality, so long as the throne was occupied, was completely absorbed in the personality of the living ruler.[47]

And if the people was made a 'subject' of rights, standing beside or above the ruler, this 'subject' could not be identified with the whole organized and unified body, since the head was excluded. Instead, a separate 'subjectivity' was attached to 'the People' as a 'subject' set over against 'the Government.' Then it is true that the people when thus conceived was by no means identified with the multitude of individuals, but instead was expressly said to be a "universitas," was brought wholly within the scope of the rules framed by jurisprudence for "universitates," and in particular was allowed to unfold its 'subjectivity' of rights only in a duly corporative assembly and by formal collective acts.[48] But despite some few traces of a contrary effect of the organic idea,[49] men were in general driven steadily onward to a conception which explained this, as every other "universitas," to be in the last analysis merely a sum of individuals taken together as a juristic unit, and differing from the plurality of all its members for the time being only in that these members are not "distributive" but "collective sumuntur." Such a conception not only appears most explicitly in the most energetic champions of the political doctrine of popular sovereignty,[50] but is shown almost more sharply in the transference of this doctrine to the Church with reference to the "universitas fidelium" as the supreme 'subject' of the Church's power.[51]

Thus indeed the doctrine of popular sovereignty even in its medieval phase contained the germ, later to grow so luxuriantly, of a purely atomistic and mechanical construction of the 'People' regarded as the 'subject' of all State-power.

2. If now we ask whether and in what sense the concept of Sovereignty was already developed with reference to the rights in dispute between people and ruler, the answer is that this concept itself, wholly foreign as it was to the original system of

medieval thought, passed through the first stages of its growth within the medieval doctrine.

The external aspect of the concept of Sovereignty is only of indirect concern here. Suffice it to say that while at first the idea of the World-Society of Mankind excluded the notion of an external sovereignty of its parts, yet jurisprudence, through the distinction (specially emphasized since Bartolus) between "universitates Superiorem recognoscentes" and "non recognoscentes," gradually set up a concept of sovereignty which was at least relative, and was then made absolute partly by the philosophic reproduction of the antique idea of the State, and partly by the political opposition to the Emperor's "imperium mundi." [52]

The original system of medieval thought had no room for a concept of sovereignty even in its internal aspect. For it was filled through and through with the idea that every earthly power, even the highest, is a responsible Office borrowed directly or indirectly from God and held within certain legal bounds.[53]

But already in the twelfth century the old idea of the ruler's office was suppressed or at least modified by the rising doctrine of absolutism, which claimed a "plenitudo potestatis" for the Emperor in the Empire just as for the Pope in the Church. This monarchical omnicompetence was in fact vested more and more with all the attributes of sovereign power. Its bearer was placed above positive law; its content was declared to need no explanation; its substance was held to be inalienable, indivisible and imprescriptible; and every subordinate power was derived from it as a mere delegation.[54]

In course of time, however, the idea of Ruler's Sovereignty as thus conceived was not only applied to every independent State but was also stripped of its specifically monarchical dress. This was promoted on the one hand by the doctrine of the essential 'rights of superiority,' which was perfected by the long labor of jurisprudence and was ever more generally applied, and which conceived these rights as indestructible, inalienable and concentrated at one point by the very nature of government itself.[55] And on the other hand, with the reception of the Aristotelian doctrine of the forms of government and their classification, there was a revival of the idea that in every form of State some one ruler (imperans), whether visible as one man or as an assembly, is the 'subject' of a sovereign power over the ruled (parentes).[56]

Even the opponents of the sovereignty of monarchs did not again call in question the idea of sovereignty, but simply claimed for the People in every form of State the position of the true and proper ruler. Hence they strove with all their might against the idea of the monarchical "plenitudo potestatis," and for this purpose they revived the idea of the monarch's office by way of giving the people a superiority over offices.[57] But the same omnicompetence which they sought to wrest from the monarch was transferred with all its essential attributes to the assembly representing the people.[58] And thus indeed we are justified in speaking not only of a doctrine of sovereignty in the middle ages, but also of a doctrine of popular sovereignty.

Here we need only observe that the idea of sovereignty in the medieval doctrine was not only undeveloped in many details, but in two points of principle was far from being so exalted as it became in later times.

Firstly, it was unanimously believed that the sovereign power is not omnipotent as against the law, but while raised above positive law is nevertheless limited by Natural Law. Of this more below (Ch. VI.).

Secondly, it was as unanimously believed that the idea of the Sovereign by no means excludes an independent legal right of non-sovereign 'subjects' to share in the power of the State. On the contrary, advocates of the ruler's sovereignty expressly maintained a political right of the people, and advocates of the people's sovereignty expressly maintained a political right of the ruler, so that even in the extreme theories the State had somewhat of a 'constitutional' character. Hence it was thought possible to combine the sovereignty of the monarch with what was in principle a 'limited' monarchy.[59] Hence the idea of a 'mixed' constitution raised no awkward questions.[60] Hence also the beginnings of a doctrine of the separation of powers could grow on the soil of popular sovereignty.[61] Nevertheless the idea of sovereignty pressed forward irresistibly toward the conclusion that in the last resort some one of the several factors of the

State must be the 'subject' of the highest power, and that in cases of collision the State is visibly embodied by this factor in itself alone.

II. From the Reformation to Althusius

The medieval doctrine of popular sovereignty was at once an active and passive concomitant of powerful struggles and commotions in Church and State. It is beyond our purpose to show the interaction which here as everywhere exists between theory and practice, to follow the gradual popularization of the doctrine, and to explain its connection with the internal and external revolutions and disturbances of the Age of the Reformation. The result was that the idea of popular sovereignty, after having rendered an indispensable service in the birth of the modern world, gave way altogether to the absolutist idea. And so for a while even as a theory it disappeared from the scene.

Its revival took place in direct connection with the bloody sequel which the Reformation found in the repression of heretical sects by the strong arm of the monarchical State. The Reformed and Catholic Monarchomachi stood quite as far from the idea of tolerance as their opponents. Even they ascribed to the State the duty of maintaining the purity of the faith. Hence in order to defend themselves from the oppression of their own religion and church by the monarch, they sought to wrest the power of the State itself from the hands of the monarch and revived the doctrine of the sovereignty of the people.

Thus in the bulk of their books, written mostly for immediate effect, the theory already perfected in the middle ages was reproduced in essentials. It was but seldom that there emerged new viewpoints, sharper formulations and more far-reaching conclusions. In Althusius for the first time, not only did all the ideas previously stated, being fitted into a complete system of general public law, gain a higher scientific value and in particular a strictly juristic expression, but there were also added new ideas of great importance.

First of all, the fundamental principle was stated in the old terms, that the princeps is "major singulis minor universis," hence against the monarch the populus is major, superior, potior, dominus.[62] And some expressly assigned to the people a "major potestas ipso principatu" and hence the "summa potestas" in the State.[63] But Althusius first applied to the rights claimed for the people the precise concept of sovereignty presented in the State, and the word "majestas" which had been used as a technical term by the advocates of 'Ruler's Sovereignty.' [64]

The Monarchomachi were agreed that in relation to the people the ruler is a contractually appointed chief minister, to whom is granted an independent but 'resolutively' conditioned right to exercise the State's power.[65] At the same time they described the ruler's power as an authority limited by the scope of its mandate and the rights of the ruled, and bound by the constitution and the laws.[66] The relation of such an idea to the concept of monarchy and its incidental personal majesty was left uncertain.[67] Here also Althusius was the first to draw the full consequences of the principle. He worked out the idea of a mutually binding contract of employment, whereby the people as proprietor transfers the exercise of the rights of majesty which it cannot wield directly to a chief manager with an independent right of management within the scope of his mandate, following in every detail the forms of private law.[68] And above all he was the first to say expressly that apart from the majesty of the people there is no room for a majesty of the monarch, and that in truth there is no distinction of forms of the State but only a distinction of forms of government according as the "summus magistratus" is monarchic or polyarchic.[69]

With regard to the popular rights deduced from the superiority of the Community, all the Monarchomachi laid the chief stress on the right which they ascribed to the people to resist by force the ruler who has become a tyrant, to sit in judgment on him and if need be to depose and punish him. In this matter there was general agreement on the doctrine which was developed by the Reformed partisans from the teachings of Calvin quoted above (Ch. I. Note 4), was taken over unchanged by the champions of the Ligue, and was erected into a system by Althusius. Men taught that the legitimate ruler becomes a tyrant by violating his official duty; that against such a "tyrannus quoad exercitium" the private individual has only the right of passive resistance (while against the "tyrannus quoad titulum" any man may do anything); that on the other hand the inferior magistrates, being entrusted with the protection of the people, are empowered and bound to resist his tyrannical measures actively, and if need be by force of arms. And lastly that the people itself, through its representative assembly or in default thereof in direct assemblage, has the right to sit in judgment on him, to correct him, if necessary to depose and punish him, even to put him to death or declare him outlawed as a public enemy.[70] For the case of an obstruction of this regular process by the power of the ruler or the malfeasance of the majority of representatives, this doctrine appeared in most of its advocates as a more or less explicit appeal to revolution,[71] and in Mariana as the approval of tyrannicide,[72] while Althusius held fast here as everywhere to the idea of a formal and sacred constitutional right. In the second place all the Monarchomachi emphasized as among the people's rights not absorbed by the contract of rulership the decisive share in the making of laws.[73] Some also laid stress on the people's ownership of the domain and property of the State.[74] Then the proposition was advanced that all officers of the State (unlike officers of the royal household) are really ministers of the sovereign people, on whom alone they are dependent even though the ruler has appointed them or vested them with hereditary rank.[75] Lastly, Hotman, by way of expanding the reserved rights of the people to a system of permanent control, drew the picture of a parliamentary monarchy in which the Estates General, in the name of the people, takes an authoritative share ("auctoritatem sanctam inviolatamque") in all matters pertaining to the welfare of the whole State ("statum Reipublicae universum").[76] But Althusius worked out a scheme of popular rights necessarily reserved against the chief magistrate in all forms of government alike, assigning to the representative assembly, or in default thereof the direct assemblage of the people, not only a permanent share in the government but the exclusive decision in the weightiest matters, the ruler being obliged to execute these decisions as they are delivered to him (above, p. 43–44).

Lastly, as to the proof of the principle of popular sovereignty, there appear in the Reformed Monarchomachi not only theological arguments which are partly new, but above all there are attempts at a concrete historical proof from the legal history of particular countries. On the other hand, the rational argument remains essentially as of old. It rests throughout on the doctrine of contract, with the help of which it seeks to prove that the people's right, being the source of the ruler's right, must also be the superior right; that the ruler, existing by the people, for the people and never without the people, is subordinate to the people; that in appointing the ruler the people, contracting freely and rationally, cannot have intended a complete alienation of its liberty.[77] To this highly questionable line of argument Althusius adds a wholly new argument of lasting effect in combining with the deduction from the nature of the contract the deduction from the nature of sovereignty. In this way he arrives at the propositions which so greatly astonish his contemporaries, as to the absolute inalienability, indivisibility and imprescriptibility of the sovereign rights of the people (above, p. 34 and 42). Even in this direction it is true that various suggestions had been made before him; [78] but no one before him had expressly stated these far-reaching principles, much less supported them with such a wealth of logic.

When all is said it is evident that the doctrine of popular sovereignty in Althusius owes its new and distinctive features chiefly to the use of a more precise concept of sovereignty. Hence before tracing the later fortunes of the doctrine we must again on the one hand glance at the history of the idea of sovereignty in general, and on the other hand we must inquire as to what changes there were in the conception of the 'subjects' contending for this sovereignty.

   1. The medieval idea of sovereignty, so far as we are concerned with its application to the internal life of the State, found no new scientific expression of any importance before Bodin. The prevailing doctrine ascribed to the ruler a sovereign State-power, but tended rather to strengthen than to discard the limitations immanent in the received idea of sovereignty.

The theological revival of the theocratic idea due to the

Reformation emphasized not only the divine right of rulership but its official character as well, with the duties and limitations arising therefrom; [79] and in case of violation there was often maintained a right of active resistance on the part of the people and even the right to depose the faithless ruler.[80] Positive jurisprudence held fast to the idea of a sovereignty of the ruler grounded on an alienation of the original sovereignty of the people.[81] But its leading representatives themselves, seeking to take away the traditional meaning of the maxim "princeps legibus solutus est," argued strongly for the subjection of the sovereign power to the constitution and the law,[82] and besides the right of the sovereign there was almost universal recognition in principle of an independent right of the people in the State.[83] Among the teachers of Natural Law the Catholic school of clerics in particular weakened the idea of the ruler's sovereignty without actually denying it, in such a way that it sometimes led to results quite like those of the doctrine of popular sovereignty.[84] And among the strictly political writers Machiavelli had a truly immense influence in magnifying the idea of sovereignty, but the theoretical construction of the State was not directly touched upon by him and otherwise it remained on the basis of the Aristotelian doctrine.

Thus Bodin really did an epoch-making thing when he not only formulated the idea of "Souveraineté" or "jus majestatis" in the strict sense of the "summa in cives ac subditos legibusque soluta potestas," but also followed out all its consequences with inexorable logic. When on the one hand he declared that the nature of sovereignty is incompatible with any limitation in time or in substance, any restriction by constitution or laws, or any severance of parts by alienation, division or prescription of time, and on the other hand recognized a unitary ruler, whether one man or one assembly, as the only possible 'subject' of sovereignty, he totally extinguished the idea of a Constitutional State. For him there are only the three simple forms of the State, absolute democracy, absolute aristocracy and absolute monarchy, the last of which is the best. He altogether rejects the idea of mixed forms, which by reason of the partition of sovereign powers should rather be called "corruptiones rerumpublicarum."

In order to explain the modified forms of government existing in the world he sets up the distinction between the "status Reipublicae" and the "ratio gubernandi," which latter is to be distinguished from the form of the State but consists only in the organization of the offices which serve the Sovereign as instruments of government. At the same time he rejects as equally illogical the idea of a limited monarchy, as here the king would be a king in name only while in fact the "universitas populi" would be sovereign. To the true Monarch the Sovereignty is conveyed completely, permanently and unconditionally; he is dispensed from every human law and can by his own act annul the privileges of the whole community, of individuals and of corporations; for him the resolutions of a parliament can be no more than mere advice; there is no possible right of resistance against him for alleged tyranny.[85] Bodin's absolutist idea of sovereignty stops short only at private law; contracts bind even the Sovereign, and personal liberty and property must be recognized by him as inviolable.[86]

Bodin's idea of sovereignty was received without hesitation by the champions of absolute monarchy. It was followed out with slight moderations by Gregorius Tholosanus,[87] and was ued by Barclay in the struggle against the Monarchomachi.[88] Even in Germany it found favor,[89] and was elaborated with logical precision by Bornitz.[90]

While most writers on politics and public law held to the principle of the ruler's sovereignty, yet they were averse from absolutism and in particular they maintained the possibility of mixed or limited forms of rulership; hence even when accepting the stricter formulation of sovereignty they could not deny that it might be relaxed in one way or another.[91] Above all the German publicists, who in spite of Bodin regarded the Emperor as a true monarch in the Empire conceived as a unitary State, could not refuse such concessions. If with Bodin they rejected the mixed form of the State as impossible, as was expressly done by Fridenreich and Reinking,[92] they must, in order to save the sovereignty for the Emperor, treat constitutional limitations and even the removability of the monarch as compatible with full "majestas." [93] If conversely they maintained with Bodin the impossibility of limiting the sovereign, as was done by Arni-saeus,[94] they must, in order to regard the Emperor as a monarch, affirm the possibility of a mixed constitution with a division of sovereign powers among several 'subjects.'[95] The prevailing opinion, however, held to the old idea that sovereignty may be limited as well as divided.[96] Thus the Germanic Empire was as a rule held to be a polity compounded of monarchy and aristocracy, in which there was ever more definitely established an actual division of sovereignty among several 'subjects' which were fully sovereign only in conjunction.[97]

Molina and Suarez came to terms in their own way with the more precise concept of sovereignty, without breaking with the traditional Jesuit theory of the State. They held that the contract of rulership is a true alienation of the people's sovereignty, and thus the ruler is sovereign ("Superior tota Republica").[98] But they not only taught that, as the people may reserve the sovereignty to itself, so it may transfer it with whatever reservations it sees fit and hence may establish a limited or a merely partial 'ruler's sovereignty,'[99] but they also assumed that in all cases by the very nature of the State the ruler is bound by positive law and by the permanent rights of the people.[100] In particular they held that sovereignty when once transferred is a strict and irrevocable right, but at the same time they gave to the people the right of resistance and deposition in case of tyranny, as beyond the sphere assigned to it every right and even the right of majesty ceases and thus the original sovereignty of the people comes again into force.[101]

Thus in whatever way the rigid concept of sovereignty came to be relaxed wherever an independent political right was reserved to the people or its representatives even in a monarchy, it would seem that the Monarchomachi were least of all bound to preserve it intact. Hence at first they operated as little as possible with the technical concept and term "majestas," left the nature of the rights assigned to the monarch largely obscure, and did not impugn the traditional doctrine of the forms of State. Hotman (Francogallia, c. 12) and Daneau (Politices, I. c. 6) expressly upheld the idea of the 'mixed' form and its advantages, while Buchanan as well as Hooker fostered the growth of the English principle of the separation of powers.[102]

Thus it was truly a bold and original stroke when Althusius accepted the absolutist idea of sovereignty in all its rigor and transferred this sovereignty to the people. He was the first to speak of the 'majesty' of the people. He first expressly gave to this 'majesty' the attributes of exclusive, inalienable, indivisible and permanent which Bodin had claimed for the 'majesty' of the ruler, and rejected as strongly as his opponents the idea of the mixed constitution and the division of powers. He first broached the idea that as there can be only one rightful sovereign, there can be only one rightful form of the State, while the so-called three forms of the State are merely distinctions of forms of government.[103] And when he pointed out the contradiction between the assumption that sovereignty is inalienable and the derivation of the ruler's sovereignty from an alienation of the original sovereignty of the people, he hit upon a truly vulnerable spot in the opposing theory. It was but a paltry shift when Suarez and later Grotius answered by alleging the possibility of giving oneself into slavery.[104]

In but one important point did Althusius correct Bodin's idea of sovereignty: filled with the idea of the legal and constitutional State, he rejected the whole notion of "potestas absoluta" and treated the sovereign power itself as bound not only by Divine and Natural Law, but also by positive law and especially the fundamental law.[105] Thus while recognizing the public as well as private rights of subject persons and groups of persons as against the sovereign, despite his sharpened concept of popular sovereignty he agreed with his predecessors in ascribing to the legitimately instituted powers a right which, within its assigned limits, is not to be violated even by the people (see above, Ch. II. Note 44).

2. When we next inquire as to the conception of the 'subjects' contending for sovereignty, there is in this respect no great advance on medieval ideas to be noticed in this period.

As before, the analogy of the State with an organism was often worked out,[106] and the corporative nature of the body politic was sometimes described with juristic precision.[107] But men did not yet reach the point of conceiving the immanent vital unity of this body as a State-Personality. In the long-standing division of the State's 'right-subjectivity' between ruler and people (see above, p. 95 ff.) there were but few who expressly spoke of the personality of the State itself. And even these few construed the "persona civitatis" to mean nothing more than either the 'ruler's personality' or the 'people's personality' according to the sense of their own time.[108]

For the advocates of ruler's sovereignty the personality of the State was absorbed in the personality of the ruler. They described the ruler and him alone as the bearer of the active life of society, as the power which unifies, orders and animates the body politic, as the visible presentment of the State itself.[109] Hence in the Monarchy they had no need of the concept of juristic person for the construction of the State-power. But in the Republic they could not dispense with this concept, if indeed they wished to find in this case a unitary ruler-personality as the 'subject' of the State's power; but here they vied with each other in exalting a purely 'collective' conception, for which the unity of the republican ruler arose simply from the mechanical union of a ruling group of persons, and the ruler's personality was nothing but the artificial equation of a logical category with a real person.[110] And in like manner, in so far as they vested the people as such with a 'subjectivity' of rights against the sovereign, they conceived the people also as a collective person, seeking but to exclude it as much as possible from the presentation or co-presentation of the 'active' State.[111]

Conversely, for the advocates of popular sovereignty the State's personality was the same as the People's personality. Hence when they wished to denote the 'subject' of supreme power as distinguished from the ruler, they expressly identified the "populus," the "universitas populi" or "universitas civium et subditorum" with the "Respublica" or "Regnum." [112] If hereby in some measure the ruler as a self-subsisting 'subject' was excluded from the State, for the rest they declared that the people, as identified with the State, was a "universitas" endowed with personality and different from the sum of the "singuli." [113] And yet they could not rise above the conception of this unity as a plurality of individuals which was unified only when taken collectively, and treated by fiction after the analogy of a natural person.[114]

Althusius worked out far more distinctly and deeply than his predecessors the thought that the State is a social body, organically ordered and articulated and having a personality of its own. And often when he describes this "corpus symbioticum" as the 'subject' of sovereignty he seems to go over to the idea of State-sovereignty. But the theory of contract which he himself so greatly sharpened carries him at once far away from this goal. His idea of the contract of rulership forces him to divide the single personality of the State and to identify the sovereign body with the separately personified "universitas populi" as contrasted with the governing body. And his idea of the social contract makes him take the view that ultimately the people like any other "universitas" is nothing but a "consociata multitudo," an aggregate of "homines conjuncti, consociati et cohaerentes," a multitude connected by various mutual legal relations and in this conjunction regarded as a unity.[115]

Those writers who took an intermediate position in the question of sovereignty did not go beyond these conceptions of the State's 'right-subjectivity.' [116] When among these Molina and especially Suarez, in a fashion similar to Althusius, employed for the construction of the State the idea of a body governing its limbs, they also arrived in the end at no other concept of State-personality than that of Althusius.[117]

III. From Althusius to Rousseau

From Althusius to Rousseau there arose on the Continent no system of politics in which the doctrine of popular sovereignty was fully and completely worked out; during this period its proper home was in England, a country disturbed by revolutions and governed by Parliaments. Here Milton based on this doctrine his pamphlets advocating a democratic Republic; he declared that the fundamental power of the people "cannot be taken from them without a violation of their natural birthright";

he degraded every monarch to an hereditary minister of the people, bound and limited by the laws, accountable for the faithful discharge of his mandate and subject at all times to control by parliaments and councilors, and who bears the title of "Lord" only by arrogance or flattery. He exalted the People as the superior and judge of the king, so that in case of tyranny it may punish him and put him to death, and even without such cause may depose him and alter the government ("merely by the liberty and right of free-born men to be governed as seems to them best").[118] Here also, while Sidney in his parliamentary constitution preserved, in name at least, the monarchical factor and postulated a constitutional division of powers,[119] yet essentially he championed an equally absolute sovereignty of the people as represented by Parliament.[120] Here lastly, Locke not only derived his scheme of the three powers from the original sovereignty of the people,[121] but while making the proper division of powers yield a full supremacy of the legislative body and a partial supremacy of the bearer of executive power,[122] he also claimed in his ideal constitutional monarchy a third and highest supremacy, normally suspended but in case of necessity dissolving the legislative power itself, as the inalienable right of the people.[123]

On the Continent also the theory had made such a deep impression on the minds of men that while no one still held it in its full extent it did not by any means disappear from the literature of public law.

Until after the middle of the seventeenth century the doctrine of popular sovereignty lived on in Germany and the Netherlands in the peculiar form of the wide-spread doctrine of the distinction between "majestas realis" and "personalis." This doctrine grew in direct provenience from the Politics of Althusius and in the result, despite its altered formulation and often very different practical aims, it differed but little theoretically from the doctrine of the hated anti-monarchists themselves. Its ever-recurring theme was that in all forms of State there is a two-fold sovereignty, since by the contract of rulership the ruler has a "majestas personalis" while the "respublica" reserves the indestructible "majestas realis," and that of these two sovereignties the 'personal' is necessarily subordinate to the 'real.' In this general sense the new theory was supported by many political writers and teachers of public law and was developed with many very important differences of detail. Among the authors of systems of politics it was held already by Kirchner, Boxhorn and Alsted, and later by Tulden, Werdenhagen, Liebenthal and Berckringer; [124] among the German imperialist publicists it was held, without using these technical terms, by Regner Sixtinus and more emphatically by Paurmeister; [125] many discourses were written on it by Arumaeus and his pupils, such as Otto, Brautlacht and above all Bortius; [126] it took an independent form in Besold; [127] it was accepted by Frantzken and Benedict Carpzov; [128] and lastly it was firmly held by Limnaeus.[129]

But a closer inspection of the writings of these men shows that with all of them "majestas realis" is but a new name for the old popular sovereignty which is retained in principle. Its 'subject' indeed is always taken as the "respublica," the "regnum" or the "imperium," so that one may be tempted to think of the idea of State-sovereignty; but these terms ultimately mean nothing else than the people personified in contradistinction to the ruler, and indeed the people in the sense of the collective unity of all.[130] In this matter it is characteristic that in a democracy the popular assembly acting by majority vote is assigned only the "majestas personalis," while the "majestas realis" is reserved for the community of all 'active' citizens, and from this is deduced the requirement of unanimity for constitutional changes and dispositions of the State.[131] And besides the sovereignty of the people the older sovereignty of the ruler is also conserved in the concept of majestas personalis and is embellished with all the usual attributes, but it is subjected to the former as the supreme and ultimate political power and is thus reduced to a merely relative importance. For this reason Alsted himself, in full accord with the Monarchomachi, accepted the idea of majestas personalis. And however strongly the other champions of the new doctrine might insist that the majesty of the ruler is a true sovereignty and not a mere magistracy, they must finally, in view of the popular rights recognized to a greater or less extent, drop the essential attributes of sovereignty from the majestas personalis. When they all agreed in ascribing to its 'subject' a power bound and restrained by the laws, limitable at will by the constitutions of the several States, and everywhere empowered to alter the fundamental laws or dispose of the State's substance and property only with the consent of the people,[132] when they expressly secured to the whole people the true and full ownership of all the rights of majesty,[133] when most of them granted to the people the right to resist and depose a ruler who breaks his contract,[134] it was but empty babble when at the same time they called the majestas personalis as well as the majestas realis a potestas summa, perpetua and even absoluta,[135] and sought by logical sleight-of-hand to escape the contradiction that of two powers one is subordinate to the other as 'higher' and yet both are equally 'highest.' [136] And for the rest, in this system the more precise concept of sovereignty was always held for the majestas realis,[137] while for the majestas personalis it was often willingly given up. In particular many adherents of this doctrine found in the idea of a double majesty a handle whereby to treat the majestas personalis (in contrast to the majestas realis) as communicable and in one way or another divisible among several 'subjects,' and thus to save the idea of a mixed form of State.[138] Others at the same time held fast to the attributes of unity and indivisibility even for the majestas personalis and rejected the forma mixta, believing that this was made superfluous by the very fact that the co-operation of the majestas realis could be extended indefinitely.[139]

In this last point the imperialistic publicists also differed when they adopted the theory of double majesty in order to solve by its aid the problem of the political form of the Germanic Empire. Here they divided into two schools. The one taught, after the example set by Paurmeister,[140] that the Empire is a State compounded of monarchy and aristocracy, in which the majestas realis belongs to the people as a whole while the majestas personalis is possessed jointly by the Emperor and the Estates.[141] The other held, following the scheme worked out by Arumaeus, by way of rejecting the mixed form of State, that the Empire is a true monarchy, although limited and tempered by aristocratic modes of government, in which the majestas personalis belongs exclusively to the Emperor while the majestas realis is exercised by the Imperial Diet as the perfect representation of the people.[142] It is clear that the doctrine, especially in this second form, could follow out the system of Althusius with slight alterations and at the same time keep strictly upon the ground of the positive public law of the Empire.[143]

This being the case the opponents of the doctrine of popular sovereignty were not so wrong when they considered the theory of majestas realis and personalis as a mere variation of that doctrine and opposed it as such. In attacking the principle that the supreme power everywhere belongs to the people, they much preferred to deal with its expression in a theory whose logical untenability they could easily expose.[144] Mortally wounded by the proof of its self-contradiction, the doctrine which had once been so wide-spread finally vanished from literature after the middle of the seventeenth century.

Yet it was no less a one than Grotius who undertook to bring out and develop the true ideas which were implied or at least suggested by the notion of majestas realis. While he absolutely rejected popular sovereignty, whether pure or modified, it was obviously by the idea of double majesty, which was then well-nigh dominant, that he was led to adumbrate the theory of State-sovereignty. He held that, just as the power of vision may be said to be possessed by the whole body as well as by the eye, so also in the State there is a twofold 'subject' of supreme power: its "subjectum commune" being the whole body politic (civitas as the coetus perfectus), and its "subjectum proprium" the ruler ("persona una pluresve pro cujusque gentis legibus ac moribus").[145] But for the proper use of this idea Grotius did not have the means, as he wholly lacked the concept of State-personality. Though he started from the conception of the State as a 'moral body' analogous to the natural organism,[146] and though at every point he applied to the State the rules of corporation law,[147] yet for him a 'person' was either a natural individual or else a sum of individuals unified and held together by contract and treated as a unit by fiction.[148] Thus in particular, wherever he referred to a 'subject' of public or international rights, he specified as such either the "princeps" or else the "populus" in the sense of the collective community.[149] Thus it was that whenever he confronted the ruler with a political right located elsewhere or described him as the mere representative of the power of others, he could not conceive the rightful or represented 'subject' as other than the "populus universim sumptus" or the "populus universus." [150] It was a merely verbal difference when in this connection he sometimes put 'State' in place of 'people.' [151] Such being the case, the "subjectum commune" of Grotius was ultimately nothing else than the aggregate of the people and his State-sovereignty nothing else than the sovereignty of the people. But according to Grotius this aggregate was fully and completely represented by the ruler and this sovereignty of the people was visible and active in the sovereignty of the ruler alone. Hence the "subjectum commune" as such lost all active power and all real importance. Thus at last the distinction of which so much had been made turned out to be quite worthless and in fact it was never used in any of his later discussions. Yet the assumption that State-sovereignty is present everywhere did not hinder Grotius from asserting the possibility of a Patrimonial State, founded either on contract or on conquest, in which the State's power resides in the patrimony of the ruler and hence he may freely dispose of the State and its rights among living persons and in case of death.[152] Thus when in doubtful cases he required the concurrence of the people in alienating the domain or property of the State, setting up a Regency or altering the succession to the throne, he deduced this simply from the presumable terms of the normally existing contract of rulership, in which, until the contrary is proved, it must be assumed that the originally sovereign people has conceded only the usufruct of the State's power.[153] In like manner he based the right of resistance against the ruler, which he granted to the people under certain presuppositions, essentially on a reserved remnant of the original sovereignty of the people.[154] And wherever he found in any State a constitutional provision of permanent active rights of the people against the ruler, he traced these back to modalities of the contract of rulership as framed in concrete cases, granting the sovereignty under definite limitations compatible with its own nature,[155] or else dividing the ruler's sovereignty between King and People or among other 'subjects.' [156]

There were but few who maintained the doctrine of "subjectum commune et proprium majestatis" in the same sense as its inventor.[157] Most writers attacked it as not merely a superfluous but a harmful doctrine, which comes dangerously near to the pestilent notion of "majestas realis" and might well be regarded as its source.[158] Others, in order to clear Grotius of the reproach of even indirectly promoting popular sovereignty, endeavored as much as possible to explain or interpret his proposition in a looser sense.[159]

Thus on the Continent, after the middle of the seventeenth century, the theory of the exclusive sovereignty of the ruler was in possession of the field. The question whether and how far, outside of a pure democracy and especially within a monarchy, popular rights would be recognized as established or at least as possible, depended again simply on the conception of sovereignty on the one hand and of the State's personality on the other. In both respects Hobbes with his epoch-making deductions shook the whole structure of earlier doctrine. His propositions, partly through their own positive influence and partly through the opposition which they aroused, were the driving force in the later progress of both ideas.

1. After Bodin the concept of sovereignty, as we have shown, was weakened in all its nuances and exalted in none. Hobbes exalted it to the last degree, beyond which it was impossible to go. He described Sovereignty as the right to everything (jus ad omnia), being transmitted from the state of nature to the State and it alone, and its holder as the "mortal God" (Deus mortalis). Thus arises this all-embracing, boundless and irresponsible power of dominion, which absorbs the personality, property, rights, conscience and religion of the subjects, is bound by no law, contract or obligation, and knows no judge other than itself. In every form of State this power is the same, in every form it is necessarily concentrated in all its fullness at one point and is the exclusive source of all other powers. In its presence all subjects or groups of subjects, be they ever so unequal otherwise, are equal in rights or rather equally 'rightless.' Any contractual limitation conflicts with the very nature of the sovereign; it destroys his sovereignty and erects another sovereign.

Any division of powers is impossible, and so is any mixture of forms of the State. Absurd is the opinion that kings are "singulis majores" but "universis minores," as it is only in the king that the people is a "universitas"; without him it is nothing but a heap of "singuli." And lastly, the notion of the so-called perversions of the forms of State is also against reason, for while the sovereign has to take care of the "public interest," he is the sole judge of what is for the public interest.[160]

While before such a Ruler-sovereignty every right of the individual and of the community went down in hopeless defeat, yet scarcely any one else made such an unconditional surrender of the rights of man;[161] but at the same time, so far as concerned the extinction of the rights of the people collectively, all the strictly absolutist systems accepted the Hobbesian concept of sovereignty intact or with slight modifications. For determining the scope of sovereignty when once established, it made no difference whether they also took as its source an individualistic original contract,[162] or recurred to a direct grant from God.[163] And even the assumption, still generally maintained, of an original sovereignty of the people (see above, p. 95 ff.) was in itself no hindrance to the reception of the Hobbesian concept of sovereignty, as the sovereign people was only given the choice of either making itself the absolute ruler by setting up a direct democracy, or alienating its own sovereignty, with all its essential marks, fully and irrevocably to a ruling monarch or aristocracy.[164]

Conversely, whoever proposed any moderation of the principle of absolute rulership by popular rights, or the possibility of a Constitutional State, would find that he must grapple with the concept of sovereignty itself, and must pierce at some point or other the impregnable armor of Hobbes's iron-clad Sovereign. Accordingly Huber made a most elaborate attack on the absolutist idea of sovereignty and resumed the old idea of measuring the State's power by the tacit or express clauses of the fundamental contract.[165] Still farther went Leibniz, who, considering the relativity of all human conditions, was in principle strongly opposed to the prevailing method with its tendency to set up absolute logical categories and to govern life by the pedantry of schools, and who himself recognized only a relative concept of sovereignty.[166] Other writers who, like von Seckendorf, undertook to instruct Princes in the duties of their station, did not enter into the dispute about principles but set themselves against the exaltation of the idea of sovereignty by emphasizing anew the character of rulership as an office bound both morally and legally.[167] And even the strictly absolutist writers on politics were driven to various modifications of the rigid concept of sovereignty, according as they upheld the authority of Aristotle against the attacks of the moderns,[168] or accepted the doctrine, almost universally recognized in positive public law, as to the binding force of fundamental laws and the inalienability of the State's domain and property without the consent of the people.[169]

In Germany especially the prevailing doctrine found itself compelled to maintain the idea of the mixed form of State, owing to the fact that it could not refuse the Emperor the rank of a Monarch, and yet after the Peace of Westphalia [1648] it could not possibly vest him with an exclusive Ruler's-sovereignty. Yet it gradually found the formula whereby it hoped to avoid the reproach of rending asunder the one and indivisible Sovereignty. Ever more decidedly it stated the principle that in the mixed form of State the supreme power is not divided but simply belongs to a single 'subject' composed of two or three factors. And thus for the Germanic Empire it reached the doctrine which at last was generally and in some sort officially received, that the monarchical Head and the aristocratic Body of Estates are conjointly (conjunctim) the 'subject' of majesty, and that the Emperor as "imperans" embodies the true sovereign only when taken together with the Imperial Estates as "coimperantes." [170]

Yet this doctrine had to fight for its success in severe struggles against the two famous attacks which the whole accepted theory of imperial public law encountered in the seventeenth century. And in both cases the sharpest weapons of its opponents were taken from the theory of sovereignty.

When in the year 1640, amid the wreckage of war, Bogislaus Philipp von Chemnitz launched his fiery book on the government of the Germanic Empire, the earliest political work of

Hobbes had not yet been published. But this bold enemy of the Imperial House needed nothing more than Bodin's conception of sovereignty, accepted by him throughout, to prove that the Emperor is essentially nothing but the president of an aristocratic republic of Princes.[171] The work of Chemnitz had a great political effect; not only did its content affect the views of contemporaries but by its method it opened up an entirely new way of thinking on public affairs. At the same time it opened no new viewpoints for the doctrines of general public law, which served it merely as aids in political argumentation.[172] Even in the vexed question of the constitutional form of the Germanic Empire there were but few who accepted its positive result.[173] Yet in this respect it had so great an effect that it seemed hopeless to make any new attempt to explain the Empire as a limited monarchy, and thus the political thought of the Empire must, whether it liked it or not, submit to the idea of a mixed form of State.

Such a mixture of different forms of State was also assumed by Pufendorf as existing in the Empire, when in 1667 he published under a pseudonym his able criticisms of the Germanic State and his well-considered proposals of reform. Yet it was for this very reason that he described the imperial constitution as 'monstrous.' [174] He took this idea over into his great systematic works and wove it into his doctrine of sovereignty, which had a lasting influence on the development of political theories.

Pufendorf's doctrine of sovereignty rests on a moderation of the Hobbesian concept of sovereignty by applying the idea of contract after the manner of Grotius. For every form of State Pufendorf ascribes to the ruler a supreme, impunible, irresponsible power, exempt from every positive law, sacred and not to be infringed by the subjects, a power which exhausts in itself the content of all active political rights.[175] But first he deduces from the nature of the State-contract true (though unenforceable) obligations of the sovereign and true (though imperfectly protected) rights of the subjects against the sovereign (above, Ch. II. Notes 41 and 113). Then he accepts the theory of the distinctions in the "modus habendi" of a right which is in itself one and the same, and thus assumes that though the State-power may be "in patrimonio imperantis" yet in case of doubt it consists in the mere usufruct thereof.[176] Lastly and above all he seeks to prove that the supreme power is by no means necessarily absolute but on the contrary admits of constitutional limitations. In particular the ruler may, without losing his sovereignty, be bound by contract to ask the consent of the people or its assembly of deputies to certain acts; even a "clausula commissoria" added for the case of default does not deprive him of sovereignty, as this has the character of a 'resolutive condition,' a breach of which causes no judicial sentence to be passed but a "nuda contestatio" of forfeiture to take place. But according to Pufendorf's arguments the "imperium limitatum" remains an undivided and undiminished sovereignty only when, despite constitutional restraint, the will of the State is in the last resort exclusively represented by the free will of the ruler, so that the State wills and acts only through the ruler ("omnia quae vult civitas vult per voluntatem Regis"), and the effect of his will and act is conditioned only in certain definite respects by certain provisions ("conditio sine qua non").[177] The case is different when the ruler lacks any of the essential rights of lordship or may be bound in any positive matter to govern his will by the will of others. In this category Pufendorf includes even the case where a monarch has not the full liberty to summon or to dissolve the assembly of the people or its representatives, to make propositions to it or to reject its acts. In this case there is a division of powers. But every actual division of powers among several persons or assemblies is contrary to the nature of the State, as sovereignty, like the soul, is one and undivided ("unum et indivisum") and parts are distinguished in it only in the same sense that faculties are distinguished in the soul. Pufendorf admits that there are States with such a division of powers. But in this he perceives no new form of the State ("forma mixta"), but an irregular and monstrous formation. And thus he develops a special doctrine of "respublicae irregulares," which he declares to be morbid (like the Aristotelian παραβάσεις), but draws the distinction that here the seat of the malady is to be sought not in the administration but in the constitution itself.[178]

Pufendorf's doctrine of sovereignty, the offspring as it were of moderate and enlightened absolutism, had a powerful effect. Un-

til after the middle of the eighteenth century it was the leading
authority in general public law as systematically worked out in
Germany. Upon this foundation there built Thomasius, Hert,
Titius, Kestner, Gundling, and many others later.[179] Boehmer,
in his influential system (which Heineccius followed for the
most part), reproduced Pufendorf's doctrine of sovereignty,
merely giving it in a few points the aspect of a sharper absolutism.[180] And even Catholic text-books of general public law,
such as those of Schmier and Heincke, stood essentially on the
same ground.[181] But on the one hand, some of Pufendorf's followers wholly rejected the notion of Patrimonial States, which
they regarded as self-contradictory.[182] And on the other hand
the doctrine of irregular forms of State was only in part maintained as taught by its author,[183] being mostly developed and
transformed in such a way that at bottom it meant no more than
that certain legally valid constitutions cannot be subsumed under
the regular scheme without being thereby deprived of all their
living force and their adaptation to certain peoples and certain
times.[184]

Thus when in the prevailing doctrine the sharpening or blunt-
ing of the concept of sovereignty appeared as a measure of the
greater or less degree of absolutism, it is clear that the struggle
for popular rights, which was everywhere kindled anew in the
middle of the eighteenth century, must first press for the weakening or even the demolition of the idea of sovereignty. In this
direction there worked above all the constitutional doctrine
which was gradually conquering the minds of men. In England
it grew up slowly out of the doctrine of popular sovereignty,
due to the fact that this doctrine took up into itself two mod-
erating factors, on the one hand the idea of the mixed form of
government, and on the other hand the principle of a separation
of the different governmental powers as a complete safeguard
of the public welfare.[185] In the long dominant formulation
which Montesquieu gave it by finding a place for all these elements, it made a real and deliberate partition of sovereignty
among several 'subjects' quite independent of one another.[186]
At the same time in Germany, after Wolff, the 'Nature-Right'
theory of the State turned more and more toward a line of

thought which often mingled the principles of the ruler's sovereignty with that of the people's sovereignty, and in any case found in the idea of sovereignty, with all its rigidity taken out, no hindrance to making the State-contracts produce any desired constitutional forms with a division of powers and a mixed 'subject.' [187] And upon the ground thus leveled the doctrine of Montesquieu was even here received with greater or less modifications by political writers and the Constitutional State of this type was commended as the ideal State.[188]

In opposition to this whole development Rousseau again inverted the relation between the rights of the people and the concept of sovereignty by restoring the doctrine of the exclusive sovereignty of the people. Just as Althusius had once applied Bodin's concept of sovereignty, so Rousseau applied that of Hobbes to the indestructible right of the people. But before we discuss this we must cast a glance at the history of the concept of the State's personality.

2. The concept of the State's personality, as has been shown above, was not brought to light either by the doctrine of "majestas realis" or by the doctrine of the "subjectum commune." Hobbes, using the technical term "persona civitatis," brought it into sharp relief as no one had done before, and made it the keystone of the juristic construction of the whole 'right-subjectivity' of the State.

The State-personality of Hobbes, however, is nothing but the ruler's personality of the old doctrine, made absolute and mechanical. Hobbes is an individualist through and through, and this individualism is the source of his conception of the 'right-subjectivity' of corporations as well as the State. To be sure, in the picture of the great Leviathan he represents the State as a gigantic Body and works out in detail the analogy with a living body, but the supposed organism turns out to be nothing but a mechanism and the living body a mere automaton. Hobbes expressly uses the figure of an automaton or "artificial man" and the comparison with a watch or an engine moved by countless springs and wheels; he expressly describes the State as a skilfully contrived work of art with an artificial life and believes in the possibility of constructing it according to exact mathematical rules; and he expressly says that the covenant of the individuals is the creative act which here pronounces its "Fiat" (Leviathan, Introduction and Ch. 19–21). Thus for him the individuals are, and remain, the only true persons; in corporations as in the State there is only a "persona civilis," which is nothing but the "artificial person" of a "fictitious Body" (Lev., Ch. 16, 22). But this artificial personality cannot come into existence in any other way than when all the individuals settle by covenant that the authority, will and act of one individual or of a group of individuals united in a visible assembly and vested with power of the majority over the minority shall be legally considered as the authority, will and act of all the individuals (see Lev., Ch. 16 and 22, De Cive, Ch. 5 § 9–10, and especially the treatment of corporate delicts and liabilities). There is no other way of producing a unity in the multitude, and this applies to the State. But as the personality of every body, and of the State as well, can only be one, the person of the "one man or one assembly," erected into a "persona repraesentativa," absorbs without residue the whole possible personality of the collective body, which is a person only in and through the ruler and without him is a mere heap of individuals. It is the ruler who "personam omnium gerit," "cujus persona civium cunctorum persona est" and in whom the "tota civitas continetur" (De Cive, Ch. 5–7, 12, Lev., Ch. 16–18, 22). And hence the sovereign himself must be regarded not as the head but as the soul of this great Leviathan (Lev., Introd. and Ch. 19 ff., De Cive, Ch. 6 §19). A metaphor which, though often used before, had always been applied in a more spiritual sense to the State-power as such, and which for the first time, in this naked materialist reference to the physical personality of the ruler, developed its power to nip in the bud every idea of a real Group-Personality.

In exalting the idea of sovereignty Hobbes was not to be outdone; in the individualist structure of the State's 'right-subjectivity' he was outdone by Horn. Horn drew the last consequences of individualism when he asserted that in this world there is and can be no other 'subject' of rights than individuals, that every so-called 'social body,' and the State as well, is nothing but a sum of individuals, and that no contract has the power to change the many into a one, a multitude of men into a real whole. From this he argued that a true sovereignty in the sense of a unity superior to the individuals must on the one hand be of supermundane origin and on the other hand must belong to one man alone. At the same time he denied all possibility of a collective person distinguished in any way from the multitude of individuals comprised in it, and thus in the Republic he recognized neither a single 'right-subjectivity' of the State nor any true State-power.[189]

Horn's attack on the collective person remained isolated. The doctrine set up by Hobbes was then accepted unchanged by all writers who agreed with him in denying the continuance of a personality of the people apart from the personality of the ruler. It was brought into the field by Salmasius against Milton,[190] was inserted by Spinoza into his own system,[191] was used by Bossuet as a paraphrase of "l'État c'est moi," [192] and was held by many other publicists who added nothing of their own.[193] But it received its most important formulation from Pufendorf. This able thinker, in the doctrine of "entia moralia" which laid the basis of his system of Natural Law, taught that the human mind constructs the sphere of the moral world-order not from physical but from moral entities; hence all "entia" in this domain are attributes ("modi"), which we ascribe to natural things and motions for the purpose of regulating the freedom of the will; but these "entia moralia," which are formed, altered and dissolved by "impositio" (not by "creatio") are apprehended by our minds, immersed in matter, after the analogy of physical things ("ad normam entium physicorum"), and though in themselves they are all 'modes,' in their relations to one another they are again considered partly as subsisting "substantiae" and partly as inhering "modi." [194] Thus he came to see that personality in law is a conceptual attribute which must be sharply distinguished from natural existence, and which in relation to other legal concepts is conceived by us as a substance. And in this sense, as like all 'moral entities' it belongs to the sphere of the moral world, he gave it the name of "persona moralis" and replaced the orthodox distinction of physical and fictitious persons by the distinction of "personae morales simplices" and "compositae." [195] But when he entered into the analysis of the "persona moralis composita," the immanent individualism of the doctrine of Natural Law forced him wholly into the paths trodden by Hobbes. In contrast to the natural unity of the "persona simplex" he explained the total unity of the "persona composita" as the result of the contractual subjection of the powers and wills of all to the power and will of one man or one assembly, resolved the whole of this so-called collective personality into a representation of individuals by individuals based on relations of obligation, and thus introduced anew the element of the artificial and fictive, and hence indirectly the antithesis of the 'natural' person.[196] Thus indeed he constructed the State-personality, which he pushed into the very center, in exactly the same sense as the absorptive Ruler-personality of Hobbes. But for the sake of admitting limited forms of the State, he modified the doctrine of the perfect and exclusive representative force of the ruler's will and acts by his well-considered reasonings on the possibility of constitutional provisions for representative action.[197] In these circumstances Pufendorf's doctrine of "entia moralia" could not yield the proper fruit for the concept of personality. And while German publicists and teachers of Natural Law commonly accepted his doctrine in the result, they tended more and more to suggest that the "persona simplex" is also a "persona moralis," and set off the concept of the 'moral person' in contrast to the reintroduced 'physical person,' so as to reduce moral personality, in the State as elsewhere, to the relation of an artificial aggregation of natural persons to unity on the one hand and the contractual representation of the aggregate by an "imperans" on the other hand.[198] And after Boehmer sharpened the distinction of societas aequalis and inaequalis so that in the former he admitted only a collective relation while in the latter he laid all the more stress on the representative relation,[199] it seemed to some of the absolutist school that the hard-won concept of "persona civitatis" was quite superfluous, and that the concept of juristic person was needed for the construction of the State only when the ruler presented itself as a collective person.[200]

But Hobbes and Pufendorf were followed in their conception of the State's personality even by those advocates of ruler's-sovereignty who followed Huber in maintaining the idea of a continuing legal relation between the ruler as such and the people as a collective body (see above, p. 97). They often operated with the word and concept 'State-personality.' But even for them the State as such became visible solely in the naturally or artificially unified ruler, who was by virtue of the contract of submission the exclusive representative of all the subjects in every public will and act. And they affirmed that only apart therefrom is the people, in the sense of this aggregate of subjects taken as a collective unit, a distinct 'moral person.' [201]

Leibniz himself did not attain to any different conception of the "persona civilis seu moralis Reipublicae" of which he made so much.[202] Just as little advance was made by reviving the idea of the ruler's office.[203] And the historic-organic mode of thought, which was gradually being introduced, never attempted to make use of its own ideas on national life and spirit for the construction of the State's personality.[204]

On the other hand the more rigidly the theory of Natural Law, in the flood-tide of success, developed its abstract scheme of society (above, p. 104), the more decidedly did it construe the concept of 'moral person' in a purely mechanical and atomistic fashion. In this structure, built up of nothing but free and equal individuals and cemented only by obligations, the 'moral person' is nothing more than an abbreviated formula for any legal relation common to a sum of individuals. Hence this concept has value only from the outside, as it enables a multitude to be treated with regard to its own common sphere as a formal unit in relation to other 'subjects.' From the inside it proves to be perfectly worthless, as in this aspect legal relations cannot be conceived without dismembering the collective unit into its parts and resolving the common sphere into separate private spheres. Thus in particular the conception of the State in its totality as a 'moral person' gains a fundamental importance only in international law. In the sphere of internal public law the State's personality wholly disappears before the individualistic legal relations between different persons, which are reducible to relations of association and of mandate. Among these persons on the one hand, by virtue of the concept of "societas inaequalis" the ruling person or a group of ruling persons takes a superior position, and on the other hand the collectively competent groups of persons (and thus a ruling or jointly ruling assembly as well as the general body of the ruled) in relation to one another fall under the category of 'moral persons.' Thus the matter stands with Wolff.[205] But Nettelbladt carries out this line of thought in a most typical fashion. He sees the essence of the "persona moralis" in the fact that here a "non unum pro uno habetur" and is thus endowed with the legal capacities of the "persona singularis." [206] But he finds such a 'moral person' in every "societas," in marriage and all other family ties, in 'collegial' sovereigns, in tribunals and institutions, and in the collective body of the people as contrasted with the State, in just the same way as in corporations, communes, the Church and the State: for "quoties plurium individuorum humanorum intellectus, voluntates et vires tendunt ad idem, toties, quoad hoc idem, pro una persona sunt habenda sicque sunt persona moralis." [207] And in just the same way he always applies the idea of a single 'right-subjectivity' only in its external aspect, while internally he holds fast to the idea of contractual relations among a number of 'subjects' of rights. And thus he treats even the State in its totality as a 'moral person,' but identifies this with the mere collective unity of all the associated individuals,[208] who, according to the contract of transference, are represented only to a certain extent by certain physical or moral persons (§ 1133), and hence he affirms the unity of the State's personality only in the relations of international law.[209] For internal public law he makes no use of the State's personality as such, but resolves everything into obligations between the different physical and moral persons forming the State, whereby he finds no difficulty either in the division of sovereignty among several single or collective 'subjects' or in the radical dualism of the ruler's personality and the people's personality.[210] Quite similar views are expressed by Achenwall and other writers of this time,[211] until towards the end of the eighteenth century, with their ever wider diffusion, they attain that caricature which astonishes us in such a writer as the ingenious Schlözer.[212]

While the people, so far as it appears at all as a 'subject' of rights, is here conceived always as the mere collective unity of individuals, the English doctrine of popular sovereignty also worked out the same conception of the people without stating more precisely its relation to the concept of State-personality.[213] In this matter also Rousseau stood on the shoulders of the absolutist doctrine introduced by Hobbes and took up its strict conception of a unitary State-personality as an integral part of his own doctrine.

IV. Popular Sovereignty in Rousseau and his Successors

Thus Rousseau's doctrine of popular sovereignty appears as the outcome of a long development and as the ingenious combination of elements ready to hand.

In its groundwork the doctrine of Rousseau is directly connected with the Politics of Althusius. Like the latter it states, in terms which are often strikingly similar but repeated by no one else, that the sovereignty of the people established by the social contract is inalienable, incommunicable and indivisible;[214] that sovereignty belongs everywhere and necessarily, solely and exclusively, to the Community, and the usurpation of it by the government dissolves the whole State by a breach of the "traité social";[215] that the so-called forms of the State are nothing but forms of government.[216] But at the same time, unlike his forerunners, he teaches that the sovereignty of the people (applying the absolutist idea of sovereignty) is perfectly unlimited and illimitable,[217] is bound by no law or constitution,[218] and cannot be transferred even as to its exercise.[219] Thus by tearing down the contract of rulership he destroys, with the same radical consistency whereby Hobbes had destroyed the rights of the people, all possibility of a constitutionally established right of any other political factor as against the sovereign people, and especially any ruling person, whether an individual or a collective person.[220] Yet while he locates the substance of sovereignty in legislation alone, as the expression of the general will in general terms, and expressly divests the sovereign of the execution of laws as a specialized and necessarily dependent function, assigning it to a duly authorized non-sovereign 'subject,'[221] yet he makes it possible not only to say that the institution of a Government is an essential requisite of the State, but also to ascribe to the governing body a moral personality of its own, a real (though only derivative) life and an independent (at least a relatively independent) power over the individuals. And thus while strongly repudiating the doctrine of the division of powers, he borrows from it those ideas which can be used in his own doctrine.²²² As to the question of the 'subject' of sovereign power, Rousseau like Althusius makes the contract of union produce a social body vested with power over its members, which despite its artificial existence he often compares to the human body, and like Hobbes he carries out the idea of the necessarily single and indivisible personality of this body.²²³ But he knows no other way of reaching the unity of the State's personality than the well-worn path of a collective summation of individuals, and works out his 'individualistic collectivism' all the more rigidly as he rejects the aid of the idea of representation. While taking the "volonté générale" as the sovereign, he takes pains to show its diametrical opposition to the "volonté de tous." But on closer inspection the whole difference turns out to be that in the 'will of all' the concrete differences of particular wills are treated as co-existing, while in the 'general will' the individual differences of particular wills are cancelled out by the summation of the common elements, thus producing an average will (II. c. 3). And thus Rousseau's sovereign State-personality remains nothing but the sum of the individuals present at any given moment. He reckons that in a State composed of ten thousand citizens each one has "la dix-millième partie de l'autorité souveraine," in a State of a hundred thousand citizens each has only one hundred-thousandth part, and hence as the State is enlarged liberty diminishes (III. c. 1). He declares that the sovereign is present and can act only in the direct assemblage of all (III. c. 12). And he strikes out of his public law all subjection of the sovereign of today to the sovereign of yesterday, so that the preservation of the force of laws rests on the simple fact that the present sovereign tacitly confirms what he does not abrogate (III. c. 11), but at any moment by a simple act of the people the whole established legal system may be swept away (III. c. 18).²²⁴

With Rousseau the history of the doctrine of popular sovereignty closes, as it has reached the end of the course in which it had been steadily driven forward since the middle ages by the logical evolution of the germinal ideas latent in it. Rousseau's doctrine could be outdone in details but not in principle. In fact the extreme parties of the French Revolution could propose nothing in this line but to carry out as fully as possible the ideas of the Contrat Social, and the revolutionary theory was not only unable to augment the principles of its master but was even forced to weaken them in many ways by accommodation to real life.[225]

In Germany it was Fichte who in his system of Natural Law most decidedly took up Rousseau's doctrine of popular sovereignty. When in his draft of the only rightful constitution he offered his own version of the separation of powers, he modified in practice even more than in principle the sovereignty of the people which he also raised above all constitutional law.[226] It was in vain that he strove, on a basis of strict individualism, for a construction of the State as an organic whole,[227] and for the concept of a real Group-Personality,[228] while at the same time he did not go beyond the identification of the sovereign people with the sum of the abstractly conceived individuals,[229] and of the ruling general will with the sum of the concurrent individual wills.[230]

Kant himself, plainly following Rousseau, accepted the doctrine of popular sovereignty in principle.[231] But in its application he recast it into a peculiar and quite different system of politics. In the first place, for practical purposes he forbade to this sovereign people all 'wrangling' over the origin of the supreme power after it has once been established, and wholly rejected any supposed right of revolution, of coercion, of resistance or of disobedience toward the ruler. On the contrary he taught that all subjects are bound 'to obey the law-making power now existing, be its origin what it may.' And he not only treated but expressly described the 'supreme head of the State,' again and again, as a 'sovereign' who in fact absorbs all popular rights, even though in principle he is a mere 'agent' of the true sovereign and a mere 'representative' of the sovereign general will.[232] Thus the idea of popular sovereignty became a mere directive theorem posited by reason and a 'touchstone' of material rightfulness for the acts of the formally sovereign ruler; it became an 'idea of reason' to make the laws such 'that they could have arisen from the united will of a whole people, and to regard every subject, so far as he claims to be a citizen, as if he had given his consent to such a will.' [233] In the next place Kant indeed set up his ideal of a 'Republic' as the only rightful and definitive form of the State, which he evidently hoped would be gradually realized through the existing government, and in which the united people is itself the sovereign, not merely represents the sovereign; but this ideal State bears the marks of a Constitutional State in which the people's sovereignty is not only active in a representative assembly alone but also, by strict observance of the principle of the separation of powers, sinks into perfect impotence as against the holder of executive power.[234] And lastly Kant himself, using the concept of 'moral person' only in the atomist and mechanical sense of the individualist theory of Natural Law, could not rise to the idea of a real State-personality,[235] but rather held to the identification of the State with the sum of the united individuals and of the sovereign general will with the concurrent and united will of all.[236] But when at this point he worked out his distinction of "homo phaenomenon" and "homo noumenon," and brought the individual, 'simply by virtue of his manhood' as homo noumenon and so far as 'the pure rightly-legislating Reason' presents itself in him, to take part in forming the general will; when he conceived law-making as the collective exercise of the autonomy of the individual will, which is determinable by reason and to be determined by a categorical imperative, whereby with reference to the external limits of freedom the categorical imperative, given *a priori* in all rational beings, becomes an externally binding law: [237] in the last analysis he substituted the sovereignty of the abstract Law of Reason for the sovereignty of a living 'subject.' [238] Thus, as in the case of the social contract (above, p. 111), we may regard the Kantian formulation of the doctrine of popular sovereignty as the beginning of the theoretical downfall of this dogma.[239]

But here we stop. We should have to enter a wholly new

circle of ideas, turning more and more away from 'Nature-Right' theories of the State, if we were to show how the principles of People's-sovereignty and Ruler's-sovereignty were conceived in later days; how their strife was carried on, while the new idea of State's-sovereignty set up its claim to a theoretical solution of this strife; how the concept of sovereignty itself was remolded in all manner of ways under the influence of modern ideas of the Constitutional State; how the concept of State-personality, brought forth anew out of the historic-organic conception of the people, made it possible on the one hand to overcome the dualism of Ruler's-personality and People's-personality without giving up the legal correlation of the rights of ruler and people, and on the other hand to overcome the principle of the division of powers, which disrupts the unity of the State, without giving up the constitutional distribution of powers.

NOTES

1. See also F. v. Bezold, Die Lehre von der Volkssouveränetät während des Mittelalters, in Sybel's Historische Zeitschrift, Vol. 36 (1876), p. 313–367.

2. In particular it was always taught that the consent of the whole people is requisite for the validation of any acts of the ruler which are prejudicial to the rights of the whole; and among these acts were reckoned subjection to another lord, alienation or partition of the domain, or indeed any renunciation of the essential rights of lordship. Thus Oldradus, and following him Baldus, on Prooem. Feud. nr. 32, and II. Feud. 26 § 4 in generali, nr. 3; Picus a Monte Pico on I. Feud. 7, nr. 7; Decius, Consilia, 564 nr. 9–10; Franciscus Curtius junior, Consilia, 174 nr. 17. Thus, to support the Donation of Constantine, a consent of the people was feigned to have been given; Baldus on Prooem. Dig. nr. 44–45, and II. Feud. 26 § 4, nr. 3; Aug. Triumph., II. q. 43 a. 3; Ant. Ros., I. c. 69; Franc. Curtius, loc. cit. nr. 18. On the other hand Lupold of Bebenburg deduced from this undisputed principle the invalidity of any concessions of any Emperor to the Church which were prejudicial to the Empire; c. 8 p. 367 and c. 12 p. 381, but especially c. 14 p. 395–397; similarly Ockham, Dial. III. tr. 2, l. 1, c. 30.—Furthermore it was explained, on the basis of l. 8 Cod. 1, 14, that it was a rule, not

indeed of law but of custom, that every monarch should of his own accord bind himself not to make laws or do other important acts of government without the consent of the whole people or its representatives; see the Commentaries on l. 8 Cod. 1, 14; also Baldus on II. Feud. 26 § 1, nr. 13.

3. See for example Petrus de Vineis, Ep. I. c. 3 p. 105; Lup. Beb., c. 17 p. 406–407 (even though the rex were maior populo); Ockham, Octo qu., II. c. 7, VI. c. 2, III. c. 3; Ant. Ros., III. c. 16.—To the contrary Baldus on l. 8 Dig. 1, 3 nr. 5–11, and I. Feud. 26 nr. 15.

4. Thus the passages cited above, Ch. II. Note 24.

5. Thus the passages cited above, Ch. II. Note 25.

6. Thus the opinions of the Glossators cited in Gl. Ord. on l. 9 Dig. 1, 3 v. "non ambigitur," on l. 11 Cod. 1, 14 v. "solus imperator," and on I. Feud. 26 v. "an imperatorem"; Cinus on l. 12 Cod. 1, 14; Christof. Parcus on § 6 Inst. 1, 2 nr. 4; Zabar. on c. 34 § verum, X. 1, 6 nr. 8; Paul. Castr. on l. 8 Dig. 1, 3 nr. 4–6; Ockham, Octo qu., IV. c. 8; Lup. Beb., c. 12 and 17.

7. Thus already Manegold of Lautenbach (above, Ch. II. Note 2); Mars. Pat., I. c. 15 and 18, II. c. 26 and 30; Lup. Beb., c. 17 p. 406; Ockham, Octo qu., II. c. 8; Miles in Somn. Virid., I. c. 141; Wyclif, Art. 17; Nic. Cus., III. c. 4; see also Durandus, Tract. de legibus, concl. 10 and 11; and for elective kings Innocent IV on c. 1 X. 1, 10 nr. 1–2.—It was just this principle that the writers of the imperialist party were most anxious to prove; for here might be found an explanation of those cases in which the Pope had, or seemed to have, deposed Emperors and Kings and absolved nations from the duty of obedience, especially the case of the dethronement of the last Merovingian king. Such precedents might be regarded as legal without any recognition of papal power. The authority had in all cases come from the people or its representatives, while the Pope's action had been merely 'declaratory' ("non deposuit papa, sed deponendum consuluit et depositioni consensit; a iuramento absolvit, i. e. absolutos declaravit"). Special reference was here made to Huguccio and Gl. Ord. on c. alius, C. 15, q. 6; see Joh. Paris., c. 15; Mars. Pat., De translatio imperii, c. 6; Lup. Beb., c. 12 p. 386–389; Ockham, Octo qu., II. c. 8, VIII. c. 1 and 5, Dial. III. tr. 2, l. 1, c. 18; Somn. Virid., I. c. 72–73; Quaestio in utramque partem, p. 106 ad 15 and 16; Nic. Cus., III. c. 4.

8. Def. pac., I. c. 7–8, 12–13, 15, 18, II. c. 30, III. concl. 6.

9. De iure regni, c. 12 p. 385 and c. 17 p. 406.

10. De concordantia catholica, III. c. 4 and 41, and II. c. 12–13. His projects for the reform of the Empire are connected with these theories, and in a remarkable fashion combine the forms of the medieval 'Land-Peace' associations with the idea of popular sovereignty, III. c. 25–40.

10a. See in particular the transactions of the French Estates of 1484, and on them Bezold, p. 361 ff., and Baudrillart, p. 10; also the remarks of Philippe de Comynes in Baudrillart, p. 11 ff.; lastly Almainus, Expos. ad Occam, q. I. c. 5 and 15, Tract. de auctor. eccl., c. 1 (in Gerson, Op. II. p. 977 ff.), Quaestio resumptiva (ib. p. 964).

11. In particular, on the one hand, the system of papal elections was always recalling the idea that during a vacancy of the Holy See the General Council as "collegium universalis ecclesiae" represents the Church, is merely represented by the Cardinals in the election of the Pope, and in case of their default must make the election itself. See even Augustinus Triumphus, I. q. 3 a. 2, q. 4 a. 1–8, q. 6 a. 6, who seeks to save the strict monarchical principle by distinguishing the 'potential superiority' ("maioritas potentialis") of the Council from the 'actual superiority' ("maioritas actualis") existing only in the Pope. On the other hand, the then undoubted doctrine that in matters of faith the Church alone is infallible and that the Pope may err and be deposed (see Schulte, Die Stellung der Koncilien, Prague 1871, p. 192–194 and 253 ff.), led to the view that in this exceptional case the Pope is subjected to the judgment of the whole Church (iudicatur a tota ecclesia, condemnatur a concilio generali, iudicatur a subditis). See c. 13 C. 2, q. 7, and c. 6 D. 40; also the opinions of Canonists collected by Schulte, op. cit., Anh. nr. 299, 301–317, 319–320. Moreover Gl. Ord. on c. 9 C. 24, q. 1 v. "novitatibus"; Innocent IV on c. 23, X. de verb. sig. 5, 40 nr. 2–3; Host., de accus., nr. 7; Johannes de Anania on c. 29 X. 3, 5 nr. 9 ff. A breach with the principle "sedes apostolica omnes iudicat et a nemine iudicatur," which from another aspect men strove to conceal by means of the fiction that an heretical Pope, being spiritually dead, has ipso facto ceased to be Pope, and that the General Council merely declares this fact in the name of the Church, of which it is now the sole representative. This is suggested by Johannes Teutonicus (in Schulte, loc. cit. nr. 310), and is urged by Aug. Triumph., I. q. 5 a. 1, 2, 6, and q. 6 a. 6, and Alv. Pel., I. a. 4–6 and 34, II. a. 10; see also the Clericus in Somn. Virid., II. c. 161, and the lengthy discussions in Ockham, Octo qu., III. c. 8, VIII. c. 5–6, Dial. I. 6 c. 66–82.

12. It was inferred that though the Pope as a general rule is superior to the Church, yet in matters of faith he is inferior to the Council; see Huguccio, in Schulte p. 260; Ockham, Dial. I. 5 c. 27, 6 c. 12–13, 57, 64; Michael de Cesena, Ep. of 1331 (in Goldast, II. p. 1237); Henricus de Langenstein, Consilium pacis (1381), c. 13 and 15 (Gerson, Op. II. p. 824 and 832). The conciliar jurisdiction over the Pope was soon extended to cases of notorious crime, schism and other evils which endangered the welfare of the whole Church; Huguccio, loc. cit.; Ockham, Octo qu., I. c. 17, II. c. 7, III. c. 8, VIII. c. 5–8, Dial. I. 6 c. 86; Letter of the University of Paris, 1394

(in Schwab, Johannes Gerson, Würzburg 1858, p. 131-132, and Hübler, Die Constanzer Reformation, Leipzig 1867, p. 362); Matthaeus de Cracovia, in Hübler p. 366–367; Pierre Plaoul, in Schwab p. 147; Zabar., De schismate, in Schard, p. 697. With this was also connected the legal theory of necessity, already involving general arguments of natural right, whereby in case of need the whole Church is authorized to act without the Pope and against the Pope; see especially Hübler, p. 368 ff., and Schwab, p. 146 ff., 211, 220.

13. Joh. Paris., c. 6 p. 115–158, c. 14 p. 182, c. 21 p. 208, c. 25 p. 215–224.

14. Mars. Pat., II. c. 7, 15–22, III. c. 1–2, 5, 32, 34–36, 41; Ockham, Dial. III. tr. 2, l. 3, c. 4–13 (the election of the Pope is a right delegated to the Cardinals by the whole Community), Octo qu., I. c. 15, III. c. 9, Dial. III. tr. 1, l. 1, c. 1 (limited power of the Pope), Octo qu., I. c. 17, III. c. 8, Dial. I. 5 c. 27, 6 c. 12–13, 57, 64, 69–72, 86 (the Council binds the Pope by its decrees, and can judge him, depose him and deliver him to the secular arm for punishment), Dial. I. 6 c. 84 (right of the Church to assemble of itself by analogy with every autonomous populus, communitas or corpus); see above, Ch. I. Note 21.

15. Mars. Pat., II. c. 2–10, 18, 20, 22, III. c. 2, 3, 5, 13–14; Ockham, Dial. I. 5 c. 1–35, 6 c. 57, 84–85, 91–100, III. tr. 2, l. 3, c. 4–15, Octo qu., III. c. 8.

16. Zabar., De schismate, in Schard, p. 703, and on c. 6 X. 1, 6 nr. 16 (the plenitudo potestatis is "in ipsa universitate tanquam in fundamento," in the Pope "tanquam ministro"); Petr. Alliac., De pot. eccl. (in Gerson, Op. II. p. 949 ff.); Gerson, De pot. eccl. (Op. II. p. 225 ff.), c. 1–11, also Concordia quod plenitudo eccl. pot. sit in summo pontifice et in ecclesia (ib. p. 259); Theod. de Niem, De schismate (ed. Basel 1566).—Still farther goes Randuf, c. 2.

17. The fullest treatment of the scholastic distinctions in this idea is given by Gerson, op. cit. (Hübler's account of his trichotomy, p. 385 ff., is not wholly correct.)

18. Zabar., De schism., p. 703 and 709, and on c. 6 X. 1, 6 nr. 15–20 ("ipsa universitas totius ecclesiae" can never validly alienate these rights); Gerson, De auferibilitate papae (Op. II. p. 209), cons. 10 and 12–19, De unitate ecclesiae (ib. p. 113), De pot. eccl., c. 11, with reference to the teaching of Aristotle that every free community has the same inalienable rights against its ruler. See already Somn. Virid., I. c. 161; Henr. de Langenstein, c. 15; Anonymus De aetatibus ecclesiae, c. 6 (in Goldast, I. p. 30 ff.). Also Randuf, c. 5 and 9; Pierre du Mont de St. Michel (1406), in Hübler p. 380, and the transactions at Constance, ib. p. 101–102 and 262.

19. Petr. Alliac., Propos. util. (in Gerson, Op. II. p. 112), appealing to the natural right of every "corpus civile seu civilis communitas vel politia rite ordinata" (somewhat differently at an earlier date, ib. I. p. 661–662); Zabar., De schism., p. 689–694; Randuf, c. 3; also Henr. de Langenstein, c. 15; and Conrad of Gelnhausen (in Martène, Thesaur., II. p. 1200); less absolutely Gerson, Op. II. p. 113, 123, 211, 249.

20. Gerson, De pot. eccl., c. 11; Zabar., De schism., p. 688–689 (with application to the 'quasi-vacancy' of a schism); Domin. Gem., Cons., 65 nr. 7.

21. Octo conclusiones per plures doctores in Italiae part. approb., 1409 (in Gerson, Op. II. p. 110); Zabar. on c. 6 X. 1, 6 nr. 9; Panormitanus on eod. c. nr. 15; also Henr. de Langenstein, c. 14. According to Gerson (Op. II. p. 123 and 293) the Council could "statuere alium modi eligendi"; according to Randuf (c. 9) it could itself elect.

22. According to Gerson, De pot. eccl., c. 7–9 and 11, De aufer. pap., c. 8 and 20, this must not be infringed even by the Council, as it is of divine right; see also Op. II. p. 130, 146, 529–530, and IV. p. 694. Of a different opinion are those who regard the Primacy as a human institution, as Ockham and Randuf (above, Ch. I. Note 21).

23. Thus Petr. Alliac., De pot. eccl., II. c. 1 (in Gerson, Op. II. p. 946), and Gerson, De pot. eccl., c. 13; both drawing the full analogy with the 'polities' of Aristotle. (The Aristocracy consists of the Cardinals.)

24. Zabar., De schism., p. 703 and 709; Octo conclus., loc. cit.; Pierre du Mont de St. Michel, loc. cit.; Gerson, De unit. eccl. (Op. II. p. 113), Quomodo et an liceat etc. (ib. p. 303), De pot. eccl., c. 7 and 11; also the famous decree of the fourth session of the Council of Constance, and Gerson (II. p. 275) thereon.—Randuf allows to the Pope no more power than "ab universali ecclesia conceditur" to him, that is, a power which is "quasi instrumentalis et operativa seu executiva" (c. 2), binds him to unconditional obedience to the Council (c. 9), and declares that all Canon law contrary to the inalienable sovereignty of the Council is void (c. 17 and 23).

25. The 'subject' of the Church's mandate and right, in all gradations, is the general body (I. c. 12–17); therefore in the Church as in the State, all superiority rests on voluntary consent and submission (II. c. 13–14). It is true that God co-operates with man in the institution of offices (II. c. 19), but it is only the grace that is bestowed directly by God, the coercive force is bestowed through the medium of the general will (II. c. 34 and 19). In every transference of power the means of declaring the "communis consensus" is election (II. c. 14, 18–19). By election are ordained the heads of the smaller and larger organizations of the Church, and thereby at the same time they receive the mandate to represent the communities of their respec-

tive districts in synodal assemblies and thus to stand as a visible presentment of
their particular churches and also of the Universal Church (II. c. 1, 16–19).
Thus the authority of all Councils comes not from their Heads but from
the "communis consensus omnium" (II. c. 8 and 13). The synodal assemblies in the first place exercise the legislative power, as the whole binding
force of a law rests on the "concordantia subiectionalis eorum qui per eam
legem ligantur" (II. c. 8–12). And further, they are the source of all the
powers of "iurisdictio et administratio" conferred on the several prelates; by
virtue of these powers the prelates become the heads of their communities and
the presidents of their respective assemblies, but they are bound by the decrees
of these assemblies and are responsible to these assemblies for the due exercise
of entrusted offices (II. c. 2, 13–15). In like manner the General Council,
representing the infallible Church in its totality (II. c. 3–7), is independent
of the authority of the Supreme Head (II. c. 25) and can assemble by its
own right (II. c. 2 and 8). The Pope himself has no other power than the
'administration and jurisdiction' conferred on him by the voluntary consent
of the ecclesia universalis through the election performed in its name (II.
c. 13–14 and 34). Like the King, he stands above the individuals but is
the servant of the community as a whole (II. c. 34); he is bound and limited
by the canons and decrees of Councils (II. c. 9–10 and 20); the Council
can judge him and depose him (II. c. 17–18). However, like Gerson,
he regards this monarchical Head as essential and divinely ordained (I.
c. 14), and, also like him, he inserts an aristocratic element, which in
the particular churches consists of the Chapters and in the universal Church
consists of the Cardinals regarded as elected provincial delegates (II. c. 15).

26. Thus Aeneas Sylvius in his earlier days, Comment. de gestis Basil.
concilii libri duo (the analogy with the relation between People and King
is followed out in full). Then especially Gregory of Heimburg in his
polemical writings concerning the quarrel about the bishopric of Brixen
[1460–1461]; see Goldast, II. p. 1591, 1604 ff., 1615 ff. and 1626 ff.
[On this quarrel Maitland refers to Creighton, History of the Papacy, London 1897, III. p. 237.] Also Almainus, Expos. ad Octo qu., I. c. 15, and
Tract. de auctor. eccl. et conc. gen., c. 1 (in Gerson, Op. II. p. 977 ff.).

27. See for example Panorm. on c. 2 X. 1, 6 nr. 2, c. 3 eod. nr. 2–4,
c. 6 eod. nr. 15, c. 17 X. 1, 33 nr. 2; Decius on c. 4 X. 1, 6 nr. 1–22,
c. 5 eod. nr. 3, Cons. 151; Henricus de Bouhic on c. 6 X. 1, 6; Marcus,
Dec., I. q. 935.—It is significant that even the constitutional theory of
Antonius Rosellus, while strictly monarchical and based on positive law, is
pervaded by the thought of a popular sovereignty within the Church; see
Monarchia, I. c. 48, II. c. 4, 13–30, III. c. 1–6, 15–18, 21–22, 26–27.

28. See above, Notes 14, 18, 19, 23, 25, 26.

29. Joh. a Turrecremata (d. 1468), De potestate papae, c. 38. Likewise Nicolas of Cues in his later days, Op. p. 825 ff. (for all plurality is evolved from unity, and the Body from the Head).

30. Quite overlooked by van Krieken, Die sogenannte organische Staatstheorie (Leipzig 1873), p. 26 ff.; Held, Staat und Gesellschaft (Leipzig 1861), p. 575, is also incorrect.

31. See S. Bernard, Ep. to Conrad (in Goldast, II. p. 67–68); Thom. Aquin., Op. IV. p. 48, q. 8 a. 1–2; Gl. Ord. on c. 14 X. 5, 31 v. "unum corpus"; Innocent IV on c. 4 X. 2, 12 nr. 3; Alv. Pel., I. a. 13; Johannes Andreae on c. 4 X. 1, 6 nr. 13; Domin. Gem. on c. 17 in Sexto, 1, 6 nr. 4–6.

32. Thus the papalists deduced from the monstrosity of the 'two-headed animal' ("animal biceps") the subordination of the Emperor to the earthly Vicar of Christ (Alv. Pel., I. a. 13 F. and a. 37 O–Q; the Clerk in Somn. Virid., II. c. 6 ff.; Aug. Triumph., I. q. 5 a. 1 and q. 19 a. 2; Cardinalis Alexandrinus on D. 15, and c. 3 D. 21; Ludovicus de Ponte Romanus, Cons. 345 nr. 3 ff.; Petrus a Monte, De primatu papae, I. nr. 16 (in Tract. univ. juris, XIII., 1 p. 144). The imperialists used this same argument in behalf of the imperium mundi as against inferior rulers (Eng. Volk., De ortu, c. 15, 17, 18; Petrarca, Ep. VII. and VIII.; Nic. Cus., III. c. 1 and 41; Ant. Ros., I. c. 67; Petr. Andl., II. c. 2). At the same time they argued that the unity of the whole Body is preserved in Christ as its Head, while under Him the partial Organisms are again constituted, according to the nature of the Mystical Body, as particular Bodies under separate Heads (Ockham, Dial. III. tr. 1, l. 2, c. 1 and 30; Miles in Somn. Virid., II. c. 305–312; Lup. Beb., c. 15 p. 399 and 401; Quaestio in utramque partem, p. 103). Then upon the nature of mankind as a single organic Body was based the postulate of the union of Church and State in one and the same life. At this point the clericalist theory, from the old comparison of the sacerdotium and regnum to the soul and body of the one organism, deduced the subjection of the secular to the spiritual power (thus Joh. Saresb., V. c. 2, 3–5; Innocent III on c. 6 X. 1, 33; Alv. Pel., I. a. 37 R; Clerk in Somn. Virid., I. c. 37, 43, 45, 47, 101). Their opponents sometimes substituted other images (thus Miles in Somn. Virid., I. c. 38, 44, 46, 48, 102, and II. c. 102, made a comparison with the head and heart, both being ruled by Christ as the Soul), but Nicolas of Cues unfolded the idea of the 'harmonious concord' of the spiritual and corporal life, which pervade each other in the whole and in every part of the corpus mysticum made one in the Spirit of God (I. c. 1–6, III. c. 1, 10, 41).

33. Joh. Saresb., V. c. 2; Hugo Floriac., I. c. 2; Thom. Aquin., De reg. pr., I. c. 1, 12–14; Ptol. Luc., II. c. 7 ("assimilatur corpori humano"), and IV. c. 33; Eng. Volk., De reg. pr., III. c. 16 ("civitas vel regnum est quasi

quoddam unum corpus animatum"), and c. 19 "corpus morale et politi-
cum"); Mars. Pat., I. c. 15; Ockham, Octo qu., VIII. c. 5 p. 385, Dial.
III. tr. 1, l. 2, c. 1, tr. 2, l. 1, c. 1; Gerson, V. p. 598, 600, 601; Zabar.
on c. 4 X. 3, 10 nr. 2–3 ("ad similitudinem corporis humani"); Aen. Sylv.,
De ortu, c. 18; Ant. Ros., I. c. 6; Martinus Laudensis, De represaliis (in
Tract. univ. juris, XII. p. 279), nr. 5–6.

34. Thus first Joh. Saresb., V. c. 1–19 and VI. c. 1–25; after him Ptol.
Luc., II. c. 7, IV. c. 11 and 25; Eng. Volk., III. c. 16; Aen. Sylv., c. 18;
lastly, bringing into play all the medical lore of his time, Nic. Cus., I. c. 10,
14–17, and III. c. 41.

35. Thus already Joh. Saresb., VI. c. 20–25; then Ptol. Luc., IV. c. 23;
but above all Aegid. Col., I. 2 c. 12 ("sicut enim videmus corpus animalis
constare ex diversis membris connexis et ordinatis ad se invicem, sic quodlibet
regnum et quaelibet congregatio constat ex diversis personis connexis et
ordinatis ad unum aliquid"), also I. 1 c. 13, III. 1 c. 5 and 8, 2 c. 34,
3 c. 1 and 23. And in the highest perfection Mars. Pat., 1. c. 2 (by reason
in the State, as by nature in the organism, a number of proportionately ad-
justed parts is so arranged in a whole that they communicate to one another
and to the whole the results of their activity; their "optima dispositio" produces health in the natural body and tranquillity in the State, whereby
every part of the State, like every part of the body, performs perfectly the
functions proper to it in the life of the whole); further particulars in I. c. 15,
also c. 8, 17, II. c. 24.—Compare Ockham's use of the organic idea in his
own theory of the substitution of functions, Octo qu. I. c. 11, and VIII. c. 5
p. 385. See also Eng. Volk., III. c. 16-31, and Nic. Cus., loc. cit.

36. Thus Joh. Saresb., V. c. 1 ff.; Thom. Aquin., De reg. pr., I. c. 12,
also Op., XVI. p. 147 and IV. p. 48 ff.; Aegid. Col., I. 2 c. 12; Eng. Volk.,
III. c. 16; Alv. Pel., I. a. 63; Baldus on Prooem. Feud., nr. 32; Nic. Cus.,
III. c. 41; Aen. Sylv., c. 18; Ant. Ros., I. c. 67 and 69. It is urged that,
while the whole is independent of the changes of its members, yet every
member has value for the life of the whole.

37. Thus Hugo Floriac., I. c. 1 and 12, p. 45; Ptol. Luc., IV. c. 9;
Thom. Aquin., loc. cit.; Mars. Pat., II. c. 5; Alv. Pel., I. a. 63 G; Randuf,
c. 2, 7 and 17.

38. Thus Mars. Pat., II. c. 24; Alv. Pel., I. a. 36 C ("membra divisi-
bilia" and "membra indivisibilia"); Antonius de Butrio on c. 4 X. 1, 6
nr. 14–15 ("membra de membro"); Nic. Cus., II. c. 27. Hence it is argued
from the analogy of the organism that the papal centralization, joining the
finger directly to the head, is a monstrosity; thus already S. Bernard, De
consideratione, III. (in Goldast, II. p. 82); in detail Mars. Pat., loc. cit.;
also Randuf, c. 17; Greg. Heimb., loc. cit. p. 1615 ff.

39. Thus Ptol. Luc., II. c. 26; Mars. Pat., I. c. 2 and 5; Alv. Pel., I. a. 63 C; Eng. Volk., III. c. 21; Nic. Cus., III. c. 1; Petr. Andl., I. c. 3.

40. Thus Joh. Saresb., loc. cit.; Thom. Aquin., Op. VIII. p. 821; Ptol. Luc., II. c. 23; Mars. Pat., I. c. 2 and 8; Alv. Pel., I. a. 63 G; Ockham, Octo qu., I. c. 11, VIII. c. 5.

41. Eng. Volk., III. c. 16 ("pars civitatis" distinguished from "pars regni"); Mars. Pat., I. c. 5.

42. Ptol. Luc., IV. c. 23; Aegid. Col., III. 2 c. 34; Mars. Pat., I. c. 17; Joh. Paris., c. 1; Petr. Andl., I. c. 3. Comparison now with the head, now with the heart, now with the soul; and fallacies as in Alv. Pel., I. a. 7, 13, 24, 28, 36, 38, against which Ockham, Dial. 1. 5 c. 13 and 24, urges that, despite all resemblance, there is a difference between mystical and natural bodies.

43. Thus Baldus, Consilia, III. c. 159: in the king we must distinguish the persona regis and the persona privata; "et persona regis est organum et instrumentum illius personae intellectualis et publicae," that is, of the "ipsa respublica"; therefore, since "magis attenditur actus seu virtus principalis quam virtus organica," the acts of the ruler are at bottom acts of the State itself as a Juristic Person; and thus they bind a subsequent ruler. See ib. c. 371, and I. c. 326–327 and 271. Also Jason, Cons., III. c. 10 (especially nr. 14).

44. For the history of the idea of the 'juristic person' I may refer, here as in general, to the continuation of my work "Das deutsche Genossen-schaftsrecht."—That Baldus himself conceives the State's personality merely in the sense of the Romanist 'fiction theory' is shown by his comments on Rubr. Cod. 10, 1 nr. 15–16 ("voluntas non est imperii, sed imperatoris," for "imperium non habet animum"; will is matter of fact, and "id quod facti est," as distinguished from "id quod iuris est," is not thus to be transferred from Emperor to Empire).

45. Thus Baldus, Cons., II. c. 271 nr. 4, and III. c. 159 nr. 5 ("loco duarum personarum rex fungitur"); Alexander Tartagnus on l. 25 § 1 Dig. 29, 2 nr. 4 ("tanquam imperatorem non tanquam Titium"); Marcus, Dec., I. q. 338 nr. 1–7; and the lengthy argument in support of the distinction between the State's property and the private property of the ruler, in Ockham, Octo qu., II. c. 8; also the discussions as to whether a ruler is bound by the acts of his predecessor, in Baldus, loc. cit., I. c. 271, 326, 327, III. c. 159, 371; Joh. Andr. on c. 34 X. 1, 6 nr. 38–39; Gl. Ord. on c. 36 X. 1, 3; Jason, Cons., III. c. 10; Bologninus, Cons. 6.

46. The formation of this concept of "dignitas," and of the distinction as to whether a right does or does not exist and an act is or is not done 'by virtue of the office' ("intuitu dignitatis"), and so on, belongs to the Canonists.

But others commonly operated therewith. Thus even Baldus, loc. cit., III. c. 159 nr. 3–5, despite the argumentation cited above, Note 43; compare on Rubr. Cod. 10, 1, nr. 11, 13, 14 ("dignitas . . . vice personae fungitur"). Likewise Jason, loc. cit., and Ockham, loc. cit. [The office or dignity can be 'objectified,' i. e. conceived as a 'thing' in which rights exist, and which remains the same while men successively hold it; and then again it can be 'subjectified' and conceived as a person (or substitute for a person) capable of owning things.—Maitland.]

47. Thus it is said that within the sphere of his competence the princeps represents the whole people (Mars. Pat., I. c. 15; Zabar., De schism., p. 689 ff.; Baldus on Rubr. Cod. 10, 1, nr. 12, 13, 18); and the champions of an absolute Ruler's-sovereignty already deduce from the plenitude of this representation the proposition that the Ruler is the State (thus Baldus, loc. cit.: "princeps est imperium, est fiscus").—In like manner the champions of the sovereignty of the Pope say that as Head he represents the whole Body and in this sense he himself is the Church (see Guilelmus Durantis, Speculum iudiciale, I. 1 de leg. § 5, nr. 1; Joh. Andr., Nov. s. c. 1 in Sexto 2, 12 nr. 1; Card. Alex., in summa D. 15; Jacobatius, De conc., IV. a. 7 nr. 29–31, VI. a. 3 nr. 41 and 58 ff.). Their opponents likewise ascribe to him, though only to a limited extent, the character of a "persona publica totius communitatis gerens vicem" (see Ockham, Dial. I. 5 c. 25; also Zabar. on c. 6 X. 1, 6 nr. 16; Gerson, De aufer., c. 8–20, De pot. eccl., c. 7; Nic. Cus., I. c. 14 ff., II. c. 27 ff.; Ant. Ros., II. c. 20 ff., III. c. 16 ff.).

48. Thus Mars. Pat., I. c. 12–13, 17, III. c. 6; Aegid. Col., II. 1 c. 3; application of the rules of law touching the acts of majorities, in Eng. Volk., De reg. pr., I. c. 5, 7, 10, 14; Mars. Pat., loc. cit.; Lup. Beb., c. 6 and 12; Ockham, Dial. III. tr. 2, l. 1, c. 27; Ant. Ros., V. c. 2; and even of the lore of corporate delicts in Ockham, Dial. III. tr. 2, l. 1, c. 29–30, l. 2, c. 5. —Even in the smallest details the general theory of Corporations is applied to the assembly of the ecclesia universalis in the concilium generale, and is used by the opposing parties in support of quite different conclusions; see above, Note 14; Zabar., De schism., p. 689 ff.; Nic. Cus., I. c. 4 and II. c. 15; Ludov. Rom., Cons. 352 and 522; Card. Alex. on c. 2 D. 17; Ant. Ros., II. c. 4, III. c. 1–4, 7–14; Jacobatius, loc. cit., IV. a. 3 and 7.

49. Such as the separation of one's capacity as an individual and as "membrum corporis et pars totius," in Eng. Volk., IV. c. 21–29; the measurement of 'active' citizenship by the right of suffrage, in Mars. Pat., I. c. 12; the consideration of grades of rank and station, in Lup. Beb., c. 17 p. 406, and even in Mars. Pat., I. c. 12 ("secundum gradum suum"), 13 and 15.

50. See especially Nic. Cus., as above in Note 10, also III. c. 4 ("vice

omnium"), 12 and 25; Mars. Pat., I. c. 12–13; Lup. Beb., c. 5–6; Ockham, Dial. I. 6 c. 84. See also Patric. Sen., De inst. reip., I. 1, 5 ("multitudo universa potestatem habet collecta in unum, . . . dimissi autem singuli rem suam agunt").

51. D'Ailly, Gerson (De pot. eccl., c. 10, Conc., p. 259), and Nic. Cus. (II. c. 34) expressly ascribe the rights of the Church to "omnes collective sumpti." And Mars. Pat., Randuf and others also leave no room for doubt that for them the sovereign universal Church is identical with the sum of all the faithful. And while most of these writers avoid further consequences by supposing a perfect representation of this "universitas fidelium" by the Council, yet Ockham, who holds that even the Council is only a "pars ecclesiae," standing below the "communitas" in matters of faith, follows these consequences out to the end (Dial. I. 5 c. 25–28).—And thus Turrecremata can undertake to prove that the "ecclesia universalis" is not even possibly competent to hold the ecclesiastical power ascribed to it in the conciliar theory. For, he argues, a "communitas" cannot have rights of which the major part of its members are incapable, and of the faithful the major part will consist of women and laymen; besides it would follow that all the members of the Church would have equal rights and the consent of all would be necessary for every single act of sovereignty (op. cit., c. 71–72).

52. See further below, Ch. V.

53. Thus Joh. Saresb., IV. c. 1, 2, 3, 5 (minister populi, publicae utilitatis minister); Hugo Floriac., I. c. 4, 6, 7; Dante, I. c. 12 (Princes "respectu viae sint domini aliorum, respectu autem termini aliorum ministri sunt," the Emperor is "minister omnium"); also Thom. Aquin., De reg. pr., I. c. 14, De regimine Iudaeorum, q. 6, Op. XXI. p. 592 and 595 ff., Ptol. Luc., II. c. 5–16, III. c. 11; Alv. Pel., I. a. 62 I; Eng. Volk., II. c. 18, IV. c. 33–34, V. c. 9; Ant. Ros., I. c. 64; Petr. Andl., I. c. 3, II. c. 16–18.

54. See for example, on the papal "plenitudo potestatis," Innocent IV on c. 1 X. 1, 7, c. 10 X. 2, 2, c. 27 X. 2, 27 nr. 6; Durantis, Spec., I. 1 de legato § 6, nr. 1–58; Thom. Aquin., III. p. 8–9, IX. p. 514, XV. p. 22–23; Aug. Triumph., I. q. 1, 8, 10–34, II. q. 48–75; Alv. Pel., I. a. 5–7, 11–12, 52–58 (potestas sine numero, pondere et mensura).—On the imperial "plenitudo potestatis" the pronouncements of the Hohenstaufen and the imperialistic jurists are well known; these could have been taken directly from the Roman texts. The doctrine is developed in its most extreme form by Aen. Sylv. (c. 14–23), who argues that the Emperor together with the Princes can do no more than the Emperor alone, on the ground that "amat enim unitatem suprema potestas." It may be noted that Frederick II not only realizes already the idea that absolute monarchy is an office, but claims

the sovereign ubiquity: the employment of instruments is necessary, for "non possumus per universas mundi partes personaliter interesse, licet simus potentialiter ubique nos" (Petr. de Vin., III. c. 68).

55. This doctrine grew up gradually out of the discussions on the validity of the Donation of Constantine and on the possibility of an exemption from the power of the State. Here we may see an ever more distinct apprehension of the rule that every contract which purports to sacrifice án essential right of sovereignty is void, and that no title can give protection against that claim to submission which follows from the very idea of government. Such writers as Baldus, who state this rule most precisely, also apply it in favor of City-republics. See Baldus on Prooem. Dig. nr. 36 ff., l. 5 Cod. 7, 53 nr. 13; also Bartolus on Prooem. Dig. nr. 13 ff., l. 3 § 2 Dig. 43, 23 nr. 5, l. 2 Dig. 50, 6 nr. 2 and 6; Jason, Cons., III. c. 10, 16, 24–25; Crottus, Cons., III. c. 223, nr. 11 and 21–22; Joh. Paris., c. 22; Dante, III. c. 10, also c. 7; Lup. Beb., c. 13–15; Somn. Virid., II. c. 293; Ockham, Octo qu., I. c. 12, III. c. 7 and 9, IV. c. 3–5, VIII. c. 1, Dial. III. tr. 2, l. 1, c. 18 and 27, l. 2, c. 5 and 23; Ant. Ros., I. c. 64–70; Aen. Sylv., c. 11–12.— Hand in hand with this goes a theoretical separation of those rights of sovereignty which belong essentially to the State from the rights which belong to the Fiscus in private law; see Baldus on II. Feud. 51, pr. nr. 4 ("sicut ipsa civitas"—"iure privato"), and on l. 1 Cod. 4, 39 nr. 4; Ockham, Dial. III. tr. 2, l. 2, c. 23; Vocabularius Juris (Paris 1520), v. "fiscus"; Paul. Castr. on l. 4 Cod. 2, 54; Martinus Laudensis, De fisco (in Tract. univ. juris, XII. p. 2), q. 141.

56. See Thom. Aquin., I. c. 1–3; Aegid. Col., III. 2 c. 2; Eng. Volk., I. c. 5–18; Mars. Pat., I. c. 8–9; Ockham, Dial. III. tr. 1, l. 2, c. 6–8. With special reference to the conception of the ruling assembly as a collective sovereign, Aegid. Col., III. 2 c. 3 ("plures homines principantes quasi constituunt unum hominem multorum oculorum et multarum manuum"); Mars. Pat., I. c. 17; Ockham, Dial. III. tr. 2, l. 3, c. 17; Patric. Sen., op. cit., I. 1 and 4, III. 3.

57. See especially Ockham, Octo qu., III. c. 5, VIII. c. 4, Dial. III. tr. 2, l. 2, c. 20, 26–28 ("potestas limitata"); Nic. Cus., III. c. 5; Gerson, IV. p. 597 ff. and 601; Decius, Cons., 72 nr. 2; Manegold of Lautenbach already uses the notion of office ("vocabulum officii") in this sense.— Especially against the papal plenitude, Joh. Paris., c. 3 and 6; Mars. Pat., II. c. 22 ff.; Ockham, Octo qu., I. c. 6, 15, III. c. 4–5, 9, Dial. III. tr. 1, l. 1, c. 2–15, tr. 2, l. 1, c. 23; Somn. Virid., I. c. 156–161; Randuf, c. 5, 10, 23, 28; Nic. Cus., III. c. 13; Greg. Heimb., II. p. 1604 ff.

58. This may be compared with the account given above as to the rights ascribed to the people. It should be noted that the freedom of the sovereign

Assembly from the restraints of positive [Canon] law is most sharply defined by the Conciliar theorists in the doctrine of "epikeia"; see Henr. de Langenstein, c. 15; Randuf, c. 5; and especially Gerson, De unit. eccl., Op. II. p. 115, also ib. p. 241 and 276. The attribute of inalienability and indestructibility is most distinctly transferred by Nic. Cus. (above, Notes 10 and 25) to the sovereign rights of the people; but see also Mars. Pat., I. c. 12 (in the words "nec esse possunt") ; Ockham, Dial. III. tr. 1, l. 1, c. 29; and the passages cited above, Note 16.

59. See especially Thom. Aquin., De reg. pr., I. c. 6; also Jason on l. 5 Cod. 1, 2, lect. 2, nr. 10–13.

60. See the independent development and application of the doctrine of the formae mixtae in Eng. Volk., I. c. 14–16; also Joh. Paris., c. 20; Petr. Alliac., De pot. eccl., II. c. 1; Gerson, De pot. eccl., cons. 13.

61. See the distinction of the legislative and the executive power in Mars. Pat., I. c. 11, 14, 15, 18; in Nic. Cus., and others; also the doctrine of the Scotsman John Mair (Disput. of 1518, in Gerson, Op. II. p. 1131 ff.) : there are two supreme powers, that of the people being the more unlimited.

62. Junius Brutus, q. III. p. 131–147; De jure Magistratuum, q. 5 and 6; Danaeus, I. c. 4 and III. c. 6 ("supra Regem") ; Hooker, in Ranke, loc. cit. p. 240 ff.; Buchanan, p. 79 ff.; Rossaeus, c. 2 § 11; Boucher, I. c. 10–17; Mariana, I. c. 8.

63. The first expression occurs in Salamonius, p. 16 ff. (compare p. 28: the People is the "Superior") ; the second expression in Hotman, Francog., c. 19.

64. See above, p. 42–43, 53, 57–58, 90–91. After him Hoenonius, II. § 39 and 42, IX. § 5; Alstedius, p. 14 and 18.

65. See De jure Mag., q. 4 p. 9 ff. ("supremus magistratus") ; q. 6 p. 9 (only the "summus gradus" among the ministers of the people) ; ib. p. 37 ff. and 74 (only a 'resolutively' conditioned summum imperium; conditio expressa aut tacita, "si juste sancteque populum rexerit"). Buchanan, p. 16 ff., 59 ff. (responsible and revocable "munus"), p. 78. Salamonius, p. 20 (comparison with "servus universitatis"), p. 30 ("mandatarius" and "minister"), p. 42 (praepositus or institor of civilis societas). Junius Brutus, q. II. p. 84 ff., III. p. 143 ff. ("Minister Reipublicae," servus regni), 248 ff., 261 ("contractus mutuus obligatorius, ut bene imperanti bene obediatur," "conditio tacita vel expressa . . . qua deficiente contractus solvitur"), 297 ff.; also p. 174–183 on the purpose and scope of the transferred "officium" or "ministerium." Rossaeus, c. 2 § 3 (power of government "sub conditione et stipulatione"), § 6 ("obligatio reciproca"), § 11 (the king's obligation of obedience to the "Respublica universa et leges"). Boucher, I. c. 19. Hoenonius, II. § 1–5, III. § 38.

66. Poynet, q. 2–5; De jure Mag., q. 6 p. 33, 74, 82 ff., q. 9 p. 107 ff.; Buchanan, p. 25 ff., 47 ff., 76 ff.; Salamonius, lib. I. and II.; Junius Brutus, q. III. p. 184–200 (Rex organum legis, leges a populo accipit, therefore he is bound by them), p. 200 ff. (non est dominus vitae), p. 212 ff. (neque dominus bonorum); Boucher, I. c. 3 and II. c. 20; Rossaeus, c. 1 § 6, c. 2 § 9–10, c. 3 (personality and property as limitations of the ruler, whose power is·restricted by its purpose and must not destroy liberty); Danaeus, I. c. 4 p. 42–43 (potestas limitata et legibus adstricta); Mariana, I. c. 2, 5, 8, 9, III. c. 7; Hoenonius, I. § 17, IX. § 6–15.

67. Hotman, c. 13, ascribes to the king a "majestas" as head of the Estates General, and Alstedius, p. 14, a "majestas personalis"; Danaeus sets forth the usual doctrine of the forms of State.

68. Above, p. 44 ff.—He overlooks the fact that in private law the "mandatarius" does not gain a right to carry out the "mandatum."

69. Above, p. 47. Buchanan also practically wipes out the distinction between monarchy and republic (p. 20).

70. These teachings are most fully developed in the work De jure Mag., q. 6 p. 26–90; in Junius Brutus, q. II. p. 84 ff., III. q. 270 ff.; and in Althusius (as above, p. 46), who has the merit of attempting a strictly juristic statement of the distinctive marks of tyranny, the steps to be taken against it, and the modes of punishment. After him in Hoenonius, IX. § 31–57 and II. § 14–16; and in Alstedius, p. 56–61. In substantial agreement Poynet, q. 6; Knox in his dialogue with Mary Stuart [in 1561]; Hotman, c. 7; Buchanan, p. 61 ff.; Salamonius, lib. II. and V.; Rossaeus, c. 1 § 6–8 and 11; Boucher, I. c. 2, III. c. 14–17; Mariana, I. c. 6; Danaeus, I. c. 4 p. 43, and especially III. c. 6 p. 216 ff.

71. As in the arguments of the work De jure Mag., q. 7 p. 90 ff., culminating in the justification of an appeal to foreign intervention; and in Junius Brutus, loc. cit.; also Buchanan, loc. cit.; but especially Rossaeus, c. 9; and still more Boucher, lib. IV. ("judiciorum formula premente negotio expectari non oportet," but rather to take up arms); other purely revolutionary pamphlets as in Baudrillart, p. 66 ff. and 73 ff.

72. Mariana, I. c. 6; also Boucher, III. c. 17 with IV. c. 1 ff.

73. See Buchanan, p. 30 ff. (strongly emphasized); Hotman, c. 25; Salamonius, p. 28 ff.; Junius Brutus, q. III. p. 192 ff. (Rex leges a populo accipit; no law "absque Reipublicae consensu"); Rossaeus, c. 2 § 8; Mariana, I. c. 8–9 and III. c. 7 (and especially in every imposition of taxes).

74. Hotman, Francog., c. 8–9 and 25, Quaest. illustr., q. 1 (as regards the res publicae and the fiscus the King is but an administrator, while in the domanium he has the "quasi ususfructus" and only "nuda proprietas

. . . penes universitatem populi sive Rempublicam"); Junius Brutus, q. III. p. 216 ff. and 235 ff. (the King is nothing but an administrator); Althusius, as above, p. 45.

75. See especially De jure Mag., q. 6 p. 26 ff.: the "magistratus subalterni" are not dependent on the summus magistratus, but only "ab ipsa supremitate," "a summa illa imperii seu regni δυνάμει et auctoritate"; they are "officiarii Regni non Regis," and with the latter they are connected by "mutua obligatio"; a breach of this by the King releases them from their oath and entitles and binds them to armed resistance in their official capacity. See Hotman, Francog., c. 19 and 26 (Ministri Regis and Regni). Althusius, Polit., c. 32 § 39 ff.

76. Hotman, c. 14 ff. and c. 25 (especially in legislation, settlement of succession to the throne, alienation of domain, pardons, removals from office, coinage).

77. De jure Mag., q. 5 p. 10 ff., q. 6 p. 37 ff. and 75 ff.; Hotman, c. 6–18 (historical evidence of the rights which "populus sibi reservavit"), and c. 19 (rational arguments from the theory of contract; also the king is mortal, fallible, liable to the weaknesses of an individual—but the people is not); Buchanan, p. 16 ff., 48 ff., 78 ff. (causa, prior, praestantior); Salamonius, p. 16–20 ("populus creat," does this freely, will have no dominus but only a princeps), and p. 40–41; Junius Brutus, q. III. p. 131–147 (Rex per populum, propter populum, non sine populo); Rossaeus, c. 2 § 3–11; Boucher, I. c. 10–17 (constituens major constituto; Rex non sine populo sed populus sine Rege esse potest; populus prior, potior, superior); Danaeus, I. c. 4 (subditi natura, tempore, fine et autoritate priores Principe; explanation of the pactum); Mariana, I. c. 8 (the people should always concede only a limited power; only a "regius principatus certis finibus cancellisque descriptus" is fit for civilized peoples; and then is the universitas major rege); Hoenonius, IX. § 5; Alstedius, p. 18.

78. Especially in the middle ages (above, Note 58). Among the Monarchomachi the author of the work De jure Mag., q. 6 p. 76 ff., argues that a forced contract of unconditional submission or a contract under "conditiones aperte irreligiosae" is void or else may be rescinded by a "restitutio in integrum" made to the people; similarly Junius Brutus, q. III. p. 263. Mariana, I. c. 8 p. 74, leaves it an open question whether the people can transfer absolute power. Furthermore Junius Brutus, q. III. p. 170 ff., seeks especially to prove that the people's rights, once established, are not lost by any prescription of time or any prevarication, as the people is immortal and has the rights of the Fiscus; similarly De jure Mag., q. 7 p. 90 ff., and Hoenonius, II. § 51, as to the nullity of collusions of the Optimates.

79. See the references given above, Ch. I. Notes 23 and 31. It is well known that Melanchthon at first (1523) wished to bind the Princes in all things by the will of the territorial Estates.

80. The vacillations of Luther and the Lutheran theologians in the question of the right of resistance are well known; see Hortleder, Handlungen von Rechtsmässigkeit, Anfang und Fortgang des deutschen Krieges, Frankfort 1617–1618, especially II. p. 1–223. As to this, indeed even the more and more prevalent affirmative opinion for the most part concedes the right of resistance in practice only to the Imperial Estates as against the Emperor; but the theoretical argument goes in part much farther; see especially the concurrent opinions of Luther, Jonas, Bucer and Melanchthon in 1539, to the effect that when the Emperor assumes 'unjust power beyond his office' he stands on a level with a private man, 'for public violence dissolves all obligations between subjects and overlords, by the law of nature.'—Zwingli expressly says of the ruling powers: 'if they be unfaithful and stray from the fold of Christ they may with God's help be deposed,' but by force only in case of extreme necessity; Bluntschli, p. 62.—On Calvin see above, Ch. I. Note 4.

81. See for example the citations from Alciatus and Cujacius given above, Ch. II. Note 16; then Molinaeus, Comm. in cons. Paris., Geneva 1613 (1st ed. 1539), des fiefs, § 1 glo. 5 nr. 54, § 3 glo. 3 nr. 15 ff.

82. Thus chiefly Zasius, Connanus, Cujacius, Donellus; see further below in Ch. VI., where we shall also find in the jurists of this period the doctrines of conditional obedience and the jus resistendi of the subjects.

83. Thus, now as before, the jurists almost always required the consent of the people to the alienation of the State's domain or of essential rights of sovereignty, as well as of the State's property; thus see Alciatus on l. 25 Cod. de pactis, nr. 35 ff. (Op., III. p. 218); Molinaeus, loc. cit. § 3 glo. 3 nr. 17 (the sovereign is only administrator, not proprietarius regni); Menochius, Cons. 426; Bursatus, Cons. 160; Surdus, Cons. 323; Zoannettus (d. 1586), Tract. de Romano Imperio (in Tract. univ. juris., XVI. p. 20 ff.), nr. 169–182; Tiraquellus, Opera, Frankfort 1597, V. p. 86; Nicol. Reusner, Sententiae, Frankfort 1599, IV. dec. 4; Petr. Heigius, Quaest. jur. tam civ. quam Sax., Wittenberg 1619, I. q. 19; but especially the full accounts of the state of this controversy in Gabrielius, Communes conclusiones, Frankfort 1616 (1st ed. 1576), III. concl. 7; Alex. Trentacinquius, Practicarum resolutionum libri tres, Frankfort 1610, lib. III. de pactis resol., 1 nr. 16–18; and Pfeffinger, Vitriarius illustratus, III. 18 § 3 N. a. The contrary is maintained by Hier. Treutler, Disput. selectae, Marburg 1592 ff., I. d. 2 q. 15.—And even for law-making, not only was it

often held that the "acceptatio populi" is required for the binding force of laws, but just from this there was sometimes deduced the requirement of a legislative co-operation of the people in every act of law-making; see the account of the state of this controversy in Suarez, IV. c. 19.

84. Thus above all in Vasquez, for whom the people, in alienating its sovereignty, has reserved to itself the legislative power in cases of doubt (c. 47), must consent to alienations of domain (c. 42–43), stands only under a power which is limited and bound by the laws (c. 45, also c. 4–5, 18, 21, 26), and may assail a tyrannical sovereign with armed force (c. 8). Similarly Covarruvias, I. c. 1 and 4. Less distinctly, but tending still more strongly to the assumption of a higher power reserved to the people, Lainez and Bellarmine, loc. cit.—Soto, I. q. 7 a. 2, and IV. q. 4 a. 1, admits the possibility of a real conveyance of sovereignty to the Princeps, such that he is the exclusive law-maker and "non solum singulis Reipublicae membris superior sit, verum et totius collectim corporis caput totique adeo supereminens, ut totam etiam simul punire valeat"; but even for this case he adds, "quare neque per rempublicam Rex potest regni jure expoliari, nisi fuerit in tyrannidem corruptus." Compare Victoria, III. nr. 15.

85. See Bodin, I. c. 8 nr. 79 ff., c. 10, II. c. 1 (especially nr. 174–184), c. 5, c. 7 nr. 233 ff., VI. c. 4 nr. 712. Further consequences are: the denial of the sovereignty of a Dictator or Regent (I. c. 8 nr. 79–81); the dissolution of sovereignty by any feudal relations (I. c. 9); the explanation that the Germanic Empire is not a Monarchy but an Aristocracy (II. c. 6 nr. 223–226, IV. c. 1 nr. 390 ff.), while in France there is an absolute Monarchy; the elimination of active political rights from the Aristotelian definition of the citizen (I. c. 6 nr. 51–65); the treatment of all non-sovereign magistracies as having the character of a mere office (III. c. 3–6).

86. See I. c. 8 nr. 99–106, and II. c. 3. Also the "respublica," while otherwise it never appears as a 'subject' distinct from the Sovereign, is regarded as the owner of the State's property, being represented as "pupilla" by the Ruler.

87. De rep., I. c. 1 § 9: the State's power is one, supreme, indivisible; all other powers are derived from it and consist only in the exercise of borrowed rights; the "summitas" and "unitas" are incommunicable; hence according to V. c. 1 § 3 there is no "formarum mixtura"; the Monarch has "suprema et absoluta potestas," and even in the weightiest matters he is not bound by the advice of the Estates except so far as a "lex electionis" binds him to consult his subjects (XXV. c. 7); limits are set to him only by the purpose of his office (IX. c. 1) and the "lex divina et naturalis" (VII. c.

20 § 1–55); the "Respublica" can neither depose nor punish him (XXVI. c. 5 § 24–25); yet it is the 'subject' of the State's property, which is only "quasi proprium Principis" (III. c. 2, and Synt., III. c. 2).

88. De regno, IV. c. 10, and VI. (the whole right of the people is transferred and thus belongs to another); II., IV., V. c. 12 (every true Monarchy is absolute and incompatible with binding "leges fundamentales" or a division of powers); III. c. 14–15 (Rex legibus solutus); IV. c. 25 (universa negotia Reipublicae demandantur Regi; what his "officiales" do, he does); III. c. 4–16, V. c. 7–8 (no right of resistance or deposition; under tyranny there only remains for the people "ut oret et patienter ferat Deique judicium exspectet").

89. See for example Vultejus, Jur. Rom., I. c. 12; "Waremund de Eren-bergk," Aulicus-politicus (1596), and Verisimilia, c. 3 p. 43 ff. (yet with inconsistent recognition of a limited monarchy in the case of "certae capitulationes," c. 11 p. 150); Winkler, V. c. 4 ("majestas" is necessarily in a single ruling 'subject,' summa, absoluta, "ex sese ipsa leges ferens," not a magistracy but "supra magistratus").

90. Partit., p. 41–45, De maj., c. 2–13: majestas is by its very nature necessarily summa, universalis, prima (like the ocean, bringing forth all other powers and taking them back into itself), perpetua, individua, in-communicabilis (it is possessed either wholly or not at all, as the circle is not a circle if the smallest part is wanting), summum imperium continens, containing "omnes functiones vel jura majestatis" (for these see De maj., c. 15–31) as "partes individuae et inseparabiles," so that only "administratio partium committi potest"; hence it is always in one Princeps, "inest uni semper $\tau\tilde{\wp}$ λόγῳ, interdum etiam persona, interdum multis," and this sovereign, unless it coincides with the "cives collectim uniti," stands even above the "universi." Hence Bornitius rejects the forma mixta as impossible; there can only be the forma administrandi status similis aut dissimilis (Partit., p. 46 ff. and 102 ff.). Limitations of majestas by laws of the constitution are possible, but as soon as they "majestati aliquid detrahunt" they lead to a "status confusus" and to downfall (Partit., p. 42, De maj., c. 9 and 26).

91. See for example Paruta, Discorsi politichi, 1579. Albergati, Discorsi politici, Venice (the copy used has no date), who especially in l. 2 c. 11 p. 291, considers Bodin's idea of "maesta" as overdrawn, and in l. 2 c. 8 ff., p. 251 ff., defends the "mischianza di stato." Then the defense of the mixtura formarum in Bellarmine, De Summo Pont., I. 3; Lipsius, Politicorum libri sex, Antwerp 1604, II. c. 2; Loys de Mayerne, La monarchie aristo-democratique, Paris 1611; P. Busius (Buis), De republica libri tres, Frane-ker 1613, II. c. 6–7. Lastly the eulogy of "monarchia temperata" in Cont-zen, I. c. 14–23, and Anton. Perez, Jus publicum, Antwerp 1657, p. 54 ff.

92. Fridenreich, c. 29; Reinking, De reg., I. cl. 2 c. 2, nr. 231 ff., and cl. 5 c. 6 (majestas is indivisible, inalienable, imprescriptible, "extra commercium," "perfectum et absolutum quid, quod neque crescere neque minui potest"; hence it belongs to the Emperor either wholly or not at all).

93. Fridenreich, c. 18 ("limitata et restricta certis pactionibus potestas"), and c. 26 (even against the 'subject' of summa potestas there is, in case of breach of the constitution, a right of active resistance and of deposition). Reinking, loc. cit., I. cl. 2 c. 2 and cl. 5 c. 9: the Emperor is major universis and toto imperio; but his majestas is compatible with limitation by leges fundamentales, which are binding as contracts (ib. cl. 3 c. 12), deposition by magistratus subordinati in case of breach (ib., cl. 1 c. 5, nr. 43–104), obligation by "foedus cum populo" under oath (ib., cl. 3 c. 9), aristocratic "modus administrationis" (ib., cl. 2 c. 2, nr. 240 ff.), and 'communicative,' not 'abdicative,' sharing of the rights of sovereignty with the several Estates "salvo jure superioritatis" (ib., cl. 5 c. 2, 3, 6). See Pruckmann, c. 2 nr. 69 ff. p. 90 ff., p. 101, p. 111, nr. 1–143, where such limitations are deduced for all rulers from the terms of the contract of rulership. Buxtorff, Diss. ad 17 priora cap. Aur. B. (in Repraesentatio Reip. Germ., Nuremberg 1657), on Aur. B. c. 1 § 6–7, c. 5 § 80. Also Knichen, l. c. 8 th. 8.

94. Arnisaeus, De jure maj., I. c. 1–7, II. c. 1–7, De rep., II. c. 2 s. 5, De auctor. principum throughout: majestas is summa and absoluta, no right of resistance or deposition is possible against the Imperans, even oaths bind him only toward God; hence if there are actual binding pacts and obligations under oath, which limit him and place him under the laws, then is "majestati aliquid detractum" and there are co-sovereigns. But for alienation of the State's domain or property the consensus subditorum is required even by Arnisaeus (De jure maj., III. c. 1).

95. Arnisaeus, De jure maj., II. c. 1, De rep., II. c. 6, s. 1 and s. 5 § 1–134, II. c. 1 s. 1, De auctor., c. 1 § 4 ff., Polit., c. 8: majestas is "individuum, non indivisible," it is a "totum potentiale, non essentiale"; hence it has parts and a "distributio jurium majestatis" may take place under the constitution, as "nihil prohibet, quin partes in hoc toto unitae secerni et divisim inter plures distribui possint"; in this case a "mixta forma status" arises; thus in the Germanic Empire, in which the Emperor is a Monarch, there are various jura majestatis which are shared by him with the Estates.

96. See for example Keckermann, I. c. 33 p. 531 ff., on the limited monarchy as it exists almost everywhere in Europe, wherein "pacta specialia cum subditis . . . restringunt monarchiam sed non tollunt," and II. c. 4–6, on the true "status mixtus"; yet he allows with various cautions a right of active resistance and deposition even against the true and full Sovereign (I. c. 28 p. 425–435). Heider, p. 982 ff., distinguishes the "mixtura essen-

tialis," where as in Germany τὸ κύριον itself is divided, and the "mixtura accidentalis," where this is the case only as to the administration.

97. See Schoenborner, I. c. 16; Arnold Clapmarus, De arcanis rerump., Jena 1665 (1st ed. 1605), V. c. 20; Koenig, Acies, d. V.–VI., Theatrum polit., Jena 1622, I. c. 9 § 15 ff.; Joh. Gerhard, Centuria quaestionum politicarum, Jena 1608, I. 9; Velstenius, VII. nr. 5–6; Joh. a Felde, IV. p. 673 ff.; Clasen, Politicae compendium, Helmstädt 1675, II. c. 9; Felwinger, Diss. de republica mixta (Diss., p. 417–484): "in qua penes uno plures divisim est summa potestas."

98. Molina, II. d. 23 § 8. Suarez, III. c. 3 nr. 7, c. 4: vera alienatio, perfecta largitio, not a mere delegatio, takes place in the true monarchy; hence "Rex superior Regno, quod illam dedit;" also the Rex, just as the Respublica ipsa before him, has a "potestas propria et ordinaria" and can delegate this, which the president of a republic cannot do.

99. Molina, II. d. 23. Suarez, III. c. 4 nr. 5, c. 19 nr. 6, IV. c. 17 nr. 4. The decisive criterion of majestas according to Suarez is the power to legislate; for this reason there is a forma mixta, in which the "Rex cum Regno" is sovereign, whenever the People or Senate has a "votum definitivum" in legislation, and on the other hand a true and merely limited monarchy (preferable to the other form) when the monarch is bound merely to consult the Assembly beforehand.

100. Molina not only declares that the ruler is a mere administrator, who "non consentiente Republica" can neither divide nor alienate the State's domain or property, and likewise has no power over the person or property of individuals (II. d. 25), but in case of doubt he even requires for every law the consent of the people, as a renunciation of this is not to be presumed (II. d. 23 § 6, V. d. 46 § 3). On the other hand Suarez considers the sovereign as in himself the sole legislator, so that the consent of the people is made necessary only by an express reservation of sovereign rights (III. c. 2–3, and c. 9 nr. 4, IV. c. 19), and follows the same idea with regard to the granting of taxes (V. c. 17); yet the people remains the source of all sovereignty (III. c. 4 nr. 2–8), and the sovereign is himself bound by the laws, which he ordains "pro tota communitate cujus est pars" (III. c. 34).

101. Molina, II. d. 23 § 8–10, III. d. 6, V. d. 3 § 2: no right of resistance or deposition, as "Rex superior tota Republica"; but whenever the ruler "potestatem sibi non concessam assumat," then (as beyond the allotted sphere of rights neither he nor the people is sovereign) just as in the case of a vacancy all jurisdiction devolves "ad ipsam Rempublicam" and hence the people can come together, resist, decree a deposition and "post latam sententiam" permit the tyrant to be slain by any man. Suarez, III. c. 4 nr. 6, c. 10 nr. 7–10: the sovereign cannot be deprived, "quia verum illius domin-

ium acquisivit"; it is different in the case of tyranny, in which "tota respublica posset insurgere," "quia tunc tota Respublica superior est Rege"; for every "potestas recepta non excedit modum donationis vel conventionis," and the people has manifestly given the power only "ex conditione," "ut politice, non tyrannice regeret, alias ab ipsa (sc. Republica) possit deponi"; similarly Opus de triplici virtute, Paris 1621, p. 1055–1056.—There is no doubt that Grotius is thinking of this theory in the formulation given to it by Suarez, when in confuting the doctrine of popular sovereignty he combats the view of those "qui mutuam quandam subjectionem sibi fingunt, ut populus universus regi recte imperanti parere debeat, rex autem male imperans populo subjiciatur" (l. c. 3 § 9).

102. See Ranke, p. 242, who overlooks the fact that Buchanan not only separates, like Hooker, the legislative and the executive power, but also (p. 31–37) is the first to assert with energy the independence of the judicial power: as the making of laws belongs to the People, the interpretation of laws belongs to the Judiciary; interpretation by the King is obnoxious, as is shown by the example of the Pope, who has grown great chiefly in this way.

103. He is followed by Hoenonius, II. § 42 (majestas as potestas summa, perpetua, individua; no division of powers or forma mixta), IX. § 2 and 16.

104. That the argumentation of Grotius, I. c. 3 § 8, attacked by Rousseau, I. c. 4, is taken from Suarez, III. c. 3 nr. 7, may be assumed with certainty in perfect harmony with what is said above, Note 101. When Suarez adds that the case of "qualitates morales," such as liberty, is different from the case of "qualitates physicae," this is obviously aimed against the analogy drawn by Althusius with the inalienability of life. In this matter neither Suarez nor Grotius mentions Althusius by name, nor does Grotius name Suarez.

105. Above, p. 40. Likewise Hoenonius, IX. § 5 ff.

106. Guevara (counsellor of Charles V), Horologium Principis, I. c. 36 (following Joh. Saresb.); and quite similarly Knichen, I. c. 6 th. 11; Modrevius, Von Verbesserung des gemeinen Nutz, 1557, p. 162; Victoria, III. nr. 4; Greg. Thol., I. c. 1 § 8–10 and 16, III. c. 1 § 1, X. c. 1 § 1, XVIII. c. 1 § 4, XXI. c. 1 § 4 and 6–10, c. 2 and so on, also Synt., III. c. 2 § 1–2 (elaboration of the analogy with the corpus humanum as regards unity, soul, nerves, articulation, differentiation, harmony, functions and so on); Buchanan, p. 13 ff. (comparison of societas civilis with the human body and of the ruler with the physician); Lessius, op. cit., dedicatio of 1605.— Vasquez, c. 47 nr. 6–8, opposes the false inferences drawn from this "similitudo."

107. Thus Greg. Thol., I. c. 1 § 6–7 (corpus civile ex pluribus ut membris compositum sub una potestate suprema); Hotman, c. 19; Soto, I. q. 1 a. 3, q. 7 a. 2, IV. q. 4 a. 1–2; but above all Althusius, as above, Part I.

p. 34, 40 and Ch. III. Note 30; Molina, II. d. 22 § 9 and d. 23; Suarez, II. c. 3 nr. 1 and 6, III. c. 2 nr. 4 and 6.

108. Salamonius alone uses the phrase "persona civitatis" to mean simply the 'subject' of sovereignty; according to him it is the persona civitatis which as mandator is the true law-maker through the medium of the "persona Principis" and in general "vere agit"; but for him the persona civitatis is identical with the "populus" which he himself conceives in a purely collective sense; see p. 28, 30, 36.—For the rest the treatment of the State as a Person is almost wholly confined to controversies as to whether monarchs are bound by the acts of their predecessors, as in this point the opinions of Baldus are more often reproduced; see for example Nic. Morosus, De treuga et pace (in Tract. univ. juris, XI. 1 p. 418, q. 55 and 56); Pruckmann, p. 98 ff. nr. 10 ("organum tantum atque instrumentum illius personae incorporeae et imaginariae nunquam non existentis"). But even here not only does the category of "dignitas" prevail, the word itself being exclusively used by most of these writers (as for example Reinking, De reg., I. cl. 3 c. 10; Trentacinquius, III. de pactis resol., 1 nr. 8–10; Benedict Carpzov [1595–1666], Decis. 88), but in fact the standpoints of private law and especially the law of inheritance are more and more introduced in a most improper fashion (see for example Peregrinus, De juribus et priv. fisci, Venice 1587, I. tit. 3; Arnisaeus, De jure maj., I. c. 7; Lud. Schrader, Consilia s. Responsa, Leipzig 1606, cons. 9, 10, 13, 25).

109. This conception was promoted by Machiavelli and the whole literature evoked by him, in which the State is never referred to as the 'subject' but always as the mere 'object' of the ruler's activity (see the first chapter of Il Principe); similarly in Botero and Hippolytus a Collibus. The usual definition of societas civilis as "certus ordo jubendi et parendi" also came to its aid; see for example Lipsius, II. c. 1; Jean de Marnix, Resolutions politique et maximes d'Estat, Rouen 1624, sect. 2 p. 46 ff. For Bodin the personality of the State is identical throughout with the 'subject' of sovereignty, whereby unity and order are first introduced into the "multitudo"; see I. c. 1 nr. 1, and II. c. 1 ff., also the very obscure discussion on the binding of rulers by acts of their predecessors, I. c. 8 nr. 100–106. Bornitius says expressly that only through the Princeps the "respublica statum adipiscitur et conservat" and is, so to speak, animated; Partit., p. 45, De maj., c. 5. Arnisaeus distinguishes the "respublica" and the "civitas," which are related as soul and body, and identifies the former throughout with the ruler, whose summa et absoluta potestas produces unity, order and life; Polit., c. 6, 7, 11, De rep., I. prooem. § 14 ff., c. 5 s. 3, II. c. 1 s. 1, De jure maj., I. c. 2. See also Keckermann, Praecog., p. 7; Fridenreich, c. 2, 10, 29 (corpus, whose spiritus vitalis is the magistracy); Koenig, Acies, d. V.; Schoenborner,

I. c. 4; Crüger, d. IV.; Heider, p. 776 ff.; Matthias, Coll. pol., d. V., Syst., p. 194 ff.

110. Bodin defines Aristocracy as the form in which the "minor pars," Democracy as that in which the "universi aut major pars . . . collectim imperant," and follows this mechanical principle of numeration so strictly that he treats the Dyarchy as an Aristocracy, while a State composed of 20,000 citizens is an Aristocracy if 9,000 citizens participate in the government, and a Democracy if 11,000 do so; see I. c. 8 nr. 99, II. c. 1 nr. 174 ff., and c. 6–7; thus also he reckons among the advantages of Monarchy the fact that in this alone the majestas is wholly undivided, VI. c. 4 nr. 710 ff.; see also VI. c. 6. According to Bornitius "unus τῷ λόγῳ" always governs, but in the republic "persona multi," that is the "cives collectim uniti"; Partit., p. 51, De maj., c. 5. Similarly in Arnisaeus, loc. cit., "aliquid unum," which is such either "natura" or "conspiratione et analogia." Keckermann says that in the Republic "plures imperant" (II. c. 1), that in this "plures ex aequo indivisim" are the 'subject' of the State-power (ib. c. 2), that in the Democracy all in turn govern and are governed (ib. c. 3). And in like manner Althusius himself describes the summus magistratus in a Republic as a collective unit; see above, p. 47. Also Hocnonius, IX. § 3, X. § 1 ff., especially § 40; Fridenreich, loc. cit.; Kirchner, d. I. § 3 and d. III.–V.; Alstedius, p. 42 ff. Carpzov, Comm. ad leg. Reg., c. 13 s. 9 nr. 28–31, proves indeed the possibility of a forma mixta with "partes pro indiviso" of several 'subjects' of the State-power, with the argument that otherwise there cannot be even the simple forms of Democracy or Aristocracy, as in these cases the sovereignty is always in "plures"!—See also Knipschildt, De juribus et privilegiis civitatum imperialium, Ulm 1657, II. c. 2 nr. 113, c. 3 nr. 83 ff., V. c. 1 (where in the Imperial Cities the fictive unity of the universi represented by the imperantes is set up as the 'subject' of State-power).

111. Farthest goes Arnisaeus, who sets the "societas" of citizens, with the name of "Civitas," over against the sovereign with the name of "Respublica," and thus formulates the question "quatenus acta Reipublicae obligent Civitatem," a question which he answers in the affirmative only in the case of co-operation of the "totus populus" or promotion of the public benefit; see De rep., I. c. 5, s. 4 and 5, Polit., I. c. 5.

112. See Hotman, c. 9: "penes universitatem populi sive Rempublicam"; c. 19: the Regnum as against the Rex is "ipsa civium ac subjectorum universitas et quasi corpus reipublicae." Junius Brutus, q. III. p. 196 ff. and elsewhere. Salamonius, loc. cit. Rossaeus, c. 2 § 11. Boucher, I. c. 9: populus is the same as Regnum or Respublica. Mariana, I. c. 8. Althusius throughout. Hoenonius, II § 39–51.

113. See above, Ch. II. Notes 30–31; then the principle, everywhere repeated with emphasis, that only the universi, not omnes singuli, stand above the ruler (thus Salamonius, p. 20 and 28; Junius Brutus, q. II. p. 91 ff.; Buchanan, p. 79–80; Danaeus, III. c. 6 p. 220; Althusius, as above, p. 40); and also the inferences as to the jus resistendi, above, p. 76.

114. See for example Salamonius, p. 36: the laws of the populus are binding on it, as they are contracts; for though "populus una interdum censetur persona," yet it is "ut ficte una, ita vere populus non aliud est quam quaedam hominum multitudo"; also p. 38 ff. Further Hotman, loc. cit., together with the strict observance of the idea of "persona ficta et imaginaria" in his Quaest. illustr., q. 32–33, 38, 42. Then Junius Brutus, q. II. p. 89 ff., III. p. 149, 171 ff., 297 ff. (yet the "universa multitudo" should be represented). Also Boucher, I. c. 9, who warns against confusing the populus with the "incondita et confusa turba" but yet defines it as the "jure coacta multitudo" of the representatives. Rossaeus, c. 2 § 11. Mariana, I. c. 8 ("universi"). Hoenonius, II. § 39.

115. See above pp. 34, 36, 37, 40, 41–43, 44, 46, 47, 55, 58 and 59.

116. Thus Soto always identifies the "Respublica," which is originally sovereign and is even later vested with rights as a "corpus" against the ruler, with the "multitudo collectim sumpta" or the "populus congregatus"; thus I. q. 1 a. 3, q. 7 a. 2, IV. q. 4 a. 1–2. Similarly Vasquez, c. 47 nr. 6–8; Victoria, III. nr. 15 ("respublica" identical with "omnes simul").—Compare the strictly collective and at the same time fictive ("affingitur persona civitati ad similitudinem personarum") conception of the populus and of every universitas, in Donellus, XI. p. 7 ff. and VIII. p. 141 (II. c. 6 §16); also the doctrine that unanimity is requisite in principle, V. p. 259 (XVIII. c. 12 § 18–19).

117. Molina ascribes to the "corpus totius Reipublicae" under the law of nature the original "potestas . . . in singulas partes ad eas gubernandum, ad leges illis ferendum jusque illis dicendum et ad eas puniendum," and describes this potestas as "longe diversa . . . a collectione particularium potestatum singulorum" (II. d. 22 § 9): but this "potestas politica, quae residet in toto Reipublicae corpore comparatione suarum partium" is for him unworkable as such, as it must always be exercised by all being together and unanimous, and therefore it must be transferred (ib. d. 23); just so the Respublica is for him simply the aggregate of all, ib. d. 23 § 8, d. 25, d. 22–23, III. d. 6 ("respublica quoad capita convenire, resistere, deponere").—Suarez, who likewise deduces the State-power from the natural relation of the body to its members (III. c. 2 and c. 3 nr. 6), makes a sharper distinction of the "communitas hominum" here set up as the original 'subject' of sovereignty, from a mere sum of men: it is a multitude of men, yet not "ut

est aggregatum" but "quatenus speciali voluntate seu communi consensu in unum corpus politicum congregantur, uno societatis vinculo et ut mutuo se juvent in ordine ad unum finem politicum, quomodo efficiunt unum corpus mysticum quod moraliter dici potest per se unum" (III. c. 2 nr. 4). Compare the general discussions on the distinction of the "rudis collectio sive aggregatum" from the "corpus mysticum" (II. c. 3, nr. 1 and 6). But even for him the 'subject' still remains in truth a "hominum collectio" (III. c. 2 nr. 3), a "multitudo" (ib. nr. 4), a sum-total of many, to which only "una persona ficta" is attributed (l. c. 6 nr. 17); and even for him, apart from the Rex and against the Rex, the concept of "Regnum" or "Respublica" is identical with the general body of the people as thus conceived (thus III. c. 3 nr. 8, c. 4 nr. 5–6 and 11, c. 9 nr. 4, IV. c. 19 nr. 6). Compare above, p. 73–74.

118. See Milton, Eikonoklastes (loc. cit., I. p. 307 ff.), Defensio of 1651 (especially c. 2), Defensio of 1654 (c. 5–7), and above all The Tenure of Kings and Magistrates (loc. cit., II. p. 2 ff., especially p. 11 and 14 ff.).

119. See Sidney, c. II. s. 8–29 (preference for a "popular or mixed government," which is compounded of the three forms of State), and s. 30–33 (the powers of the monarch are herein "limited by law"); c. III. s. 1 ff. (the king "can have no other just power than what the laws give"); c. III. s. 13–14 (the legislative power is in the people), and s. 45–46 (but it is exercised by Parliament); c. III. s. 26 (the judges, even though appointed by the king, are bound only by the laws).

120. According to Sidney the legislator is the sovereign, but the legislator is the people exclusively (c. III. s. 13–14) and in its name the Parliament (ib. s. 45–46); government is not a private right, but is a burden, office and service of the people (c. II. s. 3), created and measured by the law (ib. s. 7); the king like every magistrate is an officer appointed by the people, accountable to it for transgression of the limits of his office, and removable by it (ib. s. 32, and c. III. s. 1 ff.); the people is the judge as well as the creator of every magistrate (ib. s. 41); a free nation has the right to assemble of itself (ib. s. 31), hence Parliament as well (ib. s. 38); "the general revolt of a Nation cannot be called a Rebellion" (ib. s. 36).

121. Locke, II. c. 12: from the nature of society there arise the legislative, executive and "federative" powers; ib. c. 10 § 132: the forms of government are established according as the majority either retains the legislative power, or transfers it to one man or a few men, or else institutes mixed forms as it may see fit.

122. II. c. 13: as long as the constitution and government exist, the legislative power is alone supreme, the executive and federative powers are subordinate and accountable to it; yet the bearer of the two latter powers

is in a certain sense supreme as long as he has a share in the legislative power;
compare c. 14. § 159–168, on Prerogative. Above all these powers stands
the sovereignty of the people.

123. II. c. 13 § 149–150 (compare c. 10 § 132, c. 11 § 141): the people or community remains the source of all power, which always reverts to
it, and in this sense is "always the supreme power," though this does not
become visible "till the government be dissolved"; II. c. 19 (especially
§ 212 ff., 220 ff., 240–242): the people is the judge as to whether the
constituted powers, including the legislative power, observe their limitations, and in case of transgression and consequent forfeiture "the people
have a right to act as supreme, and continue the legislative in themselves or
place it in a new form, or new hands"; in default of formal organization
it may appeal to Heaven; it cannot alienate these rights, as such a contract
would be absurd.

124. Kirchner, d. II. § 1 (majestas realis is in the "societas populi . . .
coalita," majestas personalis in the holder of civilis potestas; the latter is
subordinate to the former). Boxhorn, I. c. 3 § 1–20 (majestas of the imperans), and § 21–24 (majestas of the Respublica). Alstedius, p. 14. Tulden,
c. 11 ("majestas reipublicae ipsius"), and c. 12 (majestas personalis of the
Monarch, the Optimates or the People). Werdenhagen, III. c. 2 § 7–9.
Liebenthal, d. VII. § 3 ff. Berckringer, I. c. 4 § 6–7 (majestas realis is in
the "respublica contrahens"), and c. 5 (majestas personalis in the ruler).
Thus also in essentials Fichlau, in the polemic of 1650 (above, Part I., Ch. I.
Note 12).

125. Regner Sixtinus, Tract. de regalibus, Cassel 1609 (earlier unauthor-
ized edition of 1602 is faulty), I. c. 1 nr. 23 ("omne regnum est possessio
reipublicae et non respublica possessio regni est;" hence the imperantes hold
even the regalia from and for the respublica); nr. 38 (only as "quasi propria"); c. 5 nr. 4 ff. (yet potestas suprema is in the imperantes). Paurmeister, I. c. 3 nr. 10 ("Reges ac optimates non suo sed Reipublicae nomine
imperium et summam potestatem obtinent"); II. c. 1 nr. 11 ("populi
nomine"); I. c. 17 nr. 1 ff. (from the original sovereignty of the people
arise the forms of State, according as the "universus populus" either retains
the "summa rerum" or commits it to uni vel pluribus, but in Europe this
never amounts to παμβασιλεία, but always to the mere exercise χατὰ νόμον);
ib. c. 18 nr. 6–10 (the substance of all jurisdiction is inalienably in the
respublica, whose majestas would otherwise be destroyed, and therefore the
"dominium verum et plenum" thereof is in the imperium, to whose essentia
it is inseparably annexed; but the utile dominium, ususfructus and other
"jura realia innominata" in the rights of sovereignty were given by the
imperium to the Emperor and the Princes, and by these to other persons);

ib. c. 19 nr. 6 ff. (princeps legibus non solutus: the lex Regia leaves the imperium in the populus); ib. c. 21, 22, 23 and 30 (similar arguments as to prescription, possession, hypothecation and loss of sovereign rights; according to c. 23 nr. 13, as against the Respublica even the Emperor and Princes are mere "privati").

126. Arumaeus, op. cit., IV. nr. 2: the "plenissima majestas" is in the "regna et respublicae" themselves, which everywhere in Europe have transferred only "certas et definitas partes," so that no ruler is legibus solutus, no taxes can be levied unless duly voted, and so on; nevertheless there arises for the monarch a "majestas individua" or personalis, which is not destroyed by constitutional limitations; see IV. nr. 1 ("summa potestas limitibus circumscribi debet"), and nr. 3 (an oath of the monarch, which holds him "intra cancellos," does not diminish his majestas). Similarly Daniel Otto, ib., II. nr. 14 § 17: majestas Regnantis majestati Regni tanquam superiori obnoxia sit et obstringatur; § 18: he is but the administrator, not the proprietarius of the respublica; § 19: therefore any "alienatio in detrimentum reipublicae" is void. Georg Brautlacht, Epitome, III. c. 2 § 5–9: majestas realis Imperii, personalis Imperantis. Quirinus Cubach, Centuriae quaestionum illustr. politico-jurid., Jena 1614, I. 9 q. 1 ff. (hence no alienation). Hilliger, in Arumaeus, II. nr. 13. Konings, ib., II. nr. 17 § 8–9. In fullest detail Bortius, De natura jurium majestatis et regalium, ib., I. nr. 30: the majestas realis belongs to the "respublica ipsa," pertains to the establishment and maintenance of its status and comprises the jura regni; the majestas personalis belongs to the Princeps, pertains to the government of the respublica and comprises the jura regia (c. 1); jura regni are the rights of the populus to elect the ruler, to determine the "modus et forma regiminis," to give its consent to acts of alienation, and to maintain the leges fundamentales (c. 2); jura regia are the regalia majora and minora (c. 3); the "subjectum absolutum majestatis" is the "tota Respublica et secundario ordines et status Regni," the "subjectum limitatum" is the ruler, so far as there has been a transference to him (c. 5 § 9); the "majestas regni" is "prima et summa," as it "pendet immediate a Deo;" the "majestas regia" is "summa et absoluta," but only "in suo ordine et genere," that is, "ratione gubernationis," hence it is limited by God, by the people, by natural and positive law; but it is not subject to compulsion (c. 6); in case of breach of the contract the people has the right of resistance and deposition (c. 7).

127. See especially Diss. de majestate. In s. 1 c. 1 he treats of majestas realis, which is indestructibly in the respublica or in the populus; even under the lex Regia it remained in the populus Romanus; only flatterers pretend that "nomen Reipublicae in principatu abolitum esse"; there is

such a thing as a "crimen majestatis contra populum"; over against the majestatis imperantis the majestas realis continues in the leges fundamentales, which are its causae efficientes, and it effects the inalienability of the jura dignitatis, territoria and domania regni (of which the ownership remains in the people), the unalterableness of the succession to the throne, and so on. In ib. c. 2–7 he treats of majestas personalis, which nevertheless he describes as summa, perpetua and legibus soluta, as the source of all other powers, as essentially different from an office, and as exempt from deprivation or forfeiture. In s. 2 he discusses its ecclesiastical and in s. 3 its political components, and ascribes to the 'subject' of a true and full majestas personalis even the right of legislation and taxation without the consent of the people (s. 3, c. 2 and 7).

128. See Frantzken, De potestate Principis, in Arumaeus, IV. nr. 42, especially § 19–22 and § 92–101. Carpzov, op. cit., c. 1 s. 14 and c. 13 s. 1 (in every State the "majestas realis imperii" continues in ipsa respublica).

129. Jus publicum, I. c. 10 nr. 14 (where in support of the ruler's mere "ususfructus" he cites Junius Brutus and the preface of Althusius); more fully in Capitulationes imperatorum et regum cum annotamentis, Strasburg 1651, p. 532 nr. 48–79: the majestas realis is not "ficta et imaginaria," but it is the power "quae Reipublicae adhaeret, hoc est universitati, quae non nisi ficte personae nomen inducere potest, ex personis tamen constat"; it is originally in the populus, which "ea salva" concedes the majestas personalis as it sees fit; hence it belongs to the "populus universus" even after the appointment of a ruler and remains the norm for the majestas personalis; it expresses itself in reversion, decision in the last resort, the right of deposition; in the Empire it is exercised by the general body of the Estates.

130. See Alstedius, p. 18: the bearer of majestas personalis is superior singulis, inferior subditis universis. Kirchner, loc. cit. ("societas . . . populi coalita"), and d. I. § 3. Paurmeister, loc. cit., and I. c. 3 nr. 3. Boxhorn, loc. cit. (respublica is the populus). Berckringer, I. c. 4 § 6–7: the "respublica contrahens" is the populus, which is collectively the 'subject' of majestas realis (hence also the singuli as members), while it remains a "persona potentia, imo actu, sed possibili"; ib. § 8: universus populus; § 10: the imperans as "unum numero vel analogia" is indeed only the caput of the corpus totum, but is the "persona actu" of the State. Bortius, loc. cit. (the respublica is always the populus universus). Limnaeus, loc. cit. nr. 49, 50, 53 (as in previous Note). Carpzov, loc. cit. (see above, Note 110.) Werdenhagen indeed describes the State as an organism like the living body, in which the "unio," which he calls "summum illud

venerandum vocabulum mysticum," is produced by the "ordinatio harmonica" of status (I. c. 24); but the populus as a 'subject' of rights is even for him a "societas civilis" (c. 3) and "collectivum quid" (c. 6), which only "in jure" is treated as a "persona" (ib. § 22–24).

131. Thus Besold, loc. cit. s. 1 c. 1 § 5; and Tulden, c. 11 (only "omnes singuli"; and yet in c. 9 the concept of "corpus").—Besold even identifies the State with the whole community; see for example loc. cit. § 7 (in the public domain there is "nuda proprietas penes universitatem populi sive rempublicam, ususfructus autem penes regem"), and Diss. de jure territor., c. 4. And he himself was the first to suggest the idea of the sovereign Personality of the State, as he conceives the State as an organized body animated by regere et subjici (Diss. praecog., c. 5 and c. 8 § 1), compares it more than once to the organic body (Diss. de republica curanda, c. 1 ff.), and in the Diss. de majestate, s. 1 c. 1 § 4, argues as follows: "nunquam censendum est, totam et universam Rempublicam per Principem repraesentari; caput est non totum corpus; et quomodo in corpore humano etiam aliarum partium functiones sunt, ita et adhuc corporis publici et populi aliqua est Majestas."

132. Thus all the writers cited in Notes 124–129 above.

133. See Paurmeister, in Note 125 (various 'real rights' of the ruler in the property of the people); Otto, in Note 126 (mere administratio); Limnaeus, in Note 129 (ususfructus); Berckringer, 1. c. 4 § 6–7: the people 'privatively' transfers only the exercitium, at most this is only a sort of "locatio," the two majestates are related to each other as dominium and ususfructus.

134. As for example Boxhorn, II. c. 4 § 45 ff. (when freedom is in danger of total loss the people may remove the tyrant and even alter the form of government); likewise Disquis. polit., c. 3. Bortius, in Arumaeus, I. nr. 30 c. 7 (when the princeps injures the salus Reipublicae, for whose promotion alone he was appointed, or violates pacta expressa, then "dissolvitur obligatio" and "populus fit potior"; "contra quod remedium est, ut resistat populus et, si opus, deponat eundem"). Hilliger, ib., II. nr. 13 c. 9. Brautlacht, VIII. c. 5. Frantzken, loc. cit. § 92–101 (even in the monarchia absoluta, whenever the purpose of the institution is disregarded; by virtue of jus naturale). Limnaeus, above, Note 129. Berckringer, I. c. 5 (the majestas personalis is accountable for "delicta publica").—A different view is taken in the case of the true monarchy by Besold, Diss. de maj., s. 1 c. 6 § 2.

135. The first two attributes are claimed for majestas personalis by all the writers cited in Notes 124–129, the attribute of potestas absoluta by Bortius (Note 126), Besold (Note 127), and Carpzov (loc. cit. c. 12 s. 2).

136. Thus Bortius, c. 6, says that each of the two majestates is "summa et absoluta," but each only "in suo ordine et genere," the one in "fundando," the other in "regendo." Similarly Limnaeus, loc. cit. nr. 57 ff., and Berckringer, I. c. 5, each is "suo ordine" supreme, but just for this reason the majestas realis is the higher. Also Brautlacht, III. c. 2 § 10, says that each of the two majestates is summa neminique subjecta, perpetua, incommunicabilis, unica, indivisibilis, but majestas personalis is "restricta et limitata" by majestas realis; see ib. c. 3 § 1–3.

137. But to make it possible to split off the majestas personalis they must consider sovereignty as at bottom divisible; see for example Arumaeus, IV. nr. 2 (for it is not natura unum, but a "collectio variarum partium"); Bortius, c. 1 § 2–5 (it is not a "totum essentiale" but a "totum potentiale," a "compages potestatum et functionum").

138. Thus Besold, Diss. de statu Reipublicae mixtae, c. 1: there may be a mere limitation of sovereignty by the "ratio gubernandi," but also there may be a mixture of the status ipse, as for example in a monarchy the Estates may have a "communicata majestatica potestas"; for while majestas is not really divisible yet "pro indiviso" it may be possessed by several together; compare c. 2–3 on true mixtures, c. 4–6 on constitutional limitations of the sovereign. Frantzken, Diss. de statu Reip. mixtae, in Arumaeus, III. nr. 27: there is a forma mixta where the majestas is divisible in so far as its parts can be jointly possessed by others through a communication of the holder of summa potestas "non separatim, sed cum Principe conjunctim." Carpzov, loc. cit., c. 13 s. 9 nr. 28–31: majestas is indivisible only "pro diviso," not "pro indiviso." Limnaeus, Jus publ., I. c. 10 nr. 11 ff., and IV., add. ad lib. I. c. 10, p. 95 ff. and 112 ff.: the "majestas simul sumpta cum omnibus partibus suis" is "unum quid" and "totum potentiale," hence it cannot be distributed among several in its entirety but the parts themselves may be distributed among several 'subjects.' Likewise Tulden, II. c. 16–23 (forma mixta and temperata); Werdenhagen, II. c. 25; Liebenthal, d. VIII. q. 1; Berckringer, I. c. 5 § 7 (indivisa, non indivisibilis), and c. 12 § 15–21 (forma mixta with a true division of powers).

139. Thus Kirchner, d. III. § 7 litt. e.; Alstedius, p. 69 ff.; Arumaeus and almost all of his pupils, as for example Otto, Diss. an mixtus detur Reipublicae status, II. nr. 22 (as the summa potestas even if limitata is yet summa, he denies that it ceases to be summa because of any "divisio et communicatio"); Bortius, c. 4; Brautlacht (above, Note 136).

140. Paurmeister, II. c. 1: sovereignty is in substance, even in the Germanic Empire, inalienably in the Respublica, hence in "omnes cives ut universi," even though they have a share in the summa potestas only

"potentia" not "actu"; but it is exercised by the "collegium civium reipublicae Romanae actu participum," that is, by the Emperor and the imperial Estates, who "in uno compendio repraesentativo" represent the general body; according to c. 2 and c. 11 nr. 18–20, of the ideal shares (pro indiviso) of the imperial power the Emperor has one-half, and the Collegium of each imperial Estate one-sixth (one-third when the throne is vacant).

141. Thus Besold, De statu Reip. mixtae, c. 2; Frantzken, De statu Reip. mixtae, in Arumaeus, III. nr. 27, and ib. IV. nr. 41 § 60 ff.; Carpzov, loc. cit., c. 13 s. 2, 6, 9, c. 1 s. 13, and De regalibus, in Arumaeus, III. nr. 15 § 103; Liebenthal, d. VIII. q. 1; also Limnaeus, loc. cit., while in the Capitulationes, loc. cit., he holds rather the view of Arumaeus.

142. See Arumaeus, I. nr. 1 and elsewhere; Otto, De jure publico Imp. Rom. (1616), c. 7 and 9, and Diss., in Arumaeus, II. nr. 22 § 44 ff.; Bortius, ib., I. nr. 30 c. 4, and Jurisprud. publ. Germ., ib., I. nr. 33 p. 998 ff. and 1013 ff.; Brautlacht, loc. cit.; Cubach, Jurisprudentiae Germano-publicae lib. I. et II., Erfurt 1617; Beindorffius, in Arumaeus, III. nr. 6 p. 227 § 38; Hilliger, ib., II. nr. 13 c. 5; Konings, ib., II. nr. 13 c. 5; Schieferer, ib. III. nr. 29.—Likewise Alstedius, p. 69–80.

143. It should be noted that the adherents of the doctrine of majestas realis, while advancing to a more or less republican construction for the Empire, at the same time championed a monarchical-absolutist conception for the Territories, and often (as in Carpzov) championed it strenuously. For while on the one hand they deduced from the peculiar structure of the Empire a large measure of independence of the parts, on the other hand they held fast to the idea of the centralized State and thus they did not apply the theory of double sovereignty to the Territories as such, as they were not really States. Hence they derived the rights of the territorial Princes from the majestas realis of the people of the Empire, not the people of the Territory, and thus could treat these rights as transferred downward in indefinite fullness and boundlessness.

144. See especially Graswinckel, op. cit. c. 10–11 (majestas realis and personalis are mutually exclusive: the former exists in republics, during an interregnum, and in the Rex sub conditione, but is absorbed by an actual majestas personalis). Micraelius, I. c. 10. Cellarius, c. 9 § 18–25. Conring and Bensen (above, Part I., Ch. I. Notes 10–12). Felwinger, De maj., p. 817 ff. (like Graswinckel). Huber, I. 3 c. 1 § 11 ff. (a duplex majestas is impossible; the majestas personalis would be a mere "dignitas ministerii"). Horn. c. 10 § 11–15 ("monstrum" and "fabulosus foetus" of majestas realis). Ziegler, I. c. 1 § 44 ff. Becmann, c. 12. Pufendorf, De jure N. et G., VII. c. 2 § 14, c. 6 § 4, De off., II. c. 9 (separating the

strict doctrine of popular sovereignty and the doctrine of majestas realis). Boecler, Inst. pol., II. c. 1. Thomasius, Inst. jur. div., III. c. 6 § 121 ff. Hert, Opusc., I. 1 p. 308. Kestner, c. 7 § 9. Stryk, Diss., XIV., nr. 7 c. 2 nr. 54. Gundling, Jus nat., c. 38 § 22 ("inventa otiosi ingenii"). Boehmer, P. spec. I. c. 4 § 22 (absurd, as they are one). Schmier, II. c. 1 s. 2 § 1 (there is only majestas personalis; it is in the people originally and in case of reversion, but otherwise in the ruler). Heincke, I. c. 2 § 15, c. 3 § 4. Heineccius, Prael., I. c. 3 § 8–9, Elem. jur. nat., II. § 130 ff. Kreittmayr, § 5. Yet Scheidemantel, I. p. 111 ff., combats the doctrine of popular sovereignty (even Rousseau's) under the name of the doctrine of 'real' as apart from 'personal' majesty.

145. Grotius, I. c. 3 § 7; here he mentions the possibility of several subjecta communia under one subjectum proprium by way of a 'personal union.' See also II. c. 6 § 6: sovereignty resides everywhere in the undivided body of the State, like the soul in the living body, but goes over with a separated part. Also ib. c. 9 § 3, c. 14 § 1 and 12, II. c. 5 § 23.

146. See II. c. 9 § 3: "plane autem corpora haec artificialia instar habent corporis naturalis"; thus the identity amid change, extinction by destruction of the corpus or of the spiritus (meaning the imperium). Also I. c. 3 § 7 and II. c. 6 § 4, where at the same time he brings out the distinction of the corpus morale from the corpus naturale (possibility of one head of several bodies, right of the parts to resist separation).

147. See for example II. c. 5 § 17–24 (votes of the majority, with-drawal), § 31, c. 8, c. 9 § 3, c. 14 (contracts), c. 21 (delicts), III. c. 2 (liability of the singuli).

148. The universitas is nothing but "singuli quique congregati, vel in summam reputati" (II. c. 21 § 7); its bond as well as its basis is the con-tract of association (II. c. 5 § 17–24, and above, Ch. II. Note 69); its unity is collective and fictive (II. c. 21 § 8).

149. Very often princeps (superior) and populus (universitas) are al-ternatively named, as in II. c. 3 § 19, c. 6, c. 9, c. 16 § 16 and 31, III. c. 20; and in just the same sense "rex aut civitas," as in II. c. 15 § 16.

150. See for example I. c. 3 § 9 and 12. Thus also it is the people that is bound by contracts of the ruler, since as coetus or universitas it has transferred this power to him; and the successor (who as such is not bound unless he is the heir, as he holds the imperium not a decesso but a populo) is bound "per interpositam civitatem" (II. c. 14 § 11); with "probabilis ratio" the "populus ipse" and therefore the successor himself as its head is bound by the auctoritas regentium as if by the authority of a tutor (ib. § 12). Likewise the State's property becomes the "patrimonium populi" and thus the "consensus populi" is requisite for its alienation (II. c. 6 § 3–

11, c. 9 § 3–11, c. 21 § 15, also I. c. 3 § 13, 15, 17, c. 4, III. c. 2). The people is also the true owner of church property (III. c. 5 § 2, c. 6, c. 8, c. 9 § 4).

151. There is not a single legal relation in which the 'right-subjectivity' of the "civitas" or "regnum" is not ascribed in exactly the same way and indeed far more often to the "populus," the "universitas" or the "universi." Likewise as to the ruler, it is said indifferently that he acts "vice civitatis" and "vice populi."

152. See I. c. 3 § 11: in the State-power the res and the modus habendi must be distinguished; it may be given "jure pleno proprietatis," "jure usufructuario" or "jure temporario"; III. c. 8 § 1: the conqueror may subdue the universos and then may acquire either the mere "imperium ut est in rege aut alio imperante" or else the patrimonial and alienable "imperium ut in populo est"; also I. c. 3 § 12–15 and II. c. 6 § 3–14, on the alienability of the "imperia in patrimonio imperantis" and its rights, as well as the possibility of disposing of it by testament.

153. See I. c. 3 § 13–15; also ib. c. 4 § 10, II. c. 6 § 3–10 (alienation of domain), and § 11–13 (alienation of property), III. c. 8 § 1, c. 20 § 5 (in treaties of peace).

154. See I. c. 4. In principle he denies the right of resistance, even for inferior magistrates (§ 1–7). But he allows it as against the ruler to whom no sovereignty has really been transferred (§ 8), who has abdicated or been derelict (§ 9), who seeks to perform an ipso jure void alienation of the State (§ 10), who has forfeited his position by virtue of a lex commissoria (§ 12), who in a divided imperium invades the pars populi aut senatus (§ 13), or against whom the people in the transference has expressly reserved to itself the right of resistance in certain cases (§ 14). In this the contractual basis is visible throughout. Furthermore, a king who acknowledges himself an enemy of the whole people and seeks to destroy it may be driven out (§ 11). But in this case, which besides should scarcely be possible except in a union of several States under one king, there is rather a plain assumption of a 'law of necessity,' and in any case the idea of the subjectum commune is not used.

155. See I. c. 3 § 16, c. 4 § 12, II. c. 14 § 2; contractual obligation does not destroy majestas, even though a contrary act should be void or the lex commissoria is added, for the nullity or the loss of rulership follows "ipso jure" and no "superior" is constituted.

156. See I. c. 3 § 17–20, c. 4 § 13; "summum imperium unum quiddam fit ac per se indivisum," but it is divisible per partes potentiales sive subjectivas; thus the fundamental contract may make a "summitatis divisio" between king and people; but this takes place only when sovereign rights

and coercive power are reserved to the people, not simply when the ruler's power is limited; only from such a division of sovereignty does a real mixed form result.

157. In particular by Becmann, c. 12 § 7: "subjectum majestatis est tum Respublica seu persona moralis, quam Respublica induit, tum personae singulares, quae moralem istam repraesentant"; but here on the one hand the Respublica is identified with the "universi" or "omnes simul" united into a 'moral person' (see also § 4–6), and on the other hand it is explained that the king is not "minor" than the "universi seu Respublica" but that, as he represents it perfectly, "eadem non minor erit sed ipsi aequalis"; it is as with the image in the mirror. See also Treuer on Pufend. De off., II. c. 7 § 9: majestatis divisio produces no "monstrum," as indeed "respublica perpetuum majestatis subjectum manet." Rachelius, tit. 32 § 2 (while the separation of majestas realis and personalis is rejected as the highest "pernicies"). Mullerus, I. c. 7 § 65 (likewise).

158. Thus Horn, II. c. 11 § 1 (as the body without the soul is a "cadaver" and can have no rights, while the soul is the imperans); Pufendorf, de jure N. et G., VII. c. 6 § 4, De off., II. c. 9; Kestner, c. 7 § 9; Boecler, loc. cit.; Alberti, c. 14 § 3; Stryk, loc. cit. nr. 55; Heincke, I. c. 2 § 15, c. 3 § 4 (Grotius is not to blame for the notion of majestas realis, but at the same time his subjectum commune is a perversion).

159. See Joh. G. Kulpis (1652–1698), Exerc. ad Grot., II. § 6 Not.; Schmier, II. c. 3 s. 1 § 1 (the phrase "subjectum commune" expresses only the inseparableness of sovereignty from the "corpus Reipublicae rite formatum," so that the ruler himself is sovereign only as ruler and, failing him, a reversion of sovereignty takes place); Hert, loc. cit. p. 298 § 12 (the subjectum commune of Grotius means only the right of the people to a reversion of the vacated sovereignty of the ruler); Ickstatt, Op., II. op. 1 c. 1 § 12 (the phrases "subjectivum constitutivum" and "subjectivum activum" would be better).

160. De cive, c. 5–7, 12–13, Lev., c. 17–19, 23, 30. See above, p. 95–96.

161. For the contractual theorists see above, p. 107 ff.; in the theocratic systems (above, p. 76) the jus divinum et naturale is always recognized as a restriction of sovereignty.

162. Quite like Hobbes, Spinoza describes sovereignty as the "ipsum jus naturae" completely given up by the individuals, as quite absolute and "translata" to the ruler exclusively, wherein "absque imperii divisione et consequenter destructione" a reservation is impossible; Tract. theol.-pol., c. 16, Tract. pol., c. 2 § 15, c. 3 § 2–5 and § 11–18. See further

Houtuynus (above, Ch. II. Note 38). Similarly but with theocratic additions Bossuet, above, Ch. II. Note 22, and also Pol., II. a. 1–3 and IV. a. 1.

163. At the same time as Hobbes, Graswinckel on a theocratic basis described majestas as a potestas una, summa in se et absoluta, of which when one knows that it is one also knows what it is; it cannot be a majus vel minus, but must be omni lege major, nullo limite circumscripta; it is indivisible and illimitable and is wholly destroyed by any constitutional restriction, so that the king who is in any way restricted is not a king but the mere administrator of a republic; see especially c. 3–4, 7, 9, 11–13. Then Horn sought to prove at length that the majestas bestowed by God on the Monarch as "Pro-Deus" is "sua essentia una et indivisibilis" and can as little be communicated as "voluntas et intellectus Petri cani communicari potest," and hence that any division of powers or mixture of forms of State dissolves the State (II. c. 2 § 1, 8, c. 10 § 5, III. c. un. § 3); he exalted this Majesty to an all-embracing power over persons, property and "regimen universale" (above, Ch. I. Note 39), even derived the succession to the throne from the presumed will of the predecessor (II. c. 9 § 15), and recognized no legal limitations of the sovereign other than the ethical obligation of divine and natural law. Nevertheless he admitted that in actual States the "modus habendi" can be a limited one, and can either fix limitations or appoint other persons to share in the exercise of the rights of majesty; but such a "pactum" can also be broken in case of necessity and even a promise on oath binds the Monarch only in his conscience (II. c. 5 § 4–15). See further James I, Wandalinus, Filmer (above, Ch. I. Note 38). Also Felwinger, p. 817 ff. (like Graswinckel, but with inconsistent admission of the respublica mixta, above, Note 97).

164. See for example Micraelius, I. c. 10 § 12–16: majestas (τὸ κύριον, supremitas, superioritas) is summa, legibus soluta, una et individua, hence it must be transferred either wholly or not at all; also ib. q. 1–7 p. 108 ff.; Cellarius, c. 9; potestas summa, soluta, individua, ubique; he who is bound by fundamental laws does not possess it; Becmann, c. 12: summa, innumerabilis, universalis, absoluta; Franc. Frid. ab Andler, Jurisprudentia, Sulzbach 1682, p. 82 ff.—Similarly but with theocratic additions Salmasius, c. 1–6 (the transference is an alienation; the people, whether vi or voluntate, is like a servus and can no more free itself than a slave can; a Rex who is a minister populi is no Rex); H. de Cocceji, Prodromus (the transference is an alienation in proper right); S. de Cocceji, Jurispr. nat., § 617–618 (potestas summa et jure proprio obtenta), and § 624 (no

status mixtus); Mevius, V. § 27 ff. (una, summa, absoluta, soluta legibus, rationibus non obnoxia); Alberti, c. 14 § 4 ff. (potestas Dei vicaria et summa).

165. See Huber, De jure imperii sine vi a populo sui juris constituti (Opera minora, I. nr. 2), and De jure civ., I. 2 c. 5–7 (also I. 2 c. 3, I. 3 c. 1 § 16 and 20): the translatio is not a mandatum but a "translatio juris," so that the sovereign is the major pars or the Imperans taking its place; but the sovereign has only so much power as the populus transferre voluit. Hence while the power of the State is summa and "legibus a se latis non obligata nisi voluntarie," it is bound by the written or unwritten constitution which contains the terms of its institution (I. 3 c. 1). From this there follow everywhere inviolable rights of the individuals (above, Ch. II. Note 95), and also of the people as a whole (above, Ch. II. Note 42) who, not merely on the ground of a lex commissoria but even without this, in case of a manifest transgression of bounds can declare the imperium forfeited and punish the imperans (I. 9 c. 4). And while majestas is truly one and indivisible, yet it may stand in joint possession (I. 3 c. 1). In all forms of government alike, and with regard to the essential rights of supremacy, it is inalienable and imprescriptible, but among the three political 'subjects' (King, Optimates, People) there may be a conveyance and usucaption of the rights of majesty (ib. c. 2 and 6–9). Hence, while there is no forma mixta in the sense of a division of powers, yet there may be: (1) States whose sovereign suffers constitutional limitations of "summitas," as in France; (2) States in which the sovereign power is "summa, non integra," in that non-sovereign factors bind the sovereign to their concurrence by virtue of a joint possession of particular rights of supremacy, as in parliamentary monarchies; (3) States in which the sovereignty, by virtue of a true "communicatio majestatis," is possessed "simul et communicative" by a number of 'subjects' as a "societas imperii," as in Germany, Poland and Venice (I. 3 c. 5, 8, 9, I. 8 c. 6).

166. Leibniz sets up, particularly in Caesarinus-Fürstenerius, a wholly relative concept of sovereignty, which not only consists with constitutional limitations (even the lex commissoria) and division, but even admits of a multiple sovereignty in one State, and can indeed be quite different internally and externally; he even attempts an analysis of the doctrinal concept of sovereignty into three different concepts, which he distinguishes as majestas, superioritas and supremitas; see especially praef., p. 329 ff., c. 10–12 and c. 26–33. In c. 11 he strongly maintains this idea against Hobbes and others (naturally Pufendorf is meant), who construct for themselves by logic an absolute notion of sovereignty and, as soon as they find something actually existing that does not correspond to this, are

quick to call it a "monstrum": according to them every existing State (even France) is at bottom an Anarchy, and a sovereignty exists only "in ea Republica, cujus Rex Deus est"; but in human affairs "mediae viae" prevail. See also Specimen demonstrationum politicorum pro Rege Polonorum eligendo (1669), prop. 16 (difference between ipsa vis et potestas and the exercitium).

167. Veit Ludwig v. Seckendorf, Teutscher Fürstenstaat, 1678 (1st ed. 1655), II. c. 1 ff.; also c. 4 (defense of the rights of provincial Diets), III. c. 3 nr. 8 (consent to taxation; 'for the sake of equality and common liberty' the Prince should not tax even his own dependents and tenants before the Estates have consented to the tax); also Christenstaat, 1685, II. c. 6 and 7.—Here we may also place Fénelon, who says indeed that the "forme mixte" or "partage de souveraineté" is impracticable, yet as against the despotism of the ruler as well as of the people he commends a limited monarchy in which an aristocratic assembly votes the laws and the people itself votes the taxes; loc. cit. c. 12 and 15.

168. This is especially true of Conring in his numerous political dissertations; however strictly he observes the idea of pure Ruler's-sovereignty and denies all popular rights even as against the tyrant, who is not distinguished from the king (Opera, III. p. 723 ff., 898, 909 ff., 955 ff., 1027), yet he finally adheres in all essentials to Aristotle (hence also the forma mixta, Diss. de republica of 1653, ib. p. 763 ff. § 13).

169. Thus Mevius, V. § 30-32, treats sovereignty as limited by its purpose, by the constitution and by the inalienability of the State's property. Likewise Alberti, c. 14 § 4 ff. Also Micràelius, I. c. 10 and c. 13 § 3 ff., recognizes not the forma mixta but rather the forma temperata, as leges fundamentales are binding as contracts and a transference cum conditione touches only the modus habendi.—Now as before, the teachers of public law are almost unanimous in requiring, at least in principle, the consent of the people to the alienation of domain; thus v. Ludewig, Consilia Hallensia, II. 2, cons. 15 of 1709 and cons. 63 of 1717 (the royal demesne is granted by the 'country' as a mere ususfructus); S. de Cocceji, loc. cit. § 633 (except in case of public necessity and in patrimonial kingdoms); see above, Note 83.

170. While even earlier suggestions of this idea occur here and there (as in Besold and Frantzken, above, Note 138), yet the idea of a divided sovereignty still prevailed (above, Notes 95, 97, 138, 140, 141, 156), and the doctrine of joint sovereignty was gradually matured for the first time in the polemics against von Chemnitz and Pufendorf. See Cellarius, c. 9 § 35: "conjunctim sumpti." Hulderichus ab Eyben, De sede majestatis Romano-Germanicae, 1664 (Scripta, III. nr. 5), c. 1 § 31 ff.: miscetur

non majestas, sed subjectum; c. 3: imperator cum statibus as the subjectum commune; yet the exercise of the supreme power may also be
divided or may in some respects be carried on jointly and in others be
divided (c. 1 § 37), and the latter is the case in Germany in so far as
the territorial Princedom is a division of imperial sovereignty for administrative purposes (c. 3). "Pacificus a Lapide" (Oldenburger), Dn. de
Monzambano illustratus et restrictus, "Utopia" 1668 (so far as concerns
the Empire as a "commune corpus civile" the Emperor and Imperial Diet
together represent the majestas). Kulpis, Diss. academ., Strasburg 1705,
nr. 7 p. 256 ff. (subjectum mixtum, potestas una). P. H. Vitriarius, Institutiones juris publici (1686), I. 19 § 2, and especially I. 7 § 4–6
(majestas is not divided, but is one and indivisible in the Emperor "conjunctim cum aliis"; it is one right with subjecta diversa et mixta, analogous
to correal obligation). Pfeffinger, I. 3 N. a (I. p. 290), I. 7 § 5 N. a-e
(ib. p. 865: the Estates as "Co-Imperantes et Majestatis participes"), ib.
§ 6 N. a (ib. p. 866–870: penes omnes conjunctim consideratos). Huber,
above, Note 165. Conring, De comitiis imperii, 1666, c. 4–5. On the
later diffusion of this doctrine see Schulze, Einl., § 67.—The idea of the
mixed form of State in the sense of the division of powers is reproduced
by Boecler, II. c. 2 and III. c. 8.

171. "Hippolithus a Lapide" (v. Chemnitz, 1605–1678), Dissertatio
de ratione status in imperio nostro Romano-Germanico, 1640, c. 1–18:
the majestas as individua, summa et absoluta potestas is not in the Emperor, who is removable, restricted, subject to a Judge, has no legislative
power, no jus sacrorum, no sovereignty in international law, no suprema
jurisdictio, no right to tax, no superiority over officers, and no right of
coinage, and whose so-called "plenitudo" consists only in a few reserved
rights; on the contrary the majestas is in the Estates "ut universitas," which
as an aristocratic body (yet "ex diversis aristocratiis mixtus") stand above
the Emperor, recognize him only as the "Director" of their Corpus, and
may by a corporate act even abolish the whole institution of the Empire.
At most in the "ratio administrandi" there are slight traces of a monarchical element.

172. "Hippolithus a Lapide" takes the definition of sovereignty, its
attributes and the distinction of status reipublicae and ratio administrandi
from Bodin; yet he opines that a status mixtus may in fact decay, it is
only "parum durabilis" and a transitional form (like an egg in incubation);
the "forma plene consummata" requires "una suprema potestas."

173. As by Rachelius, I. tit. 40 § 5 (if the Empire is to be regarded
on the whole as una Respublica).

174. "Severinus de Monzambano" (Pufendorf), De statu imperii Ger-

manici ad Laelium fratrem liber, Geneva 1667, c. 6 § 8–9: "irregulare aliquod corpus et monstro simile"; it has no simple forma mixta, which is itself monstrous, but is something midway between a decaying monarchy and a growing confederation. The latter aspect does not concern us here.

175. De jure N. et G., VII. c. 5 § 5, c. 6, c. 8; De off., II. c. 8 § 4, c. 9.

176. De jure N. et G., VII. c. 6 § 13–17 (but a temporary sovereign is impossible).

177. De jure N. et G., VII. c. 6 § 7–13; De off., II. c. 9; above, Ch. II. Note 41.

178. De jure N. et G., VII. c. 4, c. 5 § 12–15, c. 6 § 13; De off., II. c. 7, c. 8 § 12.

179. Thomasius, Inst. jur. div., III. c. 6 § 32 ff., § 115 ff., 156 ff., 162 ff. (just like Pufendorf). Hert, Opusc., I. 1 p. 307 ff. (yet it should be noted that in s. 3 § 1–5 he says that the enthronement of the king should be construed not as an "alienatio" of the sovereign rights of the people but rather, as in a democracy, a mere "declaratio" of who shall hold the supreme power); also Elem., I. s. 11. Titius, Spec. jur. publ., VII. c. 7 § 17 ff., 31 ff., 106 ff. (he holds especially to the formula that the potestas remains eadem even when the modus exercendi is different; for majestas the only attributes which are really essential are "summa et independens"). Kestner, c. 7 § 3 ff. (yet in § 19 he gives to the people a right of resistance in case of manifest tyranny). Gundling, Jus nat., c. 36–37, Disc., c. 35–36. See also Stryk, Diss., XIV. nr. 7 and IV. nr. 1. Ickstatt, Op., II. op. 1 c. 1 § 13–21. Kreittmayr, § 5 ff.—Also above, p. 97 ff. and 108 ff.

180. Boehmer, P. spec. I. c. 4: the imperans necessarily has the sovereignty as "jus proprium et independens," which externally gives the "jura libertatis" of the state of nature, internally the "jus summi imperii" with all the powers over the subjects that are requisite to attain the purpose of the State; this majestas is essentially unitary, everywhere the same, all-embracing, permanent, exempt from positive law, and irresponsible; ib. III. c. 1–2 and 4: "stante imperio" it belongs by virtue of a true "alienatio" to the ruler exclusively. The people has no remnant of majestas or summa potestas, no right of resistance or deposition (c. 4 § 32–33), no power of concurrence in the laws (II. c. 3 § 14); but at the same time, unless it has beforehand given full power to the "alienatio regni," it must give its consent to this act, as otherwise "imperium vacat" and reverts to the people (III. c. 4 § 9–11); I. c. 3: a division of powers is absurd; II. c. 3 § 15 and III. c. 4 § 15 ff.: conversely, a limitation of the sovereign is possible by binding pacta and hence also by leges fun-

damentales, if they dispense with all coercive force and are interpreted by the ruler alone, while for the rest they may ordain that assemblies be called in consultation as to certain acts of government; I. c. 4 § 1: even an added "clausula nullitatis" is immaterial; yet, while of itself it creates no right of resistance or of declaring the ruler's acts void, it has a practical importance for his successors. Compare above, Ch. II. Notes 41 and 98. —Quite similarly Heineccius, Prael. in Puf. (Op., VIII. 2), I. c. 3 § 8–9, Elem. jur. nat., II. § 130 ff.

181. According to Schmier the summa potestas, which as the anima cannot be absent from the corpus politicum without reducing it to an "informe cadaver," is the libertas of the status naturalis, irresponsible, "legibus positivis soluta," inviolabilis, indivisibilis (II. pr. and c. 1 s. 1); it must be fully and completely in the imperans, yet it may be restricted by the constitution (ib. s. 2), even with the addition of the clausula nullitatis (nr. 79–83) and of the lex commissoria (nr. 84–87); in itself the people neither has a concurrent power in law-making (III. c. 2 nr. 28–30), nor has it a right of deposition, except in the hardly possible case of the ruler becoming a "hostis apertus" (II. c. 4 s. 2 § 2); on the other hand, in case of doubt it must give its consent in altering the succession to the throne or in alienations (II. c. 2 s. 1 § 2–3, and s. 2 § 3). Heincke, I. c. 3, § 13 and 26. Also above, Ch. II. Note 99.

182. Thus v. Ludewig, Opusc., I. 1 op. 8 c. 1; Kestner, c. 7 § 11–12; and Heineccius, Elem., II. § 147–149, all of whom for this reason allow in no case a disposal of the substance of the State without the consent of the people. On the other hand Thomasius, loc. cit. § 132 ff., Boehmer, I. c. 3 § 35–36, and Schmier, II. c. 2 s. 2 § 3, hold fast to the idea, and Thomasius speaks of the "regna usufructuaria" rather than "fideicommissaria," while Boehmer wholly rejects the analogy of ususfructus and speaks only of "regna non patrimonialia."

183. Thus Thomasius, loc. cit. § 38 ff., 59 ff., 156 ff. (vitium status); Boehmer, I. c. 3 § 25–26 (monstrum Reipublicae); Heineccius, loc. cit. § 138 (disruption of the "unitas voluntatis" and a "Respublica in Republica").

184. Thus Otto, Note on Pufend. De off., II. c. 8 § 12, says that the "irregularitas" due to the mixta forma is no evil and, as in the Germanic Empire, it is "ad genium populi accommodata." Hert, Elem., I. s. 11–12, sets up a formal system of "respublicae irregulares" divided into five classes. Titius, loc. cit. § 31–33 and 53–63, says indeed that when "majestas pluribus simplici saltem obligatione connexis divisim vel indivisim competit," the State is not wholly united and there is a "vitium et morbus status": but even here there is a subjectum unum and civitas una, and

since neither nature nor the consensus gentium prescribes definite rules for the forms of the State, it would be better to replace the distinction of "respublica regularis" and "irregularis" by the distinction of "respublica adstricta" and "laxa"; see also § 106–121. Kestner, c. 7 § 5 and 8, allows "mixtiones," as the majestas may be possessed by several "in solidum." Gundling, Jus nat., c. 37 § 21–36, says that the "forma irregularis" with "majestas divisa," despite the lack of "unitas," exists in England and Germany, but that a true mixed form in Sidney's sense can at best subsist "per accidens." Schmier, I. c. 4, rejects the forma mixta as "informis," while as to the formae irregulares he accepts the teaching of Hert. Heincke, I. c. 3 § 24–25, identifies mixta and irregularis. Ickstatt, loc. cit. § 16–21, revives the old doctrine of the forma mixta, wherein the rights of sovereignty are either possessed by several 'subjects' jointly, or are divided, or in part are possessed jointly and in part divided; but in this he includes every limited monarchy.

185. See above, Notes 102 and 119–123; also James Harrington (1611–1677), Political Aphorisms (idea of the balancing of two assemblies); and compare the theory of the division of powers in the forma mixta (above, Notes 95, 97, 138, 140, 141, and above all Grotius, above, Note 156).

186. The derivation of Montesquieu's doctrine from the doctrine of popular sovereignty is shown particularly in the principle that the legislative power belongs by the very nature of things to the "peuple en corps" and is only exercised in the representation thereof by the legislative body; the idea of a separation of powers in the sense of a completely divided sovereignty shows itself in the statements that the executive and judicial powers should be just as irresponsible and irremovable as the legislative power, that these powers can operate on one another only negatively (power checks power), and that it is simply through the natural need of a united movement of the State that "elles seront forcées d'aller de concert"; the idea of the mixed constitution lastly determines the arrangement of the 'subjects' of the several powers; see XI. c. 4 and 6. See Voltaire, Idées républicaines (1765): civil government is "la volonté de tous, exécutée par un seul ou par plusieurs, en vertu des lois que tous ont portées" (Janet, II. p. 564). Likewise Abbé de Mably, Doutes (1768), lettre X., and Législ. (1776), III. ch. 3 (Janet, II. p. 701 ff.); Sir William Blackstone, Commentaries on the Laws of England, 1765; J. L. de Lolme, The Constitution of England, 1775 (in French 1771), and others.—For the rest see Ranke, loc. cit. p. 242 ff.; Mohl, I. p. 277 ff., also p. 273 N. 1.

187. Wolff has no sharply defined concept of sovereignty at all; the

power of the universi over the singuli arising from the social contract
(Inst., § 979 ff.) includes in itself indeed the rights of majesty which
are requisite for the public welfare (§ 1042 ff.), but can be transferred to
any 'subjects' under whatever conditions and restrictions may be desired,
and thus can also be divided (§ 982 ff.); constitutions are binding as
contracts and can be abrogated by the people, so far as no vested right
of the ruler is impaired (§ 984 ff.); from the limitation or division of
rulership there arise respublicae mixtae (§ 993 ff.); violations of the constitution give a right of resistance (§ 1079); but the general condition that
obedience is due only in case of good government, is inadmissible (§ 985).
Achenwall likewise says that the original sovereignty of the people may
be transferred in any manner (II. § 94 ff.); hence while sovereignty, in
absolute public law, as an "imperium summum, plenum, illimitatum"
bounded only by the purpose of the State itself, resides in the people or
in another moral or physical person (§ 112 ff.), yet by actual constitutional contracts any modalities may be established (§ 98 ff.); an "imperium
minus plenum" is possible (§ 99 and 152); also an "imperium limitatum"
is possible (§ 100), whereby in a monarchy the people or the Estates may
have a simple "corregimen" or a true "coimperium" (§ 152–153); and
lastly a true division of powers is possible, such that several physical or
moral persons each for itself have a "certa pars imperii," "independenter
a reliquis," and as mutually free and equal factors exercise an "imperium
plenum et absolutum" only when taken together (§ 186–188). Nettelbladt simply strikes out the distinctive mark of sovereignty from the concept of the State, when he argues that a "potestas non summa sed subalterna" may also be a State and that the idea of a "status in statu" is by
no means absurd (Syst. nat., § 1120 ff., 1129, 1159–1160); thus as regards the rights of majesty he allows division or joint possession or a
combination of both (§ 1142, 1155 ff., 1197); the people may transfer
the full power which is originally its own (§ 1132) as an equally full and
independent right, or concede the mere usufruct with reservation of the
"jura circa potestatem" for itself, or institute an imperium minus plenum
with reservation of popular rights, or lastly establish a mere imperium
limitatum by way of preserving a joint sovereignty (§ 1198); while thus
the ruler, as regards the power transferred to him, is always a persona
publica in statu naturali (§ 1200), and the people as a persona moralis
is sometimes subdita, sometimes partially in statu naturali, and sometimes
together with the ruler in statu naturali (§ 1201). Daries also recognizes
all kinds of mixed and limited forms (§ 655 ff., 747 ff., 767 ff., 780–
789).

188. Thus v. Justi, Der Grundriss einer guten Regierung, Frankfort

and Leipzig 1759, p. 142 ff. and 154 ff., Die Natur und das Wesen der Staaten, p. 164 ff. (mixed forms of government, division and balance of powers). Scheidemantel says that in every State there is required a Majesty which is exempt from the laws, supreme, undivided, indivisible, and including in itself all the particular rights of sovereignty (I. p. 103 ff. and 163 ff.), and rejects the division of powers because it disrupts the unity of the State (p. 156–162). Yet he recommends a joint government shared by several 'subjects' or the participation of the people in its exercise (ib.), says that the State's property is the 'property of the whole nation' and is merely administered by the sovereign (II. p. 333 ff.), and recognizes in case of actual tyranny a right of the whole nation to resist by force, as by the severance of the bond between it and the Prince it returns to the 'natural state of liberty and equality' (III. p. 364–375). At a later time Schlözer teaches that a sovereignty of the ruler is established in every State (op. cit., p. 73–78, 95, 100), as the sovereignty of the people cannot be retained and must necessarily be alienated (p. 43 § 9, 76, 97 § 3, 157–161), and just as little can the Law as an 'abstract thing' be sovereign (p. 77). Yet the ruler, as the 'depository of the common will,' is restricted by the rights of man (p. 95 ff.) as well as by a fundamental contract to be sworn with the people (p. 102); and hence in case of a breach thereof the people, 'by the concept of a contract in general,' may resist, coerce, depose and punish him (p. 105 § 8), and in some circumstances give him warning (p. 108 § 10). And though the State's power is indivisible, yet as every simple form of government leads to intolerable despotism, the "princeps compositus" was invented with a division of powers, checks and balances (p. 112 ff.); this mixed form of government, as 'the last resort of poor humanity, which must have a State,' has been established in England by 'accident, guided by good sense, favored by conjunctures' (p. 144–155).

189. See above, p. 76. Horn explains that we should speak of quasi-corpus, quasi-materia, quasi-pars, quasi-forma and the like, only "per analogiam et similitudinem" (I. c. 1 § 1), while in truth the "civitas" is nothing but a "multitudo collectim sumpta" (ib., and II. c. 1, § 1 and 18, c. 5 § 1). But in spite of all summation the "multitudo" is and remains a heap of individuals and hence the "civitas" is by no means a "totum," while the sum as such "nullam seriem Rerum intrat et ideo affectiones Entis non sustinet"; for this reason the State's power cannot be derived from the dominion of a whole over its parts any more than it can be derived from a transference from the singuli, who were not originally endowed with any imperium at all, whether "in se" or "in alios" (II. c. 1 § 18–19). Thus a true oneness above the manyness can only come from

a divine grant of majesty to one individual exalted above all other individuals. It is impossible to find a 'subject' of the so-called majestas realis (for regnum is equivalent to rex, the "lex inanimata" is no 'subject,' II. c. 10 § 11–15), the subjectum commune is absurd (ib. c. 11 § 1), and in a republic no 'subject' of majesty can be discovered, for the "universi" who are often taken for this are nothing but "conjuncti singuli" and thus would be at once 'subject' and 'object'; a really deciding majority would produce a sovereign changing with every vote; and the shares of the singuli in the State-power are not sovereign for themselves, as every "particula" cannot be "summa" at the same time nor can they all in their summation. Thus indeed there is here only a "societas" with "mutuae obligationes singulorum," without a unitary 'subjectivity' of rights and without majestas, hence also without any true 'right' over life and death (III. c. un., especially p. 563–568).

190. Salmasius, c. 7 p. 142–143: if the Rex stands above the singuli he also stands above the universus populus, as the "numerus" makes no difference and the universitas is nothing but "omnes collective sumpti"; moreover the universi can do something only as a "concio," but the concio has transferred its right to the King and without him it cannot come together again, so that now "unus est instar concionis" and therefore "instar totius populi."

191. Spinoza, above, Ch. II. Note 37; even he conceives the State as an organic body (as in Ethica, IV, prop. 18 schol.: "ut omnium mentes et corpora unam quasi mentem unumque corpus componant"; Tract. pol., c. 3 § 1, 5: "imperii corpus una veluti mente duci debet"); but only so that the imperans represents the mens and voluntas of all (ib. c. 3 § 5: "civitatis voluntas pro omnium voluntate habenda est"; also ib. c. 4 § 1–2, c. 2 § 15, c. 3 § 1–2, where the "civitas" is identified throughout with him "qui summum habet imperium"); in the democracy he ascribes the summa potestas to the "coetus universus . . . collegialiter," the "omnes collective" or the "omnes simul" (ib. c. 3 and 6, Tract. theol.-pol., c. 16, Ethica, loc. cit.).

192. Politique, V. a. 1: the Monarch is "l'État même"; also I. a. 3 prop. 1–6 (all forces must "être absorbées dans cette force unique," the gouvernement makes the State immortal, previously there is only an anarchic multitude); VI. a. 1 prop. 2–3.

193. See already Graswinckel, c. 4 and 11: the majestas of the "persona unum" or "corpore unum" is in the State, "quod in universo Deus, in corpore anima." Houtuynus, above, Ch. II. Note 38. Cellarius, c. 9 § 35. Micraelius, I. c. 10 § 14–17: majestas is like the soul and the imperantes (several "omnes simul") "repraesentant populum." Mevius,

§ 23–26 and 44: una voluntas arises when the will and act of the ruler pass for "tota communitas et omnes singuli"; "voluntas et judicium imperantium est voluntas totius societatis seu civitatis"; "imperantes totam multitudinem repraesentant et ejus vice sunt"; "repraesentant universitatem quae sui jus eis dedit."

194. De jure N. et G., I. c. 1, and already in essentials Elem. jurispr. univ., I. def. 1 ff. Then in the moral world he makes the "status" or condition of existence of the "personae morales" correspond in detail to the "spatium" (space and time) of the physical world; to the substances of the physical world there correspond the "personae morales," while the "res" do not need to be conceived as entia moralia, as their attributes (for example "sacra") are reducible to the "obligatio hominum"; all other entia moralia are also "formaliter modi" and correspond to the natural categories of "qualitas" or "quantitas." The entia moralia can be altered either by "divino arbitrio" or "hominum placito," "ipsa personarum aut rerum substantia physica haudquiquam immutata"; thus for example in the acquisition or loss of nobility there is no physical change; and for the same reason the notion of a "character moralis indelibilis" is absurd.

195. Elem., I. def. 4, and De jure N. et G., I. c. 1 § 12–15. The phrase "persona moralis" remained; but its original sense was obscured and it was more and more restricted to the "persona composita," while again the "persona simplex" was distinguished therefrom as equivalent to "persona physica."

196. Elem., I. def. 4, II. def. 12 § 26; De jure N. et G., I. c. 1 § 12–15; De off., II. c. 6 § 5–6. For the Family, Corporation, Commune, Church and State alike it is here argued that there is only a multitude and plura individua physica, until they "voluntates viresque suas univerint intervenientibus pactis" and thus introduce "una persona"; this union however is not "naturaliter" but only "moraliter" possible by a contract in which a promise of obedience reduces their energies to subjection and a transference of wills establishes the validity of the will of one as the will of all. Hence also, just like Hobbes, he describes the State as a "homo artificialis."

197. De jure N. et G., VII. c. 2 § 13, and De off., II. c. 6 § 10 (definition of the State as a "persona moralis composita, cujus voluntas, ex plurium pactis implicita et unita, pro voluntate omnium habetur, ut singulorum viribus et facultatibus ad pacem et securitatem communem uti possit"); De jure N. et G., VIII. c. 10 § 8 (application of this idea to the question of the binding of successors); ib. c. 5 § 8, and De off., II. c. 15 § 5 (likewise in the treatment of the State's property). Compare the passages cited above, Ch. II. Note 41, on the perfect representation of the

civitas by the imperans (even in "actio ex abusu ac pravitate voluntatis," if only the monarch or the ruling coetus "qua tales" will and act) and on the total absorption of the people's personality; also the passages cited there and in Note 177 of present Chapter, on the explanation of possible restraints of the ruler.

198. See already Becmann, c. 12 § 7: the respublica is a "persona moralis" which is fully and completely represented by the ruler. Thomasius, Inst. jur. div., I. c. 1 § 87 (persona moralis composita), III. c. 6 § 62–63 (definition of the State as such), ib. § 26–31 (origin through unio voluntatum et virium in the imperium), ib. § 64 (voluntas civitatis se exserit through unus or the major pars of a concilium), Fund. jur. nat., III. c. 6 § 7. Kestner, c. 7 § 3 (una quasi persona, by submission to unus homo vel coetus). Von Ludewig, Op., I. 1 op. 8. H. de Cocceji, loc. cit., and S. de Cocceji, loc. cit. § 280 (corpus artificiale seu mysticum). Heincke, I. c. 3 § 5 (imperans repraesentat totam civitatem).

199. See P. gen. c. 4 § 4 note f, P. spec. I. c. 2 § 18 note a, c. 3 § 1 note o and § 13–21: in the societas inaequalis there is such a submissio omnium voluntatum to una voluntas unius hominis vel integri concilii, ut omnium voluntas una sit voluntas et unius personae moralis vicem sustineat; for the voluntas omnium in hujus voluntate ita concentratur ut, quod imperans summus in hisce negotiis vult, omnes velle moraliter censeantur; this takes place in a monarchy more perfectly than in a republic. Boehmer makes special use of the concept of the State's "persona moralis" only in international law (P. gen. c. 2 § 3–7, P. spec. I. c. 3 § 22), in public law not even in the question as to the binding of successors (P. spec. I. c. 3 § 35, II. c. 3 § 16).

200. Thus for example Gundling, while he borrows from Hobbes the image of Leviathan (Jus nat., c. 35, Disc., c. 34), never once employs the concept of the State's personality (see especially Jus nat., c. 3 § 52, c. 36 § 211 ff.); instead he speaks simply of the persona repraesentiva of the Princeps taking the place of the totus populus (c. 12 § 40–42), while he opines the "magistratum esse mentem totius civitatis, ejus voluntatem esse voluntatem universorum et singulorum" (c. 35 § 30), and only remarks that the imperans may be a persona physica or moralis seu mystica, that is, a collegium (c. 35 § 34, c. 37 § 3–10). Thus when in the Diss. de universitate delinquente of 1724 (Exerc. academ., nr. 16 p. 829 ff.) he argues that the conception of the "persona mystica, moralis, composita" needs no "fictio juris," but that "intellectu juris," as with all res incorporales, a collective unity may be conceived as a special thing (§ 5–8)—this, the earliest explicit denial of the Fiction theory known to me, is but the expression of the highest reach of the purely 'collective' conception (compare ib. § 13–48)

and moreover does not in any way displace the idea of the artificiality of the collective person (§ 6).—Similarly Daries, Jus nat. § 24, compared with Praecog. § 24 and Jus nat. § 655 ff. (only the imperans as a persona physica or moralis is the 'subject'), § 660 and 661.—Most strictly Ickstatt, Op., II. op. 1 c. 1 § 14–15, where it is said that in the monarchical State "totius Reipublicae intellectus atque voluntas in intellectum atque voluntatem personae moralis simplicis resolvitur," as the monarch "totam Civitatem et singula Reipublicae membra repraesentat," and that only the republic, in which "plures personae conjunctim sumptae" take the same position, presents itself as a persona moralis composita; see § 6–13 and 66.—See also Kreittmayr, § 2 and 4.

201. Thus Huber argues that "civitas habet jus personae," therefore by its laws it binds the singuli but not itself (De jure civ., I. 3 c. 1 § 32), and applies the idea in the question as to the binding of successors (I. 9 c. 5 § 65–72) and in the treatment of the State's property (II. 4 c. 1 § 24 ff.). But "civitates per eos qui habent summam potestatem personae fiunt" (I. 3 c. 6 § 26), "summi imperantes personam civitatis constituunt" (I. 9 c. 5 § 67, 72), "summà potestas est ipsa civitas" (§ 51), the "voluntas imperantium" is the "voluntas civitatis" (I. 3 c. 2 § 14, c. 6 § 26), the government is related to the State as the soul to the body (I. 2 c. 2 § 1 ff. and 17 ff., c. 3 § 1); hence when "populus jus personae retinet" and remains a universitas with contractual rights and contractual capacity (above, Ch. II. Note 42) it falls, so to speak, out of the State. Quite similarly Titius, Otto and Treuer on Pufend. De off., II. c. 6 § 11, as well as Titius, Spec. jur. publ., IV. c. 5 (while the "respublica immortalis," which "voluit" through the ruler, "durat" and "vult" even after his death, his successor, who derives his authority always "ab ipsa civitate" and succeeds "capiti corporis liberi et adhuc durantis," remains bound; but in I. c. 1 § 43 ff. the State's personality is conceived as purely collective, and according to VII. c. 7 § 19, so long as there is an imperans it is merged in him).—Likewise Hert, who in Diss. de pluribus hominibus unam personam sustinentibus (Opusc., II. 3 p. 52 ff., s. 2 § 4–8) and Diss. de mod. const. (ib. I. 1 p. 286 ff., s. 1 § 3 and 5) explains the imperans, in the State as in a "societas rectoria," as the "anima in corpore" and vests him with the most absolute representation of the whole, which becomes a persona only through the summa potestas, nevertheless recognizes a distinct "persona populi" (see above, Ch. II. Note 42). Here as in the Annot. to Pufend. De jure N. et G., I. c. 1 § 3 note 4, he emphasizes the resemblance of the State and of every universitas to a corpus humanum, but at the same time works out a purely collective conception and brings out the artificiality of taking a "multi-

tudo" as "una persona moralis."—Not otherwise does Schmier locate the State's personality in the imperans as "anima civitatis," and only argues that the ruler may consist of all or a few "collecte considerati" as "compositum morale," wherein the "persona moralis" is always represented by the major part and despite the changes thereof it remains the same, just as a monarch whose opinions change (I. c. 3 nr. 3, 28–34, 62–72). Apart from this he recognizes the people as a legally competent 'subject,' but conceives it always in the sense of a collective unity (II. c. 2 s. 3 § 2, nr. 174–200, c. 4 s. 1 § 3); and while he speaks of the "corpus reipublicae" in organic terms (I. c. 2 s. 4 § 1, nr. 135–136), he expressly identifies this with the "civium universitas" or the "cives collectim et collegialiter accepti" (I. c. 3 nr. 67), and traces the rights of the majority back to a representation of all by it (ib. nr. 68–72).—Even Heineccius describes every societas, in virtue of the contractual union of wills, as "una persona moralis" (II. § 20 ff.), but makes a unitary personality arise in the State only from the submissio omnium voluntatum to the voluntas imperantis which is henceforth taken as the voluntas totius Reipublicae, as in this case a "conspiratio in unum" is not to be attained in any other way (§ 115 ff.), and only apart from this does he ascribe to the people a permanent collective unity in the sense of a societas aequalis (above, Ch. II. Note 42).— See also the perfect identification of the "respublica" with the "imperans" together with the distinction of "civitas" from "respublica," in Conring (especially Opera, III. p. 726, 763 ff., 898, 1027).

202. Leibniz places the essence of the State purely in the "una voluntas unitasque personae civilis, qua Respublica constat," but identifies this with the voluntas and "persona naturalis seu civilis ad instar naturalis" of the ruler vested with the power of representation by the submission of the wills of all (Caesar.-Fürst., c. 11, Einl. zum Cod. dipl., I. § 22 p. 306, Spec. dem., prop. 12); he who has the potestas has the jus Reipublicae and in him "persona Reipublicae civilis seu moralis continetur," for this persona is nothing but a persona ficta, quae in aggregatione jurium consistit (Spec. dem., prop. 1; likewise as to its fictive nature, ib. prop. 42, and Nova methodus, II. § 16); "persona summae potestatis continet in se personas subditorum civiles vel ut quidam vocant morales" (Spec. dem., prop. 57).

203. In v. Seckendorf, loc. cit., the "Stat" of the territory or of the Prince is the administrative business of the Prince himself; and just so a century later in F. K. v. Moser, Der Herr und der Diener, Frankfort 1761, the State is merged in the Prince; in J. J. Moser, Pütter and others the same idea occurs, while apart from this the provincial Estates appear as special corporative 'subjects' of rights; see also Fénelon, c. 5.—Frederick

the Great comes nearer to the idea of an organic State-personality when on the one hand he compares the State to the human body (Antimach., c. 3, 9, 12, 20, Consid., Oeuvres VIII. p. 24, Essai sur les formes, ib. IX. p. 197 ff.), and on the other hand describes the Prince as the "premier serviteur et premier magistrat de l'État" (Antimach., c. 1, Mémoires, Oeuvres I. p. 123, Last Will, ib. VI. p. 215, Essai, ib. IX. p. 197).

204. See Vico's doctrine in Bluntschli, p. 243–258. Montesquieu is acquainted with an organic view of national life (XIX. c. 14), but construes the union of forces and wills in the State (I. c. 3) and the forms of government (II. c. 1 ff.) in the traditional manner, while he does not develop the idea of State-personality at all and in fact abandons it in the doctrine of the division of powers. Justus Möser not only knows nothing of the State's personality (Patr. Phant., III. nr. 62), but even says that the Nation is 'not in itself a united being' (Vermischte Schriften, I. p. 335). Herder, despite his idea of evolution and despite his organic conception of the people, treats the State as wholly mechanical (Ideen, IX. c. 4, XIX. c. 6).

205. Wolff teaches that every society is 'to be regarded as a single person' (Inst., § 850), and is thus a persona moralis or 'moral person' (§ 96); hence the State is a 'free person' in the state of nature (§ 977) and an offense against 'the right of all and each' is an offense against the 'moral person' of the State (§ 1030); but such a 'moral person' is also formed by co-owners (§ 196). Then the 'moral person' of the State plays a special role only in international law (§ 1088 ff.), while internally it is only the relations between the ruler 'representing the whole people' (§ 991) and other moral or physical persons that are spoken of.

206. Nettelbladt, Syst. nat., § 83 and 85–86, Syst. pos., § 17 and 865. Conversely unus homo may embody plures personas, Syst. nat., § 82, 1194, Syst. pos., § 16.

207. Syst. nat., § 84; compare § 329 ff.

208. Syst. nat., § 1122: "Cives alicujus Reipublicae simul sumti persona moralis sunt, quae est ipsa Respublica"; § 1132.

209. Syst. nat., § 1403 ff.; also § 1200, where it is said that, despite the double 'right-subjectivity' of Prince and People in internal affairs, externally the princeps is "una persona cum populo."

210. Syst. nat., § 1155–1157 and 1198 (plures personae physicae vel morales may possess the State-power in common or by division); § 1200–1211 (apart from the princeps the populus is a persona moralis, whether it is "omnino subdita," or has its own share of power, or is in joint possession of the sovereignty); § 1211 (in the parliamentary monarchy the Monarch,

Estates and People are three 'subjects'); § 1220 (in the Aristocracy the "collegium optimatum" is the ruler, the senatus is a "persona moralis subdita," the populus as above).

211. Achenwall explains that every societas is a persona moralis, since, as a "complexus hominum" regarded in abstraction from the particular individuals, it is an "ens unum" (Proleg. § 92 and II. § 3); so far it underlies the rights of the singuli except where "diversa hominis individui et societatis natura" causes differences (Proleg. § 93 and II. § 16–21); the family itself is a societas composita which consists of several personae mysticae (Proleg. § 94 and II. § 78 ff.); for the State the idea of the "persona libera" is employed in international law (II. § 210 ff.); internally the imperans and the populus (but in the mixed form several imperantes) appear as 'subjects' bound in mutual obligations (II. § 174 ff. and § 187).—See also Scheidemantel, I. p. 33, 64, 157 ff., III. p. 408 ff.

212. Schlözer, who expressly describes the State as a 'machine put together very artfully' (p. 3 ff., 99, 157) and as a society for insuring the rights of man and the citizen (p. 93 § 1), identifies every juristic person with the sum of the individuals so absolutely that he explains the original sovereignty of the people as the property of 'all individuals,' the people as 'the sum of all the human beings' and the general will as 'the sum of all individual wills.' Just from this he deduces the necessity of a transference, as the people can no more take possession of its sovereignty than an infant heir can take possession of a manor; and even by the exclusion of women, the introduction of the principle of majority rule or the institution of representatives a transference is already effected (p. 43, 76 ff., 96 § 3, 97, 126, 157–161). Hence he regards the ruler as a depositary of the general will, who has the right to will for all by the fact that 'the many renounce their wills and transfer them to one man or a few or the majority' and every subject promises 'that another shall will in place of him and that he will recognize this other will as his own and, in case he breaks his word, he may be forced to this recognition' (p. 75–76, 93 § 1, 96 § 3). If this ruler is a majority 'unum morale must be feigned by the majority' (p. 75, 113 § 1); 'in the Democracy a new Ruler is created for each separate act of government' as "momentaneus" (p. 113 § 2, 125 § 9, 131 § 13); in mixed forms there are several 'subjects' of State-power (p. 115 § 3).—Even he is outdone by Christian v. Schlözer, De jure suffragii (1795), § 11.—See also Humboldt, above, Ch. II. Note 112.

213. Milton, Defensio of 1651, c. 7, vainly strives to defend himself from the reproach of Salmasius that he exalts the people, without any regard to rank or station and thus as the mere "plebs," to be the sovereign; he can only plead that he takes as the sovereign "populus universus," whose

"plus quam dimidia pars" wields the supreme power, not the "plebs solus" but "omnes ordinis cujuscunque cives", and that to the "una tantummodo populi curia suprema" men of quality could well be elected.—Locke indeed regards the State as "incorporated" and "one body politic," and from the fact that this body must act with one force in one direction he deduces that it is natural and reasonable for the majority to prevail as the "greater force"; but he construes this body as a "society" and thus in the end he traces the subjection of the minority to the majority back to a contractual obligation of the individuals: II. c. 7 § 89, c. 8 § 95–99, c. 12 § 145.

214. See II. c. 7: "le peuple même ne peut, quand il le voudrait, se dépouiller de ce droit incommunicable"; I. c. 4: confutation of Grotius and argument that a contractual alienation of liberty is absurd, illegitimate and void; II. c. 1 and III. c. 6: inalienable; II. c. 2: indivisible; I. c. 7: even in external affairs the sovereign people can validly engage itself as "un être simple, un individu," but can never effectually obligate itself to an act contrary to its own being (such as submission to another sovereign or alienation of a part of itself).—Compare above, p. 34 ff. and 42.

215. See especially III. c. 10 and compare above, p. 35; further I. c. 7, II. c. 1 and 6–7, III. c. 1 ff.

216. See III. c. 2 ff., and compare above, p. 47 (also the systematic position in Althusius).

217. As to its being unlimited see above, Ch. II. Note 106; as to its being illimitable, III. c. 16 ("la limiter, c'est la détruire").

218. See I. c. 7 and III. c. 8 (above, Ch. II. Note 107).

219. The sovereignty is "irreprésentable," as power indeed can be transferred but not will; II. c. 1 and III. c. 15. On the consequences for representative assemblies see below, Ch. IV. The government exercises no sovereign powers (below, Note 221).

220. See above, Ch. II. Notes 46–47; the sovereign people comes together periodically without summons (III. c. 13); as soon as it is assembled the whole jurisdiction of the government ceases, "la puissance exécutive est suspendue, et la personne du dernier citoyen est aussi sacrée et inviolable que celle du premier magistrat; parce qu'où se trouve le représenté, il n'y a plus de représentant" (III. c. 14); any institution of a government holds good only provisionally until the next assemblage of the people, which is to be opened with the two questions stated above, Ch. II. Note 47 (III. c. 18).

221. For this reason even in the institution of a government the sovereign people, when it has enacted this law, must, in order to execute it by electing persons, strip off its own sovereignty for the moment ("par

une conversion subite de la souveraineté en démocratie"). On the other hand Rousseau absolutely rejects the idea of the division of powers. See II. c. 2 and 6, III. c. 1 and 17.

222. See III. c. 1–5, 16 and 17; the gouvernement is a "nouveau corps" between the sovereign and the individuals, a new "personne morale" within the "personne morale" of the State, a "tout subalterne dans le tout"; it receives from the sovereign a "vie empruntée et subordonnée" but "réelle"; it remains the minister of the sovereign without a will of its own and under any limitations that may be set, but is endowed with such independent power over the individuals as is requisite for the execution of the laws; the sovereign commands, the government executes, the subject obeys. —Of the monarchy it is said, ib. c. 6, that in this "un individu représente un être collectif."

223. See I. c. 6: "un Corps moral et collectif" with "son unite, son moi commun, sa vie et sa volonté"; it is a personne publique (in various aspects called État, Souverain or Puissance); ib. c. 7: "personne morale," "être de raison," externally "un être simple, un individu"; II. c. 1 and III. c. 6: "être collectif"; II. c. 2: like a body, one and indivisible; ib. c. 4: personne morale, lives in the union of the members, has the same absolute power over its limbs as a man has; III. c. 1–5: "corps artificiel"; ib. c. 10: germs of death in the body of the State as in the human body; ib. c. 11: mortality of the State and artificial prolongation of its life; the legislative power is the heart of the State and the executive power is the brain, the cessation of the heart is fatal at once, while a man may be an imbecile and yet live.—At the same time indeed a certain breach is made in this unity of the State's personality by the assumption of the separate personality of the Government (see previous Note).

224. Compare the impossibility of representation by elected deputies (III. c. 15); the rule that no one should be excluded (II. c. 2 note); the unanimity which is postulated in itself, and which is evaded only by the fiction of a clause in the contract (IV. c. 2).

225. In particular, men could not drop the idea of representation altogether.—Sieyès holds with Rousseau that the people's sovereignty is inalienable (I. p. 202 ff.), illimitable and bound by no constitution or law (ib. p. 131 ff. and 143), and empowered to abolish all existing rights at any time (p. 138 ff.); he recognizes no essential difference in the forms of State (II. p. 199 ff. and 209 ff.); yet he contends for the principle of representation, re-introduces the division of powers under the name of the several mandates for the representation of the undivided power of the people and their "concours" (II. p. 363 ff. and 371 ff.), and protests against carrying the idea of sovereignty too far (II. p. 374–376). On

the other hand he formulates even more sharply the nature of the State as a 'mechanism' (I. p. 128, 195 ff., 217 ff., II. p. 370), the character of the sovereign people as a society (I. p. 283 ff. and 445 ff.), and the identity of this society with its 'associated members taken together' and of the general will with the sum of the uniform and equal individual wills (I. p. 144–146, 207 ff., 431 ff., II. p. 195 ff.; especially I. p. 167: 'What is the will of a nation? It is the product of the wills of the individuals, as the nation is a sum of individuals').—Rousseau's basic idea is strongly reflected in Filangieri (I. c. I and II, VII. c. 53).

226. Fichte, in the Naturrecht (1796), while rejecting pure democracy (Werke III. p. 154 ff.), proposes the transference of legislative, judicial and administrative power to an Executive who is responsible but not arbitrarily removable, and who is given full liberty of action for the public weal. At the same time the people retains the constitutive power, the right to supervise and to judge of the rightfulness of the government, and to protect these rights it appoints Ephors with absolute negative power, who by their interdict can at any moment divest the government of its constitutional representation of the sovereign general will. The people, which thereby becomes a 'Commune' and as such must be assembled at once, decides in its sovereign capacity whether the Executive or the Ephors are guilty of high treason, and constitutes the fundamental law by its decision; and when Magistrates and Ephors collude the people has the right of revolution. At the same time the people is never a rebel, and even the leaders of an uprising are cleared of the presumption of rebellion as soon as they are followed by the people, for 'what is higher than the People?'; see Werke III. p. 15 ff., 161 ff., 205 ff., 222 ff.—In later years Fichte's popular sovereignty fades away into an abstract theorem; see Rechtslehre of 1812, Nachg. Werke II. p. 627 ff. (the sovereign represents only 'the will of Right issuing forth in himself'); in the Staatslehre of 1813, Werke IV. p. 435 ff., the sovereignty of the people yields altogether to the sovereignty of what can be shown to be commonly recognized as the 'highest human wisdom of the time and the people'—that is, the teaching profession.

227. In the Naturrecht (Vol. II. of 1797, loc. cit. p. 203, 208 ff., 215 ff.), he compares the 'organized whole' of the State to a tree, but an impossible tree whose parts have knowledge and will and which as a whole is therefore 'nothing but a mere concept,' while the parts, which alone truly exist, can only be what they are in their connection and interaction (unlike the particles of a heap of sand); thus for him the organic idea means only a specific form of connection of the individuals. In the Grundzüge (1804–1805, Werke VII. p. 144 ff.), the State appears as an 'artificial

institution,' as 'a concept invisible in itself' (like 'species'), as the product of the work of rulers and ruled; it is 'not the individuals, but their continuous relation to one another.' For the first time in the Reden an die deutsche Nation (1807–1808, Werke VII. p. 374 ff.), there prevails more and more a truly organic conception of the Nation, and in the Staatslehre (Werke IV. p. 409 ff., 412, 419 ff.), the construction of the State comes into connection therewith.

228. While in the Naturrecht (Werke III. p. 202–204 and 207–208) Fichte sets off, as against 'all the individuals' in their disjunction, 'all the individuals' in their political conjunction as a 'real united Whole,' a 'totality,' a 'totum which is unified by the fact itself,' yet this unity can only result from the indefiniteness of the notion of the 'all' which is to be protected, as this may or may not be 'every individual.' Thus 'this indefiniteness, this uncertainty as to which individual will be first attacked, this suspense of imagination is the bond of union; it is the medium through which all run together into one.' Such a whole then is naturally 'nothing but an abstract idea: only the citizens as such are actual persons;' and therefore international law, public as well as private, is to be derived from the relations between individual citizens of different nations, not from the relations between the nations as such; see op. cit. p. 371, and Rechtslehre, Nachg. Werke II. p. 638. Elsewhere Fichte uses the concept of 'moral or mystical person' strictly in the sense of a collective 'subject' treated by fiction as a unit; he says that as the majority from time to time it signifies an 'often very mutable person' (Werke III. p. 159 and 162); he applies this concept to marriage (ib. p. 304–349).

229. See above, Ch. II. Note 116. He says expressly that the individuals in their conjunction form 'the genuine sovereign' and that every individual is a 'share-holder in the sovereignty'; see Werke, III. p. 205 and VII. p. 153. According to him the people as a 'truly great heap' exercises the powers of sovereignty; Werke III. p. 173 and 177. And in characteristic fashion he reckons the officials as 'not among the People,' which on the contrary is only the united multitude after subtracting the persons of the magistrates (Executives and Ephors) who by taking office are forever excluded from the people; ib. p. 175–177. Yet in 1812 he says that the whole is only the 'totality of the members' and that whatever is in none of the individuals cannot be in the whole; Nachg. Werke II. p. 495, and especially p. 632.

230. He says expressly that the ruling general will is the united wills of all, which the will of the government is taken to represent only presumptively until another true general will is ascertained; III. p. 106, 150 ff., 169 ff.; the State comes about because all wills, as willing for

themselves, agree in willing the security of the rights of all; ib. p. 122 ff. and 150 ff.; compare especially the requirement, in principle, of unanimity (above, p. 111).—Quite similarly in 1812; Nachg. Werke II. p. 627 ff.

231. For Kant, in the ideally rational and only rightful and definitive State, the people is the sovereign and the general will rules as the lawmaker (Werke, VI. p. 227 ff., VII. p. 131 ff. § 45–46); by virtue of the State-contract the 'general overlord' is the united people itself (VII. p. 133 § 47); the ruler (Rex, Princeps) is but the agent (organ) of the sovereign, stands under the law, is removable and reformable (but not by punishment or compulsion) and holds his position wholly by the fact 'that he represents the general will' (VII. p. 134 § 49, also VI. p. 332 and 336); the people is also the fountain of justice (ib.). He also claims for this sovereignty of the people, as a 'most personal' right, the attribute of inalienability, so that when it is once established any promise to give it back is void; he who exercises it as the law-maker 'can only dispose of the people through the collective will of the people, but cannot dispose of the collective will itself, which is the original ground of all public contracts' (VII. p. 159–160 § 52, also VI. p. 416 ff.). Lastly he also says that the distinction of the forms of State (formae imperii) is not essential, and that the only essential distinction is that between 'republican' and 'despotic' forms of government (formae regiminis), as set up by himself (VI. p. 418 ff., VII. p. 156 ff.).

232. See Werke, VI. p. 223, 326, 330–337, 449–450, VII. p. 136–141.

233. See VI. p. 329–330, VII. p. 158 ff.

234. See VI. p. 239, 416–420, VII. p. 131–136, 159–160. The triad of powers (trias politica) corresponds to the logical triad of major premise, minor premise and conclusion; legislation is unimpeachable, the executive is irresistible, the judicial decision is unalterable; as 'independent moral persons' they are mutually co-ordinate and yet subordinate in so far as none can usurp the functions of another; the people exercises the legislative power through its representatives while it must leave the judicial decision to a jury and transfer the executive power unreservedly to the chief Head of the State. Hence even in the rightful and definitive State there can be no possible constitutional safeguard for the sovereign people or its representatives as against the executive, as any right of resistance or coercion would make the legislator an executive (VII. p. 137).

235. Kant everywhere recognizes only the individual as a real person, and in treating of Corporations and Foundations he never mentions the idea of 'moral person' at all (VII. p. 120 ff., 142 ff.). The State as a whole he treats in its external aspect as a 'moral person' and here he draws

important consequences from its unitary personality (VI. p. 409, VII. p. 161 § 53 ff., 165 § 57; above, Ch. II. Note 123). Internally he calls 'moral persons' only the collective holders of power (a collective sovereign, the 'subjects' of the three powers, a court of justice, VI. p. 323, VII. p. 97 § 36, 131 § 45, 134 § 48–49), and says that the Chief of State and the People, 'rightly considered, are after all two distinct moral persons' (VII. p. 138). By the word 'State' he sometimes means the people (as in VII. p. 133 § 47, 134 § 49), sometimes the ruler, as against whom he sets off the people as the sum of the subjects (as in VI. p. 418, 421). The State is a 'mechanism' (VII. p. 157 § 51–52).

236. See above, Ch. II. Note 121; by the contract omnes as universi become ruler over omnes as singuli (VII. p. 133 § 47); the sovereign is the 'will of the whole people,' that is, the unity of the wills of all free and equal individuals, but only of the 'independent' individuals (not wage-laborers); the collective general will which is aprioristic in the state of Nature and is actually unified in the State; 'the concurrent and united will of all, so far as every one decides for all and all decide just the same thing for every one'; and indeed unanimously and directly in itself, not contractually by majorities and representatives (VI. p. 327–329, 416–420, VII. p. 54 § 8, 62 ff. § 14–17, 106 § 41, 131 ff. § 46).

237. See VII. p. 20 ff., 36, 153 Anm. E (hence the individual is a different person as a co-legislator and as a punished subject); on the "homo noumenon" and "homo phaenomenon" see also Tugendlehre, ib. p. 195 ff., § 3 p. 222, § 11 p. 241 ff., § 13 p. 244 ff.

238. See VII. p. 158–159 § 52: 'this is the only lasting constitution, where the Law governs of itself and depends on no particular person'; Beschluss, ib. p. 173.

239. Thus also the doctrine of Kant was taken as a basis in the teaching of positive public law by widely different schools; for example Fessmaier, Grundriss des bairischen Staatsrechts, Ingolstadt 1801, argues from it that the provincial Estates express the general will (§ 94–98, 143–154), while Gönner, Teutsches Staatsrecht, Landshut 1804, employs it in the service of enlightened despotism when he makes the ruler the representative of the general will, 'not however the empirical popular will but the rational, that is to say reason itself.'

CHAPTER FOUR

THE PRINCIPLE OF REPRESENTATION

AMONG the characteristic features of the political system of Althusius as set forth above is the universal application of the principle of Representation. The historical development of this principle also leads back into the middle ages.

After the model of the Roman-Canonist theory of Corporations which was used here as everywhere, the political theories of the middle ages made considerable use of the idea of representation in the construction of the Church and the State, just as with any "universitas." Thus they borrowed from corporation law, besides the conception of the ruler as a representative of the community,[1] and the derivation of the principle of majority rule from the representation of all by the majority,[2] the theoretical formulation of the idea, long current in the middle ages though unknown to antiquity, of the exercise of the rights belonging to a community by a representative assembly. Whenever against the right of the ruler they set up a right of the community—whether this right were higher or lower than his—they affirmed the possibility that the right of the community would be exercised by an assembly of representatives. Indeed in all cases in which it seemed that a gathering of all the people was impossible owing to the size of the community, or else that the function in hand could not properly be performed by such a gathering directly, representative action was held to be a necessity. This idea was more precisely defined as a full power of agency, so that a proper act of the assembly of representatives had exactly the same legal effect as an act of the assemblage of all would have had.

Within the Church it was on this principle that men based

the whole position of Councils; and from this especially they deduced the claims which were asserted in behalf of the General Council, to the effect that it represented in a perfect and all-sufficient manner the Community of all the members of the Church, to which belonged the rights which the Council exercised.[3] To a limited extent representative functions were also ascribed to the College of Cardinals, and in particular its power of electing the Pope was traced back to a mandate given by the community, to which this right belonged.[4] Likewise in the State, the various Assemblies of Estates of larger or smaller territories were regarded as representations of the people empowered to exercise the people's rights.[5] In the Germanic Empire, from the days of Lupold of Bebenburg onward, the special position of the Electoral Princes, and in particular their power of electing the Emperor, was grounded on a representation by them of the whole people of the Empire, to which this right belonged.[6]

In default of a matured concept of the unitary personality of the State, and while the prevailing conception of the people was 'collective' (above, p. 149–151), all such relations of representation could be construed no otherwise than in the sense of a true Surrogation or Agency. Hence, as soon as men rejected the idea of a guardianship ordained from above, they were driven more and more to seek the basis of the power of political representation in a mandate given by the represented community. Thus, as the representation of all by the ruler was derived from the contract of rulership, and the representation of all by the majority was deduced from the social contract, so the representation of all by representative assemblies was traced back to a mandate given at the election. Thus when the representative position of Councils was to be explained, men referred to the fact that they were composed of the elected Heads of the various ecclesiastical communities, smaller and larger. Each of these prelates was supposed to have received at his election a mandate to represent the community under him.[7] In Ockham there already appeared the idea of a general council of delegates elected, with the participation of the laity, to represent each and all of the ecclesias-

tical communes.[8] And Nicolas of Cues extended to the Cardinals
the elective principle, which was in his view the only possible
legal basis for a mandate in political affairs. He wished to change
them into elected provincial deputies forming an Estate.[9] Likewise in the State all the powers of representative assemblies were
traced back to a mandate given by election, a mandate given by
every section of the people to its own governors and "rectores,"
even though this may have conferred an hereditary right.[10] And
already Nicolas of Cues developed from this a formal system of
representative Parliamentarism in which, instead of mechanically
planned electoral districts, the constituencies are the organic and
corporatively constructed limbs of an articulated People.[11] In
any such view the scope of the representative powers of every
assembly must depend on the terms of the fundamental electoral
mandate. Yet for the most part it was taken for granted that,
when a gathering of the whole people was impossible, there was
a mandate of complete and 'absorptive' representation, even
though in principle men held to the idea that in the last resort
the whole community stands above its representatives as well as
above its ruler. But Marsilius of Padua, in his consistent radicalism, refused to hear of such a thing as 'absorptive' representation.[12] And with regard to the General Council, Ockham above
all protested with much force against the prevailing opinion
which treated the Council, in virtue of its representative power,
in effect as if it were quite equal to the assembled "ecclesia universalis." [13] And lastly, despite all its individualistic premises,
the medieval doctrine set up the principle that the representatives, who in the first place are charged with the representation
of the several particular communities composing a people, must,
if they are to represent the people as a whole, act as one single
assembly which resolves and decides in corporate form. From
the time of Lupold of Bebenburg onward this was supported by
the argument that, as every surrogate or substitute takes the
legal nature of that for which it stands, so also the popular Representation formed as a substitute for the "universitas populi"
(in the sense explained above, p. 151) must itself be treated in
all respects as a "universitas." [14] In this matter Nicolas of Cues

was the first to say in so many words that the assembled deputies represent the whole people "in uno compendio repraesenta-tivo." [15]

The theory of the representative principle thus formed in the middle ages was not enriched with new ideas in the sixteenth century. In so far as political rights were ascribed to the whole people, for the most part their exercise by assemblies of Estates was taken as a matter of course, without further inquiry into the basis of this representative function. The persistent cult of the antique was a hindrance to the progress of the representative idea, while the absolutist doctrine of Bodin was positively hostile.[16] Thus only the Monarchomachi, to some extent, gave fuller attention to the principle of representation, which indeed could hardly be dispensed with in the practical working of their doctrine of popular sovereignty.[17] But even they were satisfied with somewhat vague and general propositions. For the most part they were inclined to assume a perfectly 'absorptive' representation of the people by the assembled Estates.[18] It was but seldom that any one reserved the final decision to the direct assemblage of the people;[19] while Junius Brutus ascribed to the assembly of the "Repraesentantes populi" as an "Epitome Regni" the same right as to the People, yet he regarded them as dependent on the "populus constituens," and argued in particular that the people's representatives cannot validly impair the people's rights either by negligence or by positive act.[20] And for the most part, in spite of its democratic basis, the State of the Monarchomachi took a strongly aristocratic form in its representative system, partly through the influence of Calvin's doctrine of Ephors,[21] and partly by adherence to the recognized system of Estates.[22]

Althusius applied the idea of the representative constitution in a more universal and systematic fashion than any of his predecessors.[23] He expressly said that the erection of a system of popular representation apart from the chief executive is desirable in every State (above, p. 43). Yet he took care to avoid any break with the principle of popular sovereignty. With the greatest sharpness he insisted that the Ephors as well as the Chief Magistrate are nothing but ministers of the powers of sover-

eignty, appointed by the people; that in case of violation of duty
their mandate may be revoked by the community whose trust
they betray; that they must jointly and severally recognize the
people as their sovereign.[24] Hence wherever and whenever
there are no representative institutions, he at once claimed for
the direct assemblage of the people the exercise of parliamentary
powers as an imprescriptible right which cannot be destroyed by
any positive law, despite any customs or statutes of particular
States to the contrary (above, p. 44). As to the composition of
representative assemblies Althusius himself copied the existing
system of Estates. But for him the element of Estates was only
one among the factors determining the formation of the corporative organisms which unite in ascending series to produce
the State, while on the other hand, as the decisive and thorough-
going formal principle of the constitution of representative
bodies he took instead the principle of corporative delegation
(see Part I., p. 37–39 and Ch. II. Note 14). For this reason,
even when he based his constitutional structure on the system of
Estates, he applied the democratic idea in theory and in practice
so far as to support with energy not only the equality of rights
of the Burghers as compared with the Nobility, but also full
rights for the Peasantry.[25]

Althusius's doctrine of popular representation was reproduced
with some weakening by Hoenonius.[26] Other political writers
accepted it in so far that while they construed the three pure
forms of the State according to the Aristotelian scheme, in the
parliamentary monarchy conceived as a mixed form they ascribed to the assembly of Estates the nature of a popular representation which was called upon to exercise the share of sovereignty belonging to the people.[27] The imperialistic publicists,
who operated with the concept of "majestas realis," quite commonly explained the powers of the Imperial Diet in general
and the College of Electors in particular by a supposed mandate
given by the whole people, whereby they were fully empowered
to represent the whole people in the exercise of its sovereign
rights.[28] And as to the Estates of the German territories the
same idea never quite disappeared, that these were a representation of the people.[29]

Yet on the whole the evolution of the theory of the representative constitution came to a complete standstill with the triumph of the absolutist movement. The strict construction of the idea of 'Ruler's sovereignty,' which gained the ascendency from the time of Hobbes onward, left no room for any further representation of the people apart from the perfect and exclusive representation of all by the ruler.[30] And even so far as a right of the people apart from the right of the ruler was now recognized in all forms of the State, or at least in limited or mixed forms, hardly a word was said as to its possible exercise by representatives. Just as little did the theory, in treating of Aristocracy and Democracy, proceed to fix the conceptual distinction between the direct and the representative forms.

Only in England did the principle of representation remain living in theory, as it grew powerful in practice. Yet even here at first no new ideas were brought to light as to the nature of popular representation. While those doctrines which were most important for the history of general constitutional law deduced the rights of Parliament from a collective sovereignty of the people, yet they held fast to the conception of parliamentary representation as a true delegation resting on a mandate.[31] To be sure, a different principle was suggested by the weighty maxims which gradually came to prevail, to the effect that every member of Parliament should represent the whole nation and not merely his district, that he is not bound to obey instructions or to render account to his constituents. But even these maxims were combined by Sidney with the idea of a collective mandate, while he justified them partly by the unity of the great body of the Nation which, on account of its size, is divided into parts for electoral purposes, and partly by a wise ordinance of self-denial of the electorate, but never by the legal nature of popular representation as something different from the ordinary relation of agency.[32]

For the Continent the representative idea was revived by Montesquieu.[33] His remarks on the historical growth of representative institutions, noticing their absence in the republics of antiquity and disclosing their earliest germs in the primitive state of the Teutons, and his thoughts on the political importance of this great achievement of the modern world, are epoch-making strokes of genius. And as to the composition of the representative body he was the first to state with precision the idea that elections should be made by districts and on the principle of universal suffrage.[34] But as to the legal nature of representation he followed the accepted view throughout. Even for him the election of deputies is a collective mandate to act as delegates of the community which is itself vested with the legislative power.[35] Even he has nothing else to urge against the giving of binding instructions but considerations of mere expediency.[36] And in his strict observance of the principle of the division of powers he brings out more sharply than his predecessors the idea that the legislative body represents the people as a separate and self-constituted 'subject' of rights as against the active power of the State.

While in Montesquieu the representative idea became one of the chief means of transfusing the older doctrine of popular sovereignty into the constitutional doctrine, Rousseau, in conscious opposition to this, carried to the extreme the tendency shown in the more radical statements of popular sovereignty ever since the middle ages, which struggled against the absorption of the popular assemblage by the representative assembly. In rejecting the principle of representation he was a faithful disciple of absolutism. He rejected it just because it was not ancient but had taken root in the feudalism of the middle ages and grown up in aristocratic England. On the ground of his 'individualist-collectivist' premises he argued logically that the sovereignty of the general will can no more be represented than alienated; that there is no such thing as a representation of the will ("la volonté se ne représente point"); that only "commissaires" for preliminary discussion of the laws can be allowed, while "toute loi que le peuple en personne n'a pas ratifiée est nulle; ce n'est point une loi"; that "à l'instant qu'un peuple se donne des Représentants, il n'est plus libre; il n'est plus." [37]

Rousseau's doctrine remained even in this point the evangel of consistent radicalism, which even now has not given up the effort to approach as near as possible to the ideal State of direct Democracy by weakening the representative principle.[38] In Germany, under its influence, Fichte banished the idea of popular representation from his 'Nature-Right' construction of the State.[39]

But the final victory belonged to the constitutional theory of the State based on the representative principle, which now followed Montesquieu almost absolutely. In this sense even the German teachers of Natural Law after the middle of the eighteenth century more and more accepted the idea of the representative constitution,[40] until Kant exalted it to a necessary postulate of the free State.[41] At the same time the German teachers of Public Law revived, in the spirit of the constitutional doctrine, the idea (never quite extinct) of a representative character of the national Estates, grounded in positive law.[42] And lastly, on this basis arose the constitutional theory of the nineteenth century, which in its many ramifications prepared, accompanied and interpreted the practical working of the representative system in all its shades and variations.[43]

Even here it was seen that, for the comprehension of the true legal nature of popular representation, the 'Nature-Right' theories of the State, with their idea of an agency based on a collective mandate, would not avail. In truth this idea is incompatible with the organic nature of the State and the unity of the State's personality, and being at bottom mechanical and individualistic it must evermore drive on toward the goal of Radicalism. Yet even now it is neither overcome nor is the construction of a higher theory perfected, which will work out fully and completely, here as elsewhere, the concept of a real Group-Personality, and will, unreservedly and in all aspects, replace the idea of mandate by the idea of an appointment to a specialized political function, and the idea of Agency (that is, the representation of one person by another person and thus of the whole by a whole) by the idea of Organism (that is, the representation of the group-person by its constitutionally appointed member-persons and thus of the whole by the part).

NOTES

1. See above, Ch. III. Note 47. Already Joh. Saresb., IV. c. 3: the king "gerit autem ministerium fideliter, cum suae conditionis memor universitatis subiectorum se personam gerere recordatur"; compare c. 5; then Mars. Pat., I. c. 15: "hoc facientibus his id facit communitas universa"; Ockham, Dial. III. tr. 2, l. 3, c. 12: vice omnium eligentium; Zabar., De schism., p. 689 ff.: the Council should be convoked by the Emperor, "qui repraesentat totum populum Christianum, cum in eum translata sit iurisdictio et potestas universi orbis."

2. See the passages cited above, Ch. III. Note 48; thus Mars. Pat. often says, valentior pars . . . totam universitatem repraesentat.

3. See above, p. 145–147. Conrad of Gelnhausen, De congreg. conc. temp. schism., 1391 (in Martène, II. p. 1200), defines: "concilium generale est multarum vel plurium personarum rite convocatarum repraesentantium vel gerentium vicem diversorum statuum ordinum et personarum totius Christianitatis venire aut mittere volentium aut potentium ad tractandum de bono communi universalis ecclesiae in unum locum communem congregatio." See also Gerson, De aufer., c. 10, De pot. eccl., c. 7 ff.; Nic. Cus., above, Ch. III. Note 25, and De auctoritate praesidendi (in Düx, I. p. 475 ff.: the Pope is the remotest, the General Council the most direct and surest representative of the Universal Church); Decius on c. 4 X. 1, 6 nr. 21.

4. See above, Ch. III. Notes 11, 14, 21, 23; Ockham, Dial. I. 5 c. 6 and 8; Nic. Cus., Conc. cath., I. c. 14, 17, II. c. 14 (repraesentant); Ant. Ros., I. c. 48 (ab universali ecclesia, quam cardinales et electores in hoc ipsam totam repraesentant).

5. See above, Ch. III. Notes 2, 7, 10a; but especially Mars. Pat., I. c. 12–13 (vicem et auctoritatem universitatis civium repraesentant); Nic. Cus., III. c. 12 and 25.

6. According to Lup. Beb., c. 5 p. 352–353 and c. 6 p. 357–358, the Electoral Princes make the election "repraesentantes in hoc omnes principes et populum Germaniae, Italiae et aliarum provinciarum et terrarum regni et imperii, quasi vice omnium eligendo." Were it not for their institution the "universitas ipsa" would have to make the choice, but as it is the Electors choose "vice et auctoritate universitatis." When therefore they have made the choice, "proinde est ac si tota universitas principum et populi . . . fecisset"; to prove this l. 6 § 1 Dig. 3, 4, and c. ult. in Sexto de praebendis are vouched. See further c. 12 p. 386–387, on the participation of the Electors as representatives of the populus regni et

imperii in the deposition of an Emperor, and c. 14 p. 396, on the consent to alienation of rights of sovereignty.—Likewise Ockham, Octo qu., VIII. c. 3 (repraesentantes universitatem); Zabar. on c. 34 § verum, X. 1, 6 nr. 8; Nic. Cus., III. c. 4 ("qui vice omnium eligerent"); Greg. Heimb., in Goldast I. p. 561; Ant. Ros., I. c. 48.

7. Nic. Cus., above, Ch. III. Note 25; especially I. c. 15 and II. c. 18, where by virtue of their election "praesidentes figurant suam subiectam ecclesiam" and councils of such prelates represent the larger units of the Church; and so on up to a representation of the Universal Church. Ant. Butr. on c. 17 X. 1, 33 nr. 27–28: at the Provincial Councils the Prelates and "Rectores" do not appear as individuals, but "quilibet praelatus vel rector tenet vicem universitatis." Zabar. on c. ult., X. 3, 10 nr. 1–3. Panorm. on c. 17 X. 1, 33 nr. 2: in the concilium generale "praelati totius orbis conveniunt et faciunt unum corpus, repraesentantes ecclesiam universalem"; likewise the praelati et maiores of the province represent their own universitates, and thus in their assembly as unum corpus they represent the "universitates ecclesiarum" of the province; and again "in una dioecesi . . . praelati et capitula repraesentant totum clerum."

8. Ockham excludes the laity only from "ordo" and "officium divinum," not from the "iura spiritualia" which pertain to the "communis utilitas." Therefore they should be admitted to the General Council; indeed (though the Scholar in Ockham's Dialogue thought this quite absurd) even women should be admitted, if there were need of them. A General Council of this sort would by no means be impossible. It could, for example, be formed in such a way that within some limited time every Commune should elect delegates, from among whom a certain number of deputies for the Council should be chosen by the diocesan Synods or secular Parliaments. In such a Council the universitas fidelium would in fact be present in the persons of its representatives, and such a Council, like the assembly of any other community or corporation, would concentrate in itself the power of the whole society; Dial. I. 6 c. 57, 84–85, 91–100, Octo qu., III. c. 8.— See also Mars. Pat., II. c. 2, 20, III. c. 2.

9. Nic. Cus., II. c. 14–15; see above, Ch. III. Note 25. He looks upon the Cardinals just as d'Ailly and Gerson do (above, Ch. III. Note 23), as the aristocratic Upper House of Parliament in a spiritual polity.

10. The general principle is formulated in Ockham, Dial. I. 6 c. 84: every people, every commune, every corpus may assemble, not only in person but also "per aliquos electos a diversis partibus," for every community "potest aliquos eligere, qui vicem gerant totius communitatis aut corporis."—See also Mars. Pat., I. c. 12–13.

11. Nic. Cus., III. c. 12 and 25: elected governors are to represent the

communities under them; assemblies of such governors are to represent the provinces and territories; and the "universale concilium imperiale" is to represent the Empire; in this Council "praesides provinciarum suas provincias repraesentantes ac etiam universitatum magnarum rectores ac magistri" and also men of senatorial rank are to assemble; they will form the "corpus imperiale cuius caput est Caesar."

12. Mars. Pat., I. c. 12: "sive id fecerit universitas praedicta civium aut eius pars valentior per se ipsam immediate, sive id alicui vel aliquibus commiserit faciendum, qui legislator simpliciter non sunt nec esse possunt, sed solum ad aliquid et quandoque ac secundum primi legislatoris auctoritatem." Here also Marsilius makes contact with Rousseau.

13. Ockham seeks rather to prove that because the Council's position is merely representative even a General Council is only "pars ecclesiae"; it stands below the "communitas fidelium, si posset convenire"; it is summoned by human agency and can be dissolved; and it is fallible, so that resistance to, appeal from, and accusation against it are possible; Dial. I. 5 c. 25–28. Similarly at some points, Petr. Alliac., in Gerson, Op. I. p. 688 ff., and again at the Council of Constance (Sess. I. in Mansi, XXVII. p. 547). Also, with hesitation, Breviscoxa (in Gerson, Op. I. p. 898).— On the other hand Gerson and Nic. Cus. (II. c. 15–16) maintain the infallibility of the Council, its representation of the Church being 'absorptive.'

14. To confute the opinion of Canonists (such as Host. and Joh. Andr. on c. 34 X. 1, 6 nr. 25) that the Electoral Princes have to make the choice as individuals ("ut singuli") and therefore among them a mere majority does not prevail, Lup. Beb., c. 6 p. 356–358 and c. 12 p. 379–380, was the first to argue that these Electors are representatives of a universitas and must themselves act "tanquam collegium seu universitas." Likewise Zabar. on c. 34 § verum, X. 1, 6 nr. 8, citing Lupold (therefore in all respects eadem forma, quae servatur in aliis actibus universitatum, servanda); Felinus Sandaeus on c. 6 X. 1, 6 nr. 29; Bertachinus, Repertorium, v. "maior pars," nr. 27; at the greatest length Petr. Andl., II. c. 1–4, with the argument: "quum electores huiusmodi successerunt in locum populi Romani, qui ut universitas sibi elegit imperatorem, debent isti censeri eodem iure, quum surrogatum sapiat naturam eius cui surrogatur."

15. Nic. Cus., loc. cit.: "et dum simul conveniunt in uno compendio repraesentativo, totum imperium collectum est."

16. Bodin concedes no representative position either to the national "senatus" (Parlement) or to the provincial "comitia"; see III. c. 1 and c. 7 nr. 346 ff.

17. Yet Salamonius speaks of a representation only as to the relation of

Prince and People: princeps repraesentat populum, gerit ejus personam, enacts the laws universi populi auctoritate; see p. 28 ff.—Similarly Victoria, III. nr. 21, and Soto, I. q. 1 a. 3.

18. Thus Hotman, Francog., c. 13–24 (the "concilium publicum" of the three Estates exercises all the sovereign rights of the people, settles all important negotia publica, and has "sacrosancta auctoritas"). Boucher, II. c. 20 and III. c. 8 (the ordines as the "comitia Regni" have the majestas as representatives of the people), I. c. 9 (they are "idem" as the Regnum or Respublica). Likewise, apparently, Mariana, I. c. 8 (proceres or deputati). —In England, Hooker in particular supposed a full representation of all men by the Parliament (Ranke, loc. cit. p. 242).

19. See for example Buchanan, p. 30: in legislation the "universus populus" is not active; but "ex omnibus ordinibus selecti ad Regem in consilium coïrent; deinde, ubi apud eos προβούλευμα factum esset, id ad populi judicium deferretur."

20. See q. III. p. 148 ff. and 173; he describes them as "electi magistratus Regni," "officiarii Regni non Regis," and "consortes et ephori imperii," "qui a populo auctoritatem acceperunt" and "qui universum populi coetum repraesentant"; they are "ut singuli Rege inferiores, ut universi superiores"; their assembly is "Regni quasi Epitome," and therefore whatever is done by the major part of them is done by the people itself; see q. II. p. 89 ff. and 150, III. p. 297 ff.—Quite similarly the author of the work De jure Mag., q. 6–7, as to the assembly of the "ordines sive status," who as "defensores ac protectores jurium ipsius supremae potestatis" hold the chief magistrate within his bounds, but cannot surrender any of the rights of the people itself.

21. See Calvin, IV. c. 20 (above, Ch. I. Note 4), and especially ib. § 8, the remark that an Aristocratie bien temperée is now the best form of government.

22. Thus in Junius Brutus and the author of the work De jure Mag., who place everything in the hands of the hereditary or elected provincial and local magistrates, who not only represent the people in their collective capacity but also as individuals receive the fullest powers; likewise in Hotman, though he says in one passage that the three Estates, excluding the spiritual Estate, should be made up of the nobility, the bourgeoisie and infima plebs (c. 13).

23. At most Nicolas of Cues may be set beside him in this respect.

24. See above, Part I., p. 40, 41–43, 46, Ch. II. Note 6 on the constitution of cities, and p. 39 on the removability of territorial Princes (provincial governors). He says, Polit., c. 9 § 22–23: "Ab hoc corpore, post Deum, profluit omnis potestas legitima in hos, quos Reges Optimatesve

vocamus. Corpus igitur hoc consociatum Rex, Princeps Optimatesve superius agnoscunt, a quo iidem constituuntur, removentur, dejiciuntur at exauctorantur. Quis vero summam dicet potestatem, quae superiorem agnoscit aliam? Quis lege solvet eum, in quam ipsemet consensit et ad ejus obedientiam se per modum contractus obligavit? Quis propriam potestatem . . . tribuet illi, qui, quam habet, alio accepit?" The potestas concessa is always less than the potestas concedentis and is to be measured only by the terms of the concession. And ib. c. 18 nr. 124, he argues that the Ephors and Optimates cannot surrender any of the people's rights to the ruler or lose them by disuse, as "ita penes Ephoros, non Rempublicam et populum, summum Reipublicae jus esset."

25. See above, Part I., Ch. I. Note 26, and p. 38; Brenneisen, p. 463 ff. —His personal position as Syndic of the democratic city-republic of Emden and his support of the old freedom of the commoners of East Friesland were the outward causes of the wide departures at this point from the political ideal of the other Calvinistic Monarchomachi. It may be said that the spirit of his writings is much more Puritan than Huguenot.

26. See Hoenonius, II. § 46–50 and IX. § 44–54: the Ephors seu ordines regni exercise "ex jussu et consensu populi" the power to appoint, restrict, supervise, depose and punish the rulers; "hi universi, quatenus universum populum repraesentant, sunt magistratu superiores, singuli vero singillatim considerati eo sunt inferiores"; and even as individuals they receive the same powers that Althusius gives them. In case there are no Ephors, Hoenonius himself agrees that the exercise of the same powers belongs imprescriptibly to the totus populus (II. § 51 and IX. § 50).

27. As for example Keckermann, II. c. 4 p. 564, who also keeps the name "ephori."

28. Thus above all Paurmeister, II. c. 1, says that in the Empire the totality of all "cives potentia participes summae potestatis" is represented by the "collegium civium potestatis Reipublicae Romanae actu participum." As to the Imperial Diet he copies the very words quoted above (Note 15) from Nicolas of Cues (ib. nr. 17), as to the College of Electors the words of Lupold of Bebenburg (II. c. 2 nr. 36–47). Among the writings collected in Arumaeus the fullest treatment of the relation between these representations is given by Bortius, Jurispr. publ. Germ., I. nr. 33 p. 1015 ff. See further Besold, Diss. de maj., s. 1 c. 1 § 5 (consensus eorum qui repraesentant populum universum—in the Empire the imperial Estates—exercises the majestas realis); Limnaeus, Capit. imp., ad art. 32 nr. 54 ff. (status universi).

29. See for example v. Seckendorf, Teutscher Fürstenstaat, II. c. 4; add. 27 (in default of the Estates the Prince should consider himself a

representative); and especially III. c. 3 nr. 8. Vitriarius, III. 17 § 36: the assembled Estates or their select committee form "unum corpus" and as such "subditos universos ac singulos repraesentant eorumque nomine deliberant et concludunt, adeo ut quicquid constituant, ab universo populo et ab universis constitutum esse censetur."

30. The formation of a royal Council of members appointed from the various clans, as recommended for Monarchies by Spinoza, Tract. pol., c. 6–7, has nothing of the idea of a popular representation; nor has the formation of a federal Senate composed of deputies from the various local Senates, as required for the larger Aristocracies, ib. c. 9 § 13.—In Germany after the Thirty Years' War the prevailing doctrine, while still speaking of the "coimperium" of an aristocratic body of the imperial Estates, no longer spoke of their representative position in relation to the whole people of the Empire. And in the territories there prevailed more and more the conception of the provincial Estates as a privileged corpus within the subject community which was fully and exclusively represented by the Prince, and often indeed the right of this body to represent the Province as against the Prince was expressly denied; see my Genossenschaftsrecht, I. p. 580 Note 196 and p. 816 ff.; also Stryk, Diss., IV. nr. 1.

31. Thus Milton and Locke throughout. Sidney, III. § 44, also says that the power of Parliament "must be essentially and radically in the people, from whom their delegates and representatives have all that they have."

32. Thus according to Sidney, loc. cit., since the English counties and boroughs are not sovereign like those of Switzerland and the Netherlands, but are "members of that great body which comprehends the whole nation," their delegates do not serve them but the whole nation. They would be legally responsible to the whole nation if it could assemble itself, and it is only because such an assemblage is impossible that they are in fact responsible only to their own consciences and to public opinion. The people wisely refrains from giving instructions; but instead of dissolving its permanent sovereignty this only proves that the power of the mandator is reflected in the power of the mandatary and that an unlimited mandate can only flow from the unlimited power of the mandator.—Conversely, Hume says that if the members of Parliament were obliged to receive instructions from their constituents, this would reduce England to a Republic; his own view of the representative principle already approximates to the present-day mode of thinking (see Pol. Disc., "Of the First Principles of Government," also "Idea of a Perfect Commonwealth").

33. Esprit des Lois, XI. c. 6 and XIX. c. 27; also XI. c. 8.

34. XI. c. 6: argument in favor of election by districts, on the ground that everyone is better acquainted with the needs of his own locality and

with his own neighbors; "tous les citoyens, dans les divers districts, doivent avoir droit de donner leur voix pour choisir le représentant; excepté ceux qui sont dans un tel état de bassesse, qu'ils sont réputés n'avoir point de volonté propre."

35. "Comme dans un État libre, tout homme qui est censé avoir une âme libre doit être gouverné par lui-même, il faudroit que le peuple en corps eût la puissance législative. Mais comme cela est impossible dans les grands États, et est sujet à beaucoup d'inconvénients dans les petits, il faut que le peuple fasse par ses représentants tout ce qu'il ne peut faire par lui-même." At the same time this representation should be absorptive; the people should have no share in government except to elect representatives, since the masses are capable of judging the qualifications of representatives but not of taking an active part in government themselves. The "corps représentant" itself should be confined strictly to law-making and checking the Executive.

36. "Il n'est pas nécessaire que les représentants, qui ont reçu de ceux qui les ont choisis une instruction générale, en reçoivent une particulière sur chaque affaire, comme cela se pratique dans les diètes d'Allemagne. Il est vrai que, de cette manière, la parole des députés seroit plus l'expression de la voix de la nation; mais cela jetteroit dans les longueurs infinies, rendroit chaque député le maître de tous les autres, et dans les occasions les plus pressantes, toute la force de la nation pourroit être arrêtée par un caprice."—As to the duty of rendering account, he simply quotes Sidney.

37. Contrat Social, III. c. 15, II. c. 1, III. c. 13; hence he only allows small City-States, which are to be joined in confederations.

38. Of eighteenth-century writers we may here mention Thomas Paine, Rights of Man, London 1791–1792; William Godwin, Enquiry concerning Political Justice, London 1793 (1796, 1798); moreover in the course of the French Revolution many attempts were made to put Rousseau's system into practice. Against these Sieyès set himself when he asserted that every representative of the people represents the whole nation and that he is not bound by instructions; whereas in his earlier days he had held that the representatives, elected by count of heads and necessarily assembled in a single chamber, were merely the commissioned agents of their own constituents and vote-carriers with a general mandate, that their mandate could be revoked or limited at will, and that the representative body as a whole was a collective 'subject' subordinate to the sovereign people, being summoned for the mere exercise of the legislative power belonging to the whole people but not empowered to alter the constitution. See I. p. 127 ff., 195 ff., 208 ff., 375 ff. and 385 ff., II. p. 195 ff., 275 ff. and 372 ff.

39. Fichte's Ephors are not representatives.—Schlözer himself accepts

Rousseau's view that every representative system excludes the sovereignty of the general will and constitutes another sovereign or a co-sovereign, but holds that this result is desirable; see p. 106–107, 145 ff., 157–161.

40. As for example Nettelbladt, § 1163 and 1210: the ordines regni have "jura populi a populo concessa," "nomine populi exercent," "populum repraesentant et jura populi habent"; § 1211: "jura populi sunt jura statuum," as these "populum reliquum repraesentant"; § 1212; § 1278–1282 (acquisition and loss of membership in the Estates, with mention of election as possible, § 1280). Achenwall, II. § 153 ff. Daries, § 786 ff.

41. Kant, VI. p. 328 ff., 419, VII. p. 159 § 2: in a large nation representatives must by general consent take the place of the whole people, the representative system is the only means of establishing the ideal Republic; for lack of it all the so-called republics of antiquity fell into despotism; VII. p. 143: the nation can tax itself only 'through the Body of Deputies.'

42. See, in my Genossenschaftsrecht, I. p. 580 Notes 197–198 and p. 821–822, the opinions cited from J. J. Möser, Pütter, Häberlin, Jacobi, Leist, Struben and Rudhart, together with the declarations in the constitutions of several States (Schwarzburg-Rudolstadt, Brunswick and above all Würtemberg). Also Möser, Patriot. Phant., IV. nr. 51 ('national representatives,' 'who acted and decided for each and all of the inhabitants of the country'). Johann Stephan Pütter (1725–1807), Auserlesene Rechtsfälle (1775), nr. 269 § 96–102. Kreittmayr, § 182: 'Just as the whole body of the State is represented by the Prince in capite, so at the same time the Diet has to represent all the rest of the country in corpore et membris.' Fessmaier, § 143–149, where just as in Kant the national Estates are said to be representatives of all the subjects; their power rests on a tacit mandate; they are summoned to declare the general will, and therefore to take part in the making of every law which is to express the general will, in taxation, in alienations ('the rights of man' forbid the alienation of subjects as if they were chattels), in federations, war and peace. Gönner, § 253 (by reason of the State's unity the national Estates represent the whole Community, not their own class); also § 98.

43. See especially v. Mohl's account of the history and literature of general constitutional law, op. cit. I. p. 265–320.

CHAPTER FIVE

THE IDEA OF FEDERALISM

OF all the distinctive features of the political system of Althusius none is perhaps so striking as the spirit of Federalism which pervades it from bottom to top. While the construction of society in the form of a corporatively articulated whole was an essential idea of the purely medieval system, yet there was this difference, that while the medieval construction was from the top downward, we have here by means of the social contract a reconstruction from the bottom upward. It is even more remarkable that in Althusius this federalistic structure appears in conjunction with that same sharply defined and concentrated idea of sovereignty which had dissolved the medieval idea of the articulated body of society and was henceforth the great lever of all centralizing efforts.

I. The Medieval Theory

The properly medieval system of thought started from the idea of the whole and of unity, but to every lesser unit down to and including the individual it ascribed an inherent life, a purpose of its own, and an intrinsic value within the harmoniously articulated organism of the world-whole filled with the Divine Spirit. Thus in accordance with the medieval scheme of things it attained a construction of the social whole which in effect was federalistic through and through. While it postulates the visible unity of mankind in Church and Empire, yet by reason of the dualism of the two Swords it not only starts throughout from the idea of two allied Orders,[1] but it limits even this unity to those relations in which joint action is demanded by the general purpose of all mankind. Thus for it the unity is neither absolute nor exclusive, but forms the over-arching dome of a social structure organized as an independent whole. And this principle is repeated in its various gradations down to the smallest local, vocational and domestic groups. Everywhere in the Church and in the State the unitary total body consists of living member-bodies, each of which, though itself a whole, necessarily requires connection with the larger whole.[2] Each has a purpose of its own, and consists of parts which it procreates and dominates, and which in their turn are wholes.[3] Between the highest Universality or 'All-Community' and the essential unity of the individual there is a series of intermediate unities, in each of which lesser and lower units are comprised and combined. The political theories endeavor to set up a definite scheme descriptive of this articulation of mankind; for the church they follow the existing hierarchical system, and for secular societies they set up a parallel system by enlarging the Aristotelian gradation of communities.[4]

The first severe attack on this federalistic construction came from the ecclesiastical idea, which had raised the papal system on the one hand to an absorption of the State by the Church, and on the other hand to a centralization of the Church itself which deprived its parts of all independent life. But the final collapse of the proud edifice was due to the antique idea of the State which was revived in political and legal theory, and under whose influence there was a steady advance toward the conception of the State as The (exclusive) Society.

To be sure, the prevalent doctrine made a large reservation in adopting the idea that the State is simply 'human society.' It confined this universality of the political society to that aspect of human life which is concerned with temporal welfare, and secured to the Church a higher or at least an equal rank as the society devoted to eternal salvation. Yet the subsequent absorption of the Church by the State was already being prepared in theory in the fourteenth and fifteenth centuries. Among the medieval publicists there was one who dared to project a system, logically worked out even in details, in which the Church is a State-institution, Church property is State property, spiritual offices are offices of State, the government of the Church is part of the government of the State, and the sovereign ecclesiastical community is identical with the political assemblage of the citizens. He was Marsilius of Padua.[5] No one followed him the whole way. But particular consequences of the same principle were drawn even in the middle ages by other opponents of the Hierarchy.[6] And already the classical sentence to the effect that the "ius sacrum" is part of the "ius publicum" was beginning to be employed in this sense.[7]

For the rest, political philosophy borrowed from Aristotle the definition of the State as the highest and most perfect community, a community that is self-sufficient in contrast to the lower grades represented in Family and Commune.[8] When this idea came to be worked out, it followed that only one among the various subordinated and superordinated societies could be identified with the State. For a while men evaded this logical consequence by a crass inconsequence. For the philosophers rediscover the "civitas," or πόλις as defined by Aristotle, in the medieval town, but by virtue of the idea of the unitary organic structure of mankind, they subordinate this to a "regnum" and to the "imperium": that is, to higher and wider communities in which it is completed and limited. Thus at once they retract their definition without any embarrassment; they change their superlative into a comparative, and the absolute attributes into relative.[9] Then at the same time the jurists, with the Corpus Iuris Civilis before them, explain that the Empire is the one true State; [10] but they define "civitas," "populus" and "regnum" in such a way that these terms may be applied to the Commune or the Province; [11] and then, in fact, they go on applying the concept of 'The State' to communities much smaller than the Empire.[12] Nevertheless the antique idea of the State, when once it had been received, was destined to triumph. Thus indeed the philosophic theory of the State begins immediately to operate with the presupposition that there cannot be two States one above the other, and that above the State there is no room for a World-State, while below the State there is only room for mere Communes.[13] And in jurisprudence, following Bartolus [1314–1357] an ever sharper distinction is drawn between communities which have and those which have not an external "superior," and communities of the latter kind are placed on a level with the Imperium.[14] The differences between civitas, regnum and imperium become mere differences in size instead of being joints in the organic articulation of mankind, and at the same time the concept of the State is monopolized by the "universitates superiorem non recognoscentes." [15]

Thus already before the close of the middle ages the idea of the State was completely concentrated and the attribute of external sovereignty became the essential and distinctive mark of the State. Above the sovereign State the "imperium mundi," even when its bare existence was not denied, had now evaporated into an empty shadow even in theory as it had long before done in fact; at any rate it was stripped of the character of a State. For States within the State there was henceforth no room, and all the smaller societies had to fall within the rubric 'Communes and Corporations.'

But the concentration of State-life at a single point did not by any means imply a concentration of all community-life at this point. The medieval idea of the organic articulation of mankind could continue in miniature within the sovereign State, as the idea of the organic articulation of the nation. And to a certain degree this was indeed the case. The theory of corporations, which was elaborated in the fullest detail by jurisprudence on the basis of Roman and Canon Law, and which now applied only to the smaller groups, had radically altered and decomposed the Germanic notion of the autonomous life of Communities and 'Fellowships'; but yet it retained enough of this notion to insure to all non-sovereign communities, as against the exclusively sovereign State, a certain independent life of their own, a sphere of inherent rights within the domain of public law, an organic position intermediate between the Individual and the Community of All.[16] And among the political theorists there were some who in the last centuries of the middle ages—centuries full of a vigorous corporate life—sought to oppose that centralization which had triumphed in the Church and was threatening the State, with a well-grounded statement of the idea of corporative articulation and a reasoned justification of the claims of the smaller groups to a value of their own and rights of their own.[17]

Yet on the whole, even in the middle ages, the drift of theory set steadily toward an exaltation of the exclusive sovereignty of the State to the exclusive representation of all social life by the State. Owing to the fact that the texts of the later Roman law-codes were always breaking through the medieval Germanic interpretations, jurisprudence was gradually driven to anticipate the transformation of society by recasting the theory of corporations. This theory took the form of a conception of society for which the State was the sole source and the sole 'subject' of rights in public law; while the corporation, within the sphere of public rights annexed to it, was construed as a mere delegated commission of the State, and only in the domain of private law was it treated as a distinct 'subject' of rights, as if it were an individual, by virtue of a fictitious personality bestowed on it by the State. At the same time, political philosophy was on the one hand filling itself full of the antique idea of the State, and on the other hand it was saving therefrom and developing the Christian-Germanic idea of freedom and depositing this in the individualistic theory of Natural Law. And as this work advanced toward more distinct results, medieval doctrine was girding itself for that conflict which fills the later centuries, a conflict between the sovereign State and the sovereign Individual over the demarcation of the provinces assigned to them by Natural Law. In the course of this struggle all intermediate groups were first reduced to the level of the more or less arbitrarily fashioned creatures of mere positive law, and in the end were extinguished and suppressed.[18]

II. Since the Sixteenth Century

All these theoretical defenses of the centralizing and atomistic trends, which were already fashioned in the middle ages, grew more intensive and extensive during and after the sixteenth century.

Here we may but briefly refer to the extraordinary importance in this respect of the great revolution in the relation of Church and State which was effected by the Reformation. When the Church became less and less a rival for sovereignty and more and more a secularized institution, there disappeared the last great hindrance to the exaltation of the State as the all-embracing Society. The Reformers might preserve the concept of the one Universal Church in the concept of the Invisible Church; but this was not a legal concept. They might continue the doctrine of the "potestates distinctae"; but neither in the Calvinist ideal of the republican commonwealth identical with the community of the faithful, nor in the Lutheran interpretations of territorial church-polity with the Episcopal system and the doctrine of the three Estates, did this separation of the "regimen ecclesiasticum et saeculare" mean anything more than a division in the administrative organization of the one Body. Lastly, from the side of the Catholic doctrine the whole medieval theory might be revived; but even in the Catholic world this did not deflect the universal course of development of ideas. And all along the line the pure Territorial system triumphed at last, whereby the perfect absorption of the Church by the State was theoretically completed.

With the collapse of the idea of the Universal Church restricting the State's sovereignty, there gradually perished all that was left of the idea of the Universal Monarchy restricting the State's sovereignty. It was but as a lifeless phantom that the "imperium mundi" was dragged along by the imperialistic publicists. On the other hand, in the doctrine of Natural Law the medieval idea was revived in a new form in which, without diminishing the sovereignty of the several States, it undertook to derive the connection subsisting among them in international law from a permanent and indissoluble Society of States. For since the sixteenth century it became ever more common to base the obligation of the jus gentium on the "societas gentium" of natural law, in which the original and indelible unity of mankind always gains a legal expression, while at the same time full sovereignty is secured to each nation.[19] To be sure, the idea of the Society of States constantly threatened to go over into the idea of the World-State, which was then construed as a World-Republic simply by way of contrast to the medieval World-Monarchy.[20] But the prevailing doctrine set itself expressly against the view that the Society of Nations involves any power of the whole over its members, and merely supposed that among States which remain in the state of nature toward one another there are natural obligations of a social kind, just as among individuals before there were any States.[21] In all centuries however, the stricter partisans of the doctrine of sovereignty would have as little to do with the idea of a natural Society of States as with the old idea of a World-State based on positive law,[22] or else even denied that international law is true law.[23]

Just as against the Universal Church and against the Society of Nations, so also in relation to the lesser associations of States, the concept of sovereignty was now worked out, without exception in theory, in a sense which precluded all possibility of a State composed of States.[24] Thus wherever federative structures or 'Unions' existed in the world of fact, men thought that they had only to choose between the assumption of a League (or relation of 'Union') among several fully sovereign States and the assumption of a single articulated State.[25] Therefore on the one hand, men said that even formally organized Confederations (as in the case of Switzerland [26] and the United Netherlands) were mere Leagues. For the sake of this indeed they added to the received doctrine of "foedera," besides the several categories of equal and unequal Federations, the more or less sharply distinguished concept of the Confederation of States produced by a "foedus arctissimum" and organized as a "Corpus confoederatorum" or "Systema civitatum." [27] Yet in this they always insisted strongly that, be the association ever so close, it leaves the sovereignty of the several States intact, and hence they and they alone are States, while the whole bears at most the outward show of a State.[28] And on the other hand, wherever men could not or would not deny that the whole is a State (as especially in the Germanic Empire), they generally upheld the idea of the Unitary State.[29]

Hence in the question of the centralizing or federalistic construction of the State, everything depended on whether and how far, within the unitary State, the exclusive sovereignty of the whole, which is thereby characterized as a State, was compatible with a separate and independent communal life of the partial societies. It was within this frame that Althusius built up his system of Federalism, while he set himself against the prevailing opinion on this point as decidedly as he held to the strictest formulation of the doctrine of sovereignty as regards the identification of State and Church, the negation of the World-State and the rejection of the 'State composed of States.'

For the theoretical conception of the relation between the State and lesser societies, the decisive factor was, first and foremost, the elaboration of the medieval theory of corporations by jurisprudence. The jurisprudence of the sixteenth century often defended the rights of communes and corporations when they were threatened by the growing power of the absolute State, and thereby upheld, to a considerable extent, the idea that every "universitas" has its own independent sphere of rights in public law.[30] But on the whole, all remnants of the conception of the corporation as a community were swallowed up by the idea developed from the Roman texts, that the 'right-subjectivity' of the "universitas" has in itself only the value of an individual feigned for purposes of private law, and only in special cases, by virtue of special privileges, can it be vested with certain liberties or franchises in public law which in themselves flow from the exclusive authority of the State.[31] Even the champions of the independence of corporations saw themselves ever more decidedly forced to take this ground. They merely sought on the one hand to deduce from the corporation's ownership of its property in private law the widest possible sphere of inherent rights of self-government and self-regulation, and on the other hand to protect from revocation those privileges or "jura quaesita" which went beyond this sphere.[32] But in defending the private-law conception of public-law relations and the maintenance of vested privileges, they were at once placed at an open disadvantage against their absolutist opponents, who in subduing the independence of corporations could bring into the field the ideas of public right and of the public welfare which outweighs privileges.[33]

It is easy to understand that from these schools of thought represented by the jurists the modern absolutist form of the doctrine of corporations found its way into the theories of politics and natural law.[34] But here two other factors entered in, which in principle had a sharpening effect. Firstly, in the natural structure of society planned according to the antique scheme, the Family alone took the position of a necessary medium between the Individual and the State, while the Commune was at most recognized as a natural lower grade of the State. And in the perfected State the Commune wholly disappeared as a society in natural law, reappearing as a product of mere positive law together with the other corporations which had always been regarded purely from the standpoint of positive law. Secondly, the exaltation of the idea of sovereignty drove steadily toward the conception of the State's power as an absorptive omnipotence, so that the power of other societies could be conceived only as an effluence from the State. In both respects Bodin above all, in his full and favorable treatment of "collegia, corpora et universitates," developed the consequences of the principle, and therefore, strongly as he emphasized (unlike almost all the later absolutists) their high political value and the advantages of a healthy freedom for communes and corporations, he still held in principle to the view that they are State-institutions.[35] Among his followers Gregorius already in practice went beyond him in this line,[36] and Arnisaeus and Bornitius saw in communes and corporations nothing but departments of the State for administrative purposes.[37] Quite similar views were developed by the teachers of pure Natural Law, so far as they thought it worth while to say anything at all about communes and corporations.[38] In the numerous text-books and handbooks of Politics produced after the beginning of the seventeenth century, not only did the construction of all lesser societies as mere State-institutions prevail more and more, but they were also treated mostly from the standpoint of the paramount police power, in a spirit which was ever more hostile to their freedom and independence.[39] At the same time the influence of these 'nature-rightly' and 'political' views made itself ever more distinctly felt in positive public law.[40]

To this general movement the sixteenth-century doctrine of popular sovereignty remained indifferent, inasmuch as its groundwork was as consistent with a strictly centralizing as with a purely federalistic construction of the State, and thus it set up no distinctive principles of its own either way. But with regard to

practical results, while centralizing views prevailed among the
Catholics of this school, the idea of Federalism worked its way
through in some of the Reformed Monarchomachi, in obvious
connection with the federalist character of their church-polity
based on the communal principle. It was Junius Brutus above
all who set up the several Provinces and Cities as guardians of
the covenant with God as well as of the contract with the people,
and in reviving medieval doctrines [41] claimed for them the right
and duty of armed resistance to the government which breaks
its contract, and in extreme cases even the right to secede from
the State.[42]

It was Althusius again who with creative genius embraced in
a system and grounded on a theoretical principle the federalistic
ideas fermenting in the world of events and in the opinions of
his own religious and political environment. This he achieved
by simply carrying the idea of the social contract, which was
first erected into a principle by him, unreservedly into his fundamental scheme of resolving all public law into private law. This
gave him a construction of society by pure Natural Law, in
which the family, vocational association, commune and province
are necessary organic links between the Individual and the State;
in which the larger society is always composed of smaller societies
as corporative units, and only through them does it act upon
their members; in which every smaller society, as a true and
original community, draws from itself its own communal life
and its own sphere of rights, giving up to the higher society only
so much of this as is indispensably required for the attainment
of its specific end; in which, lastly, the State is otherwise ge-
nerically of the same nature as its component societies and differs
from them only in its exclusive sovereignty. As the highest legal
power on earth the State receives many new attributes and functions of its own; but it finds an insuperable barrier in the special
rights of the smaller societies, and in case of transgression thereof
it is supplanted by the power of the members which by breach
of the contract of union is restored to a full sovereignty. This
radical inversion of the dominant theory of corporations was
made by Althusius for the relations of public law and private

law alike, and thus it is that he became the author of a quite new concept of the corporation.[43]

It was not until a century and a half later that the theory of Natural Law produced another system on a similar basis. Meanwhile there was no one else to maintain a rational and thoroughgoing federalism. Yet the doctrine of Althusius was by no means without influence; on the contrary, in two different ways it had a lasting effect on the development of political ideas.

From it, in the first place, was directly evolved the phrase and the concept of 'Composite State.' Hoenonius, following Althusius throughout, distinguished between the "Respublica simplex" consisting of one State, and every State composed of several States or enlarged to a "Regnum" or "Imperium," applying to the latter the federalist idea in the term "Respublica composita." [44] Besold accepted this concept of a "Civitas composita," but as he was otherwise far from holding the federalist idea he confined it to the case of several "gentes" with different "leges" but all conjoined in "unum corpus politicum" with "unum imperium," which differs as widely from States articulated in communes and corporations as from Confederations and 'Personal Unions.' While he held up the Germanic Empire as the great example of such a "Civitas composita," he expressly characterized this form as a State composed of States, in which the "majestas" belongs exclusively to the whole, but the members themselves are of the nature of subordinate and relative States.[45] To this effect he wrote a special dissertation "de Statu Reipublicae subalterno," in which he worked out, with special reference to the German territories, the notion of the 'Sub-State,' which is not sovereign and hence is not a true State but is otherwise analogous to the sovereign 'Super-State'; [46] while in a series of other dissertations he treated all other lesser societies as mere corporative articulations of the 'simple State.' [47] This notion of the 'State-of-States' first set up by Besold [48] was developed forty years later by Hugo in a more precise and systematic manner, in which on a similar basis he worked out the principle of a division of powers between the sovereign Super-State and the dependent Member-States and used it for the construction of the "duplex regimen"

existing in the Germanic Empire.[49] Since that time the concept
of the Composite State never quite disappeared from political
science. Many imperialistic publicists accepted it in Hugo's formulation,[50] and Leibniz expressed it in a form approaching still
nearer to modern views of the Federal State.[51] It was indeed
shaken severely by the heavy attacks which Pufendorf aimed
against it with the weapons of the strict theory of sovereignty,
while at the same time erecting his own doctrine of the "Systemata Civitatum" surpassing the simple "foedus" in duration
and organization.[52] Yet when Pufendorf said that it was impossible that a State should contain States within itself, and thus
recognized only the 'Personal Union' and the pure Confederation as normal forms of the association of States,[53] he had to admit
that in fact there are intermediate forms and that the Germanic
Empire in particular stood midway between a 'System of States'
and a unitary State. He himself, it is true, regarded every such
'irregularity' as a morbid derangement, and just for this reason he
characterized the Germanic Empire as a monstrous creature
which could only be reformed by the surgical operation of making it a 'regular System of States.' And many publicists followed
him in absolutely rejecting the idea of the Federal State,[54]
whereby those who were not willing, like him, to brand the
ever-venerated Empire as a monstrosity had but to choose between the two equally desperate devices of construing the existing Empire as a mere Confederation,[55] or of reverting to the
old conception of it as a unitary State.[56] But some influential
writers, who otherwise copied Pufendorf's doctrine and termin-
ology, covertly transfused the idea of the "Systema Civitatum irregulare," as realized in the Germanic Empire, back into the
concept of the "Respublica composita," to which the 'irregularity' was imputed merely as a tag affixed for the sake of the
academic theory.[57] Hert indeed, while reproducing in other respects the categories of Pufendorf, argued for the full validation
of a mediate category, construed as a Federal State in Hugo's
sense, between the articulated unitary State and the Confederation of States.[58] And when after the middle of the eighteenth
century, as explained above, the concept of sovereignty was
weakened and the doctrine of the division of powers gained cur-

rency, the path was cleared for the revival and advancement of the idea of the Federal State. Now indeed the idea of the Composite State was not only readmitted by the teachers of public law with special application to the Germanic Empire,[59] but it was sometimes accepted in general terms by the 'Nature-Right' theory of the State, and was developed into a formal system by Nettelbladt in his general theory of the Federal State.[60] And lastly, after the year 1777, when Pütter, on the ground thus leveled, had erected his well-known reconstruction of the positive public law of Germany in terms of the Federal State,[61] the concept of the 'State composed of States' first gained almost undisputed sway as applied to the moribund Empire.[62] Then with the new century, in practice as in theory, it opened its career of triumph, entering at the same time on its modern process of inner development with its wealth of ramifications.[63]

While the idea of the Federal State was indeed a gradual and historically continuous outgrowth of the federalistic idea as reproduced by Althusius on a basis of Natural Law, this had a lasting effect on the development of political ideas in yet another way. For by the logical elaboration of the principle of the social contract by Althusius, there was brought into the theory of the corporative articulation of the State an element which could never again be quite repressed by all the efforts of absolutism, and which evolved at last into a 'Nature-Right' theory of society which prepared directly for the modern idea of the freedom of communities and associations.

Wherever the derivation of the State from the social contract was strictly maintained, it was impossible to deny the same derivation of communes and associations. Thereby the lesser societies were treated as of equal birth with the State. To them was ascribed an original communal life which was no mere gift of the State, even though it was subject perhaps to the State's power of approval and restriction. Such a view indeed worked its way into many systems of politics.[64] But above all it was Grotius who expressed it in a form strongly reminiscent of Althusius. He not only insisted throughout that every lesser "consociatio" is similar in origin and nature to the societas perfectissima realized in the State,[65] but conceived the whole body of the State simply as a perpetual and immortal federation of its partial societies. From this he argued that while the whole body cannot alienate its sovereignty over a part of the people without its consent,[66] nevertheless the part (though as a rule it is equally forbidden to secede by its own act) in exceptional cases has the right to secede if there is evidently no other means of self-preservation. He demonstrated that the "jus partis ad se tuendam" is greater than the "jus corporis in partem," with the characteristic argument: "quia pars utitur jure quod ante societatem initam habuit, corpus non item." [67]

Hobbes himself could not avoid the consequence of the contractual idea, that the "Systems subordinate," which he describes at length and recognizes as necessary and useful, must be construed as social bodies analogous to the State, and with an existence derived ultimately from themselves even though the concession or permission of the State is required. But even at this point he knew how to perform the turn into the strictest absolutism in his epoch-making fashion. For while, unlike Althusius and Grotius, he made the State arise without intermediate steps from the contract of the individuals in their naked isolation making a full and definitive alienation of all powers, yet the power to associate must still inhere in the individuals: but in any case they have irretrievably lost the power to give an association any social power over themselves. They no longer have any power to give away; it is the omnipotent State alone that has such power. Thus indeed Hobbes taught that in every "System subordinate" all power is granted and determined by the State, that the representative capacity which stamps the association as a civil person is derived from the mandate of the State, and that the competence of all corporate organs is defined solely by the authority conceded to them by the State, not by a mandate of the subject body itself. Otherwise there would result a State within the State, which is incompatible with the very idea of sovereignty.[68]

While those absolutists who started from a different basis also agreed with the results reached by Hobbes,[69] the arguments and conclusions together gained entrance into the 'Nature-Right' theories of the State dominated by the idea of contract.[70] Even the liberal-minded Huber, who was by no means averse to a certain practical independence of communes and corporate bodies, which he treats fully and favorably,[71] not only adhered in principle to the Concession theory in the fullest sense but derived all the representative powers of the officers of a lesser social body from a mandate given to them directly by the sovereign. And hence, despite the similar social basis of State and universitas, he defined their essential difference to be that the former derives its "persona" from the people, the latter from the State.[72] But it was of the greatest importance that Pufendorf himself, while projecting a general theory of "personae morales compositae" which was rich in new ideas, and offering it as a valid basis for the construction of the State and all corporate bodies alike (above, Ch. II. Note 74), nevertheless followed Hobbes throughout in the theoretical conception of the relations of the lesser societies in public law.[73] In like manner Thomasius strongly emphasized the distinction between the simple "societas aequalis" and the Society vested with power over its members, and at the same time insisted that the communes as mere "partes Reipublicae" are not societies of a special grade and were for this reason wholly omitted by Aristotle, while the 'Fellowships' or "societates arbitrariae" found no place at all in the Law of Nature.[74] In a still more striking fashion Hert combined a purely 'social' construction of all moral personality with the doctrine that every lesser society is in itself a mere "societas aequalis" and whatever power it may have comes entirely from the State.[75] From this he inferred that while the State is a body animated by the ruler, the corporation has no soul and exists only as a "persona mystica": "quoniam universitas pars est tantum civitatis et quicquid juris spiritumve habet, accepit concessu vel expresso vel tacito compotum summae potestatis." [76] And the systematists of general public law, under the influence of Pufendorf, also moved within the same circle of ideas.[77]

As against this development of the 'Nature-Right' theories of the State, positive jurisprudence often appeared in the seventeenth and even in the eighteenth century as the conservative guardian of established corporative rights. But in this it fought with the old weapons of the private-law conception on the one hand and the doctrine of Privilege on the other, and had not even a remote idea of reviving in principle the notion of the group-life of 'Fellowships'; [78] it was only privileged corporations, and not the corporative idea, with which it was concerned.[79] All the more complete was the victory of the opposing movement, pushing steadily on after the middle of the seventeenth century, which filled itself with the spirit of the absolutist doctrine of Natural Law, and drew out the consequences of it step by step with reference to the relations, in positive law, of Corporations in general and the several traditional species of Societies in particular.[80] Ever more decidedly did it operate to transform the privileged Corporation into the State-institution of public law with its artificial 'subjectivity' of rights in private law. Ever more distinctly did it teach that every vested privilege becomes void as soon as it conflicts with the "salus publica," and that the public welfare absolutely requires the concentration of all public power in the hands of the sovereign. Ever more strictly was the theory of "persona ficta" developed for the sphere of capacities still left to the corporation in its own right, while its perpetual wardship was claimed to imply the most stringent guardianship on the part of the State. What made all this possible, however, was just the fact that the federative conception prevailed as regards the Empire and, at least after the Peace of Westphalia, the territories were regarded as States, which were essentially different from the lesser societies and to which there accrued just so much of legal right as was taken from the communes and corporations.

But during the eighteenth century even the 'Nature-Right' theory of the State by no means stood still at the point which it had reached, but instead advanced in two contrary directions. The first of these completed the centralizing-atomistic idea and finally arrived at the theoretical destruction of all intermediate links between the sovereign Individual and the Sovereign Community of All. The other developed from the 'individualist-collectivist' view the principle of Free Association, and with its help undertook to reconstruct the system of corporative articulation.

The first of these tendencies prevailed chiefly in France. First of all Turgot, in the well-known article in which he claimed for the State the right to dissolve every "corps particulier," asserted openly that between the sacred natural rights of the Individual and the sovereignty of the civil society embodied in the State there is no room for a special right of the lesser societies to exist.[81] Then Rousseau, drawing the last consequences here as elsewhere, rejected every "association partielle" as a disruption and perversion of the general will.[82] And lastly the Revolution, in many controversies on the relation of parts of the State to the whole, still followed in theory and practice the centralizing idea of doing away with the concept of the organic corporate body, and replacing it by the concept of a division arranged from the center within the sum of free and equal individuals united in one collective Body.[83] Even in Germany, in the second half of the eighteenth century, there was an approximation to the tendency prevailing in France in the same measure that the ideas of enlightened despotism became current.[84] More and more, even here, every safeguard of vested rights went down before the natural rights which were alone regarded as perpetual and sacred. More and more there appeared as natural rights only the 'rights of man' on the one hand and the sovereignty of civil society on the other. More and more did these great rival principles work together in the deadly combat against the independent mediate bodies, in which the State perceived an intolerable obstacle to its sovereignty and the Individual a galling fetter on his liberty and equality. Under the influence of the French revolutionary doctrine in this very point, neither could Fichte rise to a higher view,[85] nor could Kant replace the Corporation (which he identified with the Foundation [*Stiftung*] and then radically destroyed) by a new vital principle of social articulation.[86] And lastly the theory and practice of the States of the Rhenish Confederation, in their treatment of the lesser societies, copied the French pattern with the blindest servility.

But meanwhile in Germany itself the 'Nature-Right' theory of the State advanced in another direction, in which it carried out the principle of Free Association in all gradations and finally approximated to the social structure of Althusius built from the bottom upward. This process of evolution prepared above all for the ever fuller development of a general theory of natural

society based on the idea of the social contract, which placed all
societies, including the State, under the same generic concept and
construed them according to the same scheme.[87] If thereby, now
as before, in virtue of the sharp distinction of societas aequalis
and inaequalis (above, p. 104) the lesser societies were denied
all power of their own and the action of the State was thrust deep
into their inner life, yet it was by no means a small thing that in
principle the corporate body was ever more decidedly treated as
a community which, like the State, grew out of free association
and was self-existent; that the Commune in particular entered
again into possession of an original sphere of rights; that in the
Church the 'Collegial' system, though often in a purely Territorial form, began its career of triumph. In this sense J. H.
Boehmer, even though (partly owing to the derivation of all
power from the State and partly owing to the sharp assertion of
the State's power over corporations) he destroyed all independent social life in practice, may yet be named as one of the first
who in theory restored the old idea that every lesser society is of
the nature of a 'Fellowship' [*Genossenschaft*].[88] Then in Wolff
and his school the general theory of natural society began even
in practice to come to the aid of communes and corporate bodies.[89]
But the decisive turn was made by Nettelbladt. On the one hand
he claimed for the lesser societies as well as for the individual
and the State a sphere of existence in natural law, and thus he
even ascribed to them original social rights (jura originaria, ex
natura societatis consequentia, socialia sive collegialia), prior to
all acquired rights (jura contracta) and parallel with the innate
rights of the individual. And on the other hand he included
among these self-established social rights, in all cases and even
in the societas aequalis, a "potestas" of the community over its
members. Thus indeed Nettelbladt was placed in the position of
planning, on the basis of free association, a system of social construction reproducing in many respects the ideas of Althusius.[90]
And in like manner in the German school of Natural Law there
prevailed more and more the tendency to construct the social
body from the bottom upward, to set up every community having material or local limitation as a society already self-created,
and to introduce the State for the first time at the close as the

dome arching over all, with its "jura majestatica" often, in the result, almost stifling the "jura collegialia." [91]

This wide-spread tendency in the German school of Natural Law exerted no small influence on political opinions also. While the greatest French champion of corporative mediate groups, Montesquieu, conceived the corporation (which he held to be indispensable only in monarchies) in no other sense than that of the privilege of incorporated Estates,[92] in Germany Möser, with all his predilection for the existing system of Estates and with all his aversion from the uniformitarian and leveling tendencies of Natural Law, nevertheless upheld the corporative idea in a much more liberal and modern spirit. And surely this great man was inspired more than he himself knew by the ideas developed among the teachers of Natural Law, when he not only based the State upon the autonomous and independent organization of all spheres of social life as 'Fellowships,' but in an often prophetic manner gave expression to his faith in the power of free association.[93] Toward the end of the century Schlözer preached already the freest right of association, declaring with reference to all groups (and especially religious societies): 'the great Community must not only allow them to be formed, it must even protect them; it is not concerned with the ideas and acts of the several gilds except that they shall not be contrary to the Contract of Citizenship.' [94] Humboldt himself asserted the view that the State is a subsidiary society, and said that wherever a free association suffices it is far better than an institution created by the State.[95]

After the last decade of the eighteenth century positive jurisprudence, like political theory, was so deeply penetrated by the 'Nature-Right' theory of society that the whole structure of the Roman theory of Corporations threatened to crumble.[96]

And lastly, in the social system constructed from the bottom upward, which the great legislative work of the Prussian State elaborated in a fashion so liberal for its time, who could fail to recognize the spirit of the 'Nature-Right' social doctrine? [97]

Now indeed this 'Nature-Right' theory of society, like the theory of the State derived from it, was given an individualistic and mechanical form. When it wiped out all sharp distinctions

between "societas" and "universitas," it amounted inwardly to
the idea of the social contract as a bond of obligation between
individuals, and outwardly to the idea of the 'moral person'
which makes the sum total of individuals a collective unit.[98]
Hence in its inmost essence and its final goal it was alien and
even hostile to the historical and organic factor in corporative
life, to the idea of a Group-Personality outlasting the changing
generations of individuals and of a communal Being which
merges the individual beings in a higher unity of life. In fact
Humboldt voiced the inmost feelings of this school when he
said that it would be most desirable to replace the corporation
altogether by the freely formed and freely dissolved association
of individuals, and thus avoid the perpetual binding of free individuals and future generations by weaving social 'ties' instead
of corporative 'fetters'; [99] when he proposed to escape all the
disadvantages of 'moral persons,' whose mere unity is harmful
even apart from their privileges, by a law expressly declaring
'that every moral person or society is to be regarded as nothing
more than the sum of its existing members, and hence nothing
can hinder them from deciding at pleasure, by majority vote,
as to the use of the common powers and resources;' [100] when
lastly he rejected all special rules of law on Corporations and
Foundations as superfluous, since the rubrics of Contract and
Testamentary Disposition are quite sufficient.[101]

Yet this school of thought, which by no means went to such
lengths everywhere, gained immortal honor for its emphasis on
free association, not only as against the obsolete privileged corporations but also against the centralizing-atomistic trend. And
above all it brought forth certain principles which are indispensable in the modern world, and whose reception enabled the
historic-organic view of intermediate groups, so highly developed
in our century, to prevail more and more against the centralizing
as well as the individualist counter-currents.

NOTES

1. See above, Ch. I. Note 13.

2. See for example Aegid. Col. II. 1 c. 2; Eng. Volk., De ortu, c. 15, 17, 18 (after the exemplum universalis naturae the ordo totius communitatis publicae shows an ever-recurring "subalternatio" until the summit is reached: above every general weal stands one more general, every lower end is at the same time a means to a higher end, the totality of this-worldly ends is a means to an other-worldly end; the "felicitas" of every narrower community always depends on that of some wider community, and thus finally on the felicitas imperii); Dante, I. c. 3 and 5; Aug. Triumph., I. q. 1 a. 6.

3. This is explained by Eng. Volk., loc. cit.; and especially Dante, I. c. 3, 5 and 16. For him every composite Being ("plura ordinata ad unum") has a specific final cause which makes it a unit; this holds true of the homo singularis, the communitas domestica, the vicus, the civitas, the regnum and the Community of all Mankind. No one however asserts more forcibly the idea of an organic articulation in unity and a relative independence of members in the 'harmonious concord' of the whole Body than does Nicolas of Cues (as in II. c. 27–28). See also Ant. Ros., I. c. 6; and above, Ch. III. Note 38.

4. Most commonly there is inserted, between the Empire and the Family (domus), the triple gradation of the local community (vicus, villa, oppidum), the city-community (civitas), and the territorial community (provincia, regnum); see Aegid. Col., II. 1 c. 2; Dante, loc. cit.; Ockham, Dial. III. tr. 1, l. 2, c. 3–5. Among the jurists this articulation became current chiefly through Bartolus, who comprised the three intermediate bodies as "universitas triplex" under the technical names of universitas larga, minus larga, and minima; see Comment. on l. 1 Dig. 39, 2 nr. 3, l. 23 Dig. 49, 15 nr. 1–16, l. 2 Dig. de V. S., nr. 4–7, l. 5 Cod. 10, 63, l. un. Cod. 11, 21 nr. 5–6, Auth. Coll. VII. 1 (Nov. 89), praef. nr. 4–7; also Tract. super const. ad reprim., v. "Lombardiae" nr. 1–7; Consilia, I. cons. 189 nr. 1–2. —Thom. Aquin., De reg. pr., I. c. 1 i. f., distinguishes 'familia, civitas, provincia (regnum). Eng. Volk. in one of his writings (De reg. pr., II. c. 2–3) stops at the civitas, under which rubric he includes the regnum; while in another (De ortu, c. 7 and 12) he says that Aristotle distinguishes five communities (domus, vicus, civitas, provincia, regnum), to which the imperium should be added, while Augustine reckons only three (domus, urbs, orbis). Then it becomes more and more usual to separate the Province and the territorial State as two grades; thus Aug. Triumph., I. q. 1 a. 6, makes five "communitates" in the corpus mysticum ecclesiae (the vicus with a

Parson, civitas with Bishop, provincia with Archbishop, regnum with Patriarch, the communitas totius orbis with the Pope). Likewise Ant. Ros., I. c. 6, arranges above the "individuum corpus humanum" and the "domus" five "corpora mystica universitatum": communitas unius vici, castri or oppidi under parochus and magister; civitatis under episcopus and defensor; provinciae under archiepiscopus and praeses; regni under primas and rex; and universi orbis under Papa and Caesar.

5. Mars. Pat., I. c. 5–6 (pars et officium civitatis), c. 19, II. throughout, III. concl. 7, 12–13, 16–17, 21–22, 27–28, 33–35, 37–41.

6. Thus John of Paris, c. 21, teaches that the State has an unlimited right to suppress abuses of the 'spiritual sword' by the use of the 'material sword.' In Disput. inter mil. et cler., p. 682–686, and in Somn. Virid., c. 31–32, the confiscation of church property for the "salus publica" is defended, with a strong premonitory suggestion of the "propriété de la nation" [1789]. See also Wyclif, Art. 16; and Hus, Determinatio de ablatione temporalium a clericis, in Goldast I. p. 232–242. Joh. Paris., c. 20, and Nic. Cus., III. c. 39, argue only for the taxation of church property; Quaestio in utramque partem, p. 106 ad 17, justifies statutes of mortmain. And the doctrine that in temporal matters the church is subject to the temporal Magistrate often led to the assumption of far-reaching powers of the State even as to the internal affairs of the Church. See for example the powers ascribed to the State with regard to the Reform of the Church, in Nic. Cus., III. c. 8–24, 33 and 40, wherein it is said (II. c. 40) that to the State belongs the care of all things pertaining "ad bonum publicum," and this is true "etiam in ecclesiasticis negotiis"; Greg. Heimb., in Goldast I. p. 559–560; Peter Bertrand, ib. II. p. 1261–1283; Patric. Sen., op. cit., III. 4; also Hübler, p. 281–288 and 318–322.

7. Taken over from Ulpian through Isidore into the medieval writings (see Fitting, Juristische Schriften des früheren Mittelalters, Halle 1876, p. 140 § 66 and p. 164 § 95), the maxim "ius publicum est in sacris, sacerdotibus et magistratibus" was accepted by the Church in order to prove its own State-like nature (Thom. Aquin., Op. II. p. 349). But already Ockham, Octo qu., IV. c. 6, says that many inferred from this same text that the Emperor "possit ordinare apostolicam sedem et facere papam et archiepiscopos et episcopos," and that no renunciation of such a "ius publicum" could have been valid.

8. See Thom. Aquin., De reg. pr., I. c. 1 i. f., and Op. XXI. p. 366 ff.; Aegid. Col., III. 1 c. 1 ("principalissima communitas"), c. 4, III. 2 c. 32; Joh. Paris., c. 1; Eng. Volk., De reg. pr., II. c. 2–3; Mars. Pat., I. c. 4 (perfecta communitas omnem habens terminum per se sufficientiae); Ockham, Dial. III. tr. 1, l. 2, c. 3–5.

9. Thus Thom. Aquin., De reg. pr., I. c. 1, sees an ascending scale of "per se sufficiens esse" in civitas, provincia, regnum; and Ptol. Luc., III. c. 10–22 and IV. c. 1–28, places the priest-kingly, the kingly (including the imperial), the 'political,' and the domestic in four grades of lordship, and in so doing applies the word "Politia" to the "civitates" which have been expressly defined as cities that are subject to the Emperor or King (IV. c. 1); but he then takes "civitas" now in this and now in a more general sense. The procedure of Aegid. Col. is clearer: for him the "civitas" is the "principalissima communitas" only "respectu domus et vici"; the "communitas regni" is yet "principalior," being related to the civitas as this is to vicus and domus (III. 1 c. 1); he also declares it highly necessary that, to secure their internal and external completion (finis et complementum), several civitates should be united in the body of one regnum or in a "confoederatio sub uno rege" (ib. c. 4–5; compare II. 1 c. 2, and III. 2 c. 32). Similarly Ockham, Dial. III. tr. 1, l. 2, c. 5: the civitas is "principalissima omnium communitatum," but only of those "simul in eodem loco habitantes"; for the rest, it is subordinate to some ducatus or some regnum, to which analogous rules apply. All the other writers cited above, Note 4, presuppose as a matter of course that the "civitas" will be completed by some "regnum" and this by the "imperium."

10. Compare the Glossa Ordinaria and the Commentaries of the later legists on l. 9 Dig. 1, 3, l. 1 Dig. 1, 4, l. un. Dig. 1, 11, l. 11 Cod. 1, 17, and I. Feud. 26; also Pillius, De ordine iudiciorum, II. § 13, and Tancredus, Ordo iudiciarius, I. 1 § 1. Lupold of Bebenburg at this point follows the legists closely; he regards the Empire as the State in the sense of Roman law, and kings as "magistratus maiores" who differ from "praesides provinciae" only in being hereditary, and who in strictness owe their positions to an imperial appointment made by way of "tacitus consensus."

11. See the definitions of "civitas" (along with urbs, oppidum, villa, etc.), populus, provincia, territorium and regnum, in Joh. Andr. on c. 17 in Sexto 5, 11, and c. 17 in Sexto 1, 6 nr. 7; Domin. Gem. on c. 17 in Sexto 5, 11 nr. 3–4; Phil. Franchus, eod. c. nr. 4–5; Archidiaconus on c. 56 C. 12, q. 2; Bartholomaeus Caepolla on l. 2 pr. Dig. de V. S., nr. 1–28; Vocab. Iuris, v. "civitas"; Baldus on l. 5 Dig. 1, 1; Bartolus on l. 1 § 12 Dig. 39, 1; Ludov. Rom. on l. 1 § 12 Dig. 39, 1 nr. 12–17; Jason on l. 73 § 1 Dig. de leg., I. nr. 1–9; Marcus, Dec., I. q. 365 aand 366. Especially favored are the definitions of "civitas" as "civium unitas" or "hominum multitudo societatis vinculo adunata ad simul iure vivendum," and of "populus" as "humanae multitudinis coetus iuris consensu et concordi communione sociatus," wherein the question is left quite open whether State or Commune is meant.

12. From of old, men help themselves out of difficulties by saying that in the 'proper' sense only the Empire and its capital city of Rome are "respublicae" with "ius publicum" and "bona publica," and all other communities are "loco privatorum"; but that in a confessedly 'improper' sense these terms may also be applied to particular populi and civitates. Placentinus, De varietate actionum, II. 2 p. 38; Pillius, Summa Cod., 11, 29 nr. 1; Gl. Ord. on l. 1 § 2 Dig. 3, 4, v. "proconsul," l. 7 pr. eod., v. "publico," l. 1, pr. Dig. de R. D., v. "aut publicae," l. 26 § 9, Dig. 4, 6, v. "non absit," l. 16 and 17, Dig. de V. S., l. 4 Cod. 2, 54, v. "respublica," l. 5 Cod. 6, 1, l. 3 Cod. 11, 29; Baldus on Const. I. Dig., pr. nr. 8, and Cons., V. c. 336; Jason on l. 71 § 5 Dig. de leg., I. nr. 29; Bartholomaeus de Saliceto on l. 4 Cod. 2, 54; Decius, Cons. 360, 403, 468, 564, 638; Joh. de Platea on l. un. Cod. 11, 21 nr. 5; Bertachinus, v. "respublica."

13. This is the procedure of John of Paris, c. 1, and other Frenchmen, who treat 'the Realm' ("regnum") as the abstract State and flatly deny the "imperium mundi" (above, Ch. I. Note 13); likewise Mars. Pat., and Patric. Sen. (I. 3 ff.), without further definition.

14. Already Bartolus says expressly of the "civitas quae superiorem non recognoscit," that it "tantam potestatem habet in populo quantam Imperator in universo." Thus on l. 7 Dig. 48, 1 nr. 14, l. 4 Dig. 50, 9 nr. 7 (populus without superior has ipse in se imperium), 8 and 14, l. 3 Cod. 11, 31 nr. 2; compare his development of the distinction with regard to particular rights of superiority, on l. 9 Dig. 1, 1, l. 1 pr. Dig. 3, 4 nr. 3, l. 7 Dig. 48, 1 nr. 14, l. 3 Dig. 48, 5 nr. 2, l. 2 Dig. 49, 14 nr. 2, l. 7 Dig. 49, 15 nr. 1–3, l. 23 eod. nr. 16, l. 3 Dig. 50, 10 nr. 4–5, l. 1 Cod. 10, 10, nr. 1, 5 and 11, Tract. de repraes., q. 1 nr. 6 and q. 2 nr. 8, compared with q. 3 nr. 5.—See further Angelus on l. 1 Cod. 10, 10 nr. 1 and 5; Lucas de Penna on ead. l. nr. 1, and l. 2 Cod. 11, 29; Baldus on § 1 Inst. 1, 2 nr. 8, Cons., V. c. 406 nr. 6; Jason, Cons., III. c. 70 nr. 6–8; Paul. Castr. on l. 86 Dig. 29, 2 nr. 3; Franc. Curtius senior, Cons. 48 nr. 21; Panorm. on c. 7 X. 1, 2 nr. 6 (sovereign kings and cities have imperial rights in their domain); Decius, Cons., 403 nr. 2, 649 nr. 3.—The dispute, as to whether such sovereignty is only "de facto" or may also be "de iure," had little real importance; Bartolus himself treats this as indifferent (thus on l. 26 Dig. 36, 1, and l. 1 Cod. 10, 10 nr. 11: in civitatibus, quae de iure vel de facto hodie non recognoscunt superiorem, et sic est populus liber); see also Albericus de Rosciate, De statutis, III. q. 19, and on l. 2 Cod. 6, 35 nr. 1–3.

15. Thus Paul. Castr. on l. 1 § 1–3 Dig. 3, 4 nr. 1, l. 5 Dig. 1, 1, lect. 2, and l. 86 Dig. 29, 2 nr. 3, expressly says that according to modern law every "populus superiorem non recognoscens" has a real and true "respublica" of its own, while other communes have "largo modo rempublicam," and the

lesser collegia are only "partes reipublicae" with a certain "similitudo" to States. Similarly Jason on l. 19 Cod. 1, 2 nr. 15, and l. 1 Dig. 2, 1 nr. 18.

16. Here, as in the subsequent remarks on the history of the theory of corporations, I may again refer once for all to the continuation of my work on Genossenschaftsrecht.

17. In the Church the writers of the Conciliar party strongly resist the centralizing theory and defend the independent rights of the particular churches; see Joh. Paris., c. 6; Petr. Alliac., in Gerson I. p. 666 ff. and 692, and De pot. eccl., II. c. 1; Gerson, II. p. 256; and with the deepest reasoning Nic. Cus., II. c. 13 and 22–28; compare already the citations above, Ch. III. Note 38. For the State, besides Dante, Nic. Cus. and Ant. Ros., who hold to the medieval idea of a Community comprising all mankind (above, Note 3), even Marsilius maintains the principle of mediate organic articulation (II. c. 24, for the regimen civile as well as ecclesiasticum). According to Ockham, Dial. III. tr. 2, l. 1, c. 30, even "ipsa tota communitas Romanorum" ought not to infringe the "iura partialia Romanorum personarum vel congregationum seu collegiorum aut communitatum particularium"; compare ib. l. 2, c. 28: "quaelibet privata persona et quodlibet particulare collegium est pars totius communitatis; et idco bonum cuiuslibet particularis collegii est bonum totius communitatis." Also it is often said, in accordance with Aristotle, that the suppression of "sodalitates" and "congregationes" is a criterion of the tyrant, while the "verus rex" would have his subjècts "confoederatos et coniunctos"; thus Aegid. Col., III. 2 c. 10; likewise Thom. Aquin., De reg. pr., I. c. 3; Somn. Virid., c. 134; Gerson, IV. p. 600.

18. In sharpest opposition to the medieval system of mediates Patric. Sen., I. 6, antiquarian through and through, proclaims the equality of all citizens before the law (aequalitas iuris inter cives), and even their equal capacity for all public offices and their equal civic duties.—Most of the abstract social constructions framed by medieval publicists and philosophers under the influence of Natural Law have nothing to say of intermediate groups; but this silence itself is of far-reaching importance. For so far as the corporation finds no place in the system of Natural Law, its whole existence falls within positive law and is thus treated more and more as something which the State has arbitrarily created and may alter at will. And so far as the sphere of the State's power on the one hand, and the sphere of the individual's freedom on the other, become the exclusive and all-sufficient starting-points for a philosophy of law, the corporation can find a place in public law only as a part of the State and a place in private law only as an artificial individual; while everything in actual life that may seem contrary to this doctrine is regarded as the result of privileges which the State has granted and which it may at any time revoke in the public interest. (An application of this is made

by Petrus de Andlo, I. c. 12, when he says that, according to the maxim "contra absolutam potestatem principis non potest praescribi," the Emperor can withdraw all public powers from any commune or corporation however long the usage, as in the case of that odious jurisdiction over life and limb which is held by "plures communitates, imo castella et exiguae villae terrarum, ubi per simplicissimos rusticos ius reddi consuevit.")

19. Thus Connanus, op. cit., I. c. 5, nr. 1 and 4, places the source of the jus gentium in "humana societas"; herein is preserved (I. c. 6 nr. 2–3) the original unity and a vestige of the primeval community: "mundus hic quasi omnium urbs et civitas"; in so far as Paris belongs not merely to the Parisians but to the world, omnes homines are "concives" (as Socrates called himself a 'citizen of the world') and the Law of Nations is a "jus quasi civile." See Omphalus, op. cit., I. c. 38: "societas omnium hominum"; Greg. Thol., I. c. 3 § 11 ff.: "commune jus gentium" as a vestige of the "civitas mundana"; Winkler, I. c. 9: all men and nations are "una societate juris naturaliter devincti"; Joh. a Felde, I. c. 1 p. 5.—With more precision Suarez dilates on the Society of Mankind, which he also believes to continue in the jus gentium (I. c. 6 nr. 18, III. c. 2 nr. 5–6); there is "aliqua unitas" and "societas ac communicatio," which as "quasi politica et moralis" is the bearer of the Law of Nations and, although "unaquaeque civitas perfecta, respublica aut regnum sit in se communitas perfecta et suis membris constans, nihilominus quaelibet illarum est etiam membrum alioquo modo hujus universi" (III. c. 19 nr. 9); yet sovereign States are only the particular nations, which are connected with one another merely by the "naturalis ordo rerum humanarum" and not by "leges civiles universales" (III. c. 4 nr. 7), and above which there is no world-dominion of any kind, whether of the Pope or of the Emperor (ib. c. 6–8).—Then it was of special importance that Grotius accepted this idea; see II. c. 8 § 26, c. 15 § 5 and § 12 ("omnes Christiani unius corporis membra"), c. 20 (societas humana), c. 21 § 3; also c. 3 § 6 (the jus gentium, unlike the pure jus naturale, gives infants and insane persons the right to own property, "personam illorum interim quasi sustinente genere humano").—See further Leibniz, in Dutens, IV. 3 p. 294 ff., and in Guhrauer, I. p. 414 ff. ('like unto a Community'); Mevius, V. § 18–20 (societas communis inter omnes populos is the source of the jus gentium), also § 4; Bossuet, I. a. 1 (société générale du genre humain).

20. Thus already says Albericus Gentilis (1552–1608), De jure belli, Hanau 1612 (1st ed. 1588), p. 11–13: "orbis rectio est penes congregationem majoris partis orbis." Victoria, III. nr. 12, also treats all States as members of one human Respublica. Likewise Boxhorn, I. c. 2 § 3–8, derives the jus gentium from the "universalis Republica omnium hominum." Junius Brutus makes use of the notion of "humana societas" in order to prove the

right and duty of neighboring States to intervene against tyrants (q. III. p. 348–358); in cases of religious oppression he already deduces the same result from the concept of the "ecclesia unica" (ib. p. 329–348).—Thereafter it is Wolff who revives the idea of the World-State in the concept of the "Civitas maxima" with "imperium universale," contradicting indeed his own reasonings on the continuance of the state of nature among States (Inst. § 1090 ff.); see the development of his thoughts by Joh. Heumann, Disquisitio de civitate gentium, in Exercitationes juris, Altdorf 1749, II. nr. 4; also Achenwall, Proleg. § 82–90 and I. § 43–44.—Lastly, Kant declares that the 'State-of-Nations' ("Völkerstaat") with binding laws is a dictate of reason *in thesi*, even though *in hypothesi* he is content with a Confederation ("Bund," "Genossenschaft," "Foederalismus freier Staaten"); Werke, VI. p. 340–346, 405–454, VII. p. 162, 168 ff.; compare above, Ch. II. Note 123.

21. For this reason all the writers quoted in Note 19 above, whenever they use the words civitas, respublica, civis, membrum, etc., insert a "quasi." Thomasius expressly says that the societas gentium does not perfect the State but only confirms and modifies the "officia" of natural law, that it is thus "imperfectior civitate," a mere "societas aequalis" without imperium and not a "respublica universalis"; Inst. jur. div., III. c. 2 § 38–56, also I. c. 2 § 104 ff., Fund. jur. nat., III. c. 6 § 5. Nettelbladt opines that the "societas natura constituta" of States with the purpose of "conservatio generis humani" is a "systema gentium" rather than a "civitas maxima"; yet the "leges sociales seu systematicae gentium" springing from this Society must be distinguished from the "leges gentium stricte naturales"; Syst. nat., § 1420–1424. Even Fichte, to secure perpetual peace, would set up only a Confederation, not a 'State-of-Nations'; Werke, II. p. 261 ff., and Nachg. Werke, II. p. 644 ff.—For the rest see above, Ch. II. Notes 82, 83.

22. Thus there is nothing of this in Bodin and his school.

23. This is chiefly the consequence of the Hobbesian doctrine; above, Ch. II. Note 82.

24. See S. Brie, Der Bundesstaat, Part I., Leipzig 1874, p. 14 ff.

25. This is most clearly stated by Bodin, II. c. 6 nr. 224, when he recounts that he had formerly taken the German Princes and Cities as sovereign and for this reason merely "jure foederis ac societatis inter se obligati," but that now, in view of the jura majestatis openly exercised by the Imperial Diet, he must admit that the Empire is an aristocratic Unitary State. See Althusius as above, Part I., Ch. II. Note 11; Casmannus, c. 66; Hoenonius, d. XII. and XIII.; Grotius, Apologeticus, Paris 1622, c. 1 (compare this with the argument from the impossibility of double sovereignty in Brie, p. 15 note 25); Huber, I. 2 c. 2 § 20–28, I. 3 c. 3; a "foedus" and a "unio" never

constitute a State, even though there is the outward show of a State; the "divisio unius corporis in diversa membra" never makes States but only "jurisdictiones."

26. As to different opinions on Switzerland compare the view attacked as erroneous by Bodin, I. c. 7, and the remarks on Simler in Brie, p. 16 note 26.

27. Even in the middle ages mention is made of "ligae et confoederationes" among corpora or universitates; see Bartolus on l. 4 Dig. 47, 22 nr. 6–11; Baldus, Super pace Constantiae, v. "ego," nr. 1; Angelus, Cons. 269 nr. 1–2. Bodin, I. c. 7, even in the case of the closest confederations, speaks only of "societas et amicitia." On the other hand, for example, a decision of the Imperial Camera (Reichskammergericht) in Meichsner, Decis., I. dec. 46 p. 758–803, treats even the Schmalkaldic League as a "universitas vel corpus." See König, in Arumaeus, II. nr. 19: "confoederati corpus quidem efficiunt sed non unam Rempublicam"; likewise König, Acies, d. III. § 1–119, and Theatrum pol., I. c. 5 § 1–185. Similarly Werdenhagen, III. c. 25 § 16 (Corpus foederatorum, but not a Respublica). But Grotius in particular sets up the concepts of the "systema civitatum foederatorum" and the 'personal union,' and treats of them in another passage (De jure belli ac pacis, I. c. 3 § 7) as of the ordinary "foedera" (II. c. 15).

28. See all the writers cited in Notes 25 and 27, especially Bodin, Althusius, König, Werdenhagen, Grotius ("neque tamen singulae desinant statum perfectae civitatis retinere"), and Huber.—See also Kirchner, d. XVII.; Arnisaeus, De rep., II. c. 4 s. 2 § 22 ff.; Otto, De jure publ., c. 11; Gryphiander, in Arumaeus, I. nr. 38; Brautlacht, VIII. c. 1–3; Besold, Diss. de praecog. philos., c. 8 § 3 (foedus not a State), and § 5 (likewise the personal union of several States), Diss. de jure territorium, c. 4 § 7, and Diss. de foederum jure (Opus politicum, ed. of 1620, II. c. 4); Cellarius, c. 13; Horn, II., c. 2 §14, c. 5 § 7.

29. The imperialistic publicists all agree that the Empire is "una Respublica." And even among the political writers until the time of Pufendorf ("Severinus"), Bodin alone suggests a doubt, which he himself at the same time rejects (above, Note 25). See also Arnisaeus, loc. cit. § 42. Even "Hippolithus a Lapide" does not contest the unitary nature of the Empire which he regards as a pure Aristocracy of Princes.

30. This idea often appears in Zasius, Cantiuncula (see Consilia s. Responsa, Cologne 1571, cons. 25), Wesembeck (see Cons. 260), Cothmann (see Resp. of 1598, in Resp. II. nr. 64, according to which every City is respublica, non privatus), Donellus, Vultejus and others, even in Gail and Mynsinger; most precisely in Connanus (see I. c. 10 nr. 7 p. 59, autonomy in the sense of a true self-legislation); and likewise in the two earliest monographs on "universitates": Losaeus, Tractatus de jure universitatum,

Venice 1601, and Bruningus, De variis universitatum speciebus earumque juribus, Marburg 1609.

31. This mode of thought already appears very distinctly in Alciatus (see on l. 27 Dig. de R. C., nr. 8, Opera I. p. 378, along with the 'collectivistic' Fiction theory, III. p. 700); likewise in Cujacius (rather an 'institutionally' fictive structure and at the same time purely under private law); Duarenus, Anton. Faber and others; compare the grounding of all the powers of universitates in public law upon express privilegium or an equivalent praescriptio or consuetudo, in Matth. Coler, Cons. 1, 33 and 42, and Georg. Everhardus, I. cons. 12.

32. Upon this basis rest many highly interesting professional opinions which in sixteenth-century Germany were rendered by several Faculties and individual Doctors of Law in support of provincial Estates disputing against their Princes; see Gutachten Mainzer Doktoren (dating perhaps from the end of the fifteenth century), in Goede, Consilia, Wittenberg 1542, cons. 30; Kölner Gutachten (beginning of sixteenth century), ib. cons. 31; Gutachten of Goede himself, ib. cons. 32; Marburger Gutachten of 1568, in Kirchovius, Consilia s. Responsa, Frankfort 1605, I. cons. 1 (also in Consilia Marpurgensia, Marburg 1605, I. cons. 7); Ingolstädter Gutachten of 1569, in Kirchovius, V. cons. 24; Frankfurter Gutachten, ib. V. cons. 25; Gutachten of Joh. Ferrarius in Consilia Marpurgensia, l. cons. 1.—Compare the derivation of the public rights of universitates (the power to make by-laws, free choice of officers, right of self-taxation, freedom from accountability to the superior, free disposal of its common property, and so on), from the idea of the juristic person's private ownership of its property, in Modestinus Pistoris, Illustr. quaest., q. 134; Thomas Maul, De homagio, reverentia, obsequio . . . inter dominos et subditos, Giessen 1614 (especially tit. 12, free choice of officers, and tit. 13, no accountability), and Tract. de collectis, tit. 3 (in Thesaurus theoretico-practicus, Mainz 1666); Matth. Berlich, Caspar Klock, Petr. Heigius and others.—Even Carpzov derives the right of a city to enact market-regulations from its ownership of the market-place in private law (Def., P. II., const. 6 def. 2), while for the rest he traces all powers of autonomy and jurisdiction back to a special grant from the State (Proc. juris, II. a. 2 nr. 178 ff.).

33. Thus see the Gutachten of Ludwig Gremp von Freudenstein (middle of sixteenth century), in Besold, Consilia Tubingensia, I. cons. 4 (with the constant refrain, 'that the cities have no independent government for themselves'); Tübinger Gutachten of 1629, ib. III. cons. 91 (ex justa causa the Princeps may interfere even in the administration of the city's property); Thomingius, Responsa, I. cons. 24; the writings of Treutler and other jurists strongly inclined to absolutism.

34. Such utterances as that of Ferrarius, that the Gilds are Communes for themselves and at the same time members of the whole Body (De rep., German ed. of 1601, c. 10 p. 141 ff.), are quite isolated.

35. Bodin treats the Family as the indestructible basis and "imago" of the State (I. c. 2 ff.), and on the other hand, though he says that the collegium, corpus (plurium collegiorum conjunctio) and universitas (or Commune) are older than the State, he speaks of them first under the head of administrative law (III. c. 7), and sees in them creatures of civil law; he derives all their powers from an indispensable State-concession (III. c. 7 nr. 331). While he warmly supports their independent powers and rights within certain limits, he is just as strongly in favor of the regulation and suppression of abuses of corporate power by the State (ib. nr. 337 ff., also I. c. 8 nr. 85 ff.). He holds that they are quite as necessary to the State as they are dangerous if wrongly managed, and that the good monarch should rely upon them, and thus should take a wise middle course between the tyrannical suppression of all associations and the grant of full corporative freedom (III. c. 7 nr. 342 ff.); under this rubric he also discusses and favors provincial and imperial Diets as existing in Spain, England, France, Germany and elsewhere (ib. nr. 346–348). See Baudrillart, p. 324 ff.

36. See De rep., XIII. c. 2–4 (attacks the abuses of corporations, discusses their reformation and dissolution, favors careful investigation before permitting their establishment anew); also ib. XXIII. c. 3–4, and Syntagma, XV. c. 32–35.

37. According to Arnisaeus every lesser political power (including the whole power of territorial Princes and of Cities) is no more than a partial "delegatio" or "concessio" from the "majestas" without impairing its substance (De jure maj., II. c. 2 and 4, also III. c. 7 § 10, Polit., c. 15); for him all "collegia, corpora et universitates" result merely from the division of the subjects "in certas classes, ut scilicet commode gubernari per jussa et imperia majestatis possint" (Polit., c. 12 i. f., p. 133); he has no proper conception of the Commune (De rep., I. c. 5 s. 9). Bornitius treats Communes and Corporations as "subdivisiones" and all their powers as a delegation from the State; see Partit., p. 40, 68 ff., 72 ("in alias partes subdividuntur, quae collegia dicuntur: auctoritate principis facta et concessa"); De maj., c. 14–39.

38. Most of them are silent. But Winkler sharply distinguishes the respublica majestatis and municipalis, V. c. 2, and treats all the powers of lesser societies as "commissa" from the majestas, ib. c. 4. Suarez expressly denies all true autonomy of communitates and other corpora mystica, and traces the whole power of making by-laws either to a State-function delegated with jurisdiction or else to the idea of a simple contract; III. c. 9

nr. 16–21, II. c. 1 nr. 8–10, IV. c. 26 nr. 4–13; compare I. c. 8 nr. 5; and for ecclesiastical corporations in particular, IV. c. 6, nr. 12–13, 19 and 21; derivation of the force of consuetudo from the "consensus principis," VII. c. 13; likewise of the taxing power, V. c. 14; in any case either a public or else a purely private power, I. c. 8.

39. See for example Keckermann, Polit., I. c. 15 p. 255–275, where under the rubric "de speciali cura subditorum collectim consideratorum" he treats first of the natural Family-circle, and then of Corporations and Communes existing "ex instituto civili" in a spirit of the strictest police control and guardianship. Likewise Schoenborner, I. c. 11–13; König, Acies, d. I. § 123–129, and Theatrum pol., I. c. 1 § 376 ff.; Gueinzius, Exerc., IX. (partes); Velstenius, IV. nr. 1–9; Matthias, Coll. pol., d. IV., and Syst. pol., p. 169–193; Martinus Schookius, De seditionibus, Groningen 1664, III. c. 8 p. 835 ff.; Myler ab Ehrenbach, Hyparchologia, Stuttgart 1678, c. 5 p. 198 ff.; Becmann, c. 10.—The position of the lesser societies is but little more favorable in Liebenthal, d. V.; Micraelius, I. c. 7–8; Berckringer, I. c. 17; Knichen, I. c. 5; Perez, p. 318 ff.; Felwinger, De collegiis et sodalitiis (Diss., p. 908–924).—They are not even mentioned by Tulden in his political work, while in his writings on civil law he follows the strictest Romanist view.

40. See for example Paurmeister, I. c. 6 nr. 1–13 (only by a concessio expressa or tacita from the majestas can there be autonomy or any other power in the smaller Circles). In the writings collected in Arumaeus, while the independence of the Provinces of the Empire is emphasized, yet the position of the provincial Cities is already much reduced; thus see Arumaeus, I. nr. 13 q. 10 and II. nr. 9; Beindorffius, III. nr. 13. More favorable to these and other corporations ("subditi collegiatim sumpti") is Brautlacht, II. c. 3 § 3 and VI. c. 2 § 15, besides IV. c. 7 § 11–21.

41. In the middle ages it is often said that a part of the Empire which has suffered neglect from the Emperor has the right to institute a separate Ruler for itself; thus the Miles in Somn. Virid., I. c. 141. A similar right is claimed for parts of the Church by Ockham, Dial. III. tr. 1, l. 2, c. 28.

42. Junius Brutus, q. II. p. 95 ff., 114, 228, q. III. p. 304 ff. and 326 ff.; see Baudrillart, p. 65. Similarly in effect, De jure Mag., q. 6 p. 25 ff.— Danaeus, III. c. 6 p. 223, requires the consent of all the Provinces for changes of the constitution; failing this "quidam censent, eam posse propriam sibi politiae formam eligere," but this needs caution.

43. In the Jurisprudence of Althusius for the first time this principle of Natural Law yields the following: the systematic dichotomy of the 'subjects' of rights into individual and collective persons, the replacement of the concept of an artificial individual feigned for purposes of private law by the

concept of a collective body organized as a unit with regard to powers and interests alike, and the development of the idea of an independent communal life with regard to the inner structure of every collective person. But even for him (as with all the later systems of Natural Law) there is no escape from the mechanical and 'collectivistic' consequences of the individualist basis of contract, which prevent the germs of a conception of organic unity from attaining full growth. See above, Part I., Ch. III. Notes 16, 27, 30, also p. 58–59.

44. Hoenonius treats of this "respublica composita" in disp. XII., between the "respublica simplex" in d. XI. and the mere "confoederatio" in d. XIII.; and elsewhere he goes so far as to assume that in the composite State the parts have a right to secede (d. IX. § 44–54).—And Casmannus, c. 66, already distinguishes between the "composita Respublica" and "civitates confoederatae."

45. Besold, Diss. praecog. philos. compl., c. 8 § 1, 3–4, and Diss. de jure territorium, c. 4 § 2–3; also Diss. de maj., s. 3 c. 9, where the Germanic Imperial Estates are denied a proprium jus majestatis and are conceded only the exercise and representation of the majestas imperii.

46. In the Discursus politici, Strasburg 1623, Diss. nr. IV.

47. See in the Juridico-politicae Dissertationes sex, Strasburg 1624, Diss. nr. II., de jure familiarum, nr. III., de jure collegiorum, nr. IV., de jure academiarum, nr. V., de jure universitatum (communities of all kinds). Besold derives the power of all these societies from the State, but asserts their usefulness and ascribes to them a considerable independence.

48. This priority as stated in the text, it seems to me, is undeniable in relation to his predecessors, and may also be maintained in relation to Hugo, whom Brie, p. 17, regards as the inventor of the concept of Federal State. —From Besold is taken (with much else) the concept of "Imperia subalterna" in Tulden, op. cit. II. c. 18.

49. Ludolph Hugo, De statu regionum Germaniae et regimine principum summae imperii reipublicae aemulo, etc., Helmstädt 1661. On this work general reference may be made to the analysis given in Brie, p. 17–20. It need only be noted that Hugo himself describes the Empire as the only sovereign State, and the territories as dependent States or else analogues of States (c. 2 § 5 and 9), but distinguishes the Sub-States more sharply from Provinces (c. 2 § 4 and 7), and says that they have a full and independent power and "suo munere tanquam proprio funguntur" (c. 3 § 35). While Besold, on the basis of the majestas realis of the people of the Empire, ascribes the majestas personalis as a single and undivided power to the Community formed by the Emperor and the imperial Estates under the "forma mixta" of the aggregate State, and construes the powers distributed

as special rights among the subaltern States as merely the privileged exercise and representation of the collective majesty, Hugo works out the idea of a true division of sovereign powers between Super-State and Sub-States (c. 2 § 8 ff. and c. 3).

50. See the remarks of Brie, p. 21, on the acceptance and elaboration of Hugo's doctrine by Vitriarius, Brüggemann and Oldenburger. Vitriarius (I. 19 § 3, and III. 15 § 1 and 6–8) describes the territorial Princedom as "dependens, aemula tamen summae majestatis"; Oldenburger (disc. 11 p. 384 and disc. 12 § 1) says: "tanquam vere una Respublica complectitur in ventro suo multas minores ac subalternas civitates summum imperium quoad regimen imitantes"; at the same time Brüggemann and Oldenburger (like Besold and all the later writers) emphasize the co-operation, entailed by the forma mixta, of the heads of the Member-States in the formation of the will of the aggregate State (Brie, loc. cit. note 21). Other followers of Hugo are: G. A. Struve (1619–1692), Synt. jur. feud., c. 1 aph. 6 p. 28–29; Ahasv. Fritsch, Add. ad Limn., I. c. 10 p. 35; Pfeffinger, I. 7 § 6 N. a, and III. 15 § 4 N. a; and more especially Kulpis, De unitate Reipublicae in S. Romano Imperio (Diss. Academ., nr. 7), see c. 2 § 13 (with constant polemic against Pufendorf).—In like manner Horn, II. c. 7 § 5, takes the Empire as "una respublica," the territorial Princedom as "analogum majestatis."

51. Leibniz, Caesar.-Fürst., c. 11, says that a composite State is possible, and that its unio differs from a mere confoederatio as a collegium differs from a societas, for the reason that, as in the corporation there arises a "nova quaedam persona civilis," so here is something of the nature of a "nova Respublica" above the Member-States; likewise Spec. demonstr. pol., prop. 57.—It may be added that Spinoza approximates the concept of a Federal State in his description of the Aristocracy with plures urbes; Tract. pol., c. 9 § 1–15.

52. In "Severinus de Monzambano," c. 6–8; Diss. de Systematibus Civitatum, and de Republica Irregulari; De jure N. et G., VII. c. 5 § 12–21; De off., II. c. 8 § 13–15.—See Brie, p. 21–24.

53. From the "foedus simplex" (on which see De jure N. et G., VIII. c. 9, and De off., II. c. 17) the "Systema foederatum" is distinguished by its permanence and by the constant control of certain powers of sovereignty by "communis consensus," for which reason there is also an organized federal Assembly and a federal Council; but the Member-States remain fully sovereign, withdrawal is free, all collective power rests on a delegation, and even decision by majority of votes or the institution of a Directorate are precluded.

54. Thus Boehmer, P. spec. I. c. 3 § 27–29; see also the reproduction of

the Pufendorfian doctrine of Systemata in Schmier, I. c. 4 nr. 67–88 ("irregulares ex defectu nexus"); Heincke, I. c. 3 § 27–31 (mere semblance of one Respublica); Heineccius, II. § 127 ff.; Daries, Jus nat., § 808–811; A. L. v. Schlözer, p. 117.

55. This was done chiefly by Huber, op. cit., I. 2 c. 2 § 20–23, and I. 3 c. 3 § 17–20. Also Rachelius, I. tit. 40 § 4 (hardly una respublica, but rather "plures inaequali foedere cohaerentes" and "rerum communione utentes").—At a later time Schlözer, p. 117 § 6 (who however says that every 'System of States' is precarious).

56. Thus among others, U. de Cramer, Obs. juris universi, Wetzlar 1758–1773, obs. 1410.

57. Thus in particular Titius, Spec. jur. publ., VII. c. 7–9 (the Empire is a "civitas composita" with departures from the regular "corporum sociorum systema"); likewise in the Diss. de habitu territoriorum Germanicorum et inde veniente totius Reipublicae forma, Leipzig 1705. Compare Gundling, Jus nat., c. 37 § 37–47 (between the unitary State and the Confederation there is the "respublica composita irregularis," such as the Empire).— Thomasius, though fully adhering to Pufendorf, calls the Systemata civitatum "compositae respublicae" (Inst. jur. div., III. c. 6 § 57–58), and even declares that the Confederation is a "societas perfectior" above the State, while the latter is treated in all respects as insufficient for itself and thus is denied to be perfect (ib. c. 1 § 35–37).

58. Hert, Elem., I. s. 12 § 3–9: the State must be distinguished from Provinces (see II. s. 16), Personal Unions (II. s. 17), Systemata sive civitates Achaicae (II. s. 18), and intermediate forms between State and Confederation, such as the Germanic Empire (II. s. 19); see Opuscula, II. 2 p. 55–284, especially p. 132 (the German Territories are "respublicae speciales" within one "major respublica"). See Brie, p. 21 notes 19 and 22, and p. 24 note 37.

59. Thus already by Pütter in his Elementa juris publici Germanici, 1754, § 121–122; Ickstatt in his Opuscula, Vol. II., Op. I. c. 2 § 2 (forma mixta, in which some sovereign powers are shared "conjunctim" between Emperor and Estates, others among the latter), also Op. V. § 22–30); Kreittmayr, Grundriss, I. § 4 and 86–100 (the Princes are not "absolute" but "respective" sovereign), also Anmerkungen, I. c. 2 § 6 nr. 3.

60. See Nettelbladt, Syst. elem. univ. jurispr. nat., § 1160 and 1172 ff.; here as elsewhere I cite from the fifth edition, 1785, but I have ascertained that the first edition, of which the relevant Third Part appeared in 1762, agrees in the essential points (see especially P. III. § 35–39), and the third edition, 1767, agrees almost entirely (see especially § 1309–1316). Nettelbladt defines the "Respublica composita" as "Respublicae diversae

quae simul sumtae constituunt unam Rempublicam, cujus potestati civili subjectae sunt." He distinguishes it sharply: (1) from the "Systema rerumpublicarum," in which there is a mere foederatio into a "societas quae respublica non est"; (2) from 'Unions,' in which there is "idem subjectum potestatis plurium rerumpublicarum," and which he further divides into the 'Personal Union,' the 'Real Union,' and (a form which he is the first to define precisely) the 'Chief State' ruling over 'dependent States'; (3) from the 'Incorporation,' in which the component Community ceases to be a State and is only the autonomous member of a unitary State; see § 1160, 1172–1173. The Composite State is produced either by integration or by disintegration (§ 1183). The aggregate State, as well as the respublicae minores themselves, may be monarchical or republican and they may differ from one another in organization (§ 1175). There is a "duplex potestas civilis," the "summa" and the "subordinata"; the latter, either exclusive of the former while dependent on it, or else with its concurrence, is exercised in the "regimine rerumpublicarum minorum" (§ 1176); to this there corresponds a "duplex subjectio" (§ 1177). Peculiar to the Federal State is the distinction between membra immediata and mediata (§ 1222–1223); among the "membra rerumpublicarum minorum" the "Superiores" are superior only downwards and are subditi upwards; in relation to them all inferiors are "in duplici subjectione," whereby in doubtful cases of collision the lesser Superior takes precedence for them (§ 1224–1225). Lastly, in the Law of Nations the Member-States are not sovereign, although as true "gentes" they are proper 'subjects' of international rights (§ 1408–1409); while in the systema the particular States are externally sovereign but the "societas major," although not a "gens," yet being a "libera societas," is a 'subject' of international rights (§ 1406–1407). In all this it should be observed that Nettelbladt expressly strikes out sovereignty as an essential mark of the State (§ 1159–1160). Compare Achenwall, II. § 189–190. This corrects the statements of Brie, p. 29.—For the modifications of the doctrine of Systems (as in Wieland and Meerman) see Brie, p. 30.—The somewhat unjuristic remarks of Montesquieu on the "République fédérative" (IX. x. 1–3 and X. c. 6) at any rate leave no doubt that the true Federal State is possible, which for him also accords with the weakening of the idea of Sovereignty.

61. Pütter, Beyträge zum Teutschen Staats- und Fürstenrecht, nr. II. (along with nr. III., XI., XVII., XVIII. and XIX.). See the analysis of his doctrine in Brie, p. 25–28.

62. See Brie, p. 28–29.

63. This movement of thought, unfinished even today, is well and fully explained by Brie, p. 32 ff.—Parallel with the development of the concept

of the Federal State goes the development of the concept of the 'real union' as distinct from the 'personal union,' which alone was studied at first. On this see Franz v. Juraschek, Personal- und Realunion, Berlin 1878, of which the only criticism is that the advancement which he points out in Heineccius over the suggestions of Hert (p. 13) occurs already in Titius, Note on Pufend. De off., II. c. 8 § 14, and Treuer, eod. loc.; in this as well as in the theory of the Federal State, Nettelbladt, § 1172 (above, Note 60) deserves notice.

64. See Hoenonius, above, Note 44, and d. II. § 52–57; Kirchner, d. XIV.; Werdenhagen, II. c. 13–20 (the same grades of association as in Althusius).—It should be noted that Busius, I. c. 13, defines "collegia et corpora" as "universitates plurium civium qui in certum aliquem finem contrahunt societatem ad similitudinem Civitatis," while yet on the one hand he makes them dependent on the State's permission, to be granted only with great caution, and subjects them to the strictest control (no right of assemblage and no discussion of public affairs), and on the other hand he places them under the Roman law of "societas" (modified only in a few points, such as non-dissolution by death and "major pars"), and hence also their "statuta" are mere "conventiones privatae." A contradiction which occurs in like manner in some of the political writers mentioned above, Note 39, and is constantly repeated in the writings of the jurists.

65. See above, Ch. II. Note 69 and Ch. III. Note 147.

66. Grotius, II. c. 6 § 4: for the jus partium is "ex primaeva voluntate metiendum," but the parts willed to become partes integrantes and surely not to give the whole body the right "abscindere a se et alii in ditionem dare"; § 8: in this even publica utilitas or necessitas makes no difference, despite the jurists; it merely becomes easier to infer consent from silence. Likewise III. c. 20 § 5 for the case of a treaty of peace.

67. Grotius, II. c. 6 § 5–6.—Likewise Schmier, II. c. 2 s. 2 § 3, nr. 114–121, with the difference that for him corpus partem abscindere potest.

68. Hobbes, Lev., c. 22; compare De cive, c. 5 § 10, c. 13 § 12–13; also on the equally full absorption of the Church, Lev., c. 39, De cive, c. 17.

69. As for example Horn, I. c. 4, II. c. 2 § 14 (every assemblage not approved by the sovereign is a 'lese-majesty'), II. c. 3 § 7, c. 5 § 3 (absolute absorption of the Church).—Likewise Conring, who, like all pure Aristotelians, has no room in Natural Law for intermediate societies between the societates domesticae and the State (see Diss. de republica, 1653, Op. III. p. 763 ff., and De necessariis civitatis partibus, 1679, ib. p. 748 ff.).

70. Spinoza follows Hobbes throughout, as is shown in the construction of the inferior societies in his Monarchy (Tract. pol., c. 6–7) and of the

gilds in his Aristocracy (ib. c. 8 § 5); likewise as to the Church (ib. c. 3 § 10, Tract. theol.-pol., c. 19).

71. Huber, De jure civ., II. 3 c. 1–6, and Praelectiones on Dig. 3, 4.

72. De jure civ., II. 3 c. 6 § 1–10, Prael., loc. cit. nr. 4; only the most necessary "regimen" is conceded; and always "potestas rectorum universitatis pendet a tenore mandati, quod habent a summa potestate, a qua jus suum habet universitas"; also the application of Territorialism to the Church with a recognition of the independent personality of parishes in private law (De jure civ., I. 4 c. 1–8, I. 5 c. 1–6, II. 3 c. 4, II. 4 c. 3 § 21–55).

73. See De jure N. et G., VII. c. 2 § 21–23: "quicquid juris habeant et quicquid potestatis in sua membra, id omne a summa potestate definiri et nequaquam huic posse opponi et praevalere"; "alias enim . . . daretur civitas in civitate"; when corporate bodies coalesce into a State they must give up their previous public rights; if the State grants or allows an independent public right to communes or corporate bodies it abandons its sovereignty and becomes "irregularis et biceps." Hence even in Pufendorf communes and corporate bodies do not appear in the 'Nature-Right' gradation of societies, in which the State comes immediately after the societates domesticae (ib., lib. VI., and De off., II. c. 2–4). Nevertheless he likens the lesser societies to membra of a corpus which are themselves corpora (De jure N. et G., VI. c. 1 § 1).

74. Thomasius, Inst. jur. div., I. c. 1 § 91 ff., especially § 95, III. c. 1 § 4 ff., especially § 15–32; and for his religious territorialism the writings cited above, Ch. I. Note 3, and Diss. nr. 76. III. p 123 ff.

75. Hert, Elem., I. s. 5 § 2 ff., II. s. 2 § 41, Opusc., II. 3 p. 51–57; according to him an "ens morale," which the "conventio hominum efficit," is formed not only by the State and the Corporation but also by husband and wife, "correi," and joint tenants.

76. See especially Opusc., I. 1 p. 288 § 3, and II. 3 p. 55.

77. Thus Gundling, Exerc. XVI. (1724), p. 829 ff. § 14 ff., and Jus nat., c. 36 § 78 ff.; Schmier, V. c. 1 nr. 87 ff. (see nr. 92: "quia regimen, imperium seu jurisdictio ad universitatis constitutionem necessaria nequit ex alio fonte quam summae potestatis largitate in inferiores derivari"), c. 2–3, III. c. 3 nr. 20 (the right of association holds good in the Law of Nature but not in the State).

78. In this connection see the accurate remarks of G. Schmoller, Zeitschr. f. preuss. Gesch., XI. (1874), p. 514 ff., on the theoretical defenders of the freedom of cities against the beginnings of a reform of city-administration by the absolute princes.

79. This is shown, for example, in the fact that as a rule the champions

of the independence of cities apply the doctrine of Corporations in its most sharply restrictive sense to collegia and gilds; see Sibrand, Urbis Lubecae jura publica, 1619; Knipschildt, op. cit.; Zahn, Ichnographia municipalis, Frankfort 1657; Mevius, Comm. ad jus Lub., in Decisiones et Consilia, and see Prodromus, V. § 19 (where he describes the lesser societies as the "fundamentum civilis societatis," but just for this reason requires them to conform to the State's purpose as State-institutions, and hence in § 26 he altogether denies the right of assemblage and of association and in § 34 he teaches pure Territorialism for the Church). The defenders of the rights of the provincial Estates stand upon the same ground of simple protection for the established "jura quaesita" of certain corporations. Even in the eighteenth century it is but here and there that Riccius, Struben, Cramer, J. J. Möser and others rise to other standpoints in defending the freedom of Cities and Estates against the territorial Princes.—The collegia are treated, even in the works professedly devoted to them, in a manner hostile to their autonomy and self-government, and almost always are given protection, at most, in a special private-law aspect, being conceived for the rest as institutions of the police power; see the works of Fritsch, Strauch, Beyer, F. G. Struve and others cited in my Genossenschaftsrecht, I. § 67 Note 1. —The rural communes are surrendered by the jurists themselves to the absolute control of the Princes, and by the more conservative school even the private-law ownership of their common property is saved to them with difficulty and with the largest concessions made to the State's guardianship. —It may be added that in the Church the territorial system gains exclusive sway.—Lastly and above all, even those jurists who are most favorable to the existing corporations flatly reject any right of free association.

80. This newer tendency is partly expressed already in Carpzov, G. A. Struve, Lauterbach (especially in the work De syndicis), and others, but bursts into full bloom in Brunnemann, Schilter, Conring, and above all in the Halle school, whose leader in this direction is Stryk (especially Usus modernus, 50, 8, and Diss. IV. nr. 18 and VII. nr. 22). Very influential also was the treatment of the rights of communes and corporate bodies, inspired by Pufendorf, in Titius, Juris privati Romani-Germanici libri XII, Leipzig 1724 (1st ed. 1709), VIII. c. 2–5 (on Churches, ib. IX. c. 17, and Jus publ., III. c. 6); he was followed by Kreittmayr, Grundriss § 19, and Anmerkungen.—On the struggle against the independence of cities see Schmoller, loc. cit. p. 516 ff.; and for details the theoretical treatment, as explained in my Genossenschaftsr., Vol. I., of rural communes (§ 55), provincial Cities (§ 56), bodies of Estates (§ 60), free associations (§ 64), gilds and collegia (§ 67); see also the characteristic attack on 'Cobbler-States' ("respublicae sutoriae") in G. C. Gebauer (1690–1773), Opus-

cula, nr. 27 p. 695–700, where everything comes to the argument: "omnia sane, quae ad statum civitatis pertinent, in manu Principis sunt."

81. Turgot, in the article "Fondation" (1757) in the Encyclopédie, VII. p. 75 § 6: "Les citoyens ont des droits et des droits sacrés pour le corps même de la société, ils existent indépendemmemt d'elle"; for they are its essential elements and enter it only in order to place themselves under the protection of society by sacrificing their inborn freedom; "mais les corps particuliers n'existent point par eux-mêmes ni pour eux; ils ont été formés pour la société et ils doivent cesser d'être au moment qu'ils cessent d'être utiles."

82. Rousseau, II. c. 3; if owing to the size of the State lesser associations are unavoidable, they should be made as small and as equal as possible.

83. On the views expressed in the famous debates of the National Assembly, from the 10th of October to the 2nd of November 1789, as to the nature of corporations, see Hübler, Der Eigenthümer des Kirchenguts (Leipzig 1868), p. 46 ff. and 56 ff.; Janet, in Revue des deux Mondes, Vol. 23 (1877), p. 334–349.—Sieyès, in his pamphlet "Qu'est-ce que le Tiers État," follows Rousseau closely (I. p. 167–172); in his polemic against the confiscation of church property he does not give up the principle that the existence of every "corps moral" depends on the national will, but contends for the sacredness of the private property of all persons, including 'moral persons' so long as they exist (I. p. 459 ff. and 485 ff.); in his numerous plans of municipal organization, which exposed him to the reproach of seeking to resolve France into a federation, he always follows the stereotyped pattern of bodies organized from above on a numerical basis (I. p. 208, 292 ff., 380 ff., 509 ff., II. p. 225 ff.).

84. Nowhere perhaps are these found more fully developed than in Justus Claproth (1725–1805), Ohnmassgeblicher Entwurf eines Gesetzbuchs, Frankfort-on-the-Main 1773–1776; the sections on communes and corporations read indeed almost like a satire (I. p. 556 ff.). And as an example of how far, on the ground of public welfare, the State's control over communes could be stretched, see the arguments in Georg Ludwig Boehmer, Electa juris civilis, Göttingen 1787, I. exerc. 15 p. 567–641. The same spirit prevails in v. Selchow, v. Berg, v. Gönner and others.—Hume himself recognizes only mechanical divisions in his "Idea of a Perfect Commonwealth."

85. See the passages in which Fichte in the year 1793 declares that the Church has no rights, and allows its property to be appropriated by anyone Werke, VI. p. 244–286). And yet he says that any group of persons has the right to form a 'State within the State' (ib. p. 148 ff.). When he defends gilds and corporations he construes them, as afterwards churches

and schools, as State-institutions (Werke, II. p. 555, III. p. 233, IV. p. 403 ff.).

86. Kant, Rechtslehre, Anm. B, VII. p. 142 ff., Anm. C, ib. p. 144 ff., Appendix to 2nd edition, ib. p. 120–123; Corporation, perpetual Foundation, charitable Institution for future generations, and so on, are for him identical concepts, of which the Nobility and the Church are examples; he declares that they may at any time be dissolved, altered or dispossessed; all corporative property (and even the State's own property) is repudiated; nowhere is anything said of juristic persons or societies within the State; only the Individual and the abstract Rational State exist; in short, at this point Rousseau's thought is followed out completely.

87. See above, p. 104. To some extent Pufendorf, Becmann, Thomasius, Hert, and partly in a still higher degree Rachelius and Mullerus are also to be named among the promoters of this tendency, while in Leibniz the notion of the organismic structure of Mankind appears in a form more reminiscent of the middle ages (in Guhrauer, I. p. 414–420).

88. With greater emphasis than any one before him he gives first place to the general philosophical theory of "societates"; P. spec. I. c. 2. Then as to the "universitas" he argues precisely that it is nothing but "omnes conjunctim sumpti" with a fictitious single personality (ib. II. c. 4 § 1); that in itself it is a mere "societas aequalis" with rights of its own in private law but without coercive power (ib. § 2 ff.); that when the State vests it with power it takes the nature of a State-institution as a "collegium publicum" (ib. § 9–10); but that even the "collegia privata" are subject to the State's concession and supervision (ib. § 11–12, and c. 3 § 5 N. c). More fully than any of his predecessors he develops the notion of the State's control over corporations and follows it out in detail with regard to their formation, admission of members, constitution and management, remarking by the way that corporations are more dangerous to the State than the separate individuals (ib. c. 4 § 5–13). He denies the rights of autonomy (II. c. 3 § 23 ff.), self-taxation (II. c. 9) and jurisdiction (II. c. 7–8) of the lesser communities. He makes the officers of collegia publica direct officers of the State (II. c. 6); even elected "consules" act only "ex concessione imperantis" and in his name; indeed a free and 'privative' right of election can never be conceded to communes without destroying the majestas (ib. § 6); the obligation of rendering account to the sovereign is not annulled by any privilege or custom (ib. § 7–8). Nevertheless in principle he recognizes strict legal limits to the State's power over corporations; see especially his Consult. et Decis., III. 1 dec. 177.—On these general principles he builds his whole system of church law, with a Collegialist basis and a Territorialist structure; see Jus. publ. univ., P. spec. II. c. 5,

and Jus eccl. Protest., especially Vol. I., diss. prael. § 1 ff., II. 27 § 19, III. 36 § 6–7, V. 37 esp. § 17 ff.

89. See Wolff, Inst., § 836–853 and 1129; yet for him the Communes and Fellowships remain out of the series of entities of Natural Law.—In like manner, but following J. H. Boehmer more closely in part, Heineccius, Elem. jur. nat., II. § 11 ff. and 183 ff. (also Elem. jur. civ. sec. ord. Pand., § 439, and Diss. de coll. et corp. opif., in Opera, II. p. 367 ff.); Scheidemantel, on 'Societies in the State,' I. p. 253–255 and III. p. 244 250 (also II. p. 5–59 on the Church).

90. See especially the "Jurisprudentia naturalis generalis socialis" in Syst. Nat. § 326–414, and the "Jurisprudentia positiva generalis socialis" in Syst. pos. § 846–912 (in which the generic similarity of all societies, including the State, is elaborated, all the internal and external powers of corporate bodies are derived from the social contract, the "persona moralis" is identified simply with the "socii simul sumti," among the "jura originaria" of every societas is included the potestas over its own membra, and the true and original sphere of action of a society is distinguished from the spheres of action 'transferred' to its heads by the State). Also Syst. nat., § 1226–1250, on the position of "personae morales" as "membra Reipublicae," in which it may be specially noted that, so far as they "sibi ipsis originem debent," a confirmation by the sovereign is said to be "utilis non necessaria" (§ 1241–1242, but otherwise in § 1238–1240 in the case of Communes, which are constituted by the sovereign), and that the starting-point is always the true and original "jura collegialia," over which the State's control operates only by virtue of the "jura majestatica." Lastly the corresponding elaboration of the Collegial system for the Church, ib. § 867–964 (in itself) and § 1536–1570 (in the State), together with the dissertation written under the guidance of Nettelbladt by G. S. Madihn, De imperii sacri natura, Halle 1751.

91. See for example Achenwall, Proleg. § 91 ff. and II. § 1–40 (general theory of society with a construction of the corporate body as a society internally and a mere collective sum externally, but with a full extension of the natural rights of individuals to collective bodies taken as 'moral persons,' and with a distinction between the "jura societatis absoluta" and "acquisita"); also II. § 132–140 (Collegialism in the Church). See further Daries, § 517–561 (quite similar "jus sociale in genere"), § 674–678 (the majestas comprises only the powers of control over corporations, but to this belongs the confirmation of every "societas partialis"), § 487 ff. (Collegialism in the Church).

92. Esprit des Lois, II. c. 4; also III. c. 7, V. c. 10–11, 14–16, and VIII. c. 6.

93. See in the Patriotische Phantasien the proposals for the widest variety of free associations, I. nr. 43, 50, 52, 64, III. nr. 54, and also III. nr. 20 p. 71: 'We see daily what great things can be done by Corporations, Partnerships, Brotherhoods and such-like associations': also the general ideas, II. nr. 2, III. nr. 20, 54, 66, IV. nr. 41; then on cities, I. nr. 45, 53–54, on rural communes, II. nr. 1, III. nr. 41, 43, 52–54, 66, IV. nr. 63–64, on corporations and gilds, I. nr. 2, 4, 7, 32, 48, 49, II. nr. 32–35.

94. A. L. v. Schlözer, Allg. Staatsl., p. 70 § 19.

95. Ideen, p. 41 ff., 83, 113 ff., 115, 130.

96. This is not the place to describe this process of development; in fact the 'nature-rightly' replacement of the institutional Corporation by the contractual Partnership with a collective unity of persons (as for example in Runde, Woltaer and even Glück) prevailed until Savigny achieved his restoration of the older Roman-Canonist doctrine.

97. On the use which was made of Nettelbladt's theory of society in the Prussian Landrecht [of 1794] see Dernburg, Lehrb. des preuss. Privatr., I. (2nd ed. 1879), § 52 N. 4.

98. See above, Ch. III., and in the present chapter Notes 88–91 and 96.

99. Ideen, p. 121, 123 ff., 125. (Hence also free dissolution of marriage.)

100. P. 129–130 (but members should not be confused with functionaries, such as the clergy in the church).

101. P. 132.

CHAPTER SIX

THE IDEA OF THE LEGAL STATE

THUS far in all our incursions into various regions of thought we have had to touch upon the course of ideas as to the relation of the State to Law, and have learned to recognize in Althusius one of the warmest advocates of the idea of the Legal State. We shall now proceed to trace the growth of ideas on the relation of the State to Law in consecutive order from the middle ages to the culmination of the 'Nature-Right' theories of the State.

I. In the Middle Ages

When the middle ages began to theorize on this question the old Germanic idea of a 'Right-State' had already shown itself inadequate. It was the idea of a State which existed only in the Law and for the Law, and whose whole life was bound up in a legal order governing alike all public and all private relations. After the model of the Church, in which from the beginning there had arisen a power whose origin and purpose lay outside and beyond the scheme of mere law and which was independent of that scheme, the State-power, as soon as it became conscious of itself, began to strive for a similar emancipation from the fetters of law. Jurisprudence and philosophy, as soon as they felt the first rustle of the breath of antiquity, began to vie with each other in seeking a theoretical statement and elaboration for an idea of the State which should be independent of the idea of Law.

From the beginning indeed the political scholars of the middle ages were almost all agreed that the State rests on no basis of mere law, but on moral or natural necessity,[1] and is itself the creator of law; that its end is the promotion of material and spiritual welfare; that the realization of Law is but one of the proper means to this end; [2] and that the State's relation to the legal order is not dependent and subservient, but on the contrary independent and dominant. [3]

But despite these acquisitions from antiquity—for such in essence they were—medieval doctrine never gave up the thought that Law is by its origin of equal rank with the State and does not depend on the State. The medieval theorist felt himself absolutely bound to base the State upon Law and thus to construe its origin as a legal process, while the notion that an illegitimately established government could also have legal efficacy was quite unthinkable. [4] Moreover this doctrine was pervaded by the belief that the State is charged with the mission of realizing the idea of Law, an idea which it did not create and which it could not alter, and that for the State the Law is not a mere means but an end in itself. And lastly it was never doubted that the State-power is bound by truly legal limitations, beyond which its governing power and the subjects' duty of obedience cease.

But how was it possible to think that on the one hand the Law should exist by, for and under the State, and that on the other hand the State should exist by, for and under the Law? The middle age did not arrive at the thought that State and Law exist by, for and under each other. It solved the antithesis by means of the distinction between Positive Law and Natural Law, a distinction which came down to it from antiquity but was evolved in various forms and elaborated in detail in countless controversies.

1. Positive law (ius civile) was declared to be (including customary law construed as "statutum tacitum") the freely created product of the power of a human community, an instrument changeable according to estimates of utility, a set of rules without independent force. Here lay the revolutionary change in the world of archaic German ideas.

a. Positive law in the objective aspect was now wholly subjected to the sovereign will; men asserted the principle that the lawgiver is not bound by his own law, and more and more they came to regard the exemption from all statute law as the decisive criterion of sovereignty.

The advocates of 'Ruler's sovereignty' identified positive law with the expressly or tacitly declared will of the ruler. They set the ruler before and above the statutes made by himself or his predecessors. They taught that he for his part is not bound by a statute but can in each single case apply or break it as need might be. Even from the twelfth century onward jurisprudence laid stress on those Roman texts that made for this result, particularly the maxims "omnia iura habet Princeps in pectore suo," "quod Principi placuit legis habet vigorem," and "error Principis facit ius," but above all a sentence destined to be for centuries a focus of controversial literature, namely: "Princeps legibus solutus est." Political philosophy assented. It found the difference between the true Monarch and the magistrate of a Republic in just this, that while the latter is bound by the laws made by the people, or by him and the people, the former goes about as a "lex animata" and in each single case can modify the existing law by a sentence fitted to the needs of the moment.[5] Nor were there wanting men who from this "potestas legibus soluta" drew consequences of which the Pope in the Church and the Emperor (or a little later every Sovereign) in the State would reap the benefit.[6]

Against this doctrine the advocates of 'People's sovereignty' arrayed themselves with all available weapons. Since they held that the binding force of every statute has its source in the consent of the subject community, they would have it that every ruler is bound by the laws, even the Pope and the Emperor.[7] A separation of the legislative from the executive power began to be suggested at this point, and it afterwards became of the highest importance in the development of the idea of the Legal State.[8] However, what was at issue in the first instance was merely the 'subject' of sovereignty, not the relation between the sovereign power and the law, for the one party claimed for the sovereign assembly (in Church or State as the case might be) exactly the same superiority to all law which the other party ascribed to the ruler.[9]

b. A subjective or private right based upon a rule of Positive Law was explained as being, like the rule itself, the result of a concession made by the State, and was thus subject to the free disposal of the sovereign. It was not admitted that a vested right, if acquired by a title derived from positive law, could in principle hold good as against the power of the State.

Already, as is well known, the jurist Martinus [middle of twelfth century] went so far as to ascribe to the Emperor a true ownership of all things, and therefore an absolute power of disposal over the rights of private persons. He relied chiefly on the words in the Code (l. 3, Cod. de quadr. praersr. 7, 37): "quum omnia Principis esse intelligantur." With reference to the Church the same doctrine was asserted in behalf of the Pope.[10] For all this, however, a contrary opinion, already held at the same time by Bulgarus, was steadily gaining ground. It taught that above private ownership there stands only a 'superiority' on the part of the State, which was sometimes expressly called a mere "iurisdictio vel protectio," and even when it was described as a "dominium" it was still treated as a matter of public law.[11] However, it was just from this Superiority that men evolved the theory—a theory strange to the archaic German legal mind—of a right of expropriation, by virtue of which the State, whenever its own purpose demanded this, could alter or abrogate private rights.[12]

Thus the history of the theory of expropriation consisted mainly in the process of setting strict limits to an expropriatory right. This kindled many controversies. But as a matter of principle the dispute turned not so much on the nature as on the effects of these limitations (see below, p. 305 ff.). It was generally agreed that the supreme power may interfere with acquired or vested rights "ex iusta causa," but not arbitrarily. For some this principle was an absolutely binding rule of law,[13] and even those who would allow the sovereign, either in all cases or at least in some cases, to override it, still held it to be a good rule.[14] As a sufficient cause, besides forfeiture for crime and various other grounds, men added public necessity, to which private right must yield in case of collision. Yet ever greater stress was laid on the principle that when a right is taken away on grounds of public welfare compensation should be paid from the public funds;[15] but to this rule exceptions were often admitted, sometimes for the case of general statutes affecting all individuals alike,[16] and sometimes for cases of necessity.[17]

However, it is highly characteristic of medieval doctrine that the ground of positive law did not seem to it capable of supporting such a protection of acquired rights. On the contrary, the inviolability of a subjective right was to be strictly maintained only if, and in so far as, this right could be based on some ground of Natural Law independent of positive law. In this context two principles became the groundwork of the whole doctrine. First, that the institution of private property is rooted in the "ius gentium," a Law which was when as yet the State was not, and which flowed from the pure Law of Nature without the aid of the State. And hence the particular rights which were acquired by virtue of this institution owe their existence by no means to the State alone.[18] Secondly, that the binding force of contracts comes from the Law of Nature, so that the sovereign, though he cannot bind himself or his successors by statute, can bind himself and his successors to his subjects by contract. Hence it followed that every right which the State has granted by way of contract is inviolable by the State (though here again with the exception of interferences "ex iusta causa").[19] But if a subjective right could vouch for its existence neither of such titles of Natural Law, then doctrinal consistency must deny such protection to this "ius mere positivum."[20] This struck in particular at those rights which were placed under the rubric of 'privileges' unilaterally conceded by the State and sanctioned only by positive law. On this basis an ever growing opinion deemed that such rights are freely revocable at any time for the sake of the public welfare.[21]

2. Natural Law, in contrast to Positive Law, was in the unanimous view of the middle ages prior to, beyond and above the State.

a. Natural Law in the objective aspect, whatever disputes there might otherwise be as to its source and the ground of its obligation, was always conceived on the one hand as an emanation from a principle transcending the State and on the other hand as true and perfectly binding Law. Hence men supposed that before the State existed the "lex naturalis" already prevailed, and that directly or indirectly from this flowed those rules of law to which the State itself owed the possibility of a rightful establishment of its existence. And men also taught that the rules of Natural Law are paramount even to the highest power on earth. They stand above the Pope and above the Emperor, above the Ruler and above the sovereign People, even above the whole Community of Mortals. Neither a statute nor an act of government, neither a resolution of the people nor a custom can break the bounds thus set. Anything contrary to the eternal and indestructible principles of Natural Law is utterly void and binds no one.[22]

This force was ascribed not merely to the "ius naturale" in the strict sense of the term, but also to the revealed "ius divinum" and to the "ius commune gentium" which were placed on a level with it. For the revealed Law of God stood to the Law of Nature (properly so called) in this relation, that while the latter was implanted by God in natural reason for mundane ends, the former was communicated by God to man in a supernatural way and for a supermundane end.[23] Then the "ius gentium" (meaning such law as all nations agree in recognizing) was regarded as the system of those rules which flowed from the pure Law of Nature when account was taken of the relations arising from the corruption of human nature by original sin. As the constituted powers had not created this 'law of the nations' but had merely received it, it was held to partake of the sanctity and immutability of Natural Law.[24]

The deeper the inroads that were made into the domain of ecclesiastical and secular law-making by this idea of a Law of Nature which even legislators must not infringe, the more urgent was the need for a definite principle of limitations on the law-making power. For in all the disputes as to the extent and nature of these limitations, men agreed that Positive Law, while it can never destroy the rules of Natural Law, yet can and must modify, develop, amplify and restrict these rules with regard to special cases. In this sense a distinction was often drawn between the eternal and immutable first principles and the mutable (or even merely hypothetical) secondary precepts. This distinction was applied to the true ius naturale,[25] as well as to the ius divinum [26] and the ius gentium.[27]

b. That which held true of the norms of Natural Law must equally hold true of the subjective rights derived from them. We have seen how the relative protection afforded to acquired rights, as against the State, was deduced from and measured by the foundation in Natural Law of the concrete 'title' by which such a right had been acquired. But medieval doctrine itself was even more imbued with the thought that all those rights and duties which followed directly from Natural Law as original attributes [such as the 'right to life'] have a validity which is absolute as against positive law, and which is neither conditioned by any title nor to be set aside by an adverse title. And already in the middle ages the results of this were on the one hand the original and essential rights of superiority of the sovereign community or its legal successor,[28] and on the other hand the inborn and indestructible rights of the individual.[29]

3. Thus the supreme power, despite its exaltation above positive law, was held within legal bounds, and in the universal opinion, when it transgressed these bounds it committed an 'unright' and became a 'tyranny.' But as to the effects of such a transgression medieval doctrine was divided.

The original and never wholly discarded theory held that any act of the sovereign which broke the bounds of Natural Law is formally null and void. Hence every judge and every other magistrate who had to apply the law was to treat as null and void, not only every unrightful administrative act but every unrightful statute, even though it were issued by Pope or Emperor.[30] And the unrightful act or decree was null and void for the individual subjects as well. From this arose the doctrine that all obligation of obedience is conditioned by the rightfulness of the command.[31] And if there were an attempt to enforce the unrightful measure by compulsion, this was regarded as an act of force against which resistance by force, even by force of arms, was justified. And sometimes it even affirmed (though writers zealous for the law would always deny this) that tyrannicide should be commended or at least excused.[32]

This truly medieval mode of thought was in full accord with the practice of public law in the feudal system of 'Estates,' [33] but with the sharper definition of the concept of Sovereignty it encountered the idea that in the legal sphere the sovereign is formally omnipotent. Then the prevalent doctrine found itself once more compelled to hold that in a monarchy both the legislative and the executive acts of the monarch are vested with this formal omnipotence, while here the doctrine of popular sovereignty made a fruitful use of its principle of the division of powers, in that it granted such omnipotence only to legislation. From this standpoint all limitations of power began to seem no more than the claims of righteousness upon the sovereign will. If the sovereign will consciously and unequivocally rejected these claims it made a law which was none the less formally binding, externally binding on the courts as well as on individual men.[34] This view could not be consistent with any right of active resistance to the enforcement of acts of the sovereign, even when these were in themselves unrightful; in extreme cases disobedience was allowed, but only in the form of passive resistance.[35]

Nevertheless there still was life in the notion that the obligation of the sovereign will which is deduced from the premises of Natural Law is a legal obligation. Even though it were vain to look for a sharp demarcation between Natural Law and Morals in the middle ages, yet there was the idea of a distinction between the purely ethical precepts which were regarded as self-evidently binding even on the supreme power, and the truly legal limitations which were drawn for this power; and this distinction was clearly expressed in common parlance. No one doubted that those maxims, according to which every earthly power was subject to Natural and Divine Law and was bound to protect acquired rights to a certain extent, were actual rules of Law even where they were not to be enforced by compulsion or legal process. No one doubted that there is a Law prior to, beyond and above the State. No one doubted that formal law may be material 'unlaw' and that formal 'unlaw' may be material law.[36] No one doubted that the formally unconditioned duty of obedience incumbent on subjects is materially limited by the higher precepts of Divine and Natural Law. No one doubted that the Biblical text, 'We should obey God rather than men' [Acts v. 29], contains a valid rule of Law for all times and all places; that the humblest of subjects would do right if he refused obedience to a command of the sovereign which was against God's Will and his own conscience, and steadfastly bore the consequences, and that he would do wrong if he did otherwise.[37] And this distinction between formal and material law, a distinction inherent in the very idea of a Law of Nature, was very far from being a mere abstract theory. On the contrary, to say nothing of its indirect effects on legislation, it produced a direct practical effect of the greatest magnitude. All magistrates charged with the application of law were thought to have the power and duty to bring the acts of the sovereign into the fullest possible accord with material law or substantial justice, by means of the power of 'interpretation,' which was then given an exceedingly wide scope.[38]

During the middle ages there is hardly a trace of the view which, for the sake of a higher end, would free the sovereign (when acting for the public safety) from the bonds of Natural Law and of the Moral Law in general.[39] Thus it was that when Machiavelli based his instruction for Princes on the freedom from restraint, it seemed to the men of his day an unheard-of innovation, a monstrous crime. But the opposition as well as the open or secret assent, which the ideas of the bold Florentine met with, inspired a many-sided movement of thought which made a great impression on theories as to the relation of the State to Law.

II. After the Sixteenth Century

The development of these opinions after the sixteenth century proceeded on the foundation laid in the middle ages. In particular, the distinction of Positive and Natural Law remained the unshaken basis. Yet in many respects there appeared a tendency for these accepted divisions of Law to reunite and permeate each other. But this was just what made it possible that in all particular points there was an ever sharper opposition between two movements, one of which strove for the Legal and Constitutional State and the other for free State-absolutism.

1. So far as Positive Law was concerned, men adhered fully to the view that it is derived from the power of a human society and remains subject to it. But there arose nevertheless an important divergence of views.

a. In the objective aspect the absorption of Positive Law by the State made steady progress in theory as in fact. Ever more decidedly men reduced all Positive Law to the concept of a statute, to which customary law must adjust itself as a tacit statute. At the same time all statutes were ever more distinctly reduced to the concept of an ordinance enacted by the sovereign, so that the binding force of statutes, so far as they were not conceived as mere contracts, was derived from the law-maker's delegation or confirmation, and the binding force of custom, so far as it was not exercised by a sovereign community, was derived from his tacit acceptance.

There was also a wide divergence of views as to the nature of legislation itself. For while the absolutist school perceived in legislation a freely creative activity, the school which strove for the 'Right-State' saw in it only a development of Natural Law with adaptation to times and places. In this connection the whole or the chief importance was attached to the content of a statute on the one hand and to its imperative sanction on the other. In the sixteenth century and to some extent even in the seventeenth, there still was life in the notion that in the proper sense the law-making faculty is not the will but the rational intellect of the legislator; that what makes a statute a law lies in the formal determination by the sovereign that its content accords with the idea of justice; that the command of obedience, and the eventual use of force, arise merely as consequences of this, and that at most they are essential to the concept of complete or perfect law but not to the concept of law in general.[40] Against this there prevailed more and more the opposite view that the will of the sovereign is the true substance of law; that its binding force comes exclusively from the ruler's command addressed to his subjects, while the prior considerations of reason in the mind of the lawgiver have importance only for himself; that the idea of Law (at least of Positive Law) is quite unthinkable without the elements of a command issued by a superior will and a force exerted by an irresistible power.[41] Yet not only were there various intermediate opinions, but the derivation of all positive law from the sovereign's will was compatible with the strictest subjection of this will to the dictates of Natural Law, whether it was the supreme Will of God or the power of objective Reason that was exalted as a higher authority than the legislative will. In the eighteenth century indeed the theory which steadily gained ascendency on this basis was that of the abstract Law of Reason, in the light of which Positive Law would seem to be a mere decree for putting Natural Law into effect (see below).

With such an opposition of principles the doctrine must also split into two very different schools in answering the question, whether and to what extent the State-power stands above the laws.

Men were naturally agreed that the law-maker can alter or abrogate rules of law to the same extent that he can make them. But after the beginning of the sixteenth century a lively controversy arose over the question, whether or not the law-maker himself is bound by laws which were made by himself or his predecessors and have not been abrogated.

And whereas the medieval publicists had strictly maintained the exemption of the sovereign from positive law, there now arose a radical literary movement whose aim was to annihilate the idea of "potestas legibus soluta."

In this sense a number of eminent German and French jurists raised a strong protest against the hitherto accepted interpretation of the Roman maxim "Princeps legibus solutus est." They regarded this as nothing more than an exceptional provision for special cases and sought, as a matter of principle, to replace it by the contrary maxim "Princeps legibus tenetur," while at the same time they were by no means inclined to deny the sovereignty of the Princeps and often indeed expressly asserted the same subjection of a sovereign assembly of the People or of the Optimates. With the greatest energy Ulrich Zasius attacked the doctrine of the 'Italians and other flatterers of princes,' which he could never accept ("sed mihi nunquam placuit ista sententia"); he wished to free even Emperor and Pope merely from the "juris sollennitates," otherwise binding them to Positive as well as

Natural and Divine Law: "nam jura sunt divinitus per ora principum promulgata." [42] Still more definitely Cujacius confined the maxim "Princeps legibus solutus" to the exemption from the Lex Iulia et Papia Poppaea and a few 'solemnities'; for the rest he argued that the monarch is bound by the laws inasmuch as the people itself had but a limited power before the transference of the imperium and hence could have transferred only a limited power. [43] In the same spirit Donellus and other Frenchmen ascribed to the sovereign ruler only a "potestas legibus adstricta." [44] In Germany Pruckmann carried this idea further in a fiery polemic against absolutism in the year 1591, [45] and many other writers followed him. [46]

Yet when the concept of sovereignty took a more precise form, men had to recognize a specific difference between the duty of the sovereign to observe the rules made by himself and the obligation of a subject to obey the statutes given to him from above. Men found this difference in the fact that the true sovereign is not under any external compulsion to obey the laws; in this connection they used the formula first employed by Aquinas, that the law should bind the sovereign "quoad vim directivam" but not "quoad vim coactivam." In this way many supporters of the idea of 'Ruler's-sovereignty,' following the example of Catholic theorists, sought to maintain at the same time the idea of a 'Right-State.' [47]

In opposition to them the supporters of 'People's-sovereignty' naturally placed the ruler, who was for them indeed no sovereign, in subjection to the laws even by way of coercion and punishment. [48] But even for the sovereign people itself, they did not at first by any means claim a "potestas legibus soluta." On the contrary the Monarchomachi, so far as they expressed themselves on this question, were in principle agreed that the people, while collectively beyond the reach of coercion and punishment, is yet for its own part bound by the existing Positive Law. [49] For this reason Althusius, the strongest exponent of the idea of the Legal and Constitutional State in all its aspects, sought already to strike out the attribute of "potestas legibus soluta" from the definition of "majestas," which was otherwise so precisely expressed by him. [50]

The teaching of the Monarchomachi was followed by most of the advocates of double sovereignty with the one difference, that while they subjected the bearer of 'personal majesty' to all positive laws, yet as against him they conceded a "vis coactiva" to the laws of the constitution but to all other laws a mere "vis directiva." [51] Yet there were variations among them. For on the one hand some would have the "majestas personalis" absolutely exempt from all "leges civiles" with the exception of "leges fundamentales." [52] And on the other hand the view was put forward that the 'subject' of "majestas realis" stands quite above all positive law and even above the law of the constitution.[53]

But if there was indeed a strong drift toward the rejection, in principle, of the absolutist maxim "summa potestas legibus soluta est," yet the finally triumphant school of thought held all the more decidedly to this maxim.

In this connection it should first be noticed that in jurisprudence the medieval interpretation of the Roman maxim "Princeps legibus solutus est" defied all attacks. But it was a more important matter that Bodin treated the attribute of "potestas legibus soluta" as the essential criterion of true sovereignty.[54] In this he was followed by all the strictly absolutist adherents of his doctrine of sovereignty.[55] And they often expressly asserted that this exemption from positive law did not mean simply the exclusion of all coercion or punishment of the sovereign, but that even "quoad vim directivam" the law is for him not a law but at most a rule which he voluntarily observes.[56]

For Bodin and his school there was no difference in this respect between the ordinary civil laws and the laws of the constitution; any legal subjection to "leges fundamentales" would destroy the idea of sovereignty, and for the sake of the public weal the true sovereign should have the power to break the constitution.[57] To this the strict doctrine of absolutism held fast in later times when, largely in opposition to Hobbes (who refused to allow any constitution whatever as a limitation of the sovereign's will),[58] it recognized a certain moral duty of the ruler to obey the fundamental laws of the land, or at least those which he had sworn to obey.[59]

As against this the doctrine of moderate absolutism predominant in Germany now asserted the possibility of the Constitutional State and treated the "leges fundamentales" as true legal limitations of majesty. But at the same time it sought more and more to carry out the idea of "potestas legibus soluta" to its full extent. It made this possible by setting up the theory that "leges fundamentales" are in truth not laws but contracts, whose binding force is rooted in Natural Law; that they are the ground of the existence of "summa potestas" and not an outflow from it; hence that the sovereign, despite his elevation above all law, is indeed bound by them juristically, being bound 'directively' in any case and also 'coactively' if the contract so provides.[60] Grotius himself decided to this effect, and taught that the sovereign is exempt from all civil laws but that under Natural Law he is strictly bound by contracts and thus also by the constitution; but he stated more distinctly than any of his precursors—and this was an important advance—that the exemption from "leges civiles" applies to the sovereign only as a sovereign, while to all acts which the sovereign undertakes in his private capacity the ordinary private law must apply.[61]

This doctrine, that positive laws are not binding on the sovereign at all while the laws of the constitution bind him only as contracts, was then adopted by Pufendorf and his followers and gained almost undisputed sway.[62] Yet the stricter concept of sovereignty of this school was applied throughout; and thus while it granted the possibility of clauses in a constitution whereby unconstitutional acts were declared null and void or the throne itself declared vacant in case of breach of the constitution, at the same time all "vis coactiva" over the sovereign, even for fundamental laws, was rejected as conflicting with the concept of sovereignty.[63] And besides, when even for constitutional contracts the doctrine was invoked that "ex causa" the sovereign may break his contracts, that the "salus publica" is such a cause, and that the decision as to the requirements of the public weal rests with the sovereign alone: in the last resort the observance of the constitution was left simply to the conscience and judgment of the sovereign. And thus the general doctrine of public law, which came to the aid of the Princes with arguments for destroying the constitutional position of the territorial Estates, stood upon this ground,[64] while the defenders of the existing constitutional order, when they did not wish to abandon the whole basis of the prevailing theory, set themselves chiefly against the excessive extension of the idea of "salus publica" or against the exclusive competence of the ruler to judge of what is for the public interest.[65]

While thus the absolutist movements within the 'Nature-Right' theories of the State unconditionally restored the maxim that the sovereign power stands above statutes, the only active dispute being over the legal force of constitutions, so also the liberal movements, after the middle of the seventeenth century, almost always conceived the relation of the State-power to statute law in the same way and disputed only as to the nature and force of Constitutional Law.

The pure doctrine of popular sovereignty tended more and more to give up the standpoint held by the Monarchomachi, of a Constitutional Law binding on people and ruler alike, and while strictly subjecting all other governmental factors to the law it raised the sovereign will of the people above all positive laws and above the constitution itself.[66] Hence it was pushed in the direction of pure State-absolutism, whose last consequences were drawn by Rousseau with his usual rigor.[67]

On the other hand the constitutional doctrine, the true heir of the older doctrine of popular sovereignty, worked out with energy the thought of a Constitutional Law strictly binding on all the factors of government. But even this doctrine could not overthrow the maxim that the supreme power is exempt from the laws. Hence whatever elements of the Legal and Constitutional State were preserved and continued in this doctrine were established on the basis of a contract binding by Natural Law. Thus it differed from the doctrine of moderate absolutism chiefly in two points. First, it ascribed to the fundamental laws of the constitution a "vis coactiva" in all cases, even as against the sovereign, and thus for their maintenance it allowed in extreme cases a right of active resistance. And secondly, it evolved the notion of a tacit or unwritten constitution, deducible from the tenor of the State-contract and therefore valid for every State, whereby in all circumstances indestructible legal bounds are set to the "majestas" in favor of the individuals, and endowed these unwritten fundamental laws with exactly the same force as the written. In both respects there was no one who gave earlier and sharper expression to the thoughts of what may be called the school of pure 'Nature-Right' constitutionalism than Huber in his book, De Jure Civitatis. But Huber undoubtedly took the core of this part of his political theory from the system of Althusius. Huber teaches that in every State the ruler (single or composite) is the 'subject' of majestas (see above, Ch. III. Note 165), and that majestas is a "potestas summa et legibus a se latis non nisi voluntarie obligata" (De Jure Civ., I. 3 c. 1 § 24–38, and I. 9 c. 5). But the fundamental contracts on which all majestas rests give it strict legal limits and bind it with "potestas coactiva" by Natural Law. This force inheres above all in the tacit contractual clauses, to be presumed in all cases, whereby even in an otherwise unconditioned transference of sovereignty the inviolable rights of the individual (personality, nroperty, freedom of thought, obedience to the Will of God) are reserved (I. 2 c. 3–5 and I. 3 c. 4). And exactly the same force belongs to express agreements (leges fundamentales), whereby the scope of sovereign power may be still more narrowly limited (I. 3 c. 4–5). If the sovereign oversteps these bounds of his majestas his act is null and void, he becomes a tyrant and active resistance is allowed against him; he even forfeits his title to "imperium" and may be punished (I. 9 c. 3–4). These principles apply not only in the Aristocracy as well as in the Monarchy (I. 2 c. 5), but even in the pure Democracy, in which for this reason a breach of the constitution by the majority gives the minority a "facultas resistendi" (I. 2 c. 3 § 27 ff., and c. 4 § 1–25).—Similar thoughts, in a more or less consistent form, were soon taken everywhere as a basis for the construction of the Constitutional State by Natural Law, and during the second half of the eighteenth century were ever more widely diffused, especially in Germany.[68]

Yet the more decidedly these constitutional limitations of the State-power were founded on pure Natural Law, the less did the supporters of the constitutional idea think it needful to claim for positive law as such an independent force as against the State.

Thus it was just toward the end of the eighteenth century that the absorption of positive law by the State reached its culmination.

b. This development of views on the relation of the State to Positive Law in the objective aspect was closely connected with the development of views on the relation of the State to Positive Law in the subjective aspect.

The same stream of thought, which after the beginning of the sixteenth century turned against the doctrine that laws do not bind the law-maker, set itself against the hitherto accepted doctrine of the deprivation of acquired rights. The opinion arose that the acquired right as such is in principle not to be violated even by the State, and that special grounds are needed not for its protection but for allowing the State's interference in exceptional cases. Thus it was not necessary for the "jus quaesitum" to prove its derivation from Natural Law in order to gain security for its existence as against the State. On the contrary it was in itself entitled to protection as soon as it became actually 'vested' under the existing law. At the same time an effort was made to restrict as much as possible the exceptions to this principle. In particular, while men allowed the deprivation of acquired rights on the paramount ground of the public good, yet in all circumstances they required the payment of full compensation to the one who lost his right. And with special emphasis they denied the Italian doctrine that the absence of a legal ground for expropriation could be covered by a deliberate and express use of the "plenitudo potestatis." [69]

This movement for the protection of acquired rights did not run its course without leaving permanent results. But from the standpoint of principle the views which came to prevail were more and more divergent and rested essentially on the foundation laid in the middle ages. While many jurists kept the older Italian doctrine wholly or partly unchanged,[70] the 'Nature-Right' theory of the State was driven to resume and carry forward, in two special points, the ideas developed from that doctrine.

In the first place, the more precise expression of the concept of sovereignty tended always to revive the thought that in the last resort even the best-established right sinks powerless before the "plenitudo potestatis." In this sense Bodin and his followers stated the principle of the formal omnipotence of the sovereign, though at the same time they recognized materially perfect rights and duties between the sovereign and the subjects, at least within the sphere of private law.[71] Hobbes and his school raised the formal omnipotence of the sovereign to a material omnipotence, and hence denied all possibility of any established right of the subjects against the ruler or any established duty of the ruler toward the subjects.[72] The general voice indeed was raised against this; but all the more favor was shown to the doctrine of Pufendorf, that as against the sovereign there may be true (but only imperfect) rights of the subjects, and toward the subjects true (but only imperfect) obligations of the sovereign.[73] The constitutional doctrine first restored the full legal character of the rights of subjects as against the State; but its truly permanent fruits were due not to the futile assault which it launched anew against the principle of the formal omnipotence of the supreme power, but to the fact that the sovereign powers which stood above all subjective rights were located exclusively in the sphere of legislation, a sphere which was sharply sundered from the other functions of the State.

In the second place the 'Nature-Right' theory of the State, to the same extent that it made the sovereign exempt from positive law, was forced to resume the distinction, in principle, between the "jura quaesita" based on Natural Law and those based on mere positive law. Although Grotius expressly protested against this,[74] the prevailing doctrine always came back to the thought which was dominant in the middle ages, that as the rules of Natural Law are the only limits of the State-power, the rights acquired on the ground of such rules are the only rights that could claim guaranties for their existence against the encroachments of the State. Thus again men tended more and more to base the protection of vested rights on the two great categories of property as rooted in the "jus gentium" and contracts as binding under Natural Law, while those rights which were derived neither from the institution of property nor from a contract with the sovereign were treated as mere 'privileges' subject to more or less arbitrary revocation.[75] This was of course compatible with the widest differences in determining the scope of the two categories as well as the degree of protection afforded by them. Firstly, there was a general tendency to extend the inviolability of private ownership to all proprietary rights, but to purely proprietary rights alone. Just for this reason, in order to provide a legal basis not only for compulsory expropriation in special cases but for a radical reform of the whole traditional system of property by the State, men had need of the concept of 'Eminent Domain' ("dominium eminens"), which was so greatly developed after the time of Grotius.[76] For if this "dominium eminens" was essentially nothing else than what Stein calls the 'superior right of the inherent idea of the State,' yet its expression in the Law of Things was essentially on the principle that for the correction of a system of property based on Natural Law it was necessary to have a right of superiority whereby the State itself entered into this system as the holder of an original and universal 'interest' under Natural Law.[77] And secondly, the public rights fell ever more decidedly out of the sphere of the "jura quaesita" which were protected by the law of property, though for a time their patrimonial form might cause much wavering. Thus in the last resort the answer to the question, whether and to what extent any rights acquired in the domain of public law would be recognized as against the sovereign, depended simply on how far the principle of the binding force of contracts would be invoked in behalf of the constitution and the particular right be construed as an outflow of the constitution.[78]

The strong movement which was begun by the constitutional doctrine against the advance of State-absolutism had for its chief purpose the increased protection of subjective rights against arbitrary encroachments on the part of the State. Yet what it strove for was not the strengthening of rights acquired by the titles of Positive Law, but simply the extension of rights guaranteed by their foundation in Natural Law. Indeed after it came to pass that on the one hand the inviolability of private property was placed among the indestructible rights of the individual,[79] and on the other hand these fundamental rights were built up into a 'natural' Constitutional Law valid for all States,[80] the current set steadily, in theory as in practice, toward the exclusive realization of the 'right that is born with us' and toward the abolition, by revolution or reform, of all acquired rights conflicting with the system of the Rights of Man.

2. As regards the relation of the State to Natural Law, the idea that Natural Law is the source, purpose and limitation of the State became the keystone of the whole 'Nature-Right' theory which flourished after the sixteenth century.

a. Natural Law in the objective aspect, so far as men disputed over its nature and the ground of its obligation, was conceived now as in the middle ages, as a true and externally binding law. But in the first place men found in it the legal basis of all State-power, as it was held to be anterior to the State, and the formation of the State was construed as a legal act done according to the rules of Natural Law.[81] In the next place they inferred from it that the chief end of the State is the realization of the idea of Right or Law (*Recht*), as the view was just now fully matured that civil legislation takes its fixed norms from the law which is self-evident by reason and supplemented by the revealed commands of God, that it must develop the legal ideas thus delivered to it and adjust them to the civil state, with its conditions differing from the state of Nature and changing with time and place, and that the first principles of Natural Law hold immutably for God Himself and all the more so for every earthly power, always and everywhere, even the State.[82] And lastly, from the "jus divinum, naturale et gentium" they deduced legal limitations which bind the State-power in all cases, since with all the sharpening of the concept of sovereignty the attribute of "potestas legibus soluta" always referred to positive law alone.[83] To be sure, in opposition to the movements striving for the formal limitation of sovereignty, the view came to prevail that, as against the formal omnipotence of the sovereign, even Natural Law has in the last resort only a "vis directiva" and not a "vis coactiva." [84] Yet the restraint of the supreme power was none the less regarded as a truly legal restraint. It is but seldom that we find all legal limitations sublimated into mere ethical postulates.[85]

This 'nature-rightly' mode of thought was confronted with a dangerous rival in the political doctrine of 'Reason of State' (ragione di stato, ratio status), which emanated from Italy.

Machiavelli's doctrine, allowing no higher guidance for the sovereign than the State's interest, was indeed but seldom unconditionally accepted.[86] On the contrary, most of the political writers who followed the principle of Reason of State made an express reservation for the inviolability of Divine and Natural Law.[87] Yet in the same degree that Reason of State was pushed into the foreground the idea of the State's subjection to Natural Law was weakened.[88] For this reason the advocates of the idea of Right raised many a strong protest against the doctrine of the "Statistae." [89]

If the question here was of an external danger pressing upon the self-contained theory of Natural Law, the first effort to defeat Natural Law on its own ground and with its own weapons was made by Hobbes. He reduced the pre-political "right of nature" to a "jus inutile," which contains not even the germ of a true Right; he made the State, by whose command and force law is created, absorb all rights which it does not itself create; he rejected all notions of a legal restraint of the State in its sovereign power of deciding as to right and wrong.[90]

With this emancipation of the State from all anterior and higher law the final goal of State-absolutism was reached. All later systems of pure absolutism held fast to this principle. There was often indeed a nominal return to the doctrine of limitations of the sovereign by Natural Law, as for example in Spinoza and later in Rousseau. Yet these are not really to be taken as legal limitations but as natural bounds of all external power, postulates of rational judgment as to the true interest of the State or the necessary effects of its organization as it should be.[91]

In opposition to this Pufendorf and his school strongly asserted the legal character of Natural Law, and defended with lively polemics against Hobbes the old tenets that it prevailed before the State existed, that it supplies the guiding principles of all civil legislation, and that it binds the sovereign himself.[92] Yet Pufendorf, under the influence of Hobbesian ideas, modified the older doctrine in so far that he declared Natural Law to be an 'imperfect' law, made its continuance in the State depend on the sanction of the sovereign, and imposed on the latter only an "obligatio imperfecta" to observe the rules of Natural Law.[93]

A similar line was taken by Thomasius, Boehmer and others of this school, though sometimes they insisted still more strongly that Natural Law is true law, and though in this connection they were themselves the first to labor earnestly for a sharp severance of Natural Law from the domains of Morals and Politics.[94] At the same time the idea of the 'Right-State' was weakened by the ever growing importance which was attached to the maxim "Salus publica suprema lex esto." For while this maxim was placed among the first principles of Natural Law itself, it was treated indeed as a barrier quite as much as a bulwark of absolutism, but yet it was given the power, within the circle of 'Nature-Right' ideas, to displace the idea of justice more and more by the idea of expediency.[95]

Against all such loosening of the fetters imposed on the State by Natural Law many voices were raised in protest. The opponents were by no means agreed as to the origin of the binding force of Natural Law. Whether at this point they resorted to a more or less direct derivation from the Will of God, or gave the chief place to the principle of justice as contained in the Nature of God, or developed the thought, destined to triumph in the end, of an absolute Law of Reason binding on all rational beings by virtue of its rationality: in any case they were led to the conclusion that, in and for the State as well as in the state of nature, Natural Law has a force of its own independent of, and not mediated by, the will of the ruler.[96]

This was indeed compatible with the admission of a formal omnipotence of the State which in the last resort is indefeasible even by Natural Law.[97] But when Natural Law allied itself with the constitutional doctrine it claimed anew, and ever more decidedly, a coercive force against the sovereign himself.[98]

At the same time there appeared a twofold movement making for the omnipotence of Natural Law. On the one hand the elaboration of the abstract Law of Reason produced a legal system which embraced all the relations of life and allowed Positive Law to decide independently only in minor questions, while in all essential matters it set up its own universal rules and imperatively demanded their enforcement by the State.[99] On the other hand there grew up the theory which held that the sole function of the State is the realization of the idea of Right (or Law), denied that the State has any business to promote welfare or culture, and thus, while preventing the destruction of Right by the maxim "salus publica suprema lex," gave up all those ideas of the State for which so much labor had been spent.[100]

In fact the 'Nature-Right' doctrine reverted at last to a notion of the 'Right-State' which would have been fit for the blighted and stunted State-life of the early Germans. This 'Right-State,' if its realization had been possible at all, would have been purchased at the cost of reducing the State to bondage and impotence.

Yet in Kant himself, who carried to the utmost the idea of a government of the State by the Law of Reason as well as the restriction of the State to its legal function, there appear again the beginnings of the downfall of the system of Natural Law. For on the one hand he restores the freedom of the State, when first of all he wholly discards the old division of law into natural and positive law and recognizes but one law, which is in its whole ideal content a Law of Reason given *a priori* and unalterable by the State, but gains its actual force only by the peremptory act of the State and thus goes into effect purely as Positive Law by virtue of free legislation. On the other hand he restores the sovereign power of the State, when he holds that there can be no external guaranty against transgression of the limits of this power, and in the end resolves its legal subjection into the theory that its own nature requires it to act rationally.

b. The fact that opinions on the relation of the State to Natural Law in the subjective aspect develop in strictest congruence with opinions on the meaning and force of the rules of Natural Law appears from a review of what has already been said on the history of the system of the rights of man.[101] Before the middle of the seventeenth century the subjective rights derived from Natural Law are commonly recognized as true rights, even though the perfected theory of sovereignty makes them unenforceable; they are annulled by Hobbes and his followers, are restored as 'imperfect' rights by Pufendorf and his school, are again endowed with coercive force by the constitutional school; for Kant they share in the transformation of Natural Law, as disjoined from Positive Law, into the Law of Reason as coinciding with Positive Law. At the same time there takes place that steady increase in the content and scope of the indestructible natural rights of the individual, before which all 'titles' of positive law ultimately break down while the functions of the State shrink to the functions of an institution for the protection of persons and property. With this is connected the fact that in course of time the center of gravity of the structure of Natural Law is ever more decidedly shifted from objective to subjective Natural Law.

3. With regard to the legal consequences of a transgression of the limits of law by the State-power, opinions were determined chiefly by the conflict of two basic principles, one of which held that the sovereign is not sovereign when acting beyond his sphere of competence, and the other demanded the unconditional admission of the formal omnipotence of the sovereign.

On the whole the 'Nature-Right' theories of the State were agreed only that in any case the rights of government belong only to that government whose existence rests on a legal title. The prevailing doctrine even followed the principle of Legitimacy in the strictest fashion. It held that, pending the legitimation of an usurped power, all governmental acts of the usurper are wholly null and void, asserted for the individual the right and the duty to refuse obedience, and even allowed any private man to seize and slay such a "tyrannus absque titulo," who is outlawed as a public enemy. In this the advocates of the People's sovereignty and the champions of the Ruler's sovereignty were in agreement.[102] It was only over the question of legitimation that a difference arose between them, as the one party placed the legitimating power solely in the express or tacit consent of the people to the change of the constitution, while the other party required the express or tacit abdication of the lawful ruler.[103] After Grotius there gradually arose a contrary view, which attached a greater or less degree of legal importance to possession as such, and even partly transplanted to the soil of Natural Law the idea which had grown up in the purely political field of thought, that the full possession of sovereignty gives of itself the rights of sovereignty.[104]

Now when men started from the principle that the sovereign

is not to be regarded as sovereign outside the sphere assigned to him by the constitution, it was an easy matter to place the legitimate ruler, so far as he broke the legal bounds of rulership, on a level with the usurper. For to this extent even he would lose his title. In the sixteenth and the beginning of the seventeenth century indeed such a view largely prevailed among writers who otherwise maintained the sovereignty of the ruler. Men were of opinion that all acts of the ruler transgressing the bounds of law, even though clothed in the form of law, are wholly null and void and that the judge should declare and maintain such nullity.[105] It was deemed consistent with the nature of sovereignty that the ruler who has become a tyrant by grievous and persistent violation of law should be brought to justice, compelled to keep within bounds and even be deposed.[106] It was not only for the courts but for every single subject that the duty of obedience was held to be conditioned by the lawfulness of the ruler's acts.[107] And when the further question, whether and in what cases there is a right of armed resistance against illegitimate acts of the legitimate ruler, remained in dispute after the well-known vacillations of Luther and the other Reformers, even such a "jus resistendi" was to a large extent affirmed, with greater or less cautions, by theologians and jurists who were otherwise by no means inclined to deny the absolutist principle.[108]

As against this the principle of the formal omnipotence of the sovereign must give rise to the doctrine that every ordinance made by the supreme power as such is formally binding even though materially unlawful; that there can be no judgment upon the sovereign as such; that the subject owes unconditional obedience to the State; that even violent measures of tyranny produce no right of active resistance.[109] At the same time the absolutist doctrine held faithfully to the sacred text, "We should obey God rather than men," and now as in the middle ages declared that every individual has the right and the duty to oppose commands contrary to his conscience with the passive resistance of the martyr.[110]

The Monarchomachi made the question of the right of resistance the center of their whole system. But as a result of the replacement of Ruler's-sovereignty by People's-sovereignty, the position of this question shifted to the conflict of principle as to the legal consequences of a transgression of the limits of law by the State-power. For all the rights which they gave to the people against and over the tyrant were for them consequences, not restrictions, of the principle of sovereignty.[111] As for the rights of the subjects as such, those times of agitation inspired various revolutionary opinions, which went so far as to give a general right of insurrection to individuals whose conscience is attacked, and even to justify tyrannicide.[112] But it was against the individual subject himself that the properly systematic doctrine of the Monarchomachi, as perfected by Althusius, asserted the formal omnipotence of the State. For it taught that the private person has no right of active resistance either against the sovereign people or against the legitimate ruler who exercises its sovereignty; and thus it modified the principles of its opponents in just this point, that in case of an unlawful threat of irreparable damage the natural right of self-defense is granted to the individual even against the State.[113] Peculiar ideas, however, were developed by some of the Monarchomachi, in that on the one hand the "magistratus inferiores," not only as an assembly called to represent the people but each of them in his own district, were given the right and the duty of armed resistance to tyrannical acts of the "summus magistratus," and on the other hand particular cities and provinces threatened with tyranny were granted a right of resistance and even of secession as against the aggregate State. Yet as these principles were deduced on the one hand from the constitutional powers of the Ephors transferred directly from the sovereign people, and on the other hand from the constitutional principle of federalism, it appeared, more especially in Althusius, that this did not proclaim a right of revolution but rather established a strictly formal and universally binding Constitutional Law.[114]

Like the Monarchomachi, the advocates of a double sovereignty, to the same extent that they recognized the sovereignty of the people behind or above the sovereignty of the ruler, at once deduced from this, for the people and its representatives, the right to resist the legitimate ruler who has become a tyrant, to bring him to justice, to depose and punish him.[115] And it was just by this means that they opened the way to giving full scope to the principle of sovereignty against the subjects as such, so that the individual, so far as he was not called to take part in the exercise of the sovereign rights of the community, had only the right of passive resistance and, if the worst came, of self-defense.[116]

Even the champions of the exclusive sovereignty of the ruler, in so far as they allowed its restriction, admitted the possibility, on the ground of express constitutional provisions, of more or less extensive rights of the people as a whole to annul and resist unlawful acts of the ruler and even to depose a tyrant, without conceding thereby a self-established right of resistance of subjects against the State.[117] Yet indeed it was among these that the opinion was often held that, at least in extreme cases of tyranny, even the absolute sovereign who is not restricted by any constitutional provisions may be seized and driven out by right of Natural Law.[118] In this sense Grotius himself, while in general maintaining the principle of the formal omnipotence of the State-power and normally letting a right of resistance arise only from a saving clause in the contract of rulership in favor of the originally sovereign people, yet recognized in case of extreme tyranny a necessary right of revolution.[119]

As against this, in the absolutist doctrine after the middle of the seventeenth century the principle of the omnipotence of the ruler reached its culmination. Hobbes indeed was the only one who endeavored to set aside the principle that we should obey God rather than men and that every subject is empowered and bound to disobey a sinful command.[120] For the rest, however, the doctrine gained ascendency that unconditional obedience is due to the sovereign, that every act of the ruler, however unlawful materially, is formally binding on the subjects, and that in no circumstances can there be a right to resist the State-power.[121] This position was firmly held even by Pufendorf and his school of Natural Law, however strongly they emphasized the materially legal bounds of the State-power and the indestructible natural rights of the individual.[122]

As for the strict doctrine of popular sovereignty, the more it set the popular will above all existing constitutional law while at the same time conceiving the people as a mere sum of individuals, the more decidedly did it receive into its system a formal right of revolution. But thereby the right of insurrection, which had always been conceived as a right of irregular resistance to lawless acts which is necessary in the last resort in default of legal redress, took ever more clearly the character of a paramount right in which the people's sovereignty came to expression as exempt from all legal restrictions whatever and arbitrarily overriding all constituted powers.[123]

Thus the problem of working out the principle of legal protection in all its aspects, in the form of the idea of the Legal State, devolved more and more exclusively on the constitutional theory.

In the first place the constitutional theory sought to give a general solution of this problem by way of reviving the formal and coercive effect of those legal limitations of State-power which it had systematized. Thus it reverted to the principle that unlawful acts of the sovereign are wholly null and void. For this reason it regarded even statutes as null and void if they transgressed the sphere of material competence of the legislative power.[124] But above all it revived the doctrine of the purely conditional duty of obedience and the right of active resistance with such emphasis that this persisted far into the nineteenth century as an integral part of the constitutional system.[125] And to a greater or less extent the thought was maintained that when the sovereign invades those fundamental rights of the people or of individuals which are established by nature or guaranteed by the constitution, the original state of nature takes the place of the broken social contract, reviving once more that right of armed self-protection which was given up in the State. This thought was not always followed out with the same consistency with which Huber for example deduced even in the democracy a "jus resistendi" of the minority against the majority,[126] or Locke spoke of an armed appeal to Heaven as the last resort.[127] Yet essentially the same principle lay at the root of the deductions prevailing in the German doctrine of Natural Law, which allowed the right of resistance with some few reservations, and sometimes granted it only to the whole body of the people or to a majority and sometimes confined it to extreme cases of necessity.[128] But Kant broke altogether with the idea that there can be a constitutional right of revolution in any case, and sought instead to combine the notion of the constitutional 'Right-State' (*Rechtsstaat*) with the notion of the formal omnipotence of the sovereign.[129]

In the last analysis the fact is that every appeal to resistance and rebellion is not the outcome but the negation of the idea of a 'Right-State,' and the formal omnipotence of some supreme political power is imperatively required by the 'Right-State' itself.[130] Hence the lasting contribution made by the 'Nature-Right' constitutional doctrine to the idea of legal protection lay not in these attempts to construct a legal protection against the State and outside the State. It lay rather in the postulate of an organization of legal protection within the State and by the State, a postulate which was more sharply defined in principle than ever before through the doctrine of the separation of powers. In this respect the whole later development was governed by the great principle, ever more clearly formulated, that the formal omnipotence of the State over the Law appears solely through the factors and in the forms of legislation, that the administrative power is bound by the laws, and that the judicial power as a separate function of the State needs an independent organization with its own rules of procedure.[131] For the actual erection and completion of the Legal State these abstract principles of Natural Law were indeed an inadequate basis. But they were the lodestars under whose guidance the historic foundations of the Legal State were fixed and built up, and thus not only was there a definitive refusal of the occasional temptations to a full judicial protection of private rights against the State, but also there were unfolded in modern forms those elements of a legal protection for public right which were immanent in the Germanic idea of the State and were never wholly extinguished.[132]

III. Nineteenth-Century Ideas

The development of 'Nature-Right' ideas on the relation of the State to Law reached its culminating point in the last decade of the eighteenth century. After that time there begins, in this as in all other respects, the decline and fall of the whole structure of ideas of Natural Law. It does not fall within the scope of our monograph to follow this process further.

The idea of Natural Law was supplanted in Germany by the ideas of the 'historical' school of law. By this the old bifurcation of law into natural and positive law was finally dissolved. Yet the law, now singly conceived as the positive expression of an organic group-consciousness, was not simply the continuation of one or the other branch of the older antithesis but resolved these two branches in a higher unity. Thus indeed the elements in the historic-organic idea of law which determined the relation of the State to Law were at the same time derived from the natural and positive law of the old doctrine. There arose the view that Law is not partly before and above the State and partly from and below it, but that Law and the State grew up together, were provided for each other and are bound up in each other.

The philosophic elaboration of this thought remains imperfect to this day. Yet from the most widely different sides not only are the defects of the historical school exposed but the foundations of its theory of law are again called in question. With regard to the relation of the State to Law, amid the chaos of modern opinions two opposite schools contend against the historic-organic idea of law. From one side, for some time notions of the abstract Law of Nature have pushed themselves again into the foreground and threatened the very idea of the State. From the other side, there is at present a movement gaining more and more ground in Germany, which reverts to the older conception of Positive Law but wipes out Natural Law as its complement and strikes at the very root of the concept of Right. For this new mode of thought the idea of Right (or Law) in the end loses all its meaning in the idea of Utility and loses all its efficacy in the idea of Might. If this prevails, then the sole merit of the historical school lay in its negation of natural law, and in that case the ideas of natural law were but the empty fabric of a dream and all the centuries of their development have gone for nothing.

But if on the contrary there exists a Law—a Law which is not simply adorned with the ancient high-sounding name, but is the expression of a specific, unique and intrinsically valuable idea of mankind—then a different historical perspective offers itself. Then indeed the gains which the idea of Right has acquired from Natural Law cannot be lost; they are not surrendered but generalized by the historical conception, and they can never be extinguished in the future by any changes or refinements in the conception of Law. For then, even when law is conceived as wholly positive, the idea of Justice will evermore maintain that independence which was gained for it in the conception of Natural Law, against the idea of social utility as well as against the idea of collective might.

The relation of the State to Law, when natural and positive law coincide in idea, can no longer be conceived in the dualistic fashion of the old doctrine. But the thoughts which broke through at separate points may fuse at a single point. We no longer ask whether the State was prior to Law or Law was prior to the State; for us they are equally original, their seeds were planted with mankind itself, in their development they have grown in and through each other as potencies of that group life which is inseparable from the idea of man. For us the State as well as every other organized collective power is no mere product of the law, but even the highest power appears to us to receive its confirmation and completion only when the law stamps it as a 'legal relation.' Conversely, for us all Right is completed and confirmed only by Might; but for us the State is no more the creator of Right than is any other human Might. For Right (or Law), being the system of external rules for free wills, cannot be of the substance of will itself; when will governs will, this leads always by logical necessity to nothing but the idea of Might. If there is a binding external rule, not simply for this and that will but for the will in itself, this must be rooted in a spiritual faculty independent of the will. This faculty is reason. Hence law is not the common will that something shall be, but the common conviction that something is. Law, whether manifested directly in usage or declared by a social organ appointed for this purpose, is the conviction of a human society that in it there are external rules for the will, that is, limitations of freedom which are externally binding and by hypothesis enforceable. The State as lawgiver not only acts to a great extent as that which bears and determines the legal consciousness, but also completes the formation of all law with its command and enforcement. Yet if the common will commands that that which is law shall be obeyed, the law is not thereby created but merely confirmed. And if it is only through a supreme Might that the enforceability posited in the idea of Law can be perfectly realized, yet the law is still law even though in a particular case its enforcement fails or is imperfect or even impossible in default of a competent superior Might, if only there is still a general conviction that enforcement would be right if it were possible or if a competent power were at hand. And likewise the State no longer appears to us as a mere legal institution which exists for the law alone; yet among all its functions the legal purpose presents itself as the specific and indispensable purpose of the State, just because its full realization is possible only through the supreme Might. And while we regard the Law for its own part as primarily an instrument to serve the purposes of the State's life, yet its functions are very far from being exhausted or bounded by this. When lastly, on the one hand we set the State not above and beyond but within the Law, so that even its own freedom is bounded by the legal order, and on the other hand we set the Law not above and beyond but within the State, so that the formal omnipotence of the sovereign power prevails even as against the Law, we thereby admit indeed the possibility of a conflict between material and formal law. But he who denies the possibility of such a conflict denies the very idea of Right.

Deep-seated in the spiritual nature of man is the desire for the union of Right and Might. Their severance is always felt as something abnormal. This feeling is the best witness that there is a mightless right and a rightless might. But at the same time it is the source of that healing and repairing power which evermore makes for the union of Right and Might. For the spirit of man cannot permanently endure their disjunction. Therefore, in the end, a right which cannot enforce itself fades out from the common consciousness and thereby ceases to be a right. And a might which exists without right, if it can establish itself firmly, is in the end felt by the common consciousness to exist by right, and thus converts itself into a right.

. . . . . .

The analysis of the leading political ideas which we have found expressed in the work of this half-forgotten German Monarchomach has led us far back into the middle ages and forward to the close of the eighteenth century. With special attention to the share taken by the Germans, we have traced in a few main points the history of a movement of thought, growing ever stronger and penetrating ever deeper, whose common feature is the 'Nature-Right' conception of the State.

If we cast a glance once more at the individual whose life and doctrines we took as our point of departure, his work indeed appears to us as but part of a grand intellectual labor in which all the civilized nations of Europe took part and generations after generations worked without interruption. But even the greatest and most renowned masters who devoted their powers to this work presented themselves to us in the same light. We found that, far more than is commonly supposed, they sometimes merely cast in peculiar forms thoughts which had already been expressed, and sometimes helped to bring new ideas into full bloom where the soil had been fully prepared. All the more are we obliged to count our Althusius among the masters and assign him a place in the history of political science far above the crowd of apprentices and journeymen who took part in building the structure. All of the foregoing chapters testify to this. And in conclusion one thing may be emphasized which has stood out more and more in the course of this study: this man, excelling all others of his school of thought in the intensity of his sense of right, and equaling them in his zeal for liberty, had a doctrine of his own which, if it prepared the way for the destructive political theory culminating in Rousseau, yet in many respects laid a foundation for the constructive theory of the Constitutional State.

NOTES

1. See above, Ch. I. and II.; the Divine Will, natural necessity or the dictate of reason may be taken as the original cause.

2. When, following Aristotle, men defined the State's purpose as "bene vivere," they restricted the function of the State, in contrast to the Church, to temporal felicity, but identified this with the virtuous life so far as such is possible without the means of salvation. Thus Thom. Aquin., De reg. pr., I. c. 14 ("vivere secundum virtutem"); Ptol. Luc., III. c. 3 and IV. c. 23; Aegid. Col., III. 1 c. 1–2, III. 2 c. 8 and 32; Eng. Volk., De reg. pr., II. c. 2–4; Ant. Ros., I. c. 46 and 56. Hence not only do Joh. Paris., c. 18, Somn. Virid., I. c. 154–155, and Gerson (see Schwab, p. 88 ff.) say that the State-power is also "spiritualis" and has to do with the soul as well as the body, but even Alv. Pel., I. a. 56, admits this (the spiritual power is called "spiritualis" only by prëeminence, as it operates upon the soul "secundum gratiam" while the secular power operates only "secundum naturam"). Mars. Pat., I. c. 4–6, extends the State's function to the care for welfare in the other world as well as in this world. In Patric. Sen. the State already takes to itself all the affairs of civil life (lib. IV.–VI., even the duty to see that all citizens have beautiful—of course they would be antique—names, p. 298–304).—On the other hand in Dante's definition of the purpose of the Empire, I. c. 3–4, there is an echo of the old Germanic idea that the State's only purpose is to maintain law. It should also be noted that while Eng. Volk., De ortu, c. 7–13, treats at length of the "felicitas regni" as the State's purpose, yet in c. 14 he sums up all the functions of the State in the one idea of 'peace' (pax), and in c. 19 he identifies the State's purpose simply as the "ordinatio et conservatio pacis et iustitiae." Similarly Gerson, IV. p. 649, and Petr. Andl., II. c. 16–18.

3. This is shown in the general desire for well-planned legislation, in the discussions on the best form of government, in the cry for Reform ringing through the last centuries of the middle ages.

4. See above, Ch. II., especially Note 11.

5. Thom. Aquin., II. p. 353 a. 3, XXI. p. 477, 491, 499, 518; Aegid. Col., III. 2 c. 29 (lex positiva est infra principantem sicut lex naturalis est supra; the Prince is "medium inter legem naturalem et positivam"; the latter receives its "auctoritas" from him and he must adapt it to particular cases), also III. 2 c. 2. Ptol. Luc., II. c. 8, III. c. 8 and IV. c. 1. Eng. Volk., I. c. 10–11 (the rex as a "lex animata," doing justice in all concrete cases, is better than a "lex inanimata"). See also Joh. Saresb., IV. c. 2; Ockham, Dial. III. tr. 1, l. 2, c. 6; Petr. Andl., I. c. 8; Patric. Sen., I. 5 and III. 1.

6. As to the Emperor see the doctrine of all the legists; the theories of the Hohenstaufen (Frederick I, in Otto Frising., III. c. 16 and IV. c. 4; Epist. Frider. II of 1244 and 1245, in Huillard-Bréholles, Hist. dipl. Frid. II, Vol. VI. p. 217 and 258, and Petr. de Vin., Ep., II. c. 8, III. c. 9, V. c. 1 ff.); the summary in Ockham, Dial. III. tr. 2, l. 2, c. 26, and tr. 1, l. 2, c. 6; Aen. Sylv., praef. and c. 19–21; Petr. Andl., II. c. 8; also Gloss on Sachsenspiegel, Landrecht I. a. 1, III. a. 52–54, 64, Lehnrecht a. 4.—As to the Pope, see Boniface VIII in c. 1 in Sexto 1, 2; Aug. Triumph., I. q. 22 a. 1; Alv. Pel., I. a. 58; Laelius, in Goldast II. p. 1595 ff.; Aen. Sylv. in the year 1457 (Voigt, II. p. 240 ff.).

7. See above, p. 143–147; most distinctly Mars. Pat., I. c. 7–11, 14–15, 18; Nic. Cus., II. c. 9–10 and 20, III. praef. and c. 41; Greg. Heimb., II. p. 1604 ff. Ockham, Dial. III. tr. 1, l. 2, c. 6, says that perhaps in the whole world there is no purely regal government in the sense of a monarchy unrestrained by laws, and that such a form would not deserve preference except in the case (never existing in fact) of a perfectly virtuous ruler. With this Thom. Aquin. agrees to the extent that he prefers a monarchy limited by law (Op., XXI. p. 491 and 500 ff.).

8. In particular Mars. Pat. and Nic. Cus. develop modern thoughts at this point. It should be noticed however that all the writers mentioned in Note 5 (except Joh. Saresb.) suppose that in a Republic there will be a separation of legislative from executive power, such as they do not allow in a Monarchy, and thus they make this separation the criterion of a Republic.

9. As to the Assembly of the People, this comes out most distinctly in the theory of Marsilius; as to the General Council of the Church it comes out in the doctrine of "epikeia" overriding Canon Law; see above, Ch. III. Note 58.

10. See the statement and refutation of this doctrine in Georg Meyer, Das Recht der Expropriation, Leipzig 1868, p. 86 ff.

11. Gl. Ord. on l. 3 Cod. 7, 37, v. "omnia principis," and on l. 2, Dig. de R. D., v. "littora"; Jac. Aren. on Dig. prooem. nr. 1–7; Andreas de Isernia on II. Feud. 40, nr. 27–29; Bartolus on Const. I. Dig. pr. nr. 3, l. 4 Dig. 50, 9 nr. 12, l. 6 Dig. 50, 12 (a distinction is maintained throughout between "dominium mundi ratione iurisdictionis et gubernationis" and "dominium ratione proprietatis"); Baldus on l. 2, Dig. de R. D., Const. I. Dig. pr. nr. 10–11 (a double "dominium" in "singulae res," but "diversa ratione": ius publicum Caesaris, privatum privatarum personarum), II. Feud. 51, pr. nr. 1–4; Decius, Cons. 538 nr. 8–11.—Ockham, Dial. III. tr. 2, l. 2, c. 21–25, discusses all opinions at length, and himself teaches the doctrine of a "dominium quodammodo" of the Emperor resting on a transference from the People; this is a sort of ownership (but "minus pingue"), and yet it is compatible with the ownership of "res privatorum" by private

individuals and of "res nullius" by the "totum genus humanum," and is thus
essentially the same as the later "dominium eminens." See also Alv. Pel.,
II. a. 15, 57 and 63; Somn. Virid., II. c. 23–30 and 366 ("dominium
universale" and "dominium appropriatius et specialius"); Ant. Ros., I. c.
70; Petr. Andl., II. c. 8.

12. For the history of the theory of Expropriation in the middle ages the
account in Meyer, p. 76–115, may be referred to. All that we do here is to
give some supplementary material (particularly from writings overlooked by
Meyer) and to bring out more clearly those aspects which concern the relation between positive and natural law.

13. Gl. Ord. on l. 3 Dig. 1, 14, v. "multo magis," and other citations in
Meyer, p. 88; Gl. Ord. on c. 1 D. 22, v. "iniustitiam"; Jac. Aren., loc.
cit.; Andr. Isern., loc. cit.; Host., on c. 7 X. 1, 2, and Summa de rescriptis
(1, 3) nr. 11 ff.; Oldradus, Cons. 224 and 257; Bartolus on l. 4 Dig. 50,
9, l. 6 Dig. 50, 12, l. 6 Cod. 1, 22, and Const. I. Dig. pr. nr. 4–6 (neither
"rescribendo" nor "legem condendo"); Ant. Butr. on c. 6 X. 1, 2 nr. 20–
22; Panorm., eod. c. nr. 6; Raphael Fulgosius, Cons. 6 nr. 46–47, 21 nr. 12
and 18; Bologninus, Cons. 58; Alex. Tartagnus, Cons. II. c. 190 (especially
nr. 13), and c. 226 nr. 18; Paul. Castr. on l. 23 Dig. 41, 2, l. 6 Cod. 1, 22,
Cons. I. c. 229; Jason on l. 3 Dig. 1, 14 nr. 24–34, Cons. III. c. 86 nr. 14;
Franc. Curtius senior, Cons. 20, 49, 50, 60; Christof. de Castellione, Cons.
8 nr. 16–18; Joh. Crottus, Cons. II. c. 156 nr. 28–44; Ant. Ros., IV. c. 8
and 10. And especially Ockham, loc. cit. c. 23–25, who deduces from the
Emperor's "dominium quodammodo" a right to quash or confiscate or transfer private property rights, and to forbid the occupancy of "res nullius";
such acts however are not to be done "ad libitum" but only "ex causa et pro
communi utilitate" in so far as public utility takes precedence over "privata
utilitas." And it is Ockham who brings out most clearly (ib. c. 27) that this
is not merely a restriction of the monarch but a restriction of the State itself;
for according to him the limitation of imperial powers by the "iura singulorum" rests upon the fact that the People, which transferred its power to
the Emperor, had itself no unlimited power over "quilibet de populo," but
only "de necessitate" was it entitled to invade the sphere of private rights by
an act of the majority (according to c. 6 X. 1, 2).

14. To this effect, despite a strong tendency toward absolutism, Jacobus
Buttrigarius on l. 2 Cod. 1, 19; Alber. Rosc. on Const. I. Dig., v. "omnis,"
nr. 5 ff., l. 15 Dig. 6, 1, l. 2 Cod. 1, 19; Baldus on Const. I. Dig. pr. nr.
11, l. 7 Cod. 1, 19, l. 6 Cod. 1, 22, l. 3 Cod. 7, 37. For some intermediate
opinions see Felinus on c. 7 X. 1, 2 nr. 26–45; Decius, eod. c. nr. 19–24, and
Cons. 191, 198, 269 nr. 4–5, 271 nr. 3, 352 nr. 1, 357 nr. 3, 361 nr. 7,
520 nr. 5–6, 588, 606 nr. 8, 689 nr. 8; Joh. Mar. de Riminaldis, Cons. I.

c. 73; Ludov. Rom., Cons. 310 (a "iusta causa" is necessary in case of a "lex specialis" but not in case of a "lex universalis") ; Benedictus Capra, Regulae, 10 nr. 30 ff.

15. On the fluctuations of the Gloss see Meyer, p. 92–94. Decidedly in favor of compensation are: Baldus on l. 2 Cod. 7, 13; Decius on l. 11 Dig. de R. J., and Cons. 520; Felinus on c. 6 X. 1, 2 nr. 2, c. 7 eod. nr. 28–29; Jason on l. 3 Dig. 1, 14, and Cons. III. c. 92 nr. 11; Paul. Castr. on l. 5 § 11, Dig. 39, 1 nr. 4, l. 10 Cod. 1, 2 nr. 3; Ludov. Rom., Cons. 310 nr. 4; Crottus, Cons. II. c. 156 nr. 27–31; Bertachinus, Rep., v. "civitas," nr. 88 and 96; Aen. Sylv., c. 18 (ex publico compensandum).—Against: Alber. Rosc. on l. 14 § 1, Dig. 8, 6.

16. Decius, Cons. 520 (a lex may take away rights "generaliter" even "sine compensatione privatorum," but if "particulariter alicui subdito" then it must be "cum recompensatione") ; likewise Jason on l. 3 Dig. 1, 14 nr. 44; Paris de Puteo, De syndicatu, p. 41 nr. 24; Ant. Ros., IV. c. 8 and 10.

17. Thus Aen. Sylv., c. 17–18: when "reipublicae necessitas id expostulat," though this "aliquibus fortasse durum videbitur et absurdum."

18. Thus already the Gl. Ord. on l. 2 Cod. 1, 19, and on l. 6 God. 1, 22; then Host., Jac. Aren., Oldradus, Raph. Fulgos., Andr. Isern., Bartolus, Paul. Castr., Jason, Ockham and others as cited above, Note 13; also, but with less protection for property, Alber. Rosc., Baldus, Decius and Capra as in Note 14. See further Joh. Paris., c. 7 (deriving private ownership from the labor of the individual, and thus characterizing it as an individual right which exists without regard to a connection among men or a society with a "commune caput"). Paris de Puteo, loc. cit. nr. 22–24; Somn. Virid., I. c. 156–161; Gerson, IV. p. 598; Petr. Andl., loc. cit.; Ant. Ros., IV. c. 8 and 10 (as private ownership is derived from the "ius gentium" it is protected, but being derived only from the "ius gentium secundarium" it may be withdrawn "ex causa").—When the objection was raised that it was only the institution of property that existed "ex iure gentium," and that this was not attacked if individual owners were robbed, the reply was that the "distinctio dominorum" and the permanent establishment of the particular modes of acquisition were "de iure gentium."

19. See Baldus on I. Feud. 7 (God subjected the laws, but not contracts, to the Emperor) ; Ludov. Rom., Cons. 352 nr. 15–25; Christ. Castell., Cons. 8 nr. 25; Jason, Cons. I. c. 1 and 56, II. c. 223 and 226; Decius, Cons. 184 nr. 2, 286 nr. 5, 292 nr. 8, 404 nr. 8 ("Deus ipse ex promissione obligatur"), 528 nr. 6, 689 nr. 7–27.—On breach of contract "ex iusta causa," see Jason, Cons. I. c. 1, nr. 12 and 29 ff., II. c. 226 nr. 43, l. 3 Dig. 1, 14 nr. 34; Capra, Reg. 10 nr. 43 ff.; Ant. Ros., IV. c. 14–15.

20. Thus the Gl. Ord. on l. 2 Cod. 1, 19, and l. 1 Cod. 1, 22, holds that

private rights are suspended whenever they offend against the "ius civile," and that they may be abrogated by a rescript if such intent be clearly stated; but many, it is added, hold that in the latter case the rescript must contain an express clause "lege non obstante." This last opinion is developed by Host., Paul. Castr., Jason and others. Bartolus holds that private rights arising "ex iure civili" may be abrogated 'without cause,' but only by way of legislation and not (unless the damage be slight) by way of rescript, while Baldus, Decius and others hold that such rights may be withdrawn unconditionally and in any form.—Alber. Rosc., Innocent IV and a few others opine that the State cannot "sine causa" take away the "dominium ipsum," but can make this right of ownership illusory by taking away the "actiones" which arise merely "ex iure positivo."—Ant. Ros., III. c. 14, and Capra, Reg. 10 nr. 43–52, discuss at length the abrogation of "iura mere positiva."

21. See Jason, Cons., I. c. 1 nr. 20, c. 56 nr. 1, 2, 7, 8, 21, II. c. 226 nr. 43–49 ("privilegia" given gratuitously may be revoked at any time "sine causa"; those given for value, by reason of their contractual nature, only "cum causa"); Felinus on c. 7 X. 1, 2 nr. 48–52; Capra, loc. cit. (but only as against private subjects); Aen. Sylv., c. 15 (privileges may be revoked if they be "reipublicae damnosa").—See the application of this doctrine to the privileges granted by the State to the Church, in Disput. inter Mil. et Cler., p. 686, and Somn. Virid., I. c. 33–34.

22. See above, Ch. I. Notes 44–45, and p. 98–99, 153. On Natural Law as a limitation of the State-power see Thom. Aquin., II. p. 352 q. 96 a. 4, along with IX. p. 514 (the Pope is bound), and II. p. 355 q. 97 a. 1 (the People is bound); Aegid. Col., III. 2 c. 29 (the rex is under the lex naturalis); Aug. Triumph., I. q. 22 a. 1 (the Pope is bound); Alv. Pel., I. a. 7 and 46 (likewise); Ockham, Dial. III. tr. 1, 1. 2, c. 6, and tr. 2, 1. 2, c. 26 and 28 (as to Emperor and Pope), ib. c. 29 (as to the "universitas populi"), tr. 2, 1. 1, c. 30 (even an unanimous act of the "universitas mortalium" could not wholly abolish the Roman Empire); Baldus on I. Feud. 1 § 3 nr. 2 ("potentius est ius naturale quam principatus"), and 1. 1 Cod. 1, 1 nr. 24 ff. (therefore Emperor and Pope cannot, for example, lawfully permit usury); Capra, Reg. 10 nr. 20–43 and 53 (as to princeps, papa, imperator, populus seu universitas); Felinus on c. 7 X. 1, 2 nr. 19–25 (as to the Pope), and nr. 26 ff. (as to imperator, princeps, populus liber); Petr. Alliac., in Gerson, Op. I. p. 652 ff.; Nic. Cus., III. c. 5; Ant. Ros., IV. c. 2–14; Gerson, as above, Ch. III. Note 22 (as to the Council); Gloss on Sachsensp., I. a. 25 and 55.

23. Thus Thom. Aquin., II. p. 333 ff. and III. p. 211, explains both the "lex naturalis" and the "lex divina" as emanations from that "lex aeterna" which is identical with the Nature of God, the former being grounded in the participation of man, as a rational creature, in the moral order of the

world, and the latter being established by revelation for supermundane ends. Compare Aegid. Col., III. 2 c. 24–29 (lex naturalis), and c. 30 (lex divina); Gerson, IV. p. 652–654; also the passages cited in preceding Note, in which the force of the lex divina is placed on a level with the force of the lex naturalis.

24. See for example Thom. Aquin., II. p. 344, 348–349, 359: the "lex humana" carries out in detail the "principia legis naturalis," partly as ius gentium by way of mere 'conclusions' and partly as ius civile by way of 'determinations'; Aegid. Col., III. 2 c. 25 and 29: "si dicitur, legem aliquam positivam esse supra principantem, hoc non est ut positiva, sed ut in ea reservatur virtus iuris naturalis"; Lup. Beb., c. 15 p. 401; Ockham, Dial. III. tr. 2, l. 2, c. 28: the ius gentium, whereby the supreme power is subordinate to the common weal, "non est imperatorum vel regum per institutionem, sed solum per approbationem et observationem"; Baldus on I. Feud. 1 § 3 nr. 2; Hieronymus de Tortis (1427–1484), Consilium for Florence (in the Consilia of Antonius de Butrio, Lyons 1541), nr. 25: papa et imperator non sunt supra ius gentium, therefore (nr. 20–32) a papal sentence without previous citation is void.

25. Thus Thom. Aquin., II. p. 345–346, distinguishes between the "prima principia" of the lex naturalis, which are ineradicable and everywhere identical, and the "praecepta secundaria" of the same lex, which are mutable and, in consequence of the depravation of human reason, destructible.—It is commonly said that the ius naturale is "immutabile" and can never be abrogated ("tolli") by the ius civile, but that derogation from it "quoad quid" is possible, and that "ex causa" there may be "aliquid addi vel detrahi"; thus Lup. Beb., c. 15 p. 401; Ockham, Dial. III. tr. 2, l. 2, c. 24; Ant. Ros., IV. c. 7 (with a distinction between the "ius naturale divinum" and the "ius naturale homini commune cum animalibus"); Gloss on Sachsensp., I. a. 55.—This limitation was unavoidable, since the very existence of lordship and ownership involved a breach of the pure Law of Nature.

26. See Thom. Aquin., II. p. 345 and III. p. 211; Ockham, Dial. III. tr. 2, l. 2, c. 24; Ant. Ros., IV. c. 2–6, says that, though John de Lignano denies this, the legists are all agreed that while the ius divinum cannot be abrogated, yet so far as it is not manifestly given "de necessitate," it may be "distingui, limitari, restringi in aliquo casu vel aliquid addi."

27. Very common is the distinction between the "ius gentium primaevum" and the "ius gentium secundarium"; according to Ant. Ros., IV. c. 7, the lawgiver cannot abrogate the former even "ex causa," though he may interpret it, while he may abrogate the latter "ex causa."

28. See above, Ch. III. Notes 55 and 58.

29. Even if they are not formulated on their own account, yet they fol-

low directly from the absolute and objective validity ascribed to the first principles of Natural and Divine Law. And it needs but a fleeting glance at the medieval doctrine of State and Law to perceive that through it all, in sharp contrast to the theories of antiquity, the thought of the absolute and imperishable value of the Individual already bears fruit: a thought revealed to the world by Christianity and felt in all its depth by the Germanic spirit. That every individual by virtue of his eternal destiny is in his inmost nature sacred and inviolable even in relation to the State, that the smallest unit has a value not only for the whole but also for itself, that the individual is to be regarded by the community, never as a mere means, but also as an end: all this is not merely suggested but more or less clearly expressed. See the references given above, Ch. III. Note 36; also Dante, I. c. 3; Ockham, Dial. III. tr. 2, l. 2, c. 28.

30. Thus, to a certain extent, all the writers mentioned in Note 22. And with special reference to attacks on vested rights made without "iusta causa," the writers named in Note 13: see especially Gl. Ord. on l. 2 Cod. 1, 19, and l. 6 Cod. 1, 22; Host., loc. cit.; Jac. Aren., loc. cit. (the Emperor, if he commands anything contrary to law, "quasi non facit ut imperator"); Raph. Fulgos., loc. cit. (the contrary opinion that the Emperor does a valid act even when he does unright, would practically place everything in the hands of arbitrary power). Compare Capra, Reg. 10 nr. 35–42.—Then Bartolus draws, and others accept, the distinction between invasions of right (1) "legem condendo," (2) "iudicando," (3) "rescribendo," and he allows greater force to an act of legislation than to other acts; but he himself expressly declares that in conflict with Natural Right even statutes are null and void.—See also above, Note 24 i. f.

31. Hugo de S. Victore Saxo (above, Ch. I. Note 44), I. p. 266 (rulers are to be obeyed only "in iis quae ad potestatem pertinent," "non in iis quae ad tyrannidem"); Thom. Aquin., De reg. pr., I. c. 6, and Op., III. p. 160–161, XXI. p. 553, 592, 595 ff.; Eng. Volk., I. c. 6, 8 and 10; Ockham, Dial. III. tr. 2, l. 2, c. 20 (all men owe to the Emperor immediate but conditional obedience, that is, "in licitis" and "in his quae spectant ad regimen populi temporalis," so that for example a prohibition of wine-drinking would not be binding), c. 21–28, and with reference to the Pope, Octo qu., I. c. 15 and III. c. 9; Nic. Cus., III. c. 5; Decius, Cons. 72 nr. 2 ("superiori non est obediendum quando egreditur fines sui officii"). See also above, Ch. III. Note 57.

32. See already Manegold of Lautenbach (above, Ch. II. Note 2), who says that the king who has become a tyrant may be driven away without formality; such revolutionary doctrines were also asserted by the papalist party against the holders of State-power. Joh. Saresb., III. c. 15, VI. c. 24–

26, VIII. c. 17 and 20, where tyrannicide is directly commended. Similarly, but with rejection of tyrannicide, Thom. Aquin., loc. cit. Then the elaborate theory of the right of active resistance in Ockham, Dial. III. tr. 2, l. 2, c. 26 and 28 (by the ius gentium); Somn. Virid., I. c. 141; Henr. de Langenstein, c. 15; Gerson, IV. p. 600 and 624 (as to his well-known dispute on tyrannicide with its defender Jean Petit and at the Council of Constance, see Schwab, p. 609–646); also Decius, Cons. 690 nr. 13; lastly Capra, Reg. 10 nr. 42 (the enforcement of a tyrannical measure is an act of violence which may be resisted by violence).—Compare the transference of the doctrine to the Church in Ockham, Octo qu., I. c. 15 and III. c. 9 (obedience is due to the Pope only "in his quae necessaria sunt congregationi fidelium, salvis iuribus et libertatibus aliorum"; if he exceeds his sphere of competence every man, whether prelate, king, prince or simple layman, is entitled and bound to resist, with due regard to time, place and opportunity). Then during the Great Schism the doctrine of a right of resistance given by necessity became ever more common; see Matth. de Cracovia, Pierre du Mont de St. Michel and other Gallicans (Hübler, p. 366, 370–372, 377, also p. 121 N. 8); Gerson, Trilogus, Conclus. per stud. Bonon. of 1409 (Hübler, p. 373); Theod. de Niem, De schism., III. c. 20 (resistance, as against a "bestia"); Randuf, c. 9–10; Ant. Ros., II. c. 23, 27–30, III. c. 4–6; and Nic. Cus., even after his change of party (Op. II. p. 825–829).

33. Mohl, I. p. 323, rightly remarks that in the middle ages the idea of a right of armed resistance often materialized in flesh and blood, but the idea of unconditional obedience never.

34. This is the essence of the doctrine that the lack of a "iusta causa" for any invasion of vested rights by the sovereign may be supplied by a deliberate ("ex certa scientia") or express use of his "plenitudo potestatis" (such as is manifested by the clause "lege non obstante"). This doctrine, which first appears in a rude form in Durantis, Spec., I., tit. interdicta leg. et sedi Apost. reserv., nr. 89 (see Meyer, p. 101), is attacked by the jurists cited above, Note 13 (but see the concessions made in Jason, Cons. II. c. 233: "imperator, in quo adest potestatis plenitudo, si aliquid vult ex certa scientia, nemo potest dicere, cur ita facis," also c. 236 nr. 12–13, and IV. c. 107 nr. 4). On the other hand it is defended more or less by the jurists cited in Note 14; see in particular Alber. Rosc., loc. cit. (where practically all difference between positive and natural law disappears and the same formal omnipotence is expressly claimed for rescripts as for acts of legislation); Baldus, loc. cit.; Felinus, loc. cit. nr. 60–66 (despite nr. 45–52); Riminald., Cons. I. c. 73; Capra, Reg. 10 nr. 48–52, 56–59; Decius on c. 7 X. 1, 2 nr. 27–28, Cons. 198 nr. 7, 269 nr. 4–5, 271 nr. 3, 640 nr. 6–7, and especially 588 nr. 1–14; also Aen. Sylv., c. 16–17.

35. Thus Hugh of Fleury teaches that men should suffer and pray for tyrants, but should refuse obedience to commands contrary to Divine Law and should suffer punishment and death in the spirit of martyrs; I. c. 4 p. 17–22, c. 7 p. 31, c. 12 p. 44, II. p. 66. Compare Baldus on l. 5 Dig. 1, 1 nr. 6–7.

36. Already Joh. Saresb., IV. c. 1, 2 and 4, says that the princeps remains "legi iustitiae subiectus" and "aequitatis servus," as the "aequitas et iustitia," of which the "lex" is "interpres," should govern his will. Then in Thom. Aquin., II. p. 553 a. 3, there comes to the front the formula that the princeps, even so far as he is not subject to any "vis coactiva" of the law, is yet bound "quantum ad vim directivam"; compare ib. p. 332, and 352 q. 96 a. 4, teaching that unrightful laws (such as those which are "ultra sibi commissam potestatem," which impose unjust taxes or unjust distributions of burdens, or anything "contra commune bonum") are not binding in the forum of conscience. Also Ptol. Luc., IV. c. 1; Ockham, Dial. III. tr. 2, l. 2, c. 28; Gerson, IV. p. 583 ff., especially p. 601, also p. 671.—The purely ethical obligation of the ruler was a keynote of the writings of medieval publicists, who took much pains in preparing Instructions for the Virtuous Prince.

37. Of the unanimity which prevailed in this point no proof is needed; this limitation of obedience is always treated as a matter of jurisprudence, and is deduced from the nature of divine and natural Law ("ius").

38. See for example Gl. Ord. (above, Note 20); Baldus, loc. cit.; Jason, Cons., II. c. 233 nr. 9, III. c. 24 nr. 21, IV. c. 166 nr. 9; Franciscus Aretinus, Cons. 15 nr. 9; Franc. Curtius senior, Cons. 20, 49, 50; Dom. Gem., Cons., 99 nr. 7–8 and 104 nr. 4; Decius, Cons., 292 nr. 3 and 9, 373 nr. 10, 606 nr. 17. Besides fictions that the sovereign's act had been induced by "subreptio," "circumventio" and the like.

39. For the benefit of the omnipotent Council, Randuf teaches that, if the welfare of the Church requires it, the Council may dispense with the moral law; see c. 6, 16, 20 and 22 (in Gerson, Op. II. p. 170, 182, 188, 190); to the contrary, Gerson, IV. p. 671.

40. See above, Ch. I. Note 44; also Zasius (below, Note 42); Salamonius (below, Note 49); Junius Brutus, q. III. p. 184 ff. ("certe justum est, quicquid Deus vult, eo tamen quia vult; at quicquid Rex vult, justum prius esse debet, quam ipse velit; neque enim quid justum est, quia Rex sanxit, sed justus est Rex, qui, quae per se justa sunt, sancta esse jubet"); and to some extent Huber, I. 1 c. 1 and 7 (there is a Right without a Superior and without Might).

41. See above, Ch. I. Note 44. The strictest identification of the concepts of "law" and "command" was made by Hobbes, De cive, c. 14, Lev., c. 24–26. But as regards positive law Pufendorf and his whole school agree with

him; Pufendorf says expressly: "nam ut aliquid in Civitate effectus juris civilis habeat, in solo arbitrio summae potestatis situm est"; see Elem., I. def. 12 § 6, De jure N. et G., VIII. c. 1, De off., II. c. 12; also Thomasius, Inst. jur. div., I. c. 1 § 114 ff., Fund. jur. nat., I. c. 5 § 11 ff. In like manner the later doctrine of popular sovereignty bases the law on the general will, not on the general conviction.

42. Zasius, Lect. on l. 31 Dig. 1, 3 nr. 1–12, Paratitl. Dig. 1, 4 nr. 9–10, Cons., II. c. 10 nr. 8 ff.

43. Cujacius, Op., X. p. 789–790, 1022, also III. p. 417, VII. p. 1162 and IX. p. 667.

44. Donellus, Comm., I. c. 13 (Op. I. p. 147); he adds that, even under the theory which identifies the law with the will of the ruler, the voluntary self-binding of the ruler (which according to his opponents was effected in the Lex Digna) remains positive law until abrogated. [The Lex Digna (l. 4 Cod. 1, 14) says: "Digna vox maiestate regnantis legibus alligatum se principem profiteri."] See further Connanus, I. c. 8 nr. 3 (Princeps legibus tenetur).

45. Paragraphi "potestas soluta" tractatus; the absolutist theory is explained in c. 2 and confuted in c. 3, then (ib. nr. 30 ff.) his own principle is developed: the Princeps is "solutus" only in so far as he can alter the statutes and is dispensed from 'solemnities'; otherwise the lex is binding even on him.

46. Such as Benekendorff, Repetitio et explicatio de regulis juris, Frankfort-on-the-Oder 1593, p. 221 ff.; and Hartwig von Dassell, Consultationes decisivac, Bremen 1618 (1st ed. 1605), I. cons. 1; both agreeing fully with Pruckmann. Also Reusner, Consilia s. responsa, Frankfort 1601, I. cons. 1; Meisner, IV. s. 1 q. 10; Contzen, V. c. 20; Speckhan, Opera, Frankfort 1695, I. q. 72 p. 86 (the maxim "Princeps legibus solutus" extends only to 'solemnities' and to the legislative power, which latter is indeed bounded only by the "leges naturae, justiciae et honestatis").

47. The theory appears in Soto, Covarruvias, Gregory of Valencia; in A. Fachinaeus (d. 1597), Controversiarum juris libri XIII, Cologne 1678, I. c. 2; and most completely in Suarez, III. c. 34. Suarez teaches that in State and Church the lawgiver is bound by his own laws, for the reason that, acting as "Dei minister" and "pro tota communitate cujus est pars," he sets up a "regula virtutis" which is deduced from the jus naturale by reason and which holds also for himself by "naturalis ratio"; the argument for his subjection from a presumed clause in the contract of rulership is false, for such a clause is unnecessary and a contrary clause would be void. Yet the law binds the lawgiver only "quoad vim directivam," for the "vis coactiva" (apart from divine punishment) ceases to exist when there is no superior. As to the "vis irritativa" one must distinguish whether nullification has the nature of a

punishment or merely the nature of a legal consequence; in the latter case it
affects the sovereign himself, in the former case not. The Roman maxim
"Princeps legibus solutus" extends by no means only to the exemption from
'solemnities,' but even to the extinction of vis coactiva. Similarly Contzen,
loc. cit.; Claudius de Carnin, I. c. 4 and III. c. 1 (as the law is the imperium
rationis, mens non voluntas, God's work through men, it binds the lawgiver
also; but the sovereign who breaks it suffers only "culpa," not "poena");
Christ. Haunold (a Jesuit, d. 1690), Controversiae de justitia et jure
privatorum, Ingolstadt 1671–1674, Tract. I. c. 1, controv. 6 § 1; Schmier,
III. c. 2 nr. 31–34, and V. c. 2 (true obligations of the sovereign toward
his subjects, but no enforcement by legal action, violence, deposition or
the like).—Likewise even Meisner, loc. cit.; Velstenius, VIII. nr. 6;
Strauch, Diss. acad. (1729), nr. 3 § 37 ff.; Stryk, Diss., XIV, nr. 7 c. 3;
and many others.

48. See above, Ch. III. Note 66; Vasquez, c. 45 (leges civiles bind the
Princeps "civiliter," not merely "naturaliter"), and c. 8; Alstedius, p. 19;
Hoenonius, I. § 17, IX. § 6–15.

49. See above, Ch. II. Note 44. Above all Salamonius, whose special
theme in his De Principatu is the proof that the Prince is bound not only
by "leges divinae et naturales" and "leges ab universo populo scriptae" but
also by "suae leges," supports this proposition not only with arguments drawn
from popular sovereignty, but also with the full demonstration that while
the sovereign populus itself can repeal its own laws, yet until then it is
bound by them; for the people's law is in form a contractual self-binding
of all, but receives its imperative force from God and Reason; and it is
wrong to say that "qui legibus suis obediunt sibi ipsis obediunt," as on the
contrary "imperio rationis obeditur, quae a Deo est." Compare Victoria,
III. nr. 21. Casmannus, c. 10 (the populus itself had no absolute power
which it could transfer). See the observation of Ranke, p. 244 ff., that for
the first time under Charles I the English Parliament was unwilling to be
bound by the existing laws.

50. See above, p. 75–76, 97, 161; likewise Hoenonius, IX. § 5.

51. See above, Ch. III. Note 126, and p. 165–166; Otto, An Princeps
Legibus solutus, in Arumaeus, II. nr. 14, De jure publ. Imp. Rom., c. 12;
Arumaeus, De sensu legis Princeps, ib., I. nr. 8, also I. nr. 7 and IV. nr. 1–3;
Bortius, ib., I. nr. 30 c. 6–7 (on account of the merely 'directive' force of
leges civiles over the Princeps he holds to the attribute of "legibus solutus"
for him; see above, Ch. III. Notes 135–136); Hilliger, ib., II. nr. 13 c. 8;
Brautlacht, Epitome, III. c. 1; Cubach, Centuriae quaestionum, I. 3 q. 1 ff.

52. Thus Besold argues that while the leges fundamentales, being the
basis of the whole sovereignty of the ruler, are also its limits, yet otherwise

the ruling Princeps, Senatus or Populus, so far as supreme, must also be regarded as legibus solutus; at the same time two component parts of sovereignty must be distinguished: the "ordinaria potestas majestatis" stands below the laws as a mere "executrix legum," while the "extraordinaria potestas majestatis" (plenitudo potestatis) has as "nomothetica" no other bounds than the salus publica or the so-called "ragione di Stato" of the Italians, and hence can override the laws; see Diss. de maj., s. 1 c. 1 § 5–6, c. 7 § 2–9.—See further Carpzov, Comm. ad leg. Reg., c. 12, also c. 1 s. 3–7, c. 3, c. 13 s. 2.

53. Thus Paurmeister, I. c. 19 nr. 1–5, opines that the Respublica is not bound by any law and thus, for example, transfers "sola voluntate imperium et jurisdictionem"; on the other hand for him the Emperor is "non solutus legibus," excepting the Lex Iulia et Papia Poppaea (ib. nr. 6 ff.).—Bortius, loc. cit. c. 6, says that the "majestas Regni" is limited only by the Divine Law.—When Besold and Tulden place the 'subject' of majestas realis above the constitution, it should be noted that they ascribe the majestas realis only to the sum of the concurrent 'active' citizens (or else their representatives); see above, Ch. III. Note 131.

54. Bodin, I. c. 8 nr. 82 ff.: without potestas legibus soluta there is a mere "Principatus," and then the sovereign is the "universitas populi," which itself is in this case legibus soluta. See above, p. 158–159.

55. Thus Greg. Thol., VII. c. 20 § 1–55; Barclaius, III. c. 14–15 and IV. c. 12; Arnisaeus, De jure maj., I. c. 3 and 6; Valentinus Riemer, Decades XV quaest. jurid. illustr., Jena 1617, dec. I. q. 7; Schoenborner, III. c. 5; Faber, Jurisprud. Papin., I. 2 princ. 8 ill. 2, Rationalia ad Pand., l. 31 Dig. 1, 3; Salmasius, c. 2 and 7; Brunnemann on l. 1 pr. Dig., 1, 4.

56. Thus Treutler, op. cit., I. d. 1 q. 35; Graswinckel, c. 4 (majestas cannot by its very nature be bound by any "vis externa," whether "coactiva" or "directiva," and hence is not bound by any lex), c. 6 ("supra leges," even fundamentales), and c. 12; Horn, II. c. 2 § 10–11 (differently in III. c. un. § 4, in the case of a Republic); Boehmer, P. spec., II. c. 3 § 38.

57. See above, p. 158–159, and all the writers mentioned in Note 55 of this chapter; also "Hippolithus a Lapide," I. c. 4–6, who for this reason not only deprives the Emperor of sovereignty but also gives to the "ordines universi ut corpus," being "omnibus et etiam fundamentalibus legibus soluti," the right to abolish the Empire, to annul the rights of the Electoral Princes, and so on.

58. See above, p. 169; also Spinoza, Tract. theol.-pol., c. 16 ("summam potestatem nulla lege teneri"), and Tract. pol., c. 4 § 1–3 and 6 (the sovereign may violate all laws whenever "communis salutis interest easdem violare"); Cellarius, above, Ch. III. Note 164.

59. Graswinckel, c. 12, and Salmasius, c. 7, admit at least that an oath to observe the constitution is binding in conscience; Horn says that leges fundamentales are no more than "pacta" which are morally obligatory but which may be broken for the sake of salus publica (II. c. 10 § 4 ff., and see above, Ch. III. Note 163); similarly Bossuet, IV. a. 1 and VIII. a. 2; Fénelon, ch. V., and XI. p. 183 (violation is accountable to God alone); Boecler, II. c. 1 p. 106 ff. (remarking that in the last resort the "Popularen" cannot punish the "populus peccans" itself but must appeal to God).

60. See especially the argumentation in Besold, Diss. de maj., s. 1 c. 1 § 5–6 ("nil potest Princeps utcunque summus contra Reipublicae constitutionem: pariter ut homo seipsum interficere seu destruere nequit"; his potestas is "absoluta," but only as based on the constitution); c. 7 § 8–9 (he is exempt only from leges civiles, not from the jus naturale or the jus gentium primaevum; and hence he is not exempt from the "leges fundamentales Status," such as exist in Würtemberg, as these are really contracts and the binding force of contracts is derived from the "jus gentium primaevum"); also the elaboration of the idea of the Constitutional State in the dissertations on the several forms of State. Similarly Reinking, De reg., I. cl. 3 c. 12 (free from "leges mere civiles et positivae," bound by the "leges fundamentales regni," which as "conventiones" are obligatory under the jus gentium); Carpzov, loc. cit. c. 12; Bornitius, De maj., c. 8–10, Partit., p. 42; ab Andler, p. 60 ff.; "Waremund de Erenbergk," above, Ch. III. Note 89; Keckermann, I. c. 6 (above, Ch. III. Note 96); Fridenreich, Buxtorff and Knichen, above, Ch. III. Note 93; Felwinger, De maj., § 27 ff.; Vitriarius, I. 7 § 4, and Pfeffinger, ad h. § N. a.

61. This is the underlying thought in the reasonings of Grotius, II. c. 14 § 1–2, wherein it is but consistent when the king receives the power (as king) to dispense himself (as a private person) from positive laws even in the case of "privati actus"; likewise it is said, ib. § 6, that from contracts "cum subditis" there always arises for the king a true and strict obligation, which comes under the "civiles leges" only in the case of contracts made by the king in his private capacity, and under mere natural law in the case of contracts made by the king as king; see also as to the effect of constitutional limitations, above, p. 168.

62. Pufendorf follows throughout the idea that the persona moralis composita is no more able to bind itself by its own "leges et decreta" than can the persona moralis simplex, but only binds its own members thereby; that on the other hand true obligations arise from contracts in all cases, and hence for the originally sovereign individuals from the contract of union, for the subsequently sovereign ruler (Princeps or Civitas) from international contracts, from constitutional contracts and other contracts with his sub-

jects; see especially Elem., I. def. 12 § 17–18, De jure N. et G., VII. c. 5 § 8, VIII. c. 1, De off., II. c. 12. These principles are commonly repeated; see especially Thomasius, Inst. jur. div., I. c. 1 § 128 ff., and Fund. jur. nat., I. c. 5 § 11 ff.; Gundling, Jus nat., c. 1 § 15 ff., c. 12 § 43 ff., Mevius, Alberti and Micraelius, above, Ch. III. Note 169; Kreittmayr, I. § 5, 31 and 32; but most precisely in Boehmer, P. spec., II. c. 3 § 38 (the ruler is altogether free from leges civiles, "directive" as well as "co-active"), and I. c. 5 § 31–36 ("pacta inita cum subditis" bind him "ex lege naturae").

63. See above, p. 172–173, and the passages cited in preceding Note. For this reason Pufendorf, Thomasius, Boehmer and most of the others describe the contractual obligation of the sovereign as an "obligatio imperfecta," which in case of breach gives no right of coercive redress, legal accusation, resistance or the like; and Boehmer argues consistently that, as even a "jus annullandi" against the sovereign would presuppose an equal or higher power, the contingent nullity under the constitution cannot take practical effect until his successor comes to the throne (P. spec., I. c. 4 § 21, and c. 5 § 31–36).

64. See my Genossenschaftsrecht, I. § 60, especially p. 814–815; and above all Ickstatt, Vindiciae territorialis potestatis adversus capitulationum, compactatorum et literarum abusus, Munich and Ingolstadt 1759; also Kreittmayr, § 31 (the constitution is 'not lightly' to be broken).

65. Thus already v. Seckendorf, Teut. Fürstenstaat, pref. and II. c. 4, c. 7 § 12 (against cloaking illegality under the plea of "Stat, ratione status oder Statssachen"); then above all J. J. Moser, in the passages cited in my Genossenschaftsr., I. p. 815 Notes 41–42; also F. K. v. Moser, Der Herr und der Diener, especially p. 66 and 101 ff.

66. See above, Ch. II. Note 45, and p. 163–164 on the English doctrine; also Note 53 of this Chapter.

67. See above, p. 97–98, 109, 182. Among those teachers of Natural Law who were filled with Rousseau's spirit, Fichte sought to build a sort of Constitutional State in which it is only under certain fixed presuppositions, with whose admission the representation by the ruler ceases, that the people itself becomes a 'Community' and sovereign (Werke, III. p. 161 ff.): but materially it stands above all constitutional law (ib., p. 173 ff., 182 ff., VI. p. 103 ff. and 238 ff.).

68. For Locke the people is ultimately superior to the constitution and is bound only by the inalienable rights of the individual, but yet the legislative power is limited by the constitution, so that for example it can validly act only according to prescribed forms and cannot delegate its authority (II. c. 11 § 136–141). Montesquieu and his followers, in treating of the

division of powers, lay chief stress on the constitutional checking of these powers by one another, without further discussion of the legal limitations of the State-power in general. All the more fully was this question treated by the eighteenth-century German school of Natural Law, which came more and more to agree that the sovereign power is exempt from its own laws, but is 'coactively' bound by the natural and written constitution, from whose breach there arises a right to resist and coerce the sovereign by Natural Law; thus Wolff (above, Ch. III. Note 187); Achenwall, II. § 34–35 and 98 ff., especially § 109 ("finis" and "pacta fundamentalia" as "limites" of majestas); Nettelbladt, § 1134 ff. (arguing most emphatically that the natural and the positive law of the constitution are the limits of all power); Daries, § 780–789 (limites naturales and pactitii); Scheidemantel, III. p. 172–375 ('natural' and 'arbitrary' fundamental laws are the limits of majesty; right of resistance in case of their transgression), also I. p. 116, II. p. 360 ff.; Schlözer, p. 17 ff., 93 ff., 96 § 2, 101 § 6, 105 ff., 107 § 9. —On the other hand in Kant the idea of the Constitutional State takes a much weaker form by the exclusion of all right of resistance.

69. In the essentials there is agreement at this point among the authors cited above, Notes 42–51, despite many differences of opinion as to details and differences in principle as to the consequences of an unjust invasion of jura quaesita. Above all there stands the doctrine of Zasius; he takes as his leading principle, "Princeps non potest auferre mihi rem meam, sive jure gentium sive civili sit facta mea" (Lect. on l. 31 Dig. 1, 3 nr. 13 ff., Cons., VI. c. 10, Lect. on l. 23 Dig. 41, 2). Then he admits exceptions (such as moratoria, restitutiones, "jus nondum perfecta quaesitum," prizes of war and so on, and especially "necessitas publica"), but inveighs against the Italian doctrine that in the use of the plenitudo potestatis a "justa causa" is to be presumed, holding on the contrary that such a cause must in each case "manifeste apparere" and that such a presumption is admitted, at most, in the case of revocation of privileges granted by the Princeps himself (Lect. on l. 31 Dig. 1, 3 nr. 18–25). Lastly, he leaves the question, whether an exception is well-founded, to the judge, who in the negative case must treat an act of the ruler as void even when clothed in the form of law: "Quapropter, si princeps noceret tollendo mea jura, hoc non valeret causa non apparente, etiamsi hoc per modum legis, decreti aut statuti fieret,— contra doctrinam Baldi in l. 2 Cod. de legib.—; et ita servat nostra Germania integritates legis; et vidi ita judicari in consistorio principis contra principem, secure quo pacto adulentur Itali vel alii principibus" (ib. nr. 26). —See further Vasquez, I. c. 5 nr. 15 ff.; Pruckmann, p. 78 ff. (deprivation of jura quaesita must without any exception be "ex justa causa publicae utilitatis" and for a "justum pretium"), and p. 90 ff. (contracts are binding

without any exception); Benekendorff, p. 221 ff., 275 ff., 283 ff.; Hunnius, Variarum resol. jur. civ. libri IV, Frankfort 1646, II. 1 q. 2–3.—In general Gabrielius, Comm. concl., III. concl. 1–8, p. 303–318, in the extensive essay "de jure quaesito non tollendo," describes such views as correct and as the "communis opinio"; in particular he disapproves of replacing "causa" by a decree "de plenitudine potestatis et ex certa scientia" or by the statutory form of an act of expropriation (p. 304), requires compensation in all cases (p. 310), and holds that contracts are unconditionally binding (p. 310 ff.); yet in the case of a "simplex privilegium" he allows simple revocation (p. 315). Similarly Fachinaeus, VIII. c. 63 and XI. c. 2, though emphasizing the formal omnipotence of the sovereign. See also Trentacinquius, I. p. 25 ff., 82 ff., 35 ff. (contracts bind the sovereign "civiliter," not merely "naturaliter").

70. See Mynsinger, Cent., V. obs. 97, where at all points a distinction is drawn between rights acquired by "jus divinum, naturae vel gentium" and rights acquired by mere "jus civile vel positivum," and for abrogations of the latter, whenever the Princeps acts "proprio motu" a just cause is presumed; Gail, Practic. observ., II. obs. 56 nr. 1–18 (compensation is abolished by use of potestas absoluta); Borcholten, Consil., I. p. 3, 78 ff., 112; Meichsner, I. dec. 32 nr. 18–19; Nic. Everhardus, Cons. 58 nr. 39 ff.; Restaurus Caldus, De imperatore, q. 97 and 98; Peregrinus, 1. 3 nr. 16–19 and 62–69 (the sovereign can dissolve contracts and "dominium auferre" only ex causa, but can revoke privileges at any time by virtue of his plenitudo); Zoannettus, nr. 159–160.

71. Bodin, I. c. 8 nr. 99–106, and II. c. 3–4 (above, p. 159), where it is expressly stated that pacta with subditi as well as with exteri are perfectly (not merely "naturaliter") binding on the sovereign, and that "sine justa causa" no man can be deprived of what is his own. Greg. Thol., VII. c. 20. Besold, Diss. de maj., s. 1, c. 7 § 5–17 and c. 8. Reinking, loc. cit. Arnisaeus, De jure maj., I. c. 3 and III. c. 1–2.

72. Hobbes, De cive, c. 6 (see especially § 15: "nemini proprium esse quicquam contra illum, qui habet summum imperium"), c. 7 and 12, Lev., c. 18–19; the sovereign therefore can do no injustice to his subjects and is not obligated to them by any covenants. Likewise Spinoza, Houtuynus, and in this point Horn (see especially II. c. 4 § 15–20: as private ownership and other jura quaesita spring from the State, so also they may be revoked at any time "pro lubitu" and without compensation).

73. Pufendorf, De jure N. et G., VII. c. 8–9, VIII. c. 1 and 5, also IV. c. 4, De off., II. c. 11–12 (even the relations of civil law create for the ruler only an "obligatio imperfecta"; he may validly retract, though "peccans contra legem naturae," any promise; it is only from "aequitas"

that he concedes legal process against himself; against him every jus quaesitum is but a "jus imperfectum"). Thomasius, Inst. jur. div., I. c. 1 § 103–113 and 127 (always a mere "obligatio imperfecta" of the superior toward the inferior; if he allows a legal action against himself, this is such only "improprie" and "certe non coactiva"; jura quaesita yield in all cases to the "jus eminens"). Gundling, c. 1 § 51 ff. and c. 12 § 43 ff. Boehmer, P. spec. I. c. 5: "quoad externum effectum" the imperans is omnipotent and (there being no judge, no right of resistance, and no right of coercion or cassation) all limitations are ineffectual; "quoad facultatem legitimam" he has limits, so that in a breach of contract or arbitrary injury to the rights of the subjects he acts "injuste," though he is always but "imperfecte" obligated. Schmier, II. c. 4 s. 1 § 1–2, and V. c. 2.—In like manner Bossuet, VIII. a. 2, and Fénelon, ch. XI. p. 183.

74. Grotius allows the expropriation of any jus quaesitum (apart from punishment), but only by the dominium eminens, on grounds of publica utilitas and for compensation (compensatio ex communi), and expressly says that it makes no difference whether the right is vested ex jure naturali or civili; in both cases it is equally expropriable but also equally protected, as the inviolability of lawfully established rights is itself a rule of Natural Law; see II. c. 14 § 7–9, and likewise as to the surrender of rights of subjects in treaties of peace, III. c. 20 § 7–10. Here it should be noted that Grotius derives the force of all positive law from a tacit or express promise, and therefore says that this force is grounded in Natural Law (Proleg. nr. 6–17); that in like manner he bases property upon contract (I. c. 1 § 6); that as a result he does more to overcome the duality of natural and positive law than any later teacher of natural law until Kant.—Grotius is followed in essentials by Schmier, III. c. 3, who says likewise that every jus quaesitum is inviolable by virtue of Natural Law as continued in the State, and may be withdrawn only on grounds of necessitas vel utilitas publica and for compensation.

75. The tracing of the protection of vested rights back to the categories of property and contract, and to their roots in Divine and Natural Law binding on the sovereign, appears in full precision in Bodin, and also Gregorius, Besold, Reinking and Arnisaeus (see above, Note 71); similarly in Bossuet, VIII. a. 2, and Fénelon, ch. XI.; as well as in Pufendorf and his whole school.—For a different treatment of 'privileges' see Pfeffinger, III. 17 p. 1249; Boehmer, P. spec., II. c. 3 § 62–64.

76. For the history of the lore of dominium eminens see especially Stein, Verwaltungslehre, VII. p. 164 ff.; also Meyer, p. 119 ff.

77. Thus it was that "dominium eminens" (which in Grotius was essentially the same as the right of expropriation) was enlarged by his fol-

lowers (especially Crusius, Horn, Pufendorf, Conring, Wolff) to an ever wider concept, which comprised all the powers ascribed to the State as such over the realm of Things (including legislation in matters of private law, taxation, control by police-power and the like) and yet fell under the same generic concept with private ownership. From this came on the one hand the resolution of dominium eminens into a definite element of "imperium" in pure public law (as in Wolff by co-ordinating "potestas eminens" and "jus eminens"; then by reserving the term for the special case of the right of expropriation, as in Boehmer, Heineccius, Nettelbladt and others; and lastly by rejecting the whole expression, as in Rave, Pütter, J. J. Moser, Daries, Achenwall, Posse and others). On the other hand there was an attempt to derive the whole power of the State from its true ownership of the land (Biener and his school).

78. See above, Notes 60–62.

79. Already in Bodin we see the conjunction of liberty and property as fundamental rights of the individual; see II. c. 3–4: the "Monarchia regalis" recognizes "libertas et rerum dominia" in the subditi, while Tyranny suppresses them. And likewise among the Monarchomachi (above, Ch. III. Note 66). In later days the polemic against dominium eminens rested on the view that the right of private property was not produced (as common opinion supposed) by parcellation from an original community of goods nor even by a grant from the State, but was vested as a special right by Divine and Natural Law before any societies were formed; thus Strauch, W. Leyser (see the analysis of his work De proprietate rerum, 1658, in Meyer, p. 125 ff.), Alberti, c. 7 § 19, and others. But Locke stated in epoch-making fashion the view that property is an outgrowth of personality under Natural Law and is prior to the State, and that it is entrusted by the individual to society merely for protection (see above, Ch. II. Notes 82 and 100). This view was not only accepted in England but also penetrated more and more into continental doctrine. See even Bossuet, VIII. a. 2 (liberté and propriété are protected by the lois fondamentales); Fénelon, ch. XI. ("droit de personne" and "droit de propriété"); Voltaire (1765: "Liberty and property . . . c'est le cri anglais' . . . c'est le cri de la nature"); Montesquieu, XXV. c. 15; Sieyès (above, Ch. II. Note 113), and the French 'Declaration of the Rights of Man,' 1791, art. 17; Kant (above, Ch. II. Note 121).

80. See above, p. 313–314.

81. See above, Ch. II. Note 49, and p. 100 ff.

82. Oldendorp, op. cit., regards all jus civile as an elaboration of the Natural Law which is taught by reason or revelation; Hemming, De lege naturae apodictica methodus, Wittenberg 1562, stands already on the ground of the absolute Law of Reason; Winkler, op. cit., strongly asserts

the continuance of Natural Law in the State and the ultimate oneness of all law (II. c. 9–10, V. c. 1 ff.). No less strongly do the Catholic teachers of natural law emphasize Divine and Natural Law as the norm and limit of all legislation and its principles as immutable and valid even in the State; see Soto, I. q. 5 and IV. q. 3 a. 1; Vasquez, c. 27, also c. 10, 20, 54; Bolognetus, c. 7 and 12; Lessius, II. c. 2 and 5; Connanus, I. c. 1–7 and 10; Gregorius de Valentia, II. disp. 1 q. 4–5; Molina, V. d. 47–69; Suarez, lib. I.–II. Gregorius de Valentia, Vasquez and others say (just like Grotius, I. c. 1 § 10) that Natural Law is immutable even for God Himself; Soto and others hold that the introduction of lordship and property in place of liberty and community of goods rests upon a change of conditions, not of principles.—For this reason men are also agreed not only that somewhat of the original liberty and equality still lives imperishably in the State, but that certain vestiges and after-effects of the 'Nature-Right' community of goods necessarily restrict the civil institution of property. See the expressions of medieval doctrine and of Mariana collected in Brentano, Die Arbeitsversicherung, Leipzig 1879, p. 250–259; also Molina, II. d. 20 § 13–14 (community of goods is not only a norm for congregations striving for perfection, but besides this "bona temporalia communia debent esse omnibus quoad usum tempore extremae aut pene extremae necessitatis"). Then in Grotius this gave rise to the doctrine that the original community of goods still continues not only with regard to the ocean and other things not exhausted by use, but also with regard to the use of property "in gravissima necessitate," or without involving detriment to the owner ("utilitas innoxia"), and with regard to freedom of traffic and intercourse ("jus commune ad actus"); see II. c. 2 § 3 ff. In this form the doctrine passed into the later systems, as in Wolff, Inst., § 300 ff.; Nettelbladt, § 471 ff.

83. Here it is sufficient to note that on the one hand the advocates of popular sovereignty agree in subjecting the sovereign people itself to the jus divinum, naturale et gentium, and on the other hand Bodin (see I. c. 8 and II. c. 4), and all who with him strictly maintain the ruler's "potestas legibus soluta," expressly fix the same legal limits of sovereignty (see Greg. Thol., VII. c. 20; Arnisaeus, De jure maj., I. c. 3; Reinking, loc. cit.; Besold, Diss. de maj., s. 1 c. 7 § 8; Treutler, I. d. 1 q. 35; Schoenborner, III. c. 35; Felwinger, De maj., § 27 ff.; Bornitius, De maj., c. 8–10; Carpzov, op. cit. c. 12).

84. In this connection it should be noted that Arumaeus and his pupils, while ascribing a "vis coactiva" to the fundamental laws, expressly concede to divine and natural laws only the same "vis directiva" as in the case of civil laws; see all the passages cited above, Note 51.

85. As in Riemer, Dec., I. q. 7: "Princeps omnibus omnino legibus est solutus"; even the jus naturae binds him not as lex but only in conscience. Similarly Graswinckel and Salmasius (above, Note 59).

86. For the literature on Machiavelli see v. Mohl, III. p. 519 ff.

87. Thus in Germany Besold, Diss. de maj., s. 1 c. 7 § 5–7; then especially "Hippolithus a Lapide," who in the preface to his work (otherwise holding strictly to the idea of "ratio status") asserts against Machiavelli that Divine and Natural Law must never be broken for the sake of any "publica utilitas"; also Conring, Diss. de ratione status, 1651; Godofr. v. Jena, Collegium juris publici, Frankfort-on-the-Oder 1658 (24 dissertations "de ratione status").

88. Here belong also, in part, the writings on "arcana Reipublicae" (such as Clapmarus and Obrecht in Germany).—Conversely the literature of 'Mirrors of Princes' (in Germany for example Tympe, Aureum speculum principum, Cologne 1617; Fritsch, Princeps peccans, Jena 1677; Im-Hof, Seckendorf and others), with its emphasis on the ethical limitations of the sovereign, must at the same time promote the idea of legal limitations.

89. See for example Reinking, Biblische Polizei, II. ax. 36 ff.: rescue of Justitia from 'her wicked stepsister named Ratio Status'; Holy Scripture is the best Ratio Status. Seckendorf (above, Note 65). Pfeffinger, III. 17 p. 1249 (mere ratio Status does not, as the "Statistae" would have it, suffice for the revocation of privileges).

90. See above, Ch. II. Notes 81 and 92, and p. 169; also the definition of liberty, Lev., c. 21: "The liberty of a subject lieth therefore only in those things, which in regulating their actions, the Sovereign hath praetermitted."

91. Spinoza himself insists that in opposition to Hobbes he makes natural law continue in the State and for the State; yet his natural law is not a law but a rational self-limitation of power; see Tract. theol.-pol., c. 16, 17, 20, Tract. pol., c. 3 § 4–7 and 9, c. 4 § 1 and 4, c. 5 § 1–7. Likewise in Rousseau the limits of the sovereign power (II. c. 4) are not true legal limitations (see above, Ch. II. Note 107).—Here we must also place the doctrine of the French Physiocrats and their German followers, for when they limit the sovereign by the "évidence" of "lois naturelles" what they mean by this is the laws of physical nature rather than the rules of 'Natural Law'; see Janet, II. p. 684 ff.; Roscher, p. 480 ff.—Purely Machiavellian is Gabriel Naudé, Considérations politiques sur les Coups d'État, 1712.

92. See above, p. 106 ff.

93. See Pufendorf, Elem., I. def. 12 § 6, De jure N. et G., VII. c. 8–9, VIII. c. 1, De off., II. c. 9 and 12.

94. This division was made especially by Thomasius, Fund. jur. nat., lib. I.; at the same time he separated more sharply than any one before him the concepts of 'objective' and 'subjective' natural law (as well as objective and subjective law in general), see Inst. jur. div., I. c. 1 § 82 ff. and 134 ff.; he declared that objective as well as subjective natural law is prior to the State and is a legal limitation of the sovereign, ib. § 114 ff. and 128 ff., Fund. jur. nat., I. c. 5 § 11 ff.; yet while at first he had asserted an "obligatio externa" of the sovereign by Natural Law (Inst. jur. div., I. c. 1 § 78), later he only assumed an "obligatio interna" (Fund. jur. nat., I. c. 5).—Boehmer stated most precisely the ideas of this whole school; see P. gen., c. 1 ("lex naturae" and "jus naturae"), c. 2 § 8 ff. (both are continued in the State and bind the sovereign), c. 3 (even the "jus publicum naturale" is true law, and differs from Politics in that the latter governs the relations between ruler and subjects "ratione utilis" and the former "ratione justi"); P. spec., I. c. 2 § 20 ff. ("obligatio imperfecta" of the sovereign), ib. c. 5 (omnipotence of the sovereign "quoad externum effectum," but subjection to Natural Law "quoad facultatem legitimam").—Similarly Hert, Comm. et Opusc., I. 1 p. 91 ff. and p. 292 § 6; Schmier, III. c. 3; also Gundling, c. 1, though he supposes an "obligatio externa et perfecta" of Natural Law, whose violation is followed by Nature's penalty.

95. See Pufendorf, De jure N. et G., VII. c. 9, De off., II. c. 11; Boehmer, P. spec., I. c. 5 § 20–30; Stryk, Diss. III. nr. 16; Kreittmayr, Grundriss, § 1 and 32, also Anmerkungen, I. c. 2 § 6, nr. 2 and 5.—And see even Arnisaeus, De jure maj., III. c. 1–2; also Besold, Diss. de maj., s. 1 c. 7 § 5–7, who however says elsewhere that the "salus publica" is but the remoter purpose of the State while "justitia" is the proximate purpose (Diss. praecogn., c. 4 § 1–2).

96. Thus Cumberland in his work written against Hobbes (1672); thus the systems of Natural Law, based more or less on theology and contending against Pufendorf and Thomasius, of Alberti (1678), Praschius (1688), Placcius (1695), Mueldener (1692; see Hinrichs, III. p. 311 ff.), O. H. Becker (Jus mundi seu vindiciae juris naturae, 1690), Mevius, the two Cocceji and others; thus Leibniz against Pufendorf (above, Ch. I. Note 44); thus J. G. Wachter (1704) with his attempt to construct Natural Law by a mathematical method from the nature of man; thus Strauch, Opuscula, nr. 16 (against Hobbes and Pufendorf); thus lastly Wolff and all his followers.

97. As in Mevius, Prodromus, III. § 13 and VI. § 1 ff.: Natural Law is prior to the State, is immutable for it as for God Himself and binds the lawgiver; but no subject can appeal to it against the State-power, as men have subjected everything, even their natural rights, to the ruler.—In Horn,

II. c. 2 § 10–11, it is quite doubtful whether Divine and Natural Law are taken as legal or merely ethical limitations; likewise in Bossuet, IV. a. 1, VI. a. 1, VIII. a. 2; and Fénelon, ch. V. and XI.

98. As in Huber, I. 1 c. 1–6 and I. 9 c. 3–4; Locke, II. c. 2, 9, 11; Wolff, Jus nat., I § 62 ff., VIII. § 35, 47, 1041 ff., Inst., § 68 ff., 980, 1075 ff.; Nettelbladt, § 1127 ff.; Achenwall, I. § 2 and 34 ff., II. § 98 ff.; Daries, § 780 ff.; Scheidemantel, III. p. 172 ff.; Schlözer (above, Note 68).

99. In order to see just how Natural Law was treated as a code of laws taught by reason and Positive Law as a system of ordinances issued for its enforcement, one need but compare Nettelbladt's two systems of Natural and Positive Law. Here indeed the so-called Law of Reason, curiously enough, agrees with the law as actually existing; compare the 'natural' (!) and the 'positive' law of Tenures. And as for the relations of public law in particular, in this as in the other treatises on "jus publicum naturale sive universale" written after the time of Boehmer, it is only the doctrines of the State's rights of superiority and the fundamental rights of the Individual that are conceived as apodictic, while the most widely different forms of government are left as a matter of choice. But then the Law of Reason comes to differ more and more from the existing law (which is thus largely stigmatized as positive 'unlaw'), and develops into the program of a revolution, whether violent or peaceful. And now in particular there grows up the notion—not simply of the one fittest form of government, as in Locke and Montesquieu—but of the one and only rightful form of government, such as prevails in France after the time of Rousseau and in Germany appears most sharply in Fichte (see his ideas, ever changing in substance, as to the realization of the 'Rational State' [*Vernunftstaat*], Werke, III. p. 397, IV. p. 393 ff., 419 ff., 431 ff., VII. p. 148, 152 ff., Nachg. Werke, II. p. 622). Kant likewise constructs a Law of Reason, given *a priori* and quite immutable in substance, whereby the State is bound and directed, and sets up the concept of the 'only rightful' constitution; for him all law is indeed prior to the State and not created by it, but before the law is confirmed by the State it is only 'provisory' and it is first made 'peremptory' by the State; hence there is no practicable law other than positive law, and the Law of Reason can rightfully be restored only by way of a reform to be effected by the existing powers; see Werke, VI. p. 322 ff., 338, 413 note, VII. p. 130 ff. (53 ff., 62 ff.); and above, Ch. II. Note 121, and p. 184.

100. In this narrow sense the theory that the sole function of the State is to maintain justice (which was otherwise often compatible with a practical system of benevolent paternalism [*Wohlfahrtsstaat*] or even of bureaucratic despotism [*Bevormundungsstaat*]) was developed by Locke (see above,

Ch. II. Note 100), Humboldt (ib. Note 112), and Kant. Kant most emphatically opposed the principle of 'happiness,' which leads to despotism or rebellion; the maxim "salus reipublicae suprema lex est" is valid only if the 'public good' is taken to mean not 'welfare and happiness,' but 'the state of the greatest possible conformity of the constitution to the principles of Right, for which Reason enjoins us to strive by a categorical imperative'; see Werke, VI. p. 322 and 330–334, and more sharply VII. p. 130 § 44 and p. 136 § 49. Thus public law, grounded upon *a priori* principles, has 'binding force without regard to the weal or woe that may spring from it' (VI. p. 338); 'that somewhat high-sounding, hackneyed but truthful proverb "fiat justitia pereat mundus," or as it is said, "Let justice prevail though all the rogues on earth perish together," is a good principle of law, cutting off all crooked ways marked by fraud or force' (VI. p. 446); 'if justice perish the life of man is no longer worth living' (VII. p. 150).

101. See above, p. 107–109, and Ch. II. Notes 107, 110–114, 121; Ch. III. Note 66; also in this Chapter, Notes 68 and 74–80.

102. The Monarchomachi hold the doctrine of the "tyrannus quoad titulum" in the same form as we have seen it in Althusius (above, p. 46); see especially Junius Brutus, q. III. p. 264–270 and 281 ff.; De jure Mag., p. 14–20 (until a legitimation by subsequent consensus, provided that this is not extorted by force); Boucher, III. c. 14–17; Mariana, I. c. 6; Hoenonius, IX. § 56–57 (until "Respublica in mutationem legum rite consentiat" and he thus becomes "magistratus legitimus et inviolabilis").—In like manner the Catholic teachers of Natural Law hold that it is the right and the duty of every individual to refuse obedience to the "tyrannus quoad potestatem," and that he may justly be slain; Vasquez, c. 8; Molina, III. d. 6; Suarez, III. c. 10 nr. 7 (until legitimation by consensus tacitus); Schmier, V. c. 2 nr. 28 ff.—But the same doctrine occurs in Bodin, II. c. 5; Waremund de Erenbergk, Verisimilia, c. 11 p. 149 ff.; Arnisaeus, De auctor. princ., c. 4 § 11–14, and De rep., II. c. 3 s. 7–8 (the tyrannus quoad titulum has no subjects previous to the consensus populi); Reinking, De reg., I. cl. 1 c. 5; Carpzov, c. 14 s. 3; Knipschildt, VI. c. 4 nr. 12–13 (until "subditi paulatim assenserunt"); Fénelon, ch. VIII. (while some reject the distinction between "Roi de fait" and "Roi de droit" and assert that the former is legitimate forthwith as "Roi de Providence," yet this is not true); Schoenborner, II. c. 40; Olizarovius, III. c. 8 § 2; Kestner, c. 7 § 20–21; Kreittmayr, Anm., I. c. 2 § 6 nr. 2.—Likewise the constitutional doctrine; thus Huber, I. 9 c. 1; Locke, II. c. 17 § 197–198.

103. At first men were mostly satisfied with the principle that the "consensus populi" legitimizes (see preceding Note). At a later time the advocates of the People's sovereignty specially emphasized that this consent

must be entirely free; see Locke, § 198 ("till the people are both at liberty to consent, and have actually consented"), and II. c. 16 § 175–196 (even in case of conquest, lawful title arises only from consent); Sidney (in the passages cited above, Ch. II. Note 87). At the same time the champions of the Ruler's sovereignty developed what was later given the special name of the Principle of Legitimacy, to the effect that the consent of the people must never prejudice the right of the legitimate ruler; thus Kestner, loc. cit.; H. de Cocceji, De regimine usurpatoris rege ejecto, Frankfort 1705; Schmier, II. c. 2 s. 2 §1, nr. 82–99 (legitimation takes place when the people as well as the "legitimus imperans" freely consent, or the latter ceases by dereliction or extinction); see also Nettelbladt, § 1267–1268 (so far as the people is not "sui juris"); Achenwall, II. § 98. Contrariwise Hobbes (Lev., c. 21), Conring, and Boehmer (P. spec. III. c. 2 § 17) assert the principle that the people is released from all obligation toward the legitimate ruler when he is no longer in a position to protect it.

104. Already Victoria, III. nr. 23, requires that the laws of an usurper be obeyed in the interim.—Grotius teaches that, previous to legitimation by "longa possessione aut pacto," the illegitimate ruler who finds himself in possession of power binds the people in necessary things, as there must be a government of some kind, but that in other matters obedience should be refused so far as this is possible "sine gravi periculo" (l. c. 4 § 15). At the same time he allows violent ejection and putting to death only so long as the state of war lasts and the true sovereign gives his authorization (ib. § 16–18), but otherwise not, as it may be that the rightful sovereign himself prefers the continuance of usurpation to the perils and ravages of a revolution (§ 19); "maxime autem in re controversa judicium sibi privatus sumere non debet, sed possessionem sequi" (§ 20). On contracts of the usurper, the people and the true king are liable only "de in rem verso" (II. c. 14 § 14).—Horn, II. c. 9, § 4 and 21, holds that the hitherto existing 'majesty' is simply extinguished when there is an actual acquisition of 'majesty' by another person.—Pufendorf, De jure N. et G., VIII. c. 12 § 2–4, regards the possessor of sovereignty as externally legitimized, while internally his acts may be rescinded by the "legitima potestas."—Boehmer, loc. cit., makes it a duty to obey the usurper when it is quite impossible for the true king to protect his subjects.—Kant, VII. p. 139, says distinctly that when a revolution is successful the subjects must obey the government which is now in power.

105. At any rate this was accepted if and so far as any lex was supposed to have a "vis coactiva" or at least a "vis irritativa" over the sovereign.—That the judge can declare unjust laws null and void is expressly said by Zasius (see above, Note 42). Suarez gives a specially full treatment of the limits of legislative power. For the binding force of laws he requires the "acceptatio

populi," which, however, the people is obliged to give in the case of just laws; conversely "lex injusta non est lex," thus it "non obligat ad acceptandum, imo acceptata non obligat"; and the "nimis dura et gravis lex" is regarded as a mere experiment to see if it gains acceptance, wherefore "non peccat non observans." And lastly, "si de facto major pars populi legem non observat," those who follow the majority are excused, at least if their observance of the law would lead to "seditio" or "scandalum"; see IV. c. 19 nr. 11–13, also I. c. 9, III. c. 10, and for ecclesiastical laws IV. c. 16. Compare Molina, V. d. 73.

106. See above, Ch. III. Notes 80, 84, 93, 96. In this matter it was already decisive for the German publicists that on the one hand the Emperor was commonly regarded as a true Monarch, and on the other hand it remained possible, under the imperial constitution, to sit in judgment upon him and depose him; see Buxtorff, c. 5 § 76–83.

107. Thus Luther and the other Reformers, even where they would only allow passive resistance; likewise all the schools of Natural Law, as well as many jurists; see Suarez, I. c. 9, III. c. 10 nr. 7–10; Molina, V. d. 73; Zoannettus, nr. 91 ff. (obedience is due to the Emperor only within the limits of his office); Poynet, q. 4.

108. Luther himself inclined more and more to allow resistance when there is religious oppression, an attempt to compel idolatry, or an exercise of unlawful power; see above, Ch. III. Note 80. The opinions of theologians in favor of the right of active resistance are collected and defended in Joh. Gerhardus Theologus, An licitum subditis religionis causa a Rege deficere ac contra eum arma capere, in Arumaeus, IV. nr. 15, also nr. 18. As examples of juristic deductions in favor of the jus resistendi I cite from the sixteenth century: Erfurter Gutachten, in Goede, Cons. 11 (in favor of a city); Frankfurter Gutachten, in Kirchovius, Cons., V. c. 25 nr. 369–372 (in case of peril to the public weal, even a "legitimus magistratus," when he becomes a tyrant, may be resisted and slain); Mod. Pistoris, Cons., II. c. 9; Boërius, Tr. de seditiosis, § 5 nr. 5–6 (against a "regimen tyrannicum" there is no "seditio," as the ruler himself is "seditiosus in populo"); see also the use of this principle by the Reichskammergericht itself in deciding against magistrates, in Mynsinger, Cent., V. obs. 18. For the doctrine of resistance in the Catholic school of Natural Law see above, Ch. III. Note 84.

109. At any rate these conclusions followed in so far as a legal limitation was supposed to have a mere "vis directiva"; see above, Notes 47, 51, 84. Thus for Bodin they hold for all legal limitations; see II. c. 5; yet in III. c. 4 he sets limits to the obedience of magistrates toward the sovereign, in that they have a right to refuse obedience, not indeed for mere illegality, but in

case of an offense against the "lex divina et naturalis." See further Melchior ab Ossa, Testamentum, Frankfort 1609, c. 1. Lauterbeck, c. 20 (obedience is due only in 'external things'; but even in case of oppression of conscience, active resistance is never allowed but, at most, flight). Waremund de Erenbergk, loc. cit. p. 149–160 (one can only withdraw from the "tyrannus exercitio" by emigrating, or if the worst comes one can 'pray that the evil Ruler may die'). Barclay (above, Ch. III. Note 88). Arnisaeus, De rep., II. s. 3 c. 7–8, and De autor. princ. (yet he excuses the expulsion of a manifest tyrant). Albericus Gentilis, De potestate absoluta principis, 1605. Irvinus, De jure regni diascepsis. Liebenthal, d. XV. q. 1. Bornitius, Partit., p. 53 ff. (unconditional obedience, except as being against God). Schoenborner, III. c. 37. Caspar Klock, Tract. de contributionibus, Cologne 1699 (1st ed. 1632), c. 18 nr. 345–377. Knipschildt, c. 2 and 4.

110. Thus all the passages cited in the preceding Note.

111. See above, p. 46 and 155–156.

112. See above, Ch. III. Notes 71–72.

113. The Reformed Monarchomachi were in general guided by the teaching of Calvin, IV. c. 20, that the private person has no right of resistance even against tyrants and is bound to unconditional obedience, with the sole exception of commands contrary to the Will of God. See Junius Brutus, q. II. p. 115 (privati are bound under God to refuse obedience to the "impia jubens," but not to make active resistance to him), q. III. p. 319 ff. (in worldly matters they must obey unconditionally, as for example in paying unjust taxes), also q. I. throughout. De jure Mag., q. 1–4 (God's command takes precedence), q. 6 p. 23 (but against "injuria" privati subditi have only the right of passive resistance), q. 7 p. 91 (even this only when an assemblage is prohibited by the tyrant). Althusius, as above, p. 46. Hoenonius, IX. § 55. Alstedius, p. 56 ff.—In principle the Catholic Monarchomachi agree with this; see Boucher, III. c. 14–17, and Mariana, I. c. 6, who, however, in case of pressing necessity or the obstruction of a "conventus publicus," appeal to the pure right of revolution.

114. See above, p. 46, Ch. III. Note 75, and Ch. V. Note 42.

115. Thus the Catholic theorists cited above, Ch. III. Note 84; and especially Molina and Suarez, above, Ch. III. Note 101, who deduce these rights of the community from their principle of the contingent sovereignty of the people.—Likewise most of the advocates of "majestas realis" (above, Ch. III. Note 134); while Besold and Carpzov take this view only for "regna conditionata," and do not admit the people's constitutional right of resistance and deposition in absolute monarchies; see Besold, Diss. de republ. cur., c. 7; and Carpzov, Comm. ad leg. Reg., c. 14 s. 1–2 and 4–6.

116. Thus Vasquez, c. 8, Molina, III. d. 6, and Suarez, III. c. 10 nr. 7–10, admit the right of violent resistance of individuals against the "tyrannus quoad exercitium" only in case of self-defense, and otherwise simply the right and duty of disobedience in case of oppression of conscience; naturally this does not contradict the proposition that "post latam sententiam" the tyrant who has been outlawed by a decision of the people may be slain by any man.—Likewise the advocates of "majestas realis" sometimes concede a jus resistendi to the "magistratus subordinati in partem sollicitudinis Reipublicae assumpti" but not to "subditi privati"; instead they impose on the latter the duty of obedience even toward the "magistratus iniquus," and recognize the right and duty of passive resistance only in case of commands "contra Dei et naturae leges"; see Reinking, I. cl. 1, c. 3–4 and c. 5 nr. 43–104; Carpzov, loc. cit.—But Besold, loc. cit., while setting himself against the doctrine of the absolutists as well as the unconditional admission of the "censura populi," recognizes a right of resistance against tyranny in absolute monarchies, as a substitute for the constitutional "inspectio et jurisdictio" which in this case he denies to the people.

117. See above, Ch. III. Notes 93, 166, 169, and p. 173 ff.; also in this Chapter, Notes 60 ff.

118. As in Keckermann, I. c. 25 and 28 (above, Ch. III. Note 96); Micraelius, I. c. 10 § 12, and q. 18 ff. (for the manifest tyrant is treated as a private person); Kestner, c. 7 § 17–19 (in case of manifest tyranny the people has a right of resistance against the ruler, who thereby becomes "privatus et hostis"; the individual has only the right and duty of passive disobedience in case of offenses against the jus divinum et naturale).

119. See above, Ch. III. Notes 154–155; very similarly Schmier, II. c. 4 s. 1 § 49 ff., V. c. 2 s. 1 § 19–41, c. 3 s. 1§ 1–49; compare the right, based on federalism, of the parts to secede in case of necessity (above, Ch. V. Note 67).

120. Hobbes, De cive, c. 6 § 13–16, c. 12 § 1–4; yet elsewhere (Lev., c. 21) he grants to the individual the right of self-defense, which cannot be forbidden even as against the sovereign.

121. See Graswinckel, c. 9; Salmasius, c. 2–7 and 11; Nic. Vernulaeus, Diss. polit., Louvain 1646, I. 253; Felwinger, De maj., § 39–40; Adam Pisetzki a Kranichfeld, De statu seculari, Leipzig 1667, c. 1 p. 120 (rather die than resist); Spinoza, Tract. theol.-pol., c. 16 (obedience "tametsi absurdissima imperet"), Tract. pol., c. 3, § 3 and 5; Horn, II. c. 12 § 2–13 (obedience "in omnibus," even to the tyrant; no jus resistendi, but only disobedience and martyrdom in case of command of an "evidens peccatum"); Filmer, Patriarcha; Alberti, c. 14 § 11; Bossuet, Politique, VI. a. 2, Cinq avertiss., XXXVII. (reserving only the commands of God); Fénelon, ch.

X.; Stryk, Diss., XIV. nr. 7 c. 3; S. de Cocceji, Jurispr. nat., § 638; Heincke, III. c. 1.

122. Pufendorf, De jure N. et G., VII. c. 8, De off., II. c. 9 § 4 (the State-power is sacred; the subject must patiently suffer even the greatest wrong and should fly rather than resist); Thomasius, Inst. jur. div., III. c. 6 § 119–120; Gundling, Jus nat., c. 38 § 19–23, and Diss., c. 37 (only "in limitata et irregulari Republica" can the people draw the sword; "tuetur hic unusquisque jus suum ex pactis quaesitum"; but never "in regulari Republica," though indeed no injustice would be done to the tyrant if this did happen); Boehmer, P. spec. III. c. 2 (the individual has indefeasible rights, but in case they are violated all right of resistance is excluded, even though based on express contracts; instead there is a fixed "obligatio ad patiendum injurias"; resistance is forbidden even though on the plea of religion, and thus the exceptions of Grotius must be rejected; only in case of an offense against the Divine Will is there a duty of disobedience as well as a right of emigration (subject to the statutory restrictions of this right); Heineccius, II. § 132–134; Kreittmayr, Grundriss, I. § 35. See above, Note 63.

123. Thus already Milton (above, Ch. III. Note 118). Likewise Sidney, when he not only asserts that all unjust ordinances of the ruler are void (c. III. § 11 and 20) and allows active resistance against all tyrannical measures (ib. § 4 ff.), but also says, as we have already noted more than once, "the general revolt of a Nation cannot be called a Rebellion" (ib. § 36). Rousseau indeed goes much farther when he says (III. c. 10) that as soon as the government usurps the powers of the sovereign (which inevitably happens), 'all the simple citizens, resuming the right to their natural liberty,' are entitled to resist this state of affairs by force. Fichte ascribes the right of revolution only to the people as a collective body, but the individuals who revolt are free from all guilt as soon as they find general support (above, Ch. III. Note 226).

124. Locke expressly treats the indestructible natural rights of the individual (life, liberty and property) as formal limitations even of the popularly organized legislative power; II. c. 9 § 131, c. 11 § 134 ff. Even in Huber and in all the writers named above, Note 68, statutes are by no means excluded from the category of acts which, by transgressing the limits of the law, may become tyrannical measures, thus being void and justifying resistance; see also Boeye in the following Note.

125. See Joh. Schuurbeque Boeye, Specimen politico-juridicum inaugurale, quo disquiritur, num legibus injustis populus obtemperare teneatur, ac, si non teneatur, num summis imperantibus resistere ei liceat, Leyden 1802 (apart from the mention of Mariana, he goes back only as far as Grotius).

F. Murhard, Über Widerstand, Empörung und Zwangsübung der Staatsbürger gegen die bestehende Staatsgewalt, Brunswick 1830. For the literature on purely constitutional obedience see Mohl, I. p. 320–334.

126. Huber, I. 3 c. 4 § 7, I. 9 c. 3 (above, p. 314).

127. Locke, II. c. 18 § 199–210, c. 19 § 242.—For other forms of the doctrine of resistance in England see Mohl, I. p. 327 ff.—Hume ("Of Passive Obedience") says that the whole question is only a question of the degree of necessity.

128. As in Wolff, Polit., § 433 ff., Jus nat., VIII. § 1041 ff., Inst., § 1079 ff.; he concedes to the individual only the right of passive resistance to commands contrary to what a "lex naturalis" bids or forbids; the people has the right of disobedience in case of any breach of the constitution, and of active resistance in case of an attack on its reserved rights, as a breach of the social contract brings back the state of nature in which every man defends his own rights. Nettelbladt, § 1142 and 1270 (right of resistance in case of manifest transgression of the sovereign's bounds, but no right of coercion or punishment; dethronement is allowable, not as a punishment but as a defection). Achenwall, II. § 200–207 (injured individuals have only the indefeasible right to emigrate; when the "jus universorum vel insignis partis populi" is violated, men should take up arms and drive the tyrant out, if graver perils would arise "ex continuata et tolerata imperantis injustitia" than from a revolt). Daries, § 710 ff. (denial of justice brings back the "status naturalis"). Scheidemantel and Schlözer (above, Ch. III. Note 188). Boeye, op. cit. (wholly on the ground of the contract theory). See also the passages cited by Mohl, I. p. 332–333, from writers of the last decade of the eighteenth century (Höpfner, Hufeland, Eggers, Heydenreich, Feuerbach, H. Jacob, Erhard), together with the citations from nineteenth-century literature, ib.

129. Kant, VI. p. 330–337, 449–450, VII. p. 136–141. He is opposed to any disobedience of individuals or of the whole people toward the existing government, any jurisdiction or punitive power over it, any uprising or revolutionary violence on the plea of tyranny. Even in a limited form of government he allows only 'negative,' not active, resistance. To this there is no exception on pretence of a so-called 'right of necessity,' 'which, as a supposed right to do unright in case of necessity, is a nothing.' There are indeed 'inalienable rights of the people against the Chief of the State,' but an external guaranty of these is unthinkable; 'the freedom of the pen is the only palladium of the people's rights.' Compare above, Ch. III. Note 234.

130. Where, as in the United States, laws can be treated as formally void by reason of their material unconstitutionality, there is still a formally omnipotent authority in the constitution-making power.

131. For the evolution of the idea of the judicial power see above, Ch. III. Note 102; Montesquieu, VI. c. 5–6, XI. c. 6, XII. c. 22; Hume ("Of the Origin of Government"), says that kings, parliaments and ministers have ultimately no other purpose but to support the twelve judges; Kant, above, Ch. III. Note 234.

132. This is not the place for a history of the legal protection which was actually conceded in the domain of public law, with the theory of positive law which was formed in this connection, as it existed in Germany under the Empire. For this we have two accounts, differing in many points but supplementing each other in essentials: Bähr, Der Rechtsstaat, Cassel and Göttingen 1864, and Gneist, Der Rechtsstaat, 2nd ed. Berlin 1879.

INDEX